Salesforce Certified Platform Administrator Study Guide

Launch and Elevate Your Salesforce Career

Mike Wheeler

Preface

Many years ago, I was browsing the aisles of a local bookstore, reflecting on several previous attempts to learn how to build enterprise-level applications. While I could write basic HTML, coding was never a natural fit for me. Each time I tried to dive deeper into complex programming, I found it somewhat unapproachable and ultimately lost interest. On that day in the bookstore, I came across a book about Salesforce.

Unlike typical tech books requiring extensive coding expertise, this one emphasized solving business challenges through clicks rather than code. As I flipped through its pages, I quickly realized, "I can do this." With each passing page, my confidence grew, and so began a career journey deeply intertwined with Salesforce. Now, I find myself authoring a Salesforce book of my own. I'm humbled by this opportunity to help others, beginning with you.

Founded in 1999, Salesforce has evolved from a visionary startup to a foundational tool for businesses globally and is now one of just 30 companies comprising the Dow Jones Industrial Average. Salesforce continues to transform businesses through innovations such as its AI-powered tools like Agentforce, embedding sophisticated capabilities across its entire platform. In today's rapidly changing landscape, being fundamentally sound in Salesforce is more important than ever. That is why I have written this book.

This *Salesforce Certified Platform Administrator Study Guide* is not only a study aid but also an essential reference guide for your everyday responsibilities as a platform administrator. It provides clarity, practical insights, and hands-on applications to reinforce your understanding of core Salesforce concepts, ensuring you are well-prepared both for the exam and for scenarios you'll encounter on the job.

Who This Book Is For

This book is intended for individuals preparing for the Salesforce Certified Platform Administrator exam. Whether you're entirely new to Salesforce or looking to formalize your existing knowledge, this guide is for you. It also serves as a practical reference for current Salesforce professionals seeking a solid foundation in Salesforce fundamentals.

How This Book Is Organized

The chapters in this book provide comprehensive coverage of key Salesforce topics, including configuration, object management, sales and marketing applications, and workflow automation. Each chapter specific to the exam (Chapter 2 through Chapter 12) includes a quiz to reinforce your learning. At the book's conclusion, a full-length practice test (Chapter 13) simulates the actual certification exam, helping you gauge your readiness and build exam-day confidence. An answer key for all quizzes and the practice exam can be found in Appendix A.

What You Need to Use This Book

To effectively use this study guide, you will need a Salesforce learner account, which can be obtained for free through Salesforce's Trailhead platform. Salesforce provides these learner accounts along with an extensive range of training resources, including Trailhead, a gamified learning environment, all at no charge. Throughout this guide, I will help you sign up, log in, and navigate your free Salesforce learner account.

Conventions Used in This Book

The following typographical conventions are used in this book:

Italic
: Indicates new terms, URLs, email addresses, filenames, and file extensions.

`Constant width`
: Used within paragraphs to refer to program elements such as variable or function names, databases, data types, environment variables, statements, and keywords.

 This element signifies a tip or suggestion.

This element signifies a general note.

 This element indicates a warning or caution.

O'Reilly Online Learning

 For more than 40 years, *O'Reilly Media* has provided technology and business training, knowledge, and insight to help companies succeed.

Our unique network of experts and innovators share their knowledge and expertise through books, articles, and our online learning platform. O'Reilly's online learning platform gives you on-demand access to live training courses, in-depth learning paths, interactive coding environments, and a vast collection of text and video from O'Reilly and 200+ other publishers. For more information, visit *https://oreilly.com*.

How to Contact Us

Please address comments and questions concerning this book to the publisher:

> O'Reilly Media, Inc.
> 141 Stony Circle, Suite 195
> Santa Rosa, CA 95401
> 800-889-8969 (in the United States or Canada)
> 707-827-7019 (international or local)
> 707-829-0104 (fax)
> *support@oreilly.com*
> *https://oreilly.com/about/contact.html*

We have a web page for this book, where we list errata and any additional information. You can access this page at *https://oreil.ly/salesforce_certified_admin_platform*.

For news and information about our books and courses, visit *https://oreilly.com*.

Find us on LinkedIn: *https://linkedin.com/company/oreilly-media*.

Watch us on YouTube: *https://youtube.com/oreillymedia*.

Acknowledgments

I am deeply grateful to my editor, Sara Hunter, whose expertise and careful attention have significantly improved this guide. Special thanks also to my technical reviewers: Joyce Kay Avila, Vladislav Bilay, Michael Hopkins, and Paul McCollum. Their thoughtful insights have been instrumental in improving this book greatly.

A special thanks goes to David Michelson, Senior Content Acquisitions Editor at O'Reilly Media. David was the spark behind this book, recognizing both the potential and the need and providing the encouragement that turned this idea into reality.

A heartfelt acknowledgment goes to my dedicated team at Rapid Reskill, where I serve as the founder and principal trainer. Rapid Reskill is a recognized Salesforce Trailblazer Workforce Partner, dedicated to preparing individuals for successful careers in Salesforce. To learn more, visit us at *https://rapidreskill.com*.

Additionally, sincere appreciation goes to our team at Velza, named in honor of my late father, Velza Dean Wheeler. At Velza, we specialize in resolving problematic Salesforce implementations and preparing organizations for the future with AI and Agentforce solutions. You can read more about our story at *https://velza.com*.

I would like to express deep gratitude to my wife, Christina, who has made significant sacrifices in support of my writing and various business endeavors. Her unwavering encouragement has been essential throughout this journey. Thanks also to our children, some of whom have embarked on Salesforce careers of their own. Additionally, I want to acknowledge my mother, Dianna Wheeler, whose lifelong example of helping others continues to inspire me. Her belief in me has always encouraged me to positively impact the lives of those around me.

This book marks a significant milestone in my Salesforce journey. My hope is that it conveys to you the same sense of potential and clarity that inspired me years ago. As you prepare for certification and beyond, my wish is that you'll recognize not only the remarkable opportunities Salesforce presents for any organization, but also the possibilities it unlocks for your career.

Here to help,

Mike Wheeler

CHAPTER 1

Introduction: The Salesforce Career Opportunity and Getting Started

Welcome to the rewarding journey of becoming a Salesforce Certified Platform Administrator. This chapter marks the beginning of an exciting path that can significantly reshape your professional life. Whether you are new to the world of customer relationship management (CRM) or seeking to pivot into a more technology-focused career, attaining the Salesforce Platform Administrator certification is a foundational step. This certification represents more than just a credential; it's a gateway to understanding the fundamentals of the Salesforce platform, essential for anyone aspiring to excel in the rapidly evolving landscape of cloud computing and CRM.

In this chapter, I will lay the foundation for your journey toward Salesforce mastery. You'll explore the significance of the Salesforce Platform Administrator certification and how it equips you with the knowledge and skills necessary to effectively manage and customize the Salesforce platform. This certification is not just an end in itself; it serves as a stepping-stone to further professional growth. Many advanced Salesforce certifications require the administrator certification as a prerequisite, making it the logical starting point for most in the ecosystem.

Introduction to Salesforce

Salesforce, a name that resonates with innovation in CRM and cloud computing, has fundamentally altered how businesses interact with their customers and manage their operations. Since its inception in 1999, Salesforce has evolved from a single CRM product to an extensive cloud-based ecosystem, offering a range of solutions across various industries.

At its core, Salesforce is a platform designed to bring companies and customers together. It's a suite of cloud-based applications focused on sales, service, marketing, and more, all aimed at enhancing customer engagement and streamlining business processes. With its comprehensive tools for data management, analytics, artificial intelligence, and application development, Salesforce provides businesses with everything they need to connect with their customers.

The platform's flexibility and scalability have made it a favorite among businesses of all sizes, from small startups to global corporations. Whether it's managing sales pipelines, delivering personalized customer service, creating targeted marketing campaigns, or developing custom applications, Salesforce offers a solution that can be tailored to meet many business needs.

Salesforce has transformed CRM and been a driving force in moving many companies to the cloud. This shift has enabled businesses to operate more efficiently and adapt quickly to changing market demands.

How to Use This Book to Prepare for the Salesforce Platform Administrator Certification

This book is designed to be your guide and companion as you prepare for the Salesforce Platform Administrator certification. This credential signifies a fundamental understanding of the platform and its capabilities. Whether you're new to Salesforce or looking to formalize your knowledge, this book will provide you with a comprehensive overview of the key concepts, features, and functionalities of Salesforce.

I will start by laying the groundwork with basic Salesforce concepts, gradually moving into more complex topics. Each chapter is structured to build upon the previous one, ensuring a cohesive learning journey. You'll find real-world examples, practical tips, and insights that will deepen your understanding of Salesforce.

To get the most out of this book, engage with it actively. Read the chapters, participate in the exercises, and use the quizzes at the end of Chapter 2 through Chapter 12 to test your understanding. The final practice test that concludes this book (Chapter 13) will give you a taste of what to expect in the actual certification exam and help you assess your readiness.

Additionally, this book shows you how to explore Salesforce on your own. You'll learn how to set up your own Salesforce environment, experiment with its features, and apply what you've learned in a hands-on manner. This practical approach is important, as it will help you gain the confidence and skills needed to navigate the Salesforce platform effectively.

Remember, the goal of this book is not just to help you pass the certification exam but also to provide you with a solid foundation in Salesforce that will support your future endeavors, whether you're aiming for a career as a Salesforce administrator, consultant, developer, or any other role within the Salesforce ecosystem. More than a preparation guide, this book is a resource you'll return to time and again. It will serve as an invaluable reference as you progress in your career, offering insights and knowledge that remain relevant and useful as you traverse your own path in the Salesforce world. With each new challenge and opportunity, you'll find that the concepts and strategies detailed here should continue to be a source of guidance and inspiration.

The Structure of This Book Follows the Exam Guide

I have structured this book to closely align with Salesforce's official exam guide for the Platform Administrator certification. The outline of the exam is divided into seven knowledge areas. These knowledge areas are:

- Configuration and Setup
- Object Manager and Lightning App Builder
- Sales and marketing applications
- Service and support applications
- Productivity and collaboration
- Data and analytics management
- Workflow/process automation

> The Salesforce Certified Platform Administrator Exam Guide is available at *https://oreil.ly/scpa-exam-guide*.

When you review the Salesforce Certified Platform Administrator Exam Guide, you will notice several bulleted items, which are known as learning objectives. For example, here are the learning objectives for the first knowledge area in the Exam Guide under "Configuration and Setup":

- Describe the information found in the company settings (for example, company settings fiscal year, business hours, currency management, default settings).
- Distinguish and understand the administration of declarative configuration of the User Interface. (for example, UI settings, App Menu, list views, global actions, Lightning App Builder).
- Given a scenario, demonstrate the proper setup and maintenance of users.

- Explain the various organization Security Controls (for example, Setup Audit Trail, Login Hours, Session Settings).

- Given a user request scenario, apply the appropriate security controls based on the features and capabilities of the Salesforce sharing model (for example, public groups, org-wide default, sharing: roles, subordinates, hierarchy, report, and dashboard folders).

- Given a scenario, determine the appropriate use of a custom profile or permission set using the various profile settings and permissions.

Inspecting the learning objectives above, you may notice that the first two are focused on Salesforce Organization Setup. The next learning objective focuses on User Setup. The final three learning objectives deal with Security and Access.

 You will often see the term *org* while working through this book, Trailhead modules, and other places related to Salesforce. Org is short for *organization* which refers to an instance of Salesforce. Your Salesforce learning account(s) are your own organization(s) to use for learning purposes. The next chapter will get you familiar with Organization Setup.

This book's next three chapters follow those same three focal points of:

- Organization Setup (Chapter 2)
- User Setup and Management (Chapter 3)
- Security and Access (Chapter 4)

Make no mistake, the Configuration and Setup knowledge area covers an intimidating amount of foundational information. These concepts will be revisited in the remaining chapters as you progress through the book. Due to the large scope and fundamental nature of these concepts, I have elected to divide the Configuration and Setup knowledge area into three chapters in order to adequately cover this supremely important information.

Moving forward into the other knowledge areas, you will notice that I devote one chapter for each. The only exception to this rule is Chapter 6, "Attract, Attain, Retain: The Lifecycle of a B2B/B2C Relationship". This chapter will prove helpful from a business development and marketing, sales, and service perspective.

This dance of "attract, attain, retain" is time-tested in business and is how Salesforce is designed to work from the ground up. Having that background understanding will serve you well as you move into Chapter 7, "Sales and Marketing Applications" and Chapter 8, "Service and Support Applications".

From there, I round out the remainder of the knowledge areas of the exam, chapter by chapter. The concluding chapter is a full 60-question practice test, which you can use to measure your own knowledge and exam readiness.

 I encourage you to resist the urge to skip to the end of the book and take the practice test first. Reserve practice tests for the end of your exam preparation, because once you have taken a practice test, it is hard to recreate that experience upon a retake.

The Significance of Salesforce in the World of CRM

Salesforce has become synonymous with customer relationship management, but its journey from a pioneering CRM platform to a multifaceted cloud ecosystem is a story of innovation and evolution.

Founded in 1999, Salesforce began as a tool designed to manage a salesforce—the teams responsible for sales in an organization. It focused on streamlining the process of tracking and managing sales deals and customer interactions. The platform's original mission was to replace traditional desktop CRM systems with a cloud-based solution, making CRM more accessible and user-friendly.

Salesforce's continual evolution now extends well beyond its CRM roots, emerging as a diverse platform with cloud solutions catering to most industries. Notable examples include the Health Cloud for patient-provider engagement, Financial Services Cloud for client management, and Education Cloud for personalized student experiences. These represent just a few of the many specialized clouds Salesforce offers, each now infused with AI.

The Foundation of Salesforce Knowledge

Regardless of the career path you choose from the options within the Salesforce ecosystem, the knowledge base established through attaining the Salesforce Platform Administrator certification is invaluable. This certification lays down the fundamental understanding of the platform, equipping professionals with the skills necessary to navigate the Salesforce ecosystem effectively.

In essence, Salesforce's journey from managing a team of salespeople (a salesforce) to offering a broad spectrum of cloud-based solutions reflects its transformative impact on the world of CRM and beyond. Understanding this journey is key for anyone seeking to build a career on this platform. The Salesforce Platform Administrator certification, the focus of this book, serves as the stepping-stone in this journey, providing the foundational knowledge essential for any Salesforce professional.

What Is the Cloud?

The term *cloud* has become ubiquitous, yet its true meaning often remains shrouded in a mist of misconception and overuse. Allow me to demystify this term by grounding it in tangible concepts.

At its core, the cloud refers to the vast network of remote servers around the world, interconnected through the internet and designed to store, manage, and process data. This network represents a paradigm shift from the traditional approach where data and programs were stored and run from personal computers or on-site servers.

The cloud's omnipresence in modern technology cannot be overstated. From the emails you send to the social media platforms you browse, the cloud is an invisible yet integral backdrop to these daily activities. It has revolutionized how you interact with technology, offering a flexibility and scale previously unattainable.

Despite its prevalence, the cloud is often misunderstood. Some view it as a purely abstract concept or a marketing buzzword with little substance. This misunderstanding can lead to underestimating the cloud's impact and capabilities.

The advent of cloud computing marked a new era in information technology. It shifted the focus from local storage and processing to remote, internet-based operations. This shift is not just technical but represents a change in how businesses and individuals think about and use technology.

For Salesforce administrators and other IT professionals, a clear understanding of the cloud is foundational. It is the bedrock upon which Salesforce operates and is key to unlocking its full potential. The cloud's principles of flexibility, scalability, and accessibility are reflected in every aspect of Salesforce's design and functionality.

Bridging the cloud and the internet

Imagine the cloud as a colossal, invisible digital structure, sprawling across the globe. This structure isn't just floating aimlessly in cyberspace; it's intricately woven into the fabric of the internet. At its most basic, the cloud is a vast array of remote servers, all linked together and accessible via the internet. These servers are the heavy lifters, doing the hard work behind many of your daily digital interactions.

Every time you check your email, watch a streaming video, or work on cloud-based applications like Salesforce, your computer is reaching out to these remote servers. It's a bit like having a conversation—your computer sends a request out and the cloud responds. This interaction is seamless, almost invisible, but it's happening constantly, enabling the magic of instant access to data and software from anywhere in the world.

So, what exactly are these remote servers doing?

Three key roles define their existence—storing, managing, and processing data:

Storing

Consider the cloud as a vast digital library. Instead of books, it's lined with data. This data is stored securely, ready to be accessed or retrieved whenever you need it.

Managing

The cloud keeps everything organized and running smoothly. It stores and manages the data, ensuring that everything is where it's supposed to be and accessible when needed.

Processing

It processes the data, performing calculations, running applications, and even powering complex analytics. This processing happens on remote servers, not on your personal device, allowing for more powerful computing without straining your own hardware.

Salesforce, like most modern applications, lives in the cloud. It relies on this intricate dance between your device and remote servers to provide a seamless, efficient experience. This relationship between your device and the cloud is what makes real-time collaboration, data analysis, and customer relationship management possible on a scale and with a flexibility that was unimaginable just a few decades ago.

Data centers power the cloud

It's easy to picture the cloud as this intangible, ethereal entity, floating somewhere in the digital ether. But the cloud is physically anchored in the world, inside high-tech data centers.

Think of data centers as the engine rooms of the cloud. Scattered across the globe, these facilities are where the magic happens. They're packed with rows upon rows of servers, humming away 24/7, housing the data and applications you access daily.

These centers consume an eye-watering amount of electricity, enough to power small cities. These servers generate heat, much like your laptop does, but on a gargantuan scale. Without sophisticated cooling systems, they'd overheat faster than a smartphone in a sauna.

Then there are the vast miles of cabling, intricately connecting every piece of hardware. This serves as the connective tissue of the cloud. But how many of these data centers are out there?

Estimates suggest there are thousands worldwide. The exact number is a bit of a moving target, as new ones pop up and older ones evolve. The United States leads the pack with the largest number of servers and data centers, but other countries aren't far behind.

This global spread helps provide speed and efficiency. The closer a data center is to you, the quicker you can access your data. It's like having a convenience store right around the corner instead of across town.

By having multiple data centers in various locations, the cloud ensures that even if one goes offline, others can pick up the slack, minimizing downtime. This is why, when one part of the cloud faces issues, the whole system doesn't come crashing down.

In essence, these data centers are the backbone of the cloud. They're often overlooked and taken for granted whenever you stream a video, collaborate on a document, or manage customer relationships in Salesforce. The next time you access your cloud data, remember that there is a physical world behind the seemingly intangible.

Cloud computing versus traditional computing

In the traditional computing world, everything is local. Your software, your data, and your entire digital world reside on your computer or on servers within your company's walls. It's a bit like having all your valuables in a safe at home. You know exactly where everything is, and you feel a sense of control. But what if you want to access something when you're not at home? Or what if your needs grow and that safe isn't big enough anymore?

Enter cloud computing. Instead of being confined to local servers or personal computers, you access software and store data on servers located somewhere in the cloud. These servers are maintained by third parties, and you connect to them over the internet. It's like having a safe deposit box in a highly secure, infinitely expandable vault, accessible from anywhere in the world.

This shift brings with it the benefit of scalability. In traditional computing, if your business grows and your needs increase, you would eventually need to add more hardware or upgrade your systems. In the cloud, it's more like flipping a switch to get more resources. You can scale up or down based on your needs.

There's also cost-effectiveness. With traditional computing, you're facing significant up-front costs, such as buying hardware, obtaining software licenses, and maintenance costs. But cloud computing often follows a subscription model. You pay for only what you use, much like an electricity bill.

And there are accessibility challenges with traditional setups that tie you to the physical location where your servers and computers are. Cloud computing breaks down these barriers. You can access your applications and data from anywhere. All you need is an internet connection.

Despite all of the advantages the cloud brings, it is far from a utopian experience. There are instances where computing outside of the cloud may prevail. Traditional computing offers a level of control and security that some organizations are reluctant to relinquish. When you store data on your own servers, you're in charge of its security. With cloud computing, you're entrusting this to a third party, which can be a significant leap of faith.

The shift from traditional to cloud computing has transformed how businesses operate and people interact with technology. As you delve deeper into Salesforce and its cloud-based ecosystem, this understanding of the shift in computing paradigms offers a lens through which to view the landscape of modern digital solutions.

Salesforce and the evolution of cloud computing

Salesforce has played a pivotal role in transforming the software industry's landscape. While the concept of software as a service (SaaS) had been explored by earlier technologies and companies, Salesforce, under the leadership of Marc Benioff (a former Oracle executive), brought this idea into the mainstream. Launched in 1999, Salesforce redefined the traditional software model, shifting from a product that businesses install and maintain on their systems to a service accessible via the cloud. This innovative approach, particularly in the realm of CRM, exemplified the potential of SaaS and has since profoundly influenced the evolution of cloud computing in the tech industry.

SaaS, in essence, means delivering software over the internet, on demand, and typically on a subscription basis. This was groundbreaking. Instead of companies needing to buy and maintain their software and the hardware to run it, they could now simply log in to a service online and get everything they needed. It was like switching from buying DVDs to streaming movies on Netflix.

Salesforce's approach offered an array of benefits that traditional software couldn't match. First, there was the simplicity and speed of deployment. With no software to install and no hardware to set up, companies could get up and running in record time. This was especially groundbreaking for small businesses that lacked the resources for complex installations.

Then there was the matter of updates and new features. In the traditional model, upgrades could be costly, time-consuming, and disruptive. Salesforce, however, could roll out updates seamlessly through the cloud, ensuring all users had access to the latest features and security enhancements without lifting a finger.

Another significant advantage was scalability. Traditional software often limits you to the capabilities of your local hardware. Salesforce, on the other hand, allows businesses to scale operations up or down as needed, all through the cloud. This flexibility is invaluable for businesses in a world where change is the constant.

But perhaps the most profound impact of Salesforce and SaaS was on accessibility. With Salesforce, all you needed to manage your customer relationships was an internet connection. This democratized access to advanced business tools, previously only available to large corporations.

The Salesforce story is about a company with a visionary approach that transformed an industry. As you explore the world of Salesforce administration, it's essential to appreciate this history. It is the foundation upon which the Salesforce ecosystem is built and a key to understanding its success and its future.

Dispelling common misconceptions about the cloud

When it comes to cloud computing, especially in the context of Salesforce, there's a host of myths and misconceptions floating around. The most prominent among these is the concern about security. It's a natural worry—after all, entrusting your data to a system that seems invisible and intangible can feel like a big risk. Thankfully, the reality of cloud security is far more reassuring than these myths suggest.

The notion that the cloud is inherently less secure than traditional on-premises systems is a misconception. Cloud providers like Salesforce invest massively in security measures. They employ teams of experts dedicated to safeguarding their infrastructure. This level of security is often far more robust than what individual organizations can achieve on their own. From advanced encryption techniques to rigorous compliance standards, cloud providers ensure that your data is protected with the latest and most effective security measures.

Another common myth is that the cloud is an all-or-nothing solution. However, the truth is more nuanced. Many organizations opt for a hybrid approach, combining the strengths of both cloud and on-premises solutions. Salesforce, for instance, can integrate seamlessly with on-prem systems, providing a balanced approach that leverages the cloud's flexibility while maintaining certain operations in house.

There's also a misconception about the loss of control when moving to the cloud. While it's true that the physical servers are not under your direct control, cloud platforms like Salesforce offer extensive customization and administrative control. You can configure the platform to align closely with your business processes, create custom applications, and manage user access and permissions. This level of control ensures that while the hardware might be off-site, the software's functionality and security are very much in your hands.

The idea that the cloud is a one-size-fits-all solution is far from accurate. Cloud services, especially in platforms like Salesforce, are incredibly versatile and customizable. They can be tailored to fit a wide range of business sizes and types, from small startups to global corporations. This flexibility ensures that regardless of your organization's specific needs and challenges, the cloud can be adapted to meet them.

Understanding the realities behind these common cloud computing myths allows you to make informed decisions about adopting and using platforms like Salesforce. The cloud, with its robust security measures, flexibility, and customizable nature, offers a powerful tool for businesses to grow and innovate. As you delve deeper into Salesforce, keep these truths in mind—they'll help you navigate the platform with confidence and clarity.

Salesforce updates and customization

At its inception, Salesforce disrupted the CRM landscape by offering a cloud-based solution at a time when on-premises solutions dominated. This shift to the cloud was more than a technological leap; it was a paradigm shift in how businesses interact with their customers and manage their data. Salesforce's cloud-based platform brought unprecedented accessibility, scalability, and flexibility to CRM.

Salesforce consistently delivers three major releases each year. These scheduled updates ensure that all users automatically gain access to the latest features, enhancements, and security improvements without experiencing downtime or incurring additional costs. This regular, predictable upgrade pattern keeps the Salesforce platform up-to-date while allowing organizations to plan effectively for new functionalities and optimizations, thereby maximizing their CRM investment and capabilities.

Another key aspect of Salesforce's success in the cloud is its customization capability. Salesforce allows businesses to tailor the platform to their specific needs, whether it's through simple configuration changes or by building custom applications on the platform. This level of customization ensures that Salesforce can adapt to various business models and processes, making it a versatile tool for companies across different industries.

Salesforce's commitment to security in the cloud is unwavering. Understanding the importance of data security, Salesforce implements robust security protocols and compliance measures, ensuring that customer data is protected with the highest standards.

The next key concept to explore is Salesforce's multitenant architecture. This architecture is the backbone of Salesforce's cloud platform, enabling efficient resource sharing and scalability while maintaining data security and privacy for each tenant.

Salesforce Multitenant Architecture Overview

Understanding the multitenant architecture of Salesforce is key to appreciating how this powerful platform operates efficiently and securely at scale. At its core, this architecture is what allows Salesforce to serve millions of users worldwide, each with their unique configurations and data, without compromising on performance, security, or functionality.

Imagine an apartment building: a single structure offering individual living spaces to multiple tenants. Each tenant decorates and uses their space independently, without affecting others.

Salesforce's multitenant architecture operates on a similar principle. It hosts the data and applications of multiple clients (tenants) on a single shared infrastructure and software base. This setup is efficient and cost-effective, as it maximizes the utilization of resources like servers, storage, and maintenance efforts.

A common concern with shared environments is privacy and security. How does Salesforce ensure that one client's data is not accessible to another? The answer lies in Salesforce's robust security model, which logically separates each tenant's data. Despite sharing the same physical resources, the data of each client is isolated and invisible to others. Salesforce employs rigorous security measures, including unique identifiers and advanced encryption, to maintain this segregation and protect the integrity and confidentiality of each tenant's data.

Another aspect of Salesforce's multitenant architecture is its flexibility in customization. Each client can tailor their Salesforce environment to their specific needs, from workflow processes to user interfaces, without affecting the underlying core functionality shared by all users. Salesforce allows you to highly customize its platform because of its unique architecture. In this system, changes are made to the underlying structure, known as *metadata*. Metadata is like a blueprint that defines how the software looks and operates. This approach lets you personalize the system extensively without affecting its core shared functions. You will learn more about metadata in Chapter 5.

Multitenant architecture inherently supports scalability. As a business grows, Salesforce can accommodate increased demands without the need for investing in additional hardware or infrastructure. Moreover, when Salesforce rolls out updates and new features, they are instantly available to all clients on the platform. This simultaneous upgrading ensures that all users are always on the latest version of the software, with access to the newest features and security updates.

Salesforce's multitenant architecture is central to its functionality, providing a secure, scalable, and customizable platform. This architecture efficiently supports a diverse and ever-growing global user base, maintaining the privacy and specific needs of each client. As you explore the opportunities and career paths in Salesforce administration, understanding this foundational architecture is essential. It informs the diverse roles and responsibilities of Salesforce administrators in optimizing and maintaining this advanced platform.

Opportunities and Career Paths in Salesforce Administration

Salesforce administration offers a rich and varied landscape of career opportunities, appealing to a wide range of skills and interests. As the backbone of any Salesforce implementation, administrators play an important role in configuring, managing, and optimizing the platform to meet the specific needs of an organization. This section explores the diverse career paths available within the realm of Salesforce administration, highlighting the potential for growth and specialization.

The Role of a Salesforce Platform Administrator

At the heart of Salesforce administration is the Salesforce Platform Administrator role. This role involves a deep understanding of the platform's capabilities and how they can be tailored to support various business processes. Administrators are responsible for user management, data analytics, and ensuring the smooth operation of the CRM system. They act as a bridge between the business and the technical aspects of Salesforce, making them invaluable to any organization using the platform.

Specialization and Advancement

As you gain experience in Salesforce administration, opportunities for specialization emerge. Administrators can choose to focus on specific areas such as security, data management, or user experience. Each area offers unique challenges and opportunities for deepening expertise. For those inclined toward technical development, advancing to roles like Salesforce Developer or Architect is a natural progression. These roles involve more complex tasks such as custom application development and system architecture design.

Consulting and Strategy

For individuals with a strong understanding of business processes and strategic thinking, transitioning into Salesforce consulting can be a rewarding path. Consultants work with various organizations to implement Salesforce solutions, providing strategic advice to optimize the use of the platform. They play a critical role in understanding business needs and translating them into effective Salesforce solutions.

Salesforce Ecosystem: Beyond Administration

The Salesforce ecosystem is vast, and the skills acquired in Salesforce administration open doors to roles in project management, training, and even marketing. Understanding Salesforce's capabilities allows administrators to collaborate effectively with different departments and contribute to the broader goals of an organization.

Continuous Learning and Certification Maintenance

The Salesforce platform is constantly evolving, offering new features and functionalities. This dynamic environment necessitates continuous learning and upskilling. Alongside pursuing advanced certifications, Salesforce professionals must also engage in annual certification maintenance. This ensures that your credentials remain valid and up-to-date. Salesforce mandates the completion of certification maintenance modules on its Trailhead learning platform annually.

Salesforce administration is a career path with numerous avenues for growth and exploration. Whether your interest lies in the technical, strategic, or business side of Salesforce, there is a path that aligns with your skills and career aspirations. The journey begins with a solid foundation in Salesforce administration, opening up a world of possibilities in the ever-expanding Salesforce ecosystem.

Benefits of the Salesforce Platform Administrator Certification

Achieving the Salesforce Platform Administrator certification signifies a comprehensive understanding of core concepts and fundamentals. This credential covers an extensive range of topics, from the initial setup and security to data management and analytics concepts, making it a foundational asset in the Salesforce ecosystem.

The certification ensures that individuals have a solid grasp of Salesforce essentials. It equips them with the necessary skills to configure and manage Salesforce settings effectively, enforce user and data security, and proficiently create reports and dashboards. This foundational knowledge is essential for anyone looking to manage a Salesforce environment competently and make informed decisions.

Holding the Salesforce Platform Administrator certification opens the door to advanced roles within the Salesforce domain. It is often seen as the first step in a Salesforce career, laying the groundwork for tackling more complex tasks and responsibilities. As such, certified administrators often find themselves in high demand, valued for their comprehensive understanding of the platform.

This certification also serves as a mark of professional achievement and dedication to mastering Salesforce. It enhances one's credibility and marketability in the job market, distinguishing certified individuals as committed and knowledgeable professionals in the field.

Platform Administrator Certification Required

Perhaps most importantly, the Salesforce Platform Administrator certification is a prerequisite for many other advanced Salesforce certifications. This aspect highlights its role as the foundational step in a journey of continuous learning and specialization within Salesforce. Pursuing further certifications allows for deepening expertise in specific Salesforce functionalities and roles.

Other Salesforce Certifications

Expanding upon the foundational knowledge gained from the Salesforce Platform Administrator certification, Salesforce offers a variety of certification paths tailored to specific roles. Each path provides specialized skills and knowledge, aligning with distinct career aspirations. Salesforce's Trailhead learning platform outlines these paths in detail, guiding professionals to choose a role that best fits their interests and career goals.

 You can access Trailhead at *https://trailhead.salesforce.com*.

Salesforce Foundations Certifications

Salesforce, in its continuous effort to accommodate varying levels of expertise and experience, has introduced foundational-level certifications. These certifications are strategically designed for individuals at the beginning of their Salesforce journey. The objective is to validate foundational knowledge and understanding of the Salesforce platform, making these certifications an ideal starting point for those new to Salesforce.

Salesforce Certified Platform Foundations

The Salesforce Certified Platform Foundations certification is tailored for individuals who are starting their Salesforce career. This certification focuses on the basic concepts and terminologies related to the platform. It's designed to ensure that the certified individuals have a solid understanding of the Salesforce ecosystem, including its core functionalities and how they can be applied to enhance business processes. This certification is particularly beneficial for those who are looking to establish a foundational understanding before diving into more specialized roles within the Salesforce landscape.

Salesforce Certified Marketing Cloud Engagement Foundations

The Salesforce Certified Marketing Cloud Engagement Foundations certification targets individuals keen on mastering the marketing aspects of the Salesforce platform. This certification is crafted for those beginning their journey in the digital marketing domain within the Salesforce ecosystem. It emphasizes a foundational understanding of key marketing concepts and their application within Salesforce, particularly focusing on Marketing Cloud Engagement.

Salesforce Certified Sales Foundations

For individuals focused on sales strategy and management, the Salesforce Certified Sales Foundations path offers a deep dive into Salesforce's Sales Cloud. This certification is ideal for sales managers and executives looking to leverage Salesforce to drive sales performance and increase revenue.

Salesforce Certified Platform Developer

This path is perfect for those who enjoy coding and developing custom applications. The Salesforce Certified Platform Developer exam covers programming in Apex and Visualforce, as well as understanding the logic and functionality behind the Salesforce platform. It's tailored for professionals who want to build and customize applications on Salesforce.

Upon attaining the Salesforce Certified Platform Developer credential, you can take your coding certification prowess to the next level by then attaining the Salesforce Certified Platform Developer II credential. It is designed for those who have mastered the fundamentals of Salesforce development and are ready to tackle more advanced programming challenges. This advanced credential emphasizes sophisticated Apex programming techniques, complex Visualforce solutions, integration with external systems through APIs, and performance optimization. This certification is ideal for seasoned developers seeking to solidify their advanced skills, expand their career opportunities, and position themselves as senior technical leaders within their organization.

Salesforce Certified Marketing Cloud Engagement Foundations

The Salesforce Certified Marketing Cloud Engagement Foundations path focuses on harnessing the power of Salesforce for digital marketing. It involves mastering Salesforce Marketing Cloud and understanding customer journeys, email marketing strategies, and campaign management. This path is ideal for marketing professionals seeking to enhance their digital marketing skills.

Salesforce Consultant Certifications

This path is designed for those who wish to advise businesses on various Salesforce cloud solutions. Consultant certifications involve understanding business requirements, designing Salesforce solutions, and managing implementations. It's suited for individuals with a blend of technical and business skills. There are a wide variety of consultant certifications available, such as the Salesforce Certified Data Cloud

Consultant, Salesforce Certified Sales Cloud Consultant, and the Salesforce Certified Service Cloud Consultant, to name a few.

Salesforce Designer

The Designer certification path is for those with a keen eye for user experience and design within the Salesforce platform. It covers designing user interfaces and experiences that are intuitive, efficient, and effective. This path is perfect for individuals passionate about creating engaging and user-friendly Salesforce environments.

Salesforce Certified Platform Administrator II

Building on the basic Administrator certification, this path delves deeper into advanced Salesforce functionalities and system customizations. It's ideal for those looking to master the administration of Salesforce systems and to play a key role in optimizing their organization's Salesforce usage.

Salesforce Architect

The Architect path in Salesforce offers a structured approach to mastering the platform, culminating in the esteemed Technical Architect credential. This journey is divided into two primary tracks: the Application Architect and the System Architect, each focusing on different aspects of Salesforce architecture.

Salesforce Certified Application Architect

The Application Architect track is for those who want to delve into the functional layer of Salesforce. It focuses on understanding how to build declarative and programmatic solutions within the Salesforce platform. Key areas include:

Data modeling and management
   Designing data models and managing data effectively within Salesforce

User interface
   Crafting user experiences through customized Salesforce applications

Business logic and process automation
   Developing complex business logic and automation processes

Certifications under this track include the Salesforce Certified Platform App Builder and the Salesforce Certified Platform Developer, which lay the foundation for understanding the building blocks of Salesforce applications.

Salesforce Certified System Architect

The System Architect track, on the other hand, deals with the broader technical considerations of Salesforce solutions. It emphasizes:

Integration
> Understanding and implementing various integration patterns and practices to connect Salesforce with external systems

Identity and access management
> Ensuring secure and efficient access to Salesforce applications

System lifecycle management
> Managing the development lifecycle and environments in Salesforce

Relevant certifications in this track include Salesforce Certified Platform Integration Architect and Salesforce Certified Platform Identity and Access Management Architect, among others.

Reach the peak as a Technical Architect

Upon completing both the Application and System Architect tracks, professionals are well-prepared to pursue the pinnacle of Salesforce architecture certifications: the Salesforce Certified Technical Architect (CTA). The CTA represents a comprehensive mastery of Salesforce architecture, requiring a deep understanding of the platform's capabilities, a strategic approach to solution design, and the ability to communicate complex technical solutions effectively.

The CTA certification process involves a rigorous review board examination where candidates must present a solution architecture for a hypothetical scenario. This process tests not just technical knowledge but also problem-solving skills, communication, and understanding of business processes.

Embarking on the Architect path in Salesforce is a commitment to achieving the highest level of expertise in the Salesforce ecosystem. It's a journey that challenges professionals to continuously learn and adapt, offering immense rewards in terms of career growth, opportunities, and the satisfaction of mastering one of the most comprehensive CRM platforms in the industry.

Choose Your Own Adventure

Each of these roles offers a unique way to engage with the Salesforce platform, catering to a wide range of skills and interests. Whether your passion lies in administration, architecture, development, sales, marketing, consulting, or design, Salesforce provides a certification path to help you achieve your career goals. For more detailed information on these roles and the corresponding certifications, Trailhead is an invaluable resource.

Free Salesforce Learning Account Options

Salesforce is generous with providing free learning environments to enable you to get hands on. There are two primary learning environments you will want to become familiar with. Those free environments are free developer accounts and Trailhead accounts.

Signing Up for a Free Salesforce Developer Account

Don't let the name fool you. A free developer account from Salesforce is not intended for developers only, but for anyone. Go to *https://www.salesforce.com/form/developer-signup* and fill out the form.

You will be asked for your company name; if you don't have your own company and don't wish to tie your free account to your employer, simply enter your own name.

 Whatever you put for the company name on the form will appear in the URL of your free developer account, so it is a good idea to keep it professional. This way you can use this free learning org for a portfolio in the future, to showcase the skills and solutions you've built.

Once you submit the sign-up form, check your email to confirm your account and set your password. The free developer account comes with many Salesforce features enabled for your use. Be sure to log in to your account at least every 45 days to keep it from being automatically deactivated.

Signing Up for a Free Salesforce Trailhead Account

In addition to a free developer account, you can also spin up connected Trailhead Salesforce orgs. Trailhead is Salesforce's gamified online learning platform. As you learn Salesforce through various learning trails on Trailhead, you gain points that count toward various ranks. To get started with blazing your own trail, you will want to sign up for your own free Salesforce Trailhead account.

Go to *https://trailhead.salesforce.com* to get started. You have several options as far as getting started with setting up your free Trailhead account. You can continue by using a variety of your social media accounts, or sign up via email.

Once you have signed up for your free Trailhead account and signed in, you can request a Salesforce instance of your own. These free Salesforce instances are called Hands-On Orgs in Trailhead. While some Trailhead learning modules consist of multiple choice questions serving as knowledge checks, many others give you the opportunity to work in your own org and verify that you have completed your work satisfactorily.

Creating a Salesforce Hands-On Org in Trailhead

A Salesforce Hands-On Org is where you can complete various tasks and challenges in Trailhead. These orgs are often referred to as Trailhead Playgrounds.

You can access your Hands-On Orgs by clicking your profile image at the top-right of the Trailhead screen when you are logged in and then selecting Hands-On Orgs. Any previously created orgs that are connected to your Trailhead account will display.

To create a new Hands-On Org, click Create Playground. A pop-up window displays, as shown in Figure 1-1, with a randomly generated value in the Name.

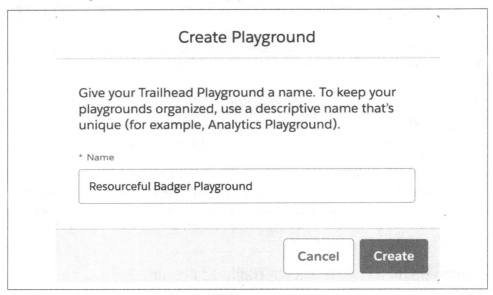

Figure 1-1. Create Playground window

You can change the name of your Trailhead Playground. Click Create to start the creation process of your new playground. Once it is ready, it will display in the list of your Connected Orgs, as shown in Figure 1-2.

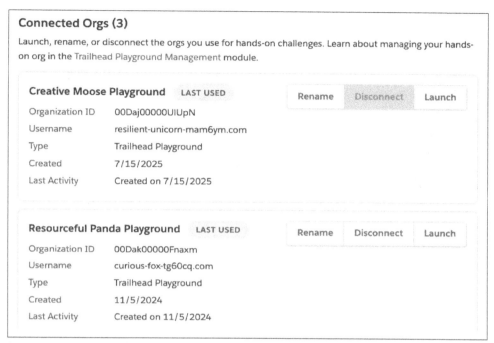

Figure 1-2. Connected Orgs screen/Trailhead Playgrounds

Launching your Trailhead Playground connected Salesforce organization

From the Hands-On Orgs screen, you can rename your Trailhead Playground by clicking the Rename button next to it, as shown in Figure 1-2. To open your Trailhead Playground, click the Launch button beside it. Your new Salesforce instance opens with the Playground Starter application displayed. You will see a welcome message, and the Welcome tab is selected (see Figure 1-3).

The Trailhead Playground Starter Welcome page provides a getting started video that you can view to get oriented. You will also find other tabs across the top of this screen. One of particular interest is the Get Your Login Credentials tab.

Figure 1-3. Trailhead Playground Starter Welcome page

Getting your login credentials to your Trailhead Playground

While you can always access your Trailhead Playground Connected Org through Trailhead by following the preceding steps, it can prove helpful to get your login credentials so you can log in directly to your connected org from anywhere.

Click the Get Your Login Credentials tab to gain access to your username and to set your password for later access. See Figure 1-4 for a sample Get Your Login Credentials screen.

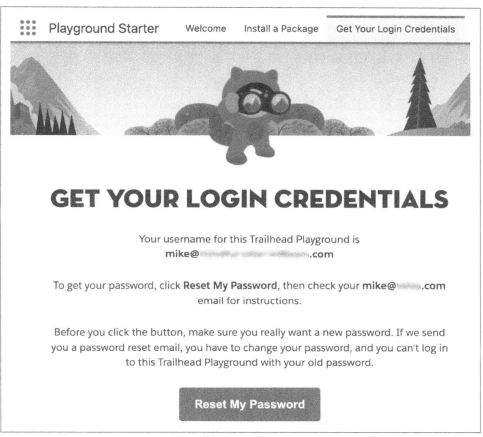

Figure 1-4. Get Your Login Credentials page with Reset My Password button

The Get Your Login Credentials screen provides you with your unique username. You can use this username in the future to log in to your Trailhead Playground org. To do so, you will also need a password.

(Re)setting your Trailhead Playground org password

As a new user in Trailhead Playground, you have your username but do not have access to whatever your default password presumably was set by Salesforce. You will need to perform a password reset. Consider this your first significant administrative task on the platform.

Click the Reset My Password button. The screen updates to inform you that a password reset link has been sent to the email address that you previously entered during Trailhead sign-up. Check your email and click the link provided to finish resetting your password.

You can now directly log in to your new Salesforce organization by going to *https://login.salesforce.com* and log in using your credentials. This is in addition to accessing your Salesforce connected orgs via Trailhead.

Salesforce User Interface Tour

Now that you are logged into your Salesforce instance, it's time to get more familiar with the user interface. When you log in to your Salesforce instance using your username and password, you will first see the Setup menu.

Salesforce Backend Setup Menu Tour

Salesforce's backend operations are akin to the behind-the-scenes workings of a restaurant's "back of the house." In Salesforce, the Setup menu represents this vital backstage area. Here, administrators manage, configure, and maintain the platform's functionalities—tasks essential to ensuring that the frontend user experience, or the "front of the house," runs smoothly and efficiently.

To access the Setup menu at any time in Salesforce, click the gear icon at the top-right of the screen to display the Setup link, as shown in Figure 1-5.

Figure 1-5. Setup accessed via the gear icon

Click the Setup link to access the Setup Home screen, as shown in Figure 1-6.

The Setup screen in Salesforce is the control center for administrators. It's where you can influence how end users in the front of the house interact with the platform through various applications launched via the App Launcher, like Marketing, Sales, Service, and custom apps. Understanding the Setup menu is critical for an effective administrator, as it provides the tools and options to configure the Salesforce environment according to business processes and user requirements. It's where you define user roles, set up security measures, customize objects and fields, and much more.

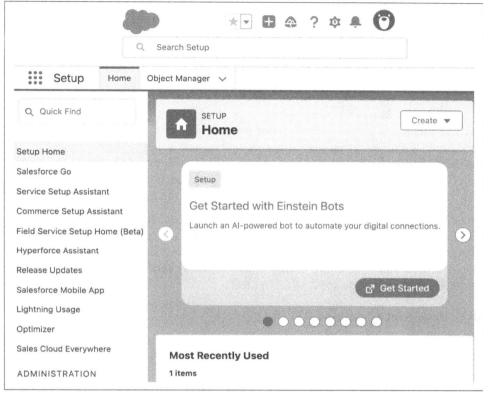

Figure 1-6. Setup Home screen with Quick Find and Setup menu

Setup Quick Find

The Setup Quick Find box in Salesforce is a powerful tool designed to streamline navigation and enhance efficiency, especially when dealing with the platform's extensive range of configuration options (see Figure 1-7). This functionality is a key component for anyone delving into the administrative side of Salesforce, as it simplifies locating specific settings and features within the vast Setup menu.

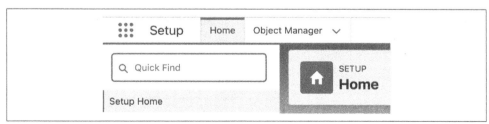

Figure 1-7. Setup Quick Find search box

Quick Find acts like a search engine for Salesforce's setup area, enabling you to quickly locate any configuration option with just a few keystrokes. Instead of manually browsing through the multitude of nested options in the Setup menu, you can type in keywords related to the setting or feature you need to access. Quick Find then presents a list of relevant options, making it easier and faster to find what you're looking for.

As an aspiring Salesforce administrator, it's important to remember that you don't need to memorize every single function within Salesforce. The platform is vast and continuously evolving, making it impractical to know every detail by heart. The real key to success lies in understanding how to effectively navigate the interface, particularly from the backend of Setup. The Quick Find box is instrumental in achieving this, empowering you to efficiently locate and manage the platform's functionalities.

Throughout this book, I will cover the core concepts and functionalities essential for the Salesforce Platform Administrator exam and for effective administration of the platform. While you explore these key areas, remember that the Quick Find tool is always at your disposal, ready to assist you in quickly accessing the specific sections of the Setup menu as you apply what you learn.

Set up Most Recently Used items

When navigating the Setup screen of Salesforce, one of the areas you'll encounter is the Most Recently Used section. It is designed to streamline your workflow by providing quick access to items you've previously worked on within the Setup environment. As you begin to familiarize yourself with Salesforce's setup and customization capabilities, the Most Recently Used section becomes an efficient way to revisit and continue your work on various configuration tasks.

Initially, when you log in to your Salesforce instance and access the Setup area, you might notice that the Most Recently Used section is empty. This is perfectly normal and simply reflects that you haven't yet interacted with any items or components within Setup. As a new Salesforce user, or even when starting work on a new Salesforce instance, this blank slate is your starting point.

When you begin exploring and interacting with different elements in Setup, such as modifying a user role, creating a new field, or adjusting security settings, your actions are automatically logged in the Most Recently Used section. The more you work within Setup, the more populated and tailored this list becomes to your specific tasks and responsibilities.

Object Manager introduction

The Object Manager in Salesforce is a central component for understanding and managing the structure and behavior of data within the platform (see Figure 1-8). Serving as a pivotal tool for administrators and developers alike, the Object Manager provides a comprehensive interface for handling standard and custom objects in Salesforce. You will learn more about objects in Chapter 5.

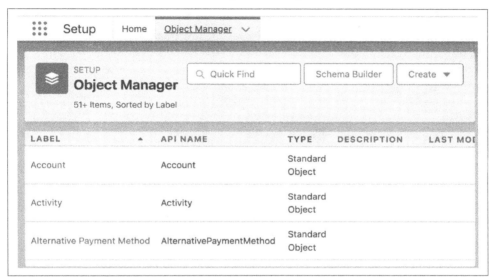

Figure 1-8. Object Manager accessed via its dedicated tab in Setup

One of the key features of the Object Manager is its accessibility. It is consistently available via the Object Manager tab located in the Setup area. This dedicated tab makes it straightforward for users to navigate directly to the Object Manager when working on object configurations. Additionally, you can also access it quickly by typing "Object Manager" into the Quick Find box within Setup. This dual access approach ensures you can reach the Object Manager with ease, whether deep in configuration tasks or just starting your Setup session.

The Object Manager is where you will spend a significant amount of time as a Salesforce administrator. You will also be using the Object Manager frequently through the duration of this book, especially in the Chapter 5.

Salesforce Frontend User Interface Tour

Now that you are more familiar with the back-of-the-house features of Salesforce Setup, it's time to move to the front of the house. It is here that the users you administer spend the majority of their time. Click the App Launcher to launch an application in Salesforce at any time.

Introducing the App Launcher

The App Launcher in Salesforce is a central feature that simplifies navigation and enhances the user experience. It serves as a gateway to the diverse applications and functionalities within the Salesforce platform. The App Launcher appears as a 3 × 3 grid located at the top-left of the interface, as shown in Figure 1-9.

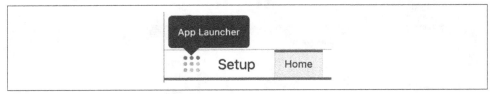

Figure 1-9. App Launcher icon

What Is an App in Salesforce?

In Salesforce, an *app* refers to a collection of tabs that work together to provide functionality for a particular business need. Think of it as a customized workspace that contains all the necessary tools and data for a specific department or process. For example, a Sales app might include tabs for accounts, contacts, Opportunities, and reports, all tailored to streamline the sales process. Apps in Salesforce are designed to be modular and user-centric, allowing users to focus on the specific tasks and information relevant to their role.

Navigating the App Launcher. When you click on the App Launcher icon (see Figure 1-9), a window pops up displaying many apps, making them quickly accessible, as shown in Figure 1-10.

The order of applications accessible via the App Launcher may vary. If you don't find the app that you are looking for, you can always click View All.

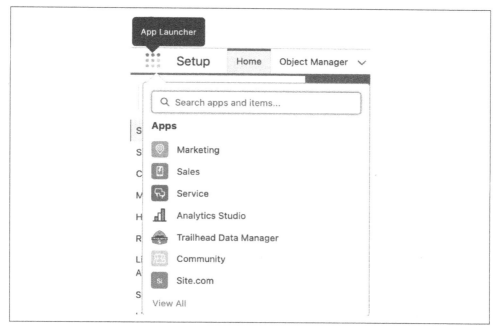

Figure 1-10. App Launcher expanded in Salesforce

Exploring All Apps and All Items from the App Launcher. Clicking View All from the App Launcher expands the App Launcher to display All Apps and All Items. All Apps reveals the full list of available applications, both standard and custom, within your Salesforce instance, as shown in Figure 1-11.

This expanded view is where you can explore and access the full range of applications that Salesforce offers.

 You can click and drag the apps lists in the App Launcher to your own desired order of appearance. This is a user-specific change and is not org-wide for all users. To change the default sort order of apps for all users, go to App Menu in Setup. Refer to "App Menu" on page 54 to learn more.

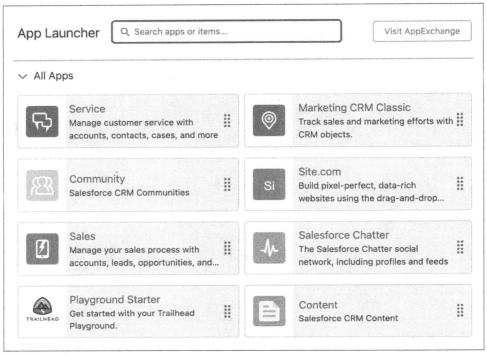

Figure 1-11. App Launcher All Apps view

Beneath the All Apps section you can scroll down to find the All Items section. The All Items section refers to individual components or objects within Salesforce. An object in Salesforce can be understood as a container for specific types of data.

From the All Items section of the App Launcher, you can click on any object in the list to access it. These objects form the building blocks of Salesforce's data model, and All Items provides a direct route to accessing these individual components.

Accessing reports and dashboards via the App Launcher. Within the All Items section of the App Launcher, you'll also find essential tools such as reports and dashboards. These powerful features are integral to Salesforce, offering visual insights and analytics into your data. Reports provide detailed data analysis, allowing you to compile and review information across various objects. Dashboards, on the other hand, present this data visually, using graphs, charts, and tables for an easy-to-understand overview.

Accessing reports and dashboards through the App Launcher is straightforward, offering quick navigation to these tools. You'll also often find dedicated tabs for reports and dashboards in standard Salesforce applications like Marketing, Sales, and Service, ensuring convenient access to real-time data analysis and decision-making insights.

Accessing the Salesforce Recycle Bin via the App Launcher. The Salesforce Recycle Bin is an essential tool for administrators, functioning much like the Recycle Bin on your computer. It is a safety net where deleted records are stored, providing you with an opportunity to recover data that may have been removed from the platform inadvertently. You can access the Recycle Bin easily via the App Launcher, making it a readily available resource in your administrative toolkit.

When records are deleted in Salesforce, they aren't immediately purged from the system. Instead, they are retained in the Recycle Bin for up to 15 days, giving you a window to restore deleted records if needed. However, it's important to note that the Recycle Bin has a storage capacity limit. If that limit is reached, older records may be permanently removed before the 15-day period expires. This built-in safeguard means that while the Recycle Bin offers a buffer for recovery, it shouldn't be relied on as a long-term backup strategy.

As an administrator, your view of the Recycle Bin is more comprehensive than that of a standard user. You have the ability to see your deleted records and those deleted by any user in your organization. This expanded view is particularly beneficial in managing data across your Salesforce environment, ensuring that no important information is lost or removed unintentionally.

App Launcher search. The App Launcher also includes a search functionality at the top, allowing you to quickly find a specific app or item by typing in keywords. This feature is incredibly useful when you know what you need but don't want to scroll through the entire list of apps and items.

List views

In Salesforce, when you click on a tab within an app, you're presented with a list view (see Figure 1-12). This view displays a list of records that fall under a specific category or criterion, like a list of all contacts or Opportunities.

When you click a tab for the first time in a new Salesforce instance, you may think that you do not have any data in your organization. That is because the default behavior is for the Recently Viewed list view to appear.

Since you have yet to view any data, your list view will be empty. You can click the down arrow, as shown in Figure 1-12, and select a different list view to see data belonging to the object/tab that you have selected.

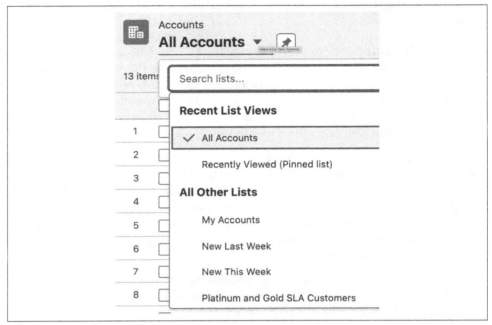

Figure 1-12. Salesforce list view of All Accounts

 Data that you will find in your free Salesforce Trailhead account is not real records of actual people and companies. This mock data is populated to closely resemble real data in a production instance of Salesforce.

Pinning a list view

One useful feature is the ability to pin a list view, as shown in Figure 1-13. Pinning sets a specific view as your default whenever you access that tab, saving you the time of searching for or setting up your preferred view each time you revisit a tab. It's especially useful if you find yourself frequently returning to the same data set.

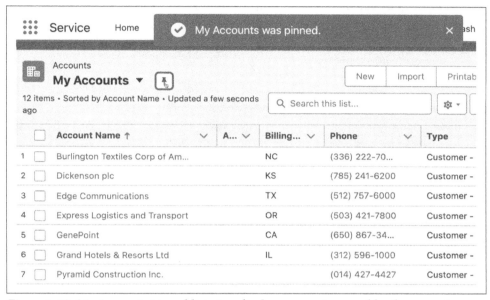

Figure 1-13. My Accounts pinned list view displays accounts owned by the current user

Record detail pages

Once you click an individual record from a list view, you are taken to the Record detail page for that particular record, as shown in Figure 1-14. This page provides comprehensive information about the specific record, organized into different sections for easy navigation. Depending on the type of record you are accessing the default view upon initial opening of a detail record may be on either the Related tab or the Details tab.

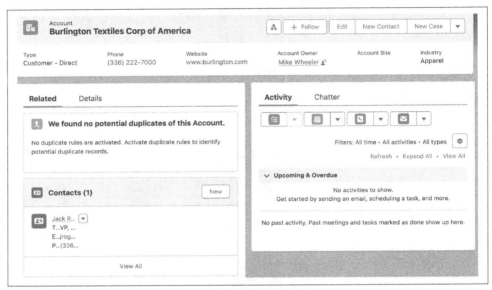

Figure 1-14. Account detail record with Related tab displayed

Related lists.   The Related tab on a Record details page houses what are known as *Related lists*. These lists display records that are linked or related to the primary record you're viewing. For instance, if you're viewing an account, the Related lists might show Opportunities or Cases that are associated with that account.

Related lists provide context and a comprehensive view of the relationships between different records in Salesforce. Understanding how to navigate and utilize these lists is key for effective data management and for gaining a holistic understanding of the relationships and interactions within your Salesforce data.

Details tab.   You can access the details of a record by clicking the Details tab, as shown in Figure 1-15, if it isn't already displayed by default upon first opening a record.

Figure 1-15. Account detail record with Details tab displayed

Hyperlinks and navigation. Throughout the Record detail page, you'll notice hyperlinked text, usually underlined and in blue. These hyperlinks enable you to navigate easily to related records or additional information, creating a connected web of data within Salesforce.

Activity management and Chatter. Two additional tabs on a Record detail page are the Activity and Chatter tabs. These tabs reside in the activity management side of a Record detail page.

The Activity tab tracks all the tasks, events, and history related to the record, while the Chatter tab serves as a collaboration space where team members can communicate and share updates about the record.

For a deeper dive into how the Activity tab can help you track tasks, events, and history related to records, be sure to explore "Activity Management" on page 294. It provides a comprehensive overview of logging calls, managing tasks and events, and utilizing Salesforce calendars for efficient activity tracking.

If you're interested in learning more about leveraging the Chatter tab for effective team collaboration and communication, see "Chatter for Collaboration" on page 306.

Summary

In this first chapter, you've explored the foundational understanding of Salesforce, its role in the tech industry, and the importance of the Salesforce Platform Administrator certification. You've been introduced to the platform's multitenant architecture and the diverse career paths it opens up. This knowledge sets the stage for a deeper exploration into the functionalities and capabilities of Salesforce.

Configuration and Setup: Organization Setup

The first knowledge area found in the Salesforce Certified Platform Administrator Exam Guide is Configuration and Setup. This knowledge area combines three core functional areas of focus, one building upon the next.

These three functional areas are:

- Organization Setup
- User Setup
- Security and Access

Since each of these three functional areas are so fundamental, large in size, and important to understand in their proper sequence, I have elected to devote a chapter to each. For that reason, this chapter focuses on the first two learning objectives of the Configuration and Setup knowledge area, which are focused on Organization Setup.

From the Exam Guide

The two Organization Setup learning objectives from the Exam Guide, and the focus of this chapter are:

- Describe the information found in the company settings (for example, company settings fiscal year, business hours, currency management, default settings).
- Distinguish and understand the administration of declarative configuration of the user interface (for example, UI settings, App Menu, list views, global actions, Lightning App Builder).

The next two chapters will focus on the User Setup and Security and Access functional aspects, respectively, with each containing their own learning objectives from the Configuration and Setup knowledge area.

It's time to begin your journey into the Configuration and Setup knowledge area by exploring the Organization Setup concepts further.

Company Settings

The Company Settings menu inside the Setup menu contains several core functions related to the setup of your company in Salesforce. See "Salesforce Backend Setup Menu Tour" on page 24 to learn more about the Setup menu.

Accessing Company Settings

You can find the Company Settings menu in the Setup menu by searching for it (see Figure 2-1). You can expand the Company Settings menu to find many fundamental configuration and setup options, such as:

- Business Hours
- Calendar Settings
- Company Information
- Data Protection and Privacy
- Fiscal Year
- Holidays
- Language Settings
- My Domain

Business Hours

Business Hours play a pivotal role in customizing the platform to mirror an organization's operational hours. Beyond ensuring your Salesforce instance accurately reflects the times when your organization is providing services to customers, Business Hours in Salesforce underpin numerous automated processes and customer service operations. These processes include managing case escalations and tracking service-level agreements (SLAs), ensuring time-sensitive operations are handled efficiently within the operational window.

Business hours and SLAs

SLAs in Salesforce work in conjunction with Entitlements, a feature that helps manage customer support agreements and service contracts. While SLAs define the expected level of service, Entitlements are used to enforce these agreements by specifying the terms of support that a customer is entitled to, such as response times and support channels.

 Entitlements in Salesforce go beyond the scope of the Salesforce Certified Platform Administrator exam, but are tested in the Service Cloud Consultant exam.

Setting organization business hours

Clicking Business Hours in the Setup menu will display the Organization Business Hours screen, as displayed in Figure 2-1.

Figure 2-1. Organization Business Hours screen

The Organization Business Hours screen displays the default business hours that are automatically set in your Trailhead learner account. You can change your business hours by clicking Edit next to your Default. This displays the Business Hours Edit screen (see Figure 2-2).

From the Business Hours Edit screen, you can update the Business Hours Name field. You can also update the Time Zone to that of your own. Additionally, you can change the start and end times of your business hours from the default operational settings of daily 24 hours to individual start and end times.

Once you have completed your adjustments, click Save to return to the Organization Business Hours screen where you will find your recent changes displayed.

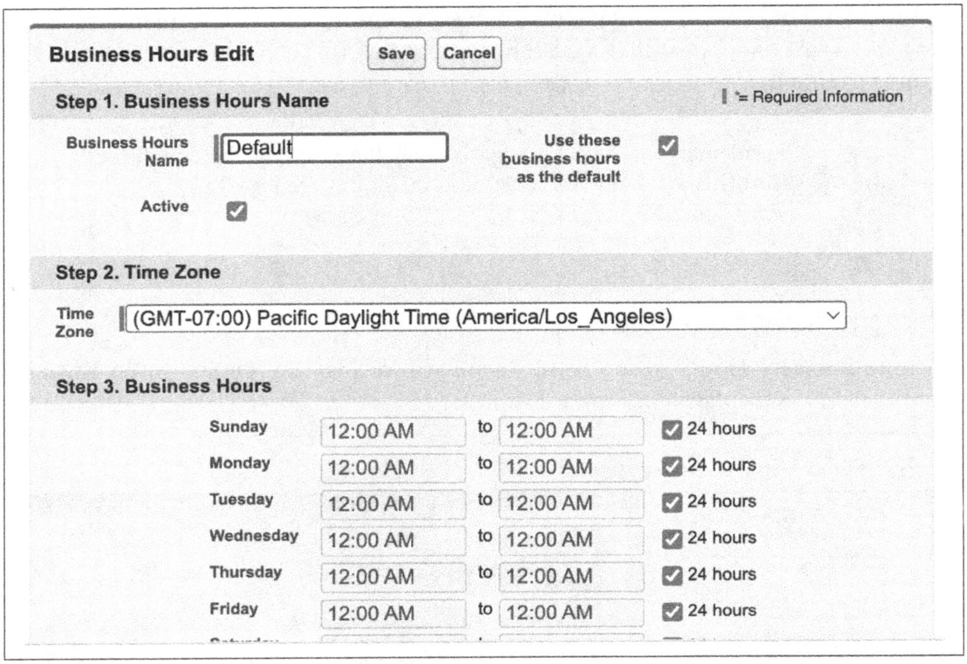

Business Hours Edit   [Save] [Cancel]

Step 1. Business Hours Name | *= Required Information

Business Hours Name [Default]   Use these business hours as the default ☑

Active ☑

Step 2. Time Zone

Time Zone [(GMT-07:00) Pacific Daylight Time (America/Los_Angeles)   ⌄]

Step 3. Business Hours

Sunday   [12:00 AM] to [12:00 AM]   ☑ 24 hours
Monday   [12:00 AM] to [12:00 AM]   ☑ 24 hours
Tuesday   [12:00 AM] to [12:00 AM]   ☑ 24 hours
Wednesday [12:00 AM] to [12:00 AM]   ☑ 24 hours
Thursday   [12:00 AM] to [12:00 AM]   ☑ 24 hours
Friday   [12:00 AM] to [12:00 AM]   ☑ 24 hours

Figure 2-2. Business Hours Edit screen

Salesforce automatically calculates daylight saving times for time zones.

Setting multiple business hours

While most organizations operate on a standard set of business hours, Salesforce offers the flexibility to support multiple business hours. This feature is needed for organizations that operate in different time zones or have various departments with distinct operational hours.

For example, a multinational corporation may have customer support centers across the globe, each with its own set of business hours. In this context, it is recommended to create one set of business hours per support center.

Setting up multiple business hours is a more advanced feature and is less common in the context of the administrator exam. The exam focus is typically on understanding and managing a standard set of business hours that reflects the main operational time frame of an organization.

Calendar Settings

The next item found in the Company Settings menu is Calendar Settings. Click Calendar Settings to reveal the submenu of "Public Calendars and Resources."

Public Calendars and Resources

In Salesforce, public calendars and resources are essential tools for managing group activities and shared resources efficiently. Clicking "Public Calendars and Resources" in the Setup menu displays the screen shown in Figure 2-3.

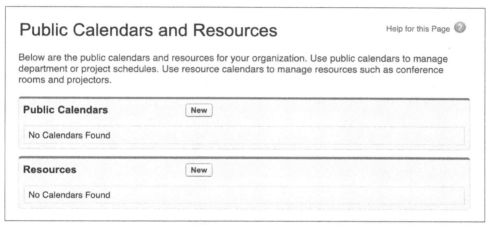

Figure 2-3. Public Calendars and Resources screen

Public calendars are used for scheduling and tracking group events in Salesforce. These events are particularly useful for organizing activities that involve multiple team members, such as marketing campaigns, training sessions, or product launches. These calendars enhance collaboration and ensure everyone is on the same page regarding upcoming events and deadlines.

Resources, on the other hand, are important for scheduling and managing assets shared within an organization. They could be physical items like conference rooms and projectors, or intangible resources like shared work hours. Proper management of resources through Salesforce prevents conflicts and optimizes their usage, contributing to smoother operational flow. I cover creating events and scheduling them in Chapter 9.

Company Information

The next Company Settings submenu is Company Information. Here is where you find details related to your company and your Salesforce instance. It's important to know that your Company Information settings are often the first point of interaction for administrators setting up a new Salesforce environment. They lay the groundwork for more complex configurations and have a cascading effect on various functionalities within Salesforce.

Clicking the Company Information submenu in Setup displays the Company Information screen, as shown in Figure 2-4.

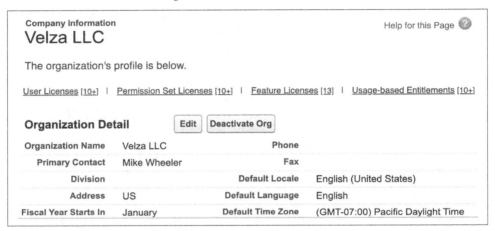

Figure 2-4. Company Information screen

The Company Information screen houses a lot of important information related to your organization. It is here that you will find specifics related to your company and Salesforce organization, such as fiscal year settings, available storage, default organization settings, and much more.

Default organization settings: locale, language, and time zone

The Company Information screen is where you can adjust your default organization settings. These default settings serve as a finely tuned engine, ensuring every aspect of your instance aligns with your organization's geographical and cultural context.

The three primary default settings found on the Company Information screen are:

- Default Locale
- Default Language
- Default Time Zone

Your company's default settings provide an operational baseline for your organization. All users in your Salesforce instance are assigned your organization's default locale, language, and time zone settings when their accounts are first created, unless specified otherwise.

You can adjust individual user locale, language, and time zone settings at the user level. I will cover user management in the next chapter.

To make changes to your company information, click Edit to display the Organization Edit screen. You can then change the locale, language, and time zone defaults for your organization, as necessary.

Default locale

Your organization's default locale setting can easily be confused with its default language. Although in some instances, these may appear similar, they control very different things.

Locale settings in Salesforce serve as a quasicultural compass directing your users' Salesforce journeys. Locale settings align the platform's environment with regional formats for dates, addresses, and names. Also, depending on your locale settings, numeric values may be comma separated, separated by periods, or have no separator.

These settings bring a sense of cultural familiarity, ensuring that your Salesforce instance resonates with your regional nuances. A misaligned locale setting can lead to significant misunderstandings and errors in data interpretation, emphasizing the need for precise configuration.

Default language

Salesforce's default language setting establishes the language that your Salesforce users will encounter in the user interface. Much like the user-specific flexibility of adjusting locale settings at the user level, you can also adjust a user's own default language to differ from the default language for your organization.

The Default Language drop-down menu in the locale settings section will display many language options to choose from, which Salesforce currently supports. This setting dictates the primary language of your Salesforce interface.

Default time zone

The default time zone setting in Salesforce plays a central role in synchronizing your global operations. Typically, you will want your default time zone to be reflective of the actual time zone for your primary global headquarters. As with the other default settings, you can set an individual user's default time zone to differ from the organizational default.

These settings offer the flexibility to tailor your Salesforce experience to diverse user groups, underlining Salesforce's commitment to delivering a user-centric platform for all. Time zone settings ensure every team member, no matter where they are in the world, is in sync.

When activities, meetings, and deadlines are correctly timed, efficient global collaboration and operational consistency becomes the norm.

 The default time zone for your organization can differ from the time zone(s) set for your business hours, which I covered earlier in this chapter. This would apply for instances where you have different business hours set for different branches or locations residing in various time zones.

Additional company information settings

Moving beyond the default settings of the Company Information screen, you will find additional settings that can be configured and maintained here. These include:

Organization Name and Address
This is where you input your organization's legal name and physical address. It's essential for correspondence, billing, and localization purposes.

Primary Contact
Designating a primary contact for your Salesforce instance is important for communication and receiving notifications from Salesforce.

Fiscal Year Starts In
Your Salesforce Fiscal Year setting defaults to a standard fiscal year with a start month of January. You will explore fiscal year settings later in this chapter.

Currency management
If your organization operates in multiple countries, you may need to enable and configure multiple currencies. Your Salesforce instance begins as a single currency environment, by default.

Used Data Space
This field displays the amount of data space consumed, such as Account, Contact, and Opportunity records, and indicates what percentage of your total allocated data storage quota is in use. Salesforce's free learning environments typically offer limited data storage capacity, making it essential to keep an eye on this field. For a detailed breakdown of data usage, the View link next to Used Data Space offers an in-depth look, helping you manage data more efficiently and plan for potential storage needs.

Used File Space

This field tracks the storage consumed by files and attachments. This includes documents, images, and other file types uploaded to Salesforce records or stored in the Salesforce Files section. These files often consume more storage space compared to standard data records.

Salesforce Organization ID (not shown in Figure 2-4)

This unique identifier is like the fingerprint of your Salesforce instance. It's a specific, alphanumeric code that Salesforce assigns to uniquely identify your organization. Essential for support cases, integrations, and identifying your organization in Salesforce ecosystems, this ID is the key to distinguishing your setup in the vast universe of all Salesforce environments.

Instance (not shown in Figure 2-4)

The instance refers to the specific Salesforce server your organization resides on. Salesforce operates multiple data centers globally, each housing a multitude of individual servers, to optimize performance and reliability. Knowing your instance is helpful during maintenance periods or service disruptions, as it helps pinpoint the server hosting your data. You can view service disruptions and scheduled maintenance for your instance at *https://status.salesforce.com*.

The Company Information screen also reveals important license information. These reference tables found beneath your Organization Detail on the Company Information screen reveal total, used, and remaining licenses in your organization.

Data Protection and Privacy

The next Company Settings submenu is "Data Protection and Privacy," as shown in Figure 2-5. Here you ensure your Salesforce environment complies with data privacy laws and respects the personal data preferences of your customers globally. This encourages trust and confidence from your customer base.

The Data Protection and Privacy screen enables administrators to access and configure aspects of data protection and privacy for leads, contacts, and personal account records. This is accomplished by way of an object called Individual, which stores details about data protection and privacy preferences for your customers.

The Individual object enables your business to handle personal data responsibly and in accordance with individual preferences. By making these data protection details available in records, Salesforce allows businesses to stay attentive to customer needs regarding personal data management. You will learn more about objects in Chapter 5.

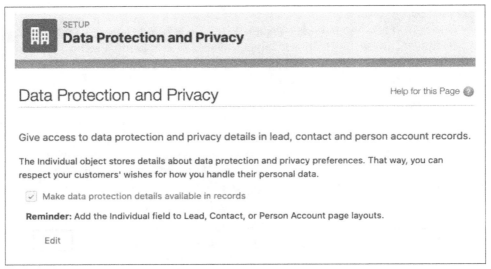

Figure 2-5. Data Protection and Privacy screen

Fiscal Year Settings in Salesforce

The next Company Settings submenu in Setup is Fiscal Year. The concept of the fiscal year is fundamental in business operations for financial planning, reporting, and analysis. Accessing Fiscal Year in Setup displays the organization's Fiscal Year Edit screen, as shown in Figure 2-6.

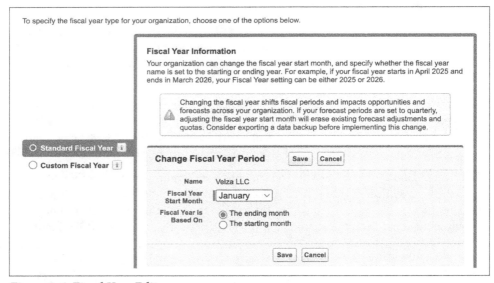

Figure 2-6. Fiscal Year Edit screen

Standard versus custom fiscal year

A standard fiscal year aligns with the calendar year, starting in January and ending in December. This is the default setting in Salesforce and is widely used by organizations whose financial reporting aligns with the calendar year.

Not all companies adhere to the standard fiscal year. Salesforce, for example, uses a custom fiscal year, aligning their financial reporting with specific business needs. Companies may choose a custom fiscal year for various reasons, such as aligning with industry standards, tax considerations, or specific operational cycles.

Considerations and implications of setting a custom fiscal year

Setting a custom fiscal year in Salesforce has significant, long-term implications. Once set, it cannot be reverted to a standard fiscal year or deleted, necessitating careful consideration before implementation.

Your fiscal year setting directly influences how sales pipelines and forecasts are managed and reported. A custom fiscal year might require adjustments in reporting and analysis practices to align with the unique financial periods.

A custom fiscal year also impacts various functionalities and data representations within the system. This decision should be taken with a long-term perspective, considering the potential need for future adjustments or realignments. Organizations should also evaluate how a custom fiscal year aligns with their operational activities, including sales cycles, budgeting processes, and performance evaluations.

Holidays

The next Company Settings submenu in Setup is Holidays. The Holidays screen, as displayed in Figure 2-7, is used to configure dates and times when your normal business hours are suspended due to various holiday observances.

Holidays impact various operational processes, such as providing for accurate scheduling and planning. They ensure business operations consider official nonworking days, which impact task assignments, SLA calculations, and customer service operations.

For organizations operating across different regions, customizing holidays according to local observances is essential for maintaining operational consistency and respecting cultural nuances. You can enter any holidays that your organization observes by clicking New, which displays the Holiday Detail screen shown in Figure 2-8.

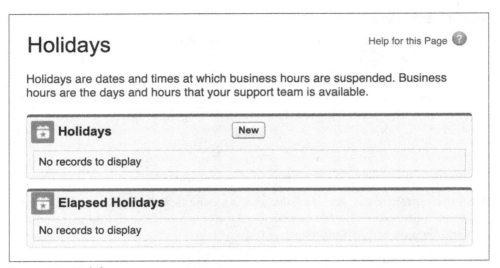

Holidays

Help for this Page ⓘ

Holidays are dates and times at which business hours are suspended. Business hours are the days and hours that your support team is available.

📅 Holidays   [New]

No records to display

📅 Elapsed Holidays

No records to display

Figure 2-7. Holidays screen

📅 Holiday Detail

Help for this Page ⓘ

Holidays are dates and times at which business hours are suspended.

Enter the dates and times at which to suspend business hours and escalation rules associated with business hours.

Holiday Detail   [Save] [Cancel]

Holiday Name	
Description	
Date	7/4/2026
Time	from [ ] to [ ] ☑ All Day
Recurring Holiday	☐

[Save] [Cancel]

Figure 2-8. Holiday Detail screen

For each observed holiday, enter the Holiday Name, Description, Date, Time, and signify if it is an All Day event and/or a Recurring Holiday.

Click Save to record the holiday details and return to the Holidays screen. Over time, previously observed holidays will display in the Elapsed Holidays section of the screen.

Language Settings

The next Company Settings submenu in Setup is Language Settings. It is here that you specify the language preferences for your organization, as shown in Figure 2-9.

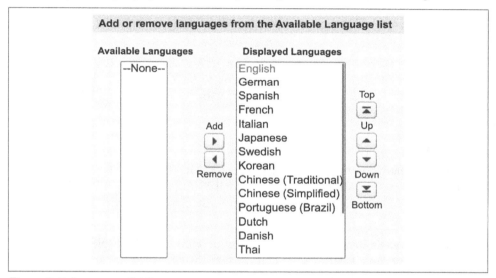

Figure 2-9. Language Settings screen

The Language Settings screen is divided into two primary sections. Toward the top you will find the end-user languages and platform-only languages. The bottom of the screen is where you will find the Available Languages list for the fully supported languages.

To make sense of this screen, it is helpful to first understand that Salesforce provides three levels of language support:

Fully supported languages (bottom of screen)
> Salesforce user interface text appears in the chosen language. The fully supported languages display at the bottom of this screen, from which you can remove languages from the Displayed Languages section back to the Available Languages section. The Displayed Languages will be those that display to your end users,

which they can select as their default language for their user interface experience in Salesforce.

End-user languages (top of screen)
Allows individual users to select a language other than the company's default language for users. Checking the "Enable end-user languages" checkbox updates the Available Languages list below to make these additional languages available to be displayed.

Platform-only languages (top of screen)
Used when Salesforce doesn't provide default translations to enable you to localize apps and custom functionality that you build. Checking the "Enable platform-only languages" checkbox updates the Available Languages list to make these additional languages available to be displayed.

Once you have finalized your Displayed Languages selections, click Save. You can verify that your changes are saved by returning to the Company Information screen and clicking the Default Language drop-down menu to find your Displayed Languages available there.

My Domain

The next Company Settings submenu in Setup is My Domain. It is a Salesforce feature that allows organizations to customize their Salesforce login URL with a unique, branded domain. Accessing My Domain from Setup displays the My Domain Settings screen.

The My Domain Settings screen, as shown in Figure 2-10, displays the current domain URL for your Salesforce instance. From this screen, you can configure and set advanced domain settings related to your Salesforce instance, such as redirections, authentication and configuration, and much more. The administration of your domain settings is generally not covered in the administrator exam.

Changing the default domain name provided by Salesforce upon creation of your Playground org may present issues in the future when checking your work on Trailhead. It is advisable not to change your domain settings in any Trailhead Playground accounts.

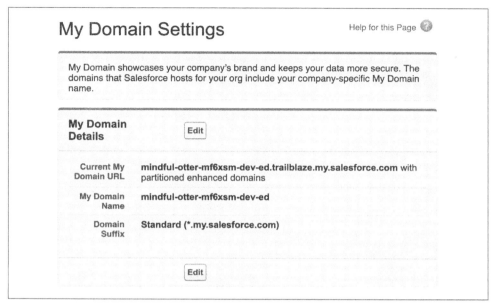

Figure 2-10. My Domain Settings screen

User Interface Settings

The next learning objective found in the Exam Guide for the Configuration and Setup knowledge area relates to Organization Setup user interface settings. Specifically, it requires that you are able to distinguish and understand the administration of declarative configuration of the user interface (i.e., UI settings, App Menu, list views, global actions, Lightning App Builder).

As you can see from the learning objective, there are several topics to unpack further. These topics are:

- UI settings
- App Menu
- List views
- Global actions
- Lightning App Builder

Continue your journey by first defining *declarative configuration*.

Declarative Configuration

Declarative configuration is a cornerstone concept for effective Salesforce administration. It is pivotal to understanding how you can tailor the platform to fit your organization's unique needs without delving into complex coding.

Declarative configuration in Salesforce is primarily characterized by its point-and-click interface. This interface enables administrators to configure and customize the Salesforce environment through an intuitive, user-friendly graphical interface. In essence, it democratizes the process of Salesforce customization, making it accessible even to those who may not have a background in programming.

At the heart of declarative configuration is the idea that complex business processes and workflows can be implemented and automated using prebuilt functionalities within Salesforce. This methodology involves using various tools and settings provided by Salesforce to define and manage various settings, such as the following:

UI settings
> Here, administrators can modify the visual layout and design of the Salesforce interface, including themes, branding, and display options. This customization ensures the platform aligns aesthetically and functionally with the organization's identity and user preferences.

App Menu
> The App Menu is used to set the default sort order of applications for your users in the App Launcher. Declarative configuration enables the customization of this menu, allowing administrators to tailor it to reflect the most frequently used apps.

List views
> These are essential for organizing and displaying data in a way that is most relevant and useful to users. Administrators use declarative configuration to create and modify list views, enabling users to easily access, sort, and analyze data based upon specific criteria or business requirements.

Global actions
> These are shortcuts that enable users to perform common tasks quickly. Declarative configuration allows the creation and customization of these actions, streamlining workflow and enhancing productivity.

Lightning App Builder
> This tool empowers administrators to create custom pages and apps by simply dragging and dropping components onto a canvas. It exemplifies the core of declarative configuration, offering a visual approach to building functional and interactive user interfaces without the need for code. By embracing declarative configuration, Salesforce administrators can tailor the platform to meet their

organization's specific requirements. This approach saves time and ensures a high degree of adaptability and scalability.

In the following sections, I will delve deeper into each of these topics, exploring how they contribute to the overall functionality and user experience of the Salesforce platform.

User Interface Settings

As you gain more experience on the Salesforce platform, you will likely discover that most key features have an accompanying Settings screen devoted to it. You can test this out for yourself by performing a search for Settings in the Setup Quick Find search box.

The user interface of Salesforce is no exception. From the User Interface screen, you can modify your organization's user interface by enabling or disabling various settings.

Locating User Interface settings

The first challenge in adjusting your user interface settings in Salesforce is locating the User Interface settings screen (see Figure 2-11). You cannot find it by searching for "user interface settings," and you will find no Setup menu item with that name. What you are looking for in Setup is "User Interface." Found as a submenu, there is an additional menu item sharing the same name of "User Interface."

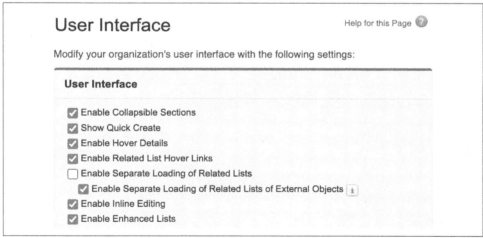

Figure 2-11. User Interface (settings) screen

Although this menu would more helpfully be named "UI Settings," clicking the sub-menu for User Interface will display the User Interface screen. Why this menu and accompanying screen are not named and discoverable via search as "user interface settings" or "UI settings" is anyone's guess.

The User Interface screen, as shown partially in Figure 2-11, contains an impressive array of dozens of checkboxes. Zooming out at a high level, these various settings are divided into the following categories:

- User Interface
- Sidebar
- Calendar
- Name Settings
- Advanced

Fortunately, the Salesforce Certified Platform Administrator exam does not test you for extensive knowledge related to the settings here. Your goal is to recognize that Salesforce does indeed provide flexibility when it comes to the adjustments available in the user interface. You can also access further details on each of these individual checkbox settings found on this screen by clicking the Help for this Page link, located at the upper-right.

App Menu

The next topic related to the User Interface learning objective in Setup is the App Menu. You learned about the App Launcher in the previous chapter. But it should be noted that the App Menu and the App Launcher are two different things.

The App Menu is accessible in Setup under User Interface and is used to set the default sort order for all of your apps accessible in the App Launcher, as shown in Figure 2-12. From this screen, you can also hide individual apps in the App Launcher.

Although the App Menu is used to set the baseline sort order of apps in the App Launcher for all users, individual users may override these defaults by dragging individual apps that are available to them in the App Launcher to their own desired order. Any users who have not made their own personal customizations will see their apps in the default sort order that has been set here in the App Menu.

Careful thought should be employed in setting a logical sort order for your App Menu. Best practice would follow that those apps most frequently accessed by your user base should be placed toward the top, with less frequently accessed applications appearing further down the list.

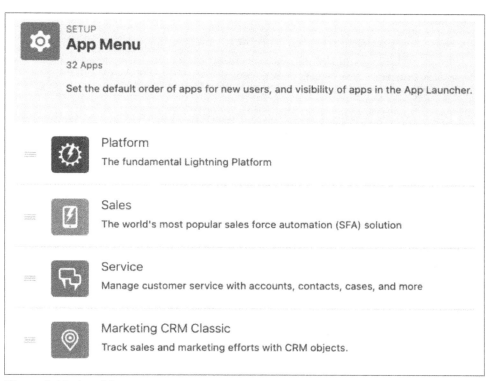

SETUP

App Menu

32 Apps

Set the default order of apps for new users, and visibility of apps in the App Launcher.

Platform
The fundamental Lightning Platform

Sales
The world's most popular sales force automation (SFA) solution

Service
Manage customer service with accounts, contacts, cases, and more

Marketing CRM Classic
Track sales and marketing efforts with CRM objects.

Figure 2-12. App Menu screen

Users may not see all of the apps that are listed in the App Menu. Their individual access to apps is controlled by their individual profile assignment, as well as any additional permission sets that they may have been assigned to. You will learn more about profiles and permission sets in Chapter 4.

List Views

In Salesforce, a list view provides a filtered list of records for a specific object, such as Accounts or Contacts. These views can be customized to show records that meet certain criteria, making it easier for users to find the information they need quickly.

List views are very versatile and can be used to perform powerful actions as an administrator. In my opinion, list views are the most under-appreciated feature of Salesforce. You can perform a lot of helpful actions with them, which I will now explore.

Accessing list views

Whenever you first click a tab for Accounts, Contacts, or other types of records in Salesforce, or a link from the All Items section of the App Launcher, a list view displays. The first time you access a list view in Salesforce, it defaults to display the Recently Viewed list view.

If you have not previously viewed any records for a certain type of record (known as an *object* in Salesforce), you are greeted with a Recently Viewed list view. This experience can prove disorienting, because you have not recently viewed any records and your list sits empty.

You can click the drop-down menu next to the Recently Viewed drop-down list to select a different list view, such as All Accounts. You can click the pin next to a list view name to pin it for later reference.

Pinning list views

A pinned list view for a user remains consistent across different applications in Salesforce. This means that if a user pins a list view in one application, this view will appear by default when they access the same object from another application.

Each Salesforce user has unique responsibilities and preferences. Pinning list views allows each user to customize their interface according to their most frequently accessed data, enhancing their overall experience and productivity.

This supports Salesforce's emphasis on personalization. Each user can tailor their experience based on their role and preferences, which is particularly beneficial in organizations where Salesforce roles are diverse.

Salesforce users also frequently switch between different types of records. Pinning list views for the most-used ones ensures they can return to their work with the relevant data immediately visible, regardless of the application they are in.

For instance, a sales representative might frequently need to view Opportunities closing this month. Pinning a Closing This Month opportunity list view would save them time otherwise spent navigating or recreating their desired view.

Sorting list views

Sorting a list view is a simple yet effective way to organize and access your data efficiently. When you're in a list view, you can sort the records by clicking on a column header. This sets the sort order of that column, allowing you to arrange the data in ascending or descending order.

This sorting proves helpful when working with extensive sets of records. You can quickly organize your view, making it easier to locate specific records or to get a better understanding of the data presented. For instance, you can sort contacts by their names, Opportunities by their expected close dates, or tasks by their due dates. This functionality saves time and enhances your ability to analyze and manage data effectively within Salesforce.

Filtering list views

Filtering list views in Salesforce allows you to refine and customize the records you see, making it easier to focus on specific data relevant to your needs. Look for the filter icon, usually found near the top-right of the list view. Clicking this will open the Filters sidebar, as shown in Figure 2-13.

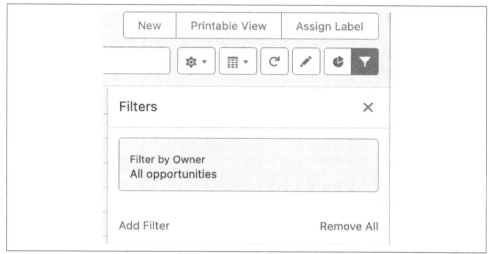

Figure 2-13. Filter icon and Filters sidebar on list view screen

You can define your filter criteria to narrow down the displayed records. For example, you might filter Contacts based on a specific city, status, or any other field relevant to your data. After setting your criteria, apply the filter to see a refined list of records that match your parameters. If this filtered view will be used frequently, you can save it for quick access later.

Rather than saving a filtered list view to update an existing list view, you can select Save As instead, to create a new version of the list view you are filtering.

Whenever you click to save a list view, you will be asked "Who sees this list view?," as shown in Figure 2-14.

Name the view appropriately for easy recognition and press the Tab key to populate the List API Name field automatically. The API name is used behind the scenes by Salesforce and can be referenced in formulas and code. You can also control who sees this list view by selecting from the bulleted list of options. I will address these options in "Setting list view visibility" on page 59.

Do not apply filters to any "All records" list view, since these are intended as nonfiltered lists of all records.

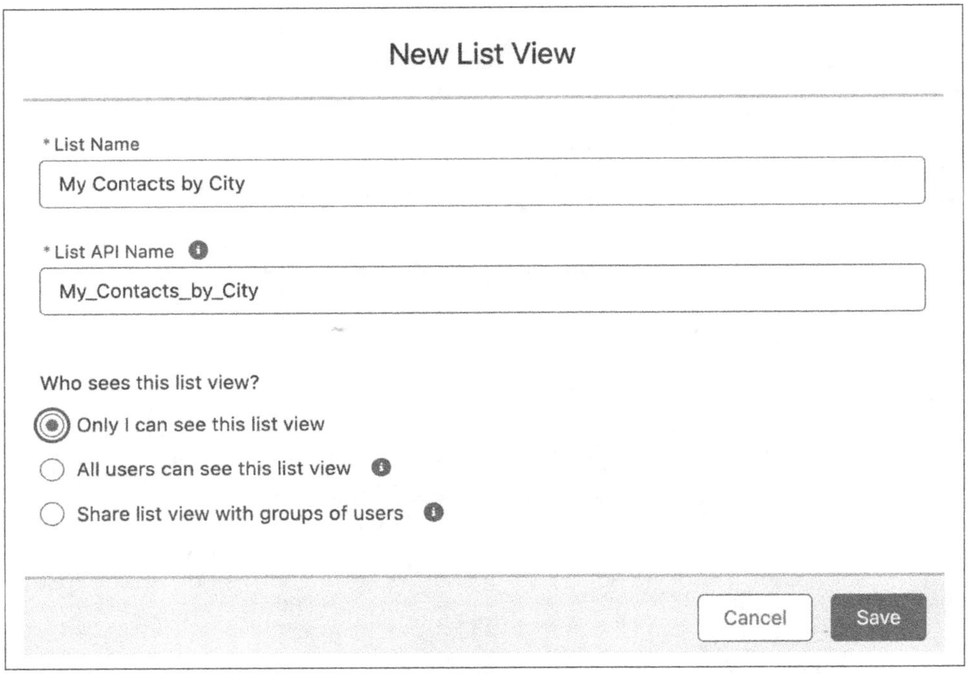

New List View

* List Name

My Contacts by City

* List API Name ⓘ

My_Contacts_by_City

Who sees this list view?

⦿ Only I can see this list view

◯ All users can see this list view ⓘ

◯ Share list view with groups of users ⓘ

Cancel   Save

Figure 2-14. New List View window

Creating new list views

Salesforce provides several sample list views in your free learner account. Situations may arise where you will need to create a new list view. To create a new list view, access the List View Controls menu by clicking the gear icon found next to the "Search this list" box.

The List View Controls displays different actions you can perform related to the list view you are currently viewing, as shown in Figure 2-15.

Figure 2-15. List View Controls accessed via the gear icon in a list view

To create a new list view from scratch, click New from the List View Controls menu. The New List View window displays. Alternatively, you can use an existing list view as a starting point to create a new list view by selecting the Clone option from the List View Controls menu. When cloning a list view, the Clone List View window displays.

For both the New List View and Clone List View windows, you will need to enter a name for the List Name. You must also provide a List API Name that Salesforce will reference behind the scenes. An informational icon is available to provide you further instruction as to the naming convention requirements for the List API Name field.

Setting list view visibility

The bottom of the New List View and Clone List View windows facilitates who can see the new list view that you are creating. As shown in Figure 2-16, your options are:

- Only I can see this list view
- All users can see this list view
- Share list view with groups of users (when selected, the window updates)

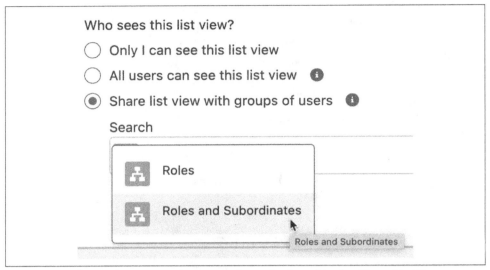

Figure 2-16. "Share list view with groups of users" selected in the Clone List View window

Once you have completed your entries for your new or cloned list view, click Save. You can now make further refinements and adjustments to your new or cloned list view.

Adding, removing, and reordering fields to display in a list view

You can add, remove, or rearrange fields in a list view to ensure that the most relevant data is immediately accessible to yourself and others. To add fields to your list view, click the gear icon to open the List View Controls menu, as displayed back in Figure 2-15.

Click the "Select Fields to Display" menu option. The "Select Fields to Display" window appears, as shown in Figure 2-17.

The Visible Fields section on the right displays the fields vertically, which corresponds with the left-to-right positioning of the fields in the resulting list view. For example, the top-most field in the Visible Fields column will display as the left-most column in your list view.

Choose the fields you want to add in your list view from the Available Fields section and move them to the Visible Fields section of the window by clicking the right arrow icon. If a field is no longer needed, removing it from the view can declutter your interface and streamline your workflow.

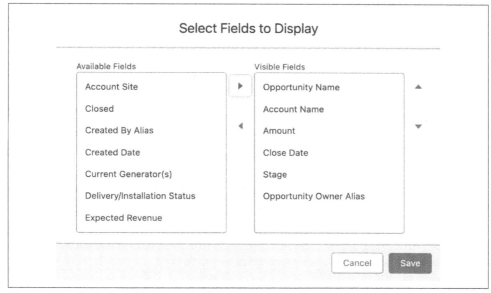

Figure 2-17. "Select Fields to Display" (in a list view) window

You may also elect to rearrange the order of the fields displayed in your list view. To do so, simply select the desired field(s) and click the up or down buttons to the right to set them in your desired sort order.

Sorting list views is incredibly useful for various scenarios. For instance, your sales team may want to see the most recent activity date or Opportunity Stage as the first field in its list view, enabling team members to quickly gauge their next actions. In contrast, a service team might prioritize case status or priority to better manage its workload.

List view printable view

The printable view feature for Salesforce list views offers a convenient way to generate printer-friendly versions of your list data. This functionality is particularly useful when you need a hard copy of your list for meetings, reports, or offline analysis.

To use this feature, navigate to the list view of your choice, and locate the Printable View button, typically found at the top of the list view. Clicking this button generates a printable version of the list, presenting the data in a clear, organized format. This view retains the order and fields displayed in the list view, making it a direct reflection of what you see on the screen.

The printable view feature respects the filters and sorting applied to the list view, ensuring the printed version matches your specific data requirements.

Creating charts from list views

Imagine you're looking at your Opportunities object tab and you want to visualize the data in a more digestible format. What you can do is pick the list view that holds the data you're interested in. It's just a matter of finding the list you need and getting ready to transform it into a visual story.

On your chosen list view page, there's a chart icon for creating visuals. Clicking this icon opens a chart panel right next to your list view, as shown in Figure 2-18.

Salesforce offers several chart options, such as bar, line, pie, or donut charts. Each of these types offers a different lens through which to view your data, and you get to pick the one that aligns best with what you're trying to convey or analyze.

Once you've chosen your chart type, you'll delve into customizing the chart settings. You decide how you want to group your data, what aspect you're focusing on (like the sum or average of certain fields), and how this information is displayed. These charts are dynamic—they update as the list view changes, giving you real-time analytics. You can also apply filters to home in on particular segments of your data, making your chart even more relevant and focused.

Once you've got your chart looking just right, you don't have to keep redoing this work. You can save your chart for future use. Plus, if you want your team to see the insights you've uncovered, you can easily share these charts with them. This feature is great for collaborative analysis and keeping everyone on the same page.

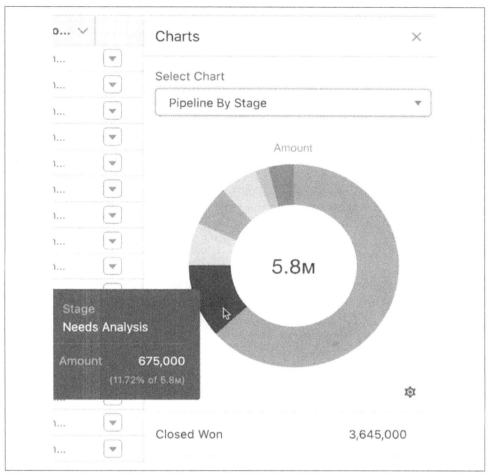

Figure 2-18. Chart added to a list view

Inline editing in list views

Inline editing in list views is a powerful convenience that enhances the efficiency of data management. It allows users to quickly modify records directly from the list view, without the need to navigate to individual record pages. This streamlined approach is useful for making quick updates to multiple records simultaneously.

How inline editing works in list views. When you are in a list view in Salesforce, you can easily edit fields of records directly. Click directly into a field on a record displayed in the list view. Fields that are available for inline editing will become editable on click, as denoted by a small pencil icon next to the field.

Modify the field as needed. You can change text, update dates, select new values from picklists, and more. After editing, you can either press Enter or click outside the field to close the edit field. You can repeat this process to make further inline edits to your list view. Once you have completed all of your edits, simply click the Save button at the bottom of your screen to save your inline edits.

Enabling/disabling inline editing in your org. As an administrator, you can control whether inline editing is available in your organization. This setting can be accessed and configured in the User Interface settings screen within Setup. Refer to "User Interface Settings" on page 51 for more details.

Mass updating records from a list view

Having explored the capability of inline editing within Salesforce's list views, it's time to elevate this functionality to the next level. Imagine not just tweaking a single entry but updating multiple records, all at once.

Consider a scenario where you're managing a multitude of leads after a successful marketing campaign. You've got a hundred new leads in your system, and after an initial review, you want to update their status to Contacted. Here's where mass updating saves your sanity, condensing a potentially mind-numbing task into a manageable moment.

You can either select the records to update by clicking the checkboxes to the left of the desired records individually or click the master checkbox at the top to select all displayed records in one go.

You can filter your list view to filter out any records you wish to not perform a mass update upon. This makes locating the desired records to select much easier.

Once selected, locate the field you wish to update and enter the new value. Salesforce will prompt for confirmation, ensuring that you are aware of the number of records that will be updated. Confirm your action, and Salesforce processes the update across all selected records.

The Kanban format

So far, you have largely interacted with the table format for list views. It's straightforward and familiar, much like an Excel spreadsheet. But Salesforce offers alternative list view formats. You will next delve into the Kanban format, which is both visually appealing and functional.

The Kanban view transforms your list views into a dynamic board. This format is beneficial for managing Opportunities or tasks, allowing you to see records represented as cards arranged in columns. Each column corresponds to a stage in your process, such as different stages of an Opportunity pipeline, as displayed in Figure 2-19.

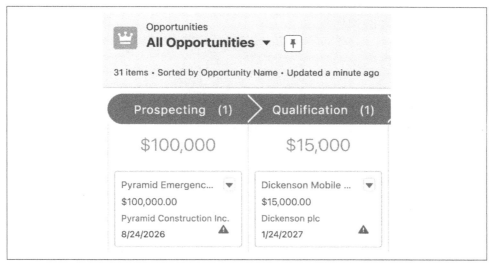

Figure 2-19. Kanban list view of All Opportunities

This list view format draws its inspiration from a Kanban board, which is a visual management tool that helps in tracking and optimizing the flow of tasks through various stages of a process. Originating from the Japanese word for *visual signal* or *card*, Kanban uses cards or other visual markers to represent work items and columns to represent each stage of a process.

Imagine you're overseeing sales Opportunities. In a Kanban view, you can see each Opportunity as a card placed in a column that reflects its current stage—be it Prospecting, Negotiation, or Closed Won. When you switch to this view, you'll see the

Opportunities neatly organized by their sales stages. Each card displays key information at a glance, like the Opportunity name, the account it's associated with, and the potential deal value.

Interactive and real-time updates.   One of the most powerful aspects of the Kanban view is its interactivity. You can click and drag an Opportunity from one stage to the next. It's not just a visual shift; dragging a card to a new column automatically updates its stage in Salesforce.

Watch as you move an Opportunity from the Value Proposition column to Closed Won. The moment you drop the card into the new column, the total values at the top of each column update, reflecting the real-time change in your pipeline by Opportunity Stage.

Split view list view format

Another innovative list view format Salesforce offers is the *split view*. This view facilitates multitasking, allowing you to see your list view and individual records side by side, as shown in Figure 2-20.

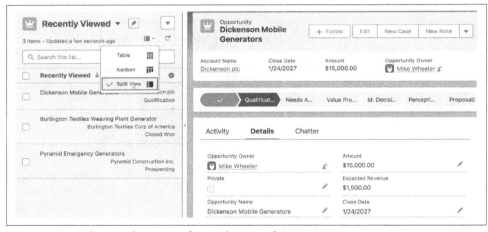

Figure 2-20. Split view list view of recently viewed Opportunities

In split view, your screen is divided into two panels. On the left, you have your list view, much like the familiar table format, but condensed. On the right, you see the details of the record you select from the list view. You can click on a record in the left panel, and immediately its details appear in the right panel. This format eliminates the need to switch back and forth between different screens or tabs, streamlining your workflow.

Split view remembers your selection. If you navigate away to another app and then return, it keeps your last viewed record open. This memory feature is particularly helpful in maintaining continuity in your work, especially if you're dealing with a large number of records.

Which list view format should I use?

There's a lot to think about when considering your viewing format. The table format is helpful for gaining an overview of your listed records and facilitates inline editing of individual or multiple records. The Kanban view brings a visual and interactive dimension, ideal for process-driven tasks. The split view excels in efficiency, keeping your workflows seamless and uninterrupted.

As you continue your Salesforce journey, exploring and adopting these formats can significantly enhance your productivity, based on varying use cases.

Global Actions

The name *global actions* is quite fitting, because these actions transcend the boundaries of specific objects or apps. Think of them as universal tools in your Salesforce toolbox, available at any time with a single click (or tap on mobile devices).

They are called *global* because no matter where you are on the platform—whether you're deep in the details of a campaign or browsing through various Opportunities—these actions are always within reach, ready to be used at a moment's notice.

The Global Actions menu is a streamlined and accessible toolbar, symbolized by a "+" icon on the Salesforce interface, as shown in Figure 2-21. From the resulting Global Actions menu, you can perform a variety of actions that are not associated with any particular record or object.

Upon opening the Global Actions menu, you'll find actions that support a variety of functions. Here is a brief rundown of each global action, its function, and the chapter in which it's discussed.

New Event
Quickly schedule events into your calendar (Chapter 9).

New Task
Set up tasks without navigating away from your current screen (Chapter 9).

New Contact
Add new contacts into your instance instantly (Chapter 7).

Log a Call
Keep track of calls with clients or team members in real time (Chapter 9).

Email
Send emails, integrating with your Salesforce records (Chapter 9).

New Opportunity
  Create Opportunities to track potential sales or deals (Chapter 7).

New Case
  Open a new Case for customer service or support inquiries (Chapter 8).

New Lead
  Input new leads as soon as you acquire them (Chapter 7).

Figure 2-21. Global Actions menu

Each option in the Global Actions menu is designed to save time and reduce the clicks required to keep your Salesforce universe well-ordered and up-to-date. With global actions, Salesforce provides instant jump points to different areas of the platform, giving you the power to act promptly and efficiently, no matter where you are in the system.

Lightning App Builder

The Lightning App Builder is a pivotal tool within Salesforce, contributing significantly to the platform's user interface configuration. It offers a declarative way to assemble various UI components, allowing administrators and developers to craft personalized pages within the Salesforce environment.

I delve more deeply into this powerful tool in Chapter 5, which covers the Object Manager and Lightning App Builder.

You can access the Lightning App Builder from Setup by searching for it in the Quick Find box. Clicking the Lightning App Builder menu in Setup displays the Lightning App Builder screen. The Lightning App Builder screen displays any previously created Lightning pages in your organization. You can create a new Lightning page by clicking New. The "Create a new Lightning page" window displays, as shown in Figure 2-22.

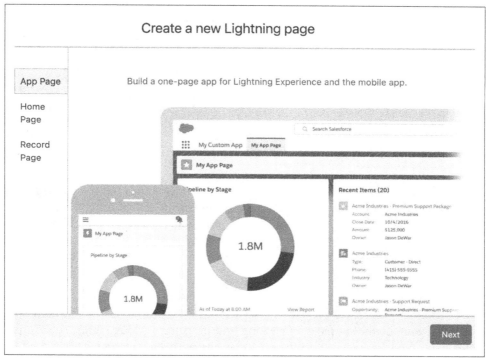

Figure 2-22. "Create a new Lightning page" window

You can start creating an app page, home page, or record page with the Lightning App Builder. Once you select your page type and click Next, you will be prompted to name your new Lightning page.

Enter the name of your new Lightning page in the Label field (and select the relevant object, if you selected to create a record page) and then click Next. From there, you can select a page template or clone a Salesforce default page. Click Done to now go to the Lightning App Builder (see Figure 2-23).

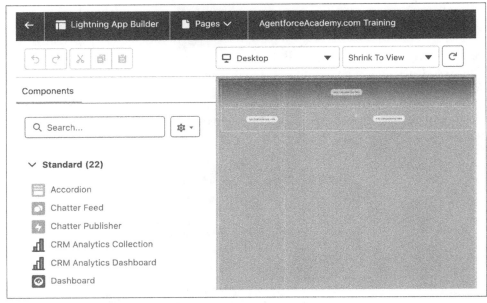

Figure 2-23. Lightning App Builder

Within the UI configuration, the Lightning App Builder stands out for its drag-and-drop interface, enabling the creation and arrangement of Lightning Components. These components range from standard components provided by Salesforce to custom components coded to meet specific business needs. You can also get more Lightning Components on the Salesforce AppExchange (*https://appex change.salesforce.com*).

The App Builder provides a visual representation of the page as you build it, ensuring a user-friendly experience even for those without a programming background. You can build your Lightning page by clicking and dragging various Lightning Components from the left sidebar onto the canvas in the middle. Once items are placed on the canvas, they can be further configured via the selected component's configuration menu on the right.

Why is a Lightning page builder called the Lightning App Builder? Although it is called the Lightning App Builder, the primary purpose of this drag-and-drop tool is to create Lightning pages. This is a frequent point of confusion, especially when considering that apps in Salesforce are built via the App Manager and not the App Builder, with the one notable exception of single-page apps, which can be created via the App Builder.

I have found it best not to question the naming conventions employed by Salesforce, as well as to not fixate on them, due to Salesforce's propensity to frequently rename items.

Summary

In Chapter 2, you dove into the Organization Setup settings. From understanding the significance of configuring company information accurately to grasping the critical aspects of business hours and user interface settings, I covered the essential components that enable Salesforce to reflect the unique needs and processes of a business. I also discussed the importance of system settings to ensure that users experience an interface that is both efficient and user-friendly. As these configurations set the stage for the rest of the Salesforce setup, a clear comprehension of these elements is paramount as you progress to the next chapter.

Chapter 2 Quiz

As you finish Chapter 2, it's time to assess the knowledge you've gathered about the organizational setup within Salesforce. These quiz questions are designed to challenge your grasp of the chapter's key points, ensuring you are well-prepared for the kind of nuanced questions you may encounter on the actual Salesforce Certified Platform Administrator exam.

Remember, each question is an opportunity to review and solidify your understanding of the foundational settings critical to Salesforce Configuration and Setup. Please carefully consider each question and select the answer that you believe is most correct.

After you've made your choices, review the answers and explanations in the Appendix to better understand the reasoning behind the correct answers. This process will reinforce your existing knowledge and clarify areas that may require additional review.

1. What functionality does the Company Settings in Salesforce provide?

    a. Managing user interface and application settings

    b. Tracking the company's fiscal year and financial reporting

    c. Defining the core identity and operational parameters of the organization

    d. Configuring data security and privacy settings

2. In Salesforce, what is the purpose of enabling Multiple Currencies?

  a. To provide translation services for global users

  b. To allow the tracking of sales data across different countries

  c. To handle the conversion between different currencies for global business operations

  d. To customize the user interface for international users

3. What feature in Salesforce allows administrators to set different business hours for various departments within an organization?

  a. Workflow automation

  b. System auditing

  c. Business Hours settings

  d. Role hierarchy

4. What is the significance of the Default Locale setting in a Salesforce organization?

  a. It sets the default format for dates, addresses, and names based on geographic location.

  b. It restricts user logins to specific geographic locations.

  c. It provides default email templates for different locales.

  d. It customizes the Salesforce interface theme based on location.

5. What is the importance of correctly configuring Business Hours in Salesforce?

  a. It allows customization of the Salesforce mobile app.

  b. It ensures accurate management of user roles and permissions.

  c. It impacts workflow, customer support, SLA tracking, and overall operational efficiency.

  d. It provides the structure for data backup and recovery processes.

6. What is the role of default organization settings in Salesforce's system settings?

  a. To manage the visibility of records and data sharing rules

  b. To configure the default locale, language, and time zone settings

  c. To determine the level of access users have to the Salesforce mobile app

  d. To set up automated workflows and approval processes

7. How is the Lightning App Builder used in Salesforce?

   a. To create and customize pages

   b. To manage user licenses

   c. To set up business hours and currency

   d. To configure data security settings

8. What is the primary benefit of customizing the App Menu in Salesforce?

   a. To improve system security

   b. To enhance user navigation and efficiency

   c. To manage data storage

   d. To configure email services

Configuration and Setup: User Setup and Management

This chapter returns to the Configuration and Setup knowledge area, now with a focus on User Setup and Management. Here you will gain the necessary skills to manage users within Salesforce.

User management encompasses a wide array of responsibilities that directly influence the efficiency and security of your Salesforce environment. From resetting passwords to resolving locked accounts, and from understanding the implications of activating or deactivating users to managing their personal customizations, this chapter provides a comprehensive walk-through of these essential administrative tasks.

From the Exam Guide

The Salesforce Certified Platform Administrator Exam Guide outlines the following learning objective for the Configuration and Setup knowledge area that aligns with this chapter: Given a scenario, *demonstrate the proper setup and maintenance of users.*

Now is the time to embark on your journey through the Configuration and Setup knowledge area by exploring the User Setup concepts further.

User Management Basics

The purpose of any software is to serve its users. Not the other way around. You should always keep your users at the forefront of your mind, viewing them as your customers. Guaranteeing customer (user) satisfaction with your work on the Salesforce platform will serve you well and ensure longevity in your career.

The singular user management learning objective is overly broad and vague. What exactly would be considered proper setup and maintenance of users? I will now pull on that thread and attempt to weave a tapestry of how-to information to equip you for the user management questions on the exam and beyond.

Access Your Own User Account

The best place to begin your user management understanding is by accessing your own Salesforce user account. I recommend that you follow along in your own free Salesforce Developer account or a Trailhead connected org. Do not work in a production environment in the workplace, for example.

To access your user account, go to the Setup menu and search for and select Users. The All Users screen displays, as shown in Figure 3-1.

	Action	Full Name ↑	Alias	Username	Role	Active	Profile
		New User		Reset Password(s)	Add Multiple Users		
☐	Edit	Chatter Expert	Chatter	chatty.00daj00000a8o9neaq.uwbdnund1lec@chatter.salesforce.com		✓	Chatter Free User
☐	Edit	User, Integration	integ	integration@00daj00000a8o9neaq.com		✓	Analytics Clc Integration L
☐	Edit	User, Security	sec	insightssecurity@00daj00000a8o9neaq.com		✓	Analytics Clc Security Use
☐	Edit	Wheeler, Mike	MWhee	mike@mindful-otter-mf6xsm.com		✓	System Administrato

Figure 3-1. All Users screen

Here you will find a list of all user accounts in your Salesforce organization. You will see listed on the screen your users' names, usernames, their active status and role (if assigned), and profile.

You will learn more about roles and profiles in Chapter 4, when I cover the Security and Access topics of the Configuration and Setup knowledge area. For now, focus on diving into your own user account.

You can either click on the Edit link next to your name in the All Users list to enter your user account in edit mode, or simply click your name to access your user account in view-only mode in the User Detail screen. I recommend clicking your name to first get familiar with your user account in view-only mode. The User Detail screen displays, as shown in Figure 3-2.

Figure 3-2. User Detail screen

Your user account contains your Name, Username, and Company name. Your Alias is a short identifier that appears in various internal locations within Salesforce, such as list views or reports, and is helpful in quickly identifying a user without displaying their full name.

There are also fields related to your Role and Profile on your User Detail screen. You will also find a large number of feature checkboxes that when checked, grant you further abilities on the platform.

The Reset Password button at the top of the User Detail screen can be used to change a password for a user account.

View User Login History

If you scroll to the bottom of your User Detail screen, you will find your Login History displayed, as shown in Figure 3-3.

Login History					
Login Time	Source IP	Login Type	Login Subtype	Status	Application
9/13/2025, 1:24:50 PM PDT	52.205. ▓ ▓	Remote Access 2.0		Success	Trailhead
9/13/2025, 1:24:50 PM PDT	52.205. ▓ ▓	Remote Access 2.0		Failed: Missing Consumer Key Parameter	Trailhead

Figure 3-3. Login History section on the User Detail screen

The Login History section displays any login attempts associated with the user account you are currently viewing. Displayed line by line are the Login Time, the Source IP address from which the login attempts were made, Login Type, and the Status, showing whether login attempts were successful or blocked due to an invalid password. You can also see the Login URL for each login attempt and further location information.

Troubleshoot Login Issues

As an administrator, one common task you will be called upon to assist with is helping your users to log in. You are able to see any individual's unsuccessful login attempts from their User Detail screen if they have entered an incorrect password. If they are entering their username incorrectly, it will not display because it will not be tied to an active user in your org.

In the example in Figure 3-3, you can see that I had an Invalid Password login attempt in my own history. This means that I did indeed enter my password incorrectly and was attempting to log in using the correct username.

Create a User Account

To effectively test administrative functionality related to user management, it's helpful to create a secondary user account in your Salesforce instance. This enables you to simulate scenarios such as locked accounts or feature permissions without risking your own administrator access.

To begin, navigate to the All Users page in Setup and click New User. The New User screen displays, where you'll enter details for this fictional user account, as shown in Figure 3-4.

The username must be in the format of an email address and must be globally unique across all Salesforce instances. Many organizations use naming conventions like adding *.dev* or *.test* to the end of usernames to keep testing and development accounts distinct and easily identifiable.

For the email address, enter one that you personally have access to if you wish to receive the activation message and set a password for this account later. Unlike usernames, which must be unique across all Salesforce instances, email addresses can be reused across multiple accounts. You can now log in to Salesforce using either a username or an email address.

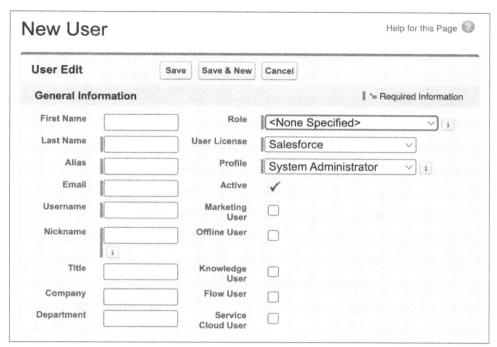

Figure 3-4. New User screen

Assign the role of chief operating officer (COO) to this user and select the Salesforce user license. Do not select Salesforce Platform, which has more limited access and is generally suited for users working with custom applications who don't require standard CRM features.

If the Salesforce license type isn't available for the selection, it may indicate that your organization has used all available licenses of that type. You can confirm current license usage on the Company Information page in Setup, which shows both total and assigned user licenses.

> Salesforce frequently updates license offerings, so always consult Salesforce Help documentation for the most current descriptions and limitations.

Next, assign this new user the System Administrator Profile to grant full administrative rights. Ensure the Active checkbox remains selected so that the account is immediately enabled upon creation. If the Active checkbox is unchecked, the user record will still be created, but will remain inactive and unusable until reactivated.

You can further configure the user by enabling specific feature licenses. These include Marketing User, Knowledge User, Flow User, and Service Cloud User. Each of these selections unlocks access to different platform features. Enabling these options allocates feature licenses from your org's available pool, which is also tracked on the Company Information page.

Scroll down to the Approver Settings section and designate yourself as the user's manager, as shown in Figure 3-5. This field isn't required but helps simulate a typical reporting relationship for approval flows.

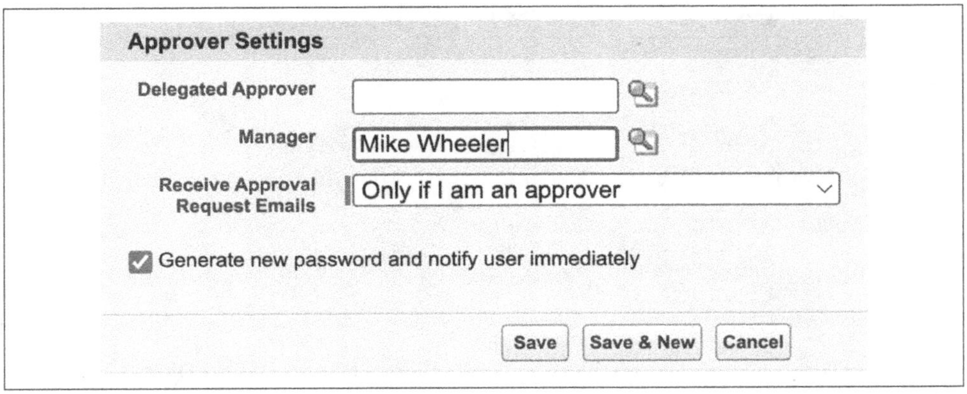

Figure 3-5. Approver Settings screen

Finally, check the "Generate a new password and notify the user immediately," box at the bottom of the screen, then click Save. The new user account now appears in the All Users list. Check your email for an account confirmation email from Salesforce. You will receive this email if you entered a working email address that you have access to for your new user account. From the confirmation email, you can set the password for your secondary fictional user account.

Set Password Policies in Your Salesforce Organization

Password policies in Salesforce determine the complexity and lifespan of user passwords, playing a key role in protecting against unauthorized access and potential security breaches. Strong password policies ensure that users create passwords that are difficult to guess or compromise. Many industries have specific requirements for password strength and rotation, making compliance a critical consideration.

Best Practices for Setting Password Policies

While strong policies enhance security, they should not hinder user productivity. Find a balance that maintains security without causing user frustration. Periodically review and update password policies to align with evolving security threats and compliance requirements.

Always educate users about the importance of password security and the rationale behind the policies to encourage compliance.

Implementing effective password policies is a critical responsibility for Salesforce administrators. It ensures the security of user accounts and the overall Salesforce environment, mitigating the risk of unauthorized access. By carefully configuring these policies, administrators can uphold high security standards while supporting a user-friendly experience.

Adjust Salesforce Password Policies

To review and adjust your organization's password policies, search for and select Password Policies in Setup. The Password Policies screen displays, as shown in Figure 3-6.

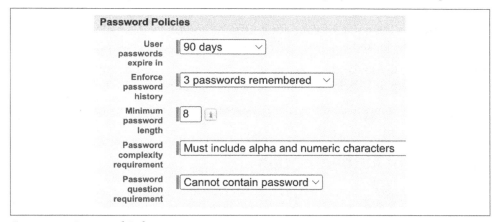

Figure 3-6. Password Policies screen

From the Password Policies screen, you can adjust settings like password longevity before they automatically expire, complexity requirements, password history enforcement, and minimum password character length, and more.

 One important picklist option on this Password Policies screen is "Maximum invalid login attempts." Options are 3, 5, 10, and "No limit." In the section "Resolve Locked User Accounts" on page 83 I will walk through the process of locking out your newly created fictional user account. For our purposes here, do not set this limit to "No limit," otherwise you will be unable to lock that user account when the time comes. Setting this to "No limit" would also not be advisable in a workplace environment, due to stricter security needs.

You can replace the boilerplate messaging that appears to your users if they forget their password or when their account is locked by entering in your own customized messaging. This is accessible at the bottom of the Password Policies screen in the Forgot Password / Locked Account Assistance section of the screen, as shown in Figure 3-7.

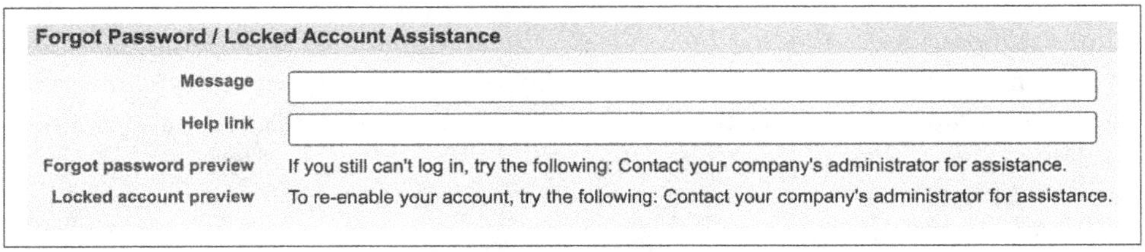

Forgot Password / Locked Account Assistance

Message	
Help link	
Forgot password preview	If you still can't log in, try the following: Contact your company's administrator for assistance.
Locked account preview	To re-enable your account, try the following: Contact your company's administrator for assistance.

Figure 3-7. Forgot Password / Locked Account Assistance screen

Whatever you enter in the Message field will appear in the email from Salesforce, which will be sent to users when they lock themselves out of their account. You may want to include the name of your administrator and/or their email address in your message for your locked out user's reference.

You can optionally make the message a clickable link by specifying the destination URL in the "Help link" field. The link can be an *http(s)* link or a *mailto* email link.

Once you have completed setting the password policies for your organization, click Save.

Multi-Factor Authentication

Multi-factor authentication (MFA) is a Salesforce requirement that enhances security by verifying user identities through multiple methods beyond the username and password combination. This additional verification typically includes using an authenticator app or a security key to confirm user identity during login. Implementing MFA significantly reduces the risk of unauthorized access caused by compromised credentials. Salesforce requires MFA for all users accessing Salesforce products.

To implement MFA in Salesforce, navigate to Setup and search for Session Settings. In the Session Settings screen, you can enable MFA under the Session Security Levels section, as shown in Figure 3-8.

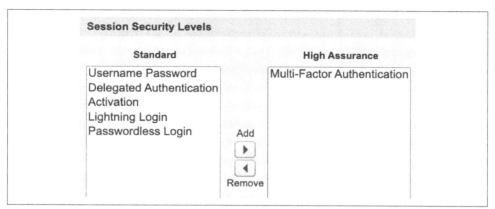

Figure 3-8. Session Security Levels screen

After MFA is enabled, users will be prompted to set up their verification method the next time they log in. Salesforce supports multiple MFA verification methods, including the Salesforce Authenticator app, third-party authenticator apps (such as Google Authenticator and Microsoft Authenticator), and security keys (such as YubiKey or other FIDO-compliant security keys).

Resolve Locked User Accounts

There are three constants in life: death, taxes, and Salesforce users will get themselves locked out of their accounts. Although you are unable to assist with the first two constants, the third will be a common area that calls for your expertise. When users exceed the number of allowed login attempts, their account is locked. Unlike a forgotten password, this situation cannot be resolved by the user through a reset link. Salesforce does not unlock accounts automatically after a period of time. Only an administrator can manually unlock a user account through Setup.

To simulate how this may play out in the future, you can now attempt to lock out your new user account by performing multiple failed login attempts. To do so, go to *https://login.salesforce.com* in a new browser window. The Salesforce login screen displays, where you can enter the correct username for your new user account for your fictional user.

Be certain you don't enter your own username so as to avoid locking yourself out of your Salesforce organization!

Enter an incorrect password for your new fictional user. In your other browser window where you are already logged in, navigate to your fictional user's detail screen. Scroll down to the bottom of their User Detail screen to view their login history and make note of the failed login attempt displayed in their history. You should see that it was made recently and from your IP address. Repeat the above steps to purposely fail at logging in as the new fictional user.

Be sure to refresh the User Detail screen to review their Login History section after each attempt. You will see that the user account has been locked once you have exceeded the maximum invalid login attempts you previously set for your organization in the Password Policies screen.

Once you have successfully locked the fictional user account, their User Detail screen will update to display an Unlock button, as shown in Figure 3-9.

Figure 3-9. User Detail screen with Unlock button

To unlock the user, click the Unlock button. The user's account will be unlocked, and they can continue to attempt to log in. If they do not know their password, you may want to also reset their password for them.

Reset User Passwords

To perform a password reset on a user account search for and select Users from Setup to display the All Users screen. Click the Edit link next to the desired user account to display the User Edit screen.

Scroll to the bottom of the User Edit screen and check the box to generate a new password and notify the user immediately. After clicking Save, the user will receive an email prompting them to set a new password.

In addition to this method, you can also reset a user's password by clicking the Reset Password button at the top of the User Detail screen. Clicking Reset Password displays a confirmation window. After you confirm, Salesforce sends the user a temporary auto-generated password via email. The user will need to log in with that temporary password, then set a new one of their choosing. While both methods ultimately lead to the same outcome, using the checkbox on the User Edit screen is often more straightforward and may be less confusing for the user.

If a user forgets their password, they can initiate a self-service reset by clicking the Forgot Your Password? link on the Salesforce login screen. After entering their username, they will receive a password reset email, provided that their email address is valid and accessible. As an administrator, it's helpful to remind users of this option when appropriate, especially for users who are not locked out but simply forgot their credentials.

 Next to the Email field on the User Detail screen, you may notice a Verify link. This link appears when a user's email address has not yet been verified by Salesforce. Clicking Verify sends an email containing a verification link to the specified address. Verification helps confirm the email address is valid and ensures the user receives system-generated emails such as password resets, notifications, and approvals. Although not required for functionality, unverified addresses may result in missed emails, particularly in restrictive email environments.

Deactivate User Accounts

Users will come and go in your organization. You will be called upon to create new user accounts and deactivate existing ones as your user base changes over time. When an employee leaves or changes roles within the organization, deactivating their account prevents unauthorized access and maintains system security.

To deactivate a user account, locate the desired account in the All Users screen and click Edit next to it. The Edit User screen displays. Uncheck the user's Active checkbox and click Save. If the user is not associated with any scheduled report deliveries or system automations, their deactivation will be complete.

When users have reports scheduled for delivery and/or automations associated with their account, you will receive a system alert that you are unable to deactivate the user. You'll see a list of issues that need to be resolved before the user can be deactivated, which you can work through. In these situations, it is advisable to freeze the user account.

Freeze User Accounts

There are scenarios where immediate action is required to discontinue a user's access to Salesforce, yet deactivating their account immediately may prove unfeasible (such as the scenario just discussed). If you are unable to deactivate a user quickly, you can freeze them.

Freezing a user account is a quick solution to prevent access while keeping the user's configuration and settings intact. It is important to keep in mind that freezing a user account does not free up a Salesforce license like deactivation does.

Freezing a user account is particularly useful in situations like a pending investigation of suspicious user activities or for the temporary leave of an employee.

To freeze a user account, locate the desired account from the All Users list and click it. The User Detail screen displays. Click the Freeze button located at the top of the screen. The user's access is now restricted and their User Detail screen refreshes to display an Unfreeze button, taking the place of the previous Freeze button.

Freezing an account maintains the user's setup and associations within Salesforce, making it a temporary and reversible action. This restricts their access while either their future status is uncertain or to provide time for the reassignment of responsibilities to other active users.

Log In As Any User

As an administrator, there will be times that you will need to see what your users are seeing (or not seeing what they should be able to see). Since you have full administrative rights in your Salesforce account, you are able to see virtually every piece of data and record. The same cannot be said for your base of users.

Record and field visibility are common issues left to you to resolve. The ability to log in as another user to, in essence, see what they see is an invaluable tool that Salesforce makes available to you.

Enable Log In As Any User

To enable administrators to be able to log in as other users in your organization, search for and select Login Access Policies in Setup. The Login Access Policies screen displays, as shown in Figure 3-10.

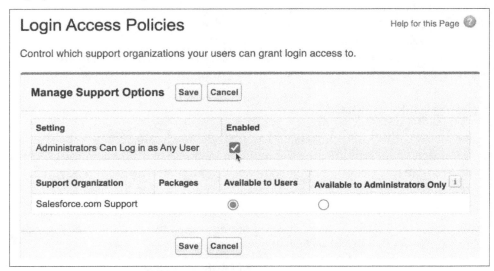

Figure 3-10. Login Access Policies screen

Select the "Administrators Can Log in as Any User" checkbox and click Save. A note displays that your changes have been saved. You can now proceed with logging in as another user.

Logging In As Any User

Now that you have enabled logging in as other users in your Salesforce organization, you are ready to experience that ability yourself. Verify that a Login link now appears next to the name of the fictional user you previously created, as shown in Figure 3-11.

Figure 3-11. Login link displayed next to fictional user account on Users screen

Clicking either the Login link from the Users screen or the Login button on the User Detail screen will log you into Salesforce as your fictional user. You will notice a banner appears at the top of the screen specifying the user you are now logged in as (see Figure 3-12).

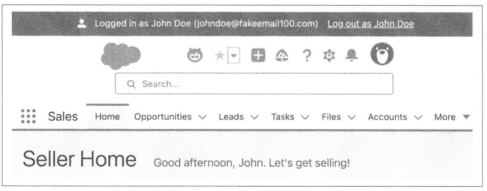

Figure 3-12. "Logged in as" banner at top of screen with "Log out" link

Now that you are logged in as another user, you can navigate to various screens in Salesforce to see what that user would see. Whenever you are ready, you can log out as the other user by clicking the log out link in the banner at the top of the screen.

If logging out as another user also logs you out of your own Salesforce account, you will be returned to the Salesforce Login screen. You can disable this feature by logging back into Salesforce as yourself and then navigating to Session Settings in Setup. On the Session Settings screen, uncheck the "Force relogin after Login-As-User" checkbox and click Save. This will keep you logged in to Salesforce upon logging out as another user.

User Personal Customizations

As an administrator, most changes you make to Salesforce are considered org-wide changes, or changes that impact all users. Personal customizations are those that you make just for yourself as an individual user and do not impact others.

Personal customizations may be made by your users as well. These also have no impact on other users. These changes can provide a more customized experience at the individual user level.

Make User Personal Customizations

To adjust your personal customizations, click your user image located at the top-right of the screen. Your personal Settings link displays in the resulting pop-up, as shown in Figure 3-13.

Figure 3-13. Settings link

Click the Settings link to display the Personal Information screen, as shown in Figure 3-14.

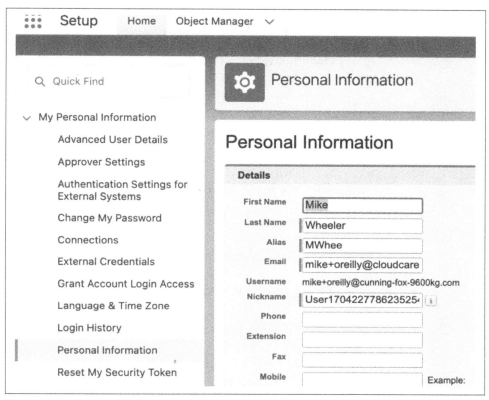

Figure 3-14. Personal Information screen

The Personal Information screen is similar in appearance to the Setup menu, complete with a Quick Find box for searching. It is especially confusing because it appears as though you are in the Setup Home tab, as you can see in Figure 3-14. Note, however, that the Quick Find box here is just for the My Personal Information menu options. To return to Setup, click the Home tab.

The Personal Information screen defaults to your user details. Your user details are divided across multiple screens, whereas your regular User Detail screen contains all of your information on a single screen. You can change your details on this screen, if needed. You can also access your full User Detail screen by clicking Advanced User Details from the My Personal Information menu on the left, as shown in Figure 3-15.

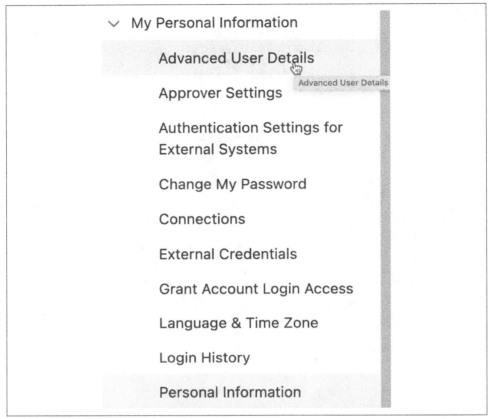

Figure 3-15. Advanced User Details option

Navigate through the various links found below the My Personal Information drop-down menu to become familiar with the personal customizations you and your users can change.

Display and Layout Personal Customizations

Salesforce enables users to adjust the display and layout of individual records as part of their personal customizations. To make display and layout personal customizations, click to expand Display & Layout, as shown in Figure 3-16.

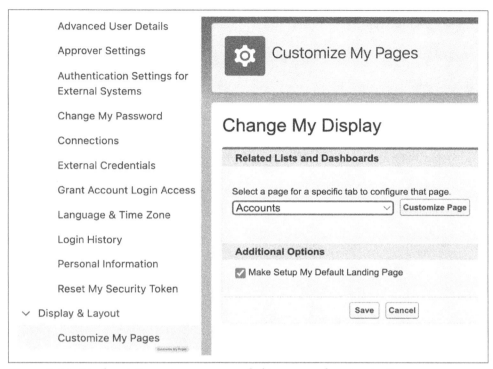

Figure 3-16. Display & Layout menu expanded in personal customizations

Clicking the Customize My Pages menu option from the Display & Layout drop-down menu displays the Change My Display screen, as shown in Figure 3-16.

Notice the Make Setup My Default Landing Page checkbox in the Additional Options section of the Change My Display screen in Figure 3-16. Selecting this checkbox ensures that you will default to going into the Setup menu each time you log into Salesforce.

You can select a page from the drop-down list and click the Customize Page button. The Customize My Pages screen displays, as shown in Figure 3-17.

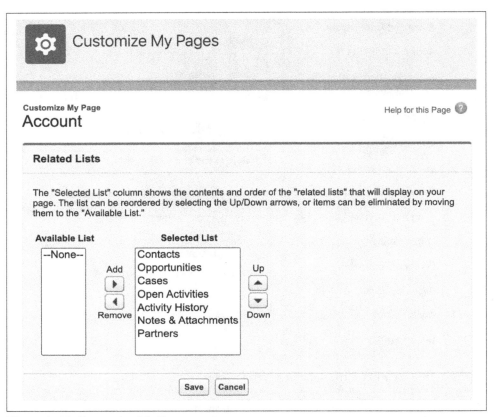

Figure 3-17. Customize My Pages screen

The Customize My Pages screen displays the Related Lists that display in the page layout for whichever page you previously selected. You can adjust the order of the Related Lists by clicking to select one on the right, and then clicking the up or down buttons to move them to the desired position. Keep in mind that since this is a personal customization, you will see the changes but these are not org-wide for all users.

You can also remove Related Lists by selecting them in the Selected List on the right side and then clicking the Remove button to move them to the Available List. Once you have finished making personal customizations to the display and layout of the Accounts page, click Save.

Additional User Settings Options

I have addressed the My Personal Information and Display & Layout menu options from the Settings menu. You will also find several more settings options available to you in this menu, as shown in Figure 3-18.

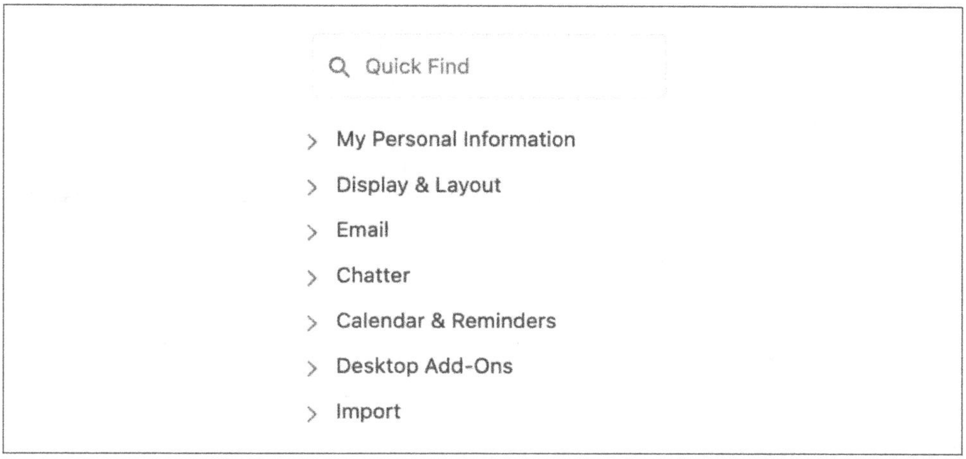

Figure 3-18. Settings menu options

I will explore many of these remaining options in later chapters. I will leave it to your own curiosity to explore them further for now. These are intended once again as individual user settings that your user base has the ability to adjust on their own behalf.

Giving users the ability to make their own personal customizations can lighten your workload as an administrator. You will want to keep these settings in mind so you can train your user base over time that they have the power to make some changes to their own user account and experience. This will help you to avoid being called upon frequently to make changes that could be performed by your users instead.

Summary

In this chapter, you explored the essentials of user management in Salesforce, from accessing your own user account to creating new users and troubleshooting login issues. You learned how to set and adjust password policies, resolve locked user accounts, and reset user passwords. Additionally, the chapter covered deactivating and freezing user accounts, as well as enabling logging in as another user for troubleshooting. Mastering these user setup and management basics is important for ensuring a secure and efficient Salesforce organization as you move forward.

Chapter 3 Quiz

As you finish Chapter 3, it's time to assess the knowledge you've gathered about user setup and management in Salesforce. This quiz is designed to test your understanding of key concepts, ensuring you're well-prepared for the kind of nuanced questions that may appear on the Salesforce Certified Platform Administrator exam.

Remember, each question is an opportunity to review and strengthen your grasp of essential user management topics, from creating new users to adjusting password policies and troubleshooting login issues. Take your time with each question and select the answer that best aligns with the principles you've learned.

After making your choices, carefully review the answers and explanations in the Appendix to solidify your understanding of the correct answers. This process will reinforce your existing knowledge and highlight areas that may require further review, ensuring you're well-prepared for real-world scenarios and exam success.

1. Which feature allows administrators to directly access a user's environment for troubleshooting purposes?

   a. Freezing User Accounts

   b. Enabling "Log in as Any User"

   c. Setting Password Policies

   d. Viewing User Login History

2. What is the recommended method to resolve a locked user account in Salesforce?

   a. Deactivate the user

   b. Freeze the user account

   c. Unlock the user account

   d. Enable "Log in as Any User"

3. Which of the following actions is possible when deactivating a user account in Salesforce?

   a. The user can still receive Chatter notifications.

   b. The user cannot log in or access Salesforce.

   c. The user's records are automatically deleted.

   d. The user's associated reports and dashboards are transferred to other users.

4. What is a key benefit of setting password policies in your Salesforce organization?

   a. Preventing users from changing their passwords

   b. Enabling "Log in as Any User"

   c. Improving overall security by enforcing strong passwords

   d. Limiting access to specific IP ranges

5. Which feature allows Salesforce administrators to monitor unsuccessful login attempts made by a particular user?

   a. User profile settings

   b. Login Access Policies

   c. User login history

   d. Permission set assignments

Configuration and Setup: Security and Access

The power of Salesforce security lies in its ability to control both what users can access and what actions they are allowed to take. As an administrator, it is your responsibility to define not only who can view a record, but who can create new records, edit existing ones, delete records, or access specific system features.

Security settings in Salesforce impact every user. They determine whether a user can see a particular record, whether they can modify information, and whether they can perform administrative functions such as managing users or customizing the platform. Controlling access and actions is essential to protecting data, maintaining system integrity, and ensuring that users can work efficiently.

This chapter concludes the Configuration and Setup knowledge area for the Salesforce Certified Platform Administrator exam. You have previously learned how to configure an organization's settings and manage user accounts. Now, the focus shifts to setting up the security model that governs what users can do within Salesforce and how data access is controlled.

By the end of this chapter, you will have a complete understanding of how Salesforce security settings work together to control both access and user capabilities across the system.

From the Exam Guide

The Salesforce Certified Platform Administrator Exam Guide outlines the following learning objectives for the Configuration and Setup knowledge area that align with this chapter:

- Describe the features and capabilities of the user access and visibility settings (for example, profiles, permission sets, and roles).

- Given a user request scenario, apply the appropriate security controls based on the features and capabilities of the Salesforce sharing model (for example, organization-wide defaults, role hierarchy, sharing rules, manual sharing).

- Apply the appropriate security controls based on the features and capabilities of the Salesforce sharing model.

Understanding the Salesforce Security Model

Before diving into the configuration of security settings, it is important to understand how Salesforce structures access across its platform. Salesforce security is built to be most restrictive by default. Users start with no access to objects, fields, or records unless explicit permission is granted. Administrators then open access intentionally, layer by layer, based on user roles, business needs, and organizational structure.

The Salesforce sharing model follows a layered approach, where each layer builds on the one before it. At the base, profiles and permission sets control whether a user can access specific objects and fields at all. Organization-wide defaults set the baseline visibility for records within those objects. Higher layers such as role hierarchy, sharing rules, manual sharing, team access, and territory hierarchy can selectively open further access where required.

Figure 4-1 illustrates this security model. As you move upward, precision gives way to broader access, following Salesforce's principle of opening up only as necessary.

Understanding this layered approach is important. It ensures that you set up security controls in a deliberate way, first determining what users can see and do at the object level, and then determining how much record-level visibility they should have within that structure.

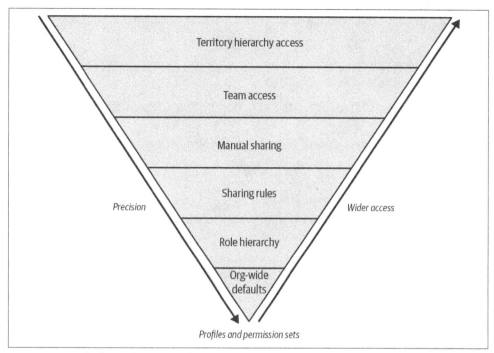

Figure 4-1. Salesforce sharing architecture visualized

Profiles

In Salesforce, a profile defines the baseline permissions for a user. It controls what the user can access and what actions they are allowed to take. Every user must be assigned exactly one profile. Profiles cannot be removed or left blank. They are required to log in and interact with Salesforce.

In most Salesforce free learner environments, users are assigned the System Administrator Profile by default. This provides broad access to nearly every feature and object in Salesforce. In a real-world environment, most users are assigned more restrictive profiles that are tailored to their job functions.

To view the profile you have been assigned, search for and select Users within Setup. The All Users screen displays, as shown in Figure 4-2.

On the All Users screen you can see your assigned profile listed to the right of your username. It is likely set to System Administrator if you are working in a learning environment.

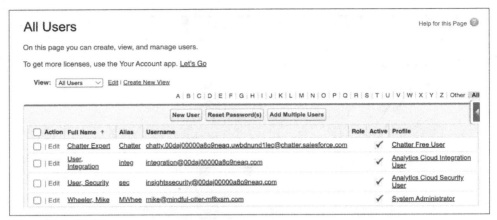

Figure 4-2. All Users screen

To inspect the permissions that are granted by your profile, click the profile name. This opens the Profile Detail screen, as shown in Figure 4-3, where all permissions and settings for that profile are listed.

Figure 4-3. Profile Detail screen

The Profile Detail screen is very lengthy and involved, in that it displays every single setting and configuration available on a profile, including page layout assignment, object access settings, field level security, and much more. Fortunately, there is an enhanced and searchable version of the Profile user interface.

Enhanced Profile User Interface

Salesforce provides an Enhanced Profile User Interface option that organizes Profile settings more cleanly and makes them easier to review and search. To enable this option in Setup, search for and select User Management Settings. The User Management Settings screen displays. Toggle the Enhanced Profile User Interface setting to the Enabled position.

After enabling the Enhanced view, return to your profile. You will now see the profile displayed in a more organized format with sections divided by functional area, as shown in Figure 4-4.

Figure 4-4. Enhanced Profile User Interface view of the System Administrator Profile

You can review which users are assigned to a profile by clicking the Assigned Users button at the top of the profile. You can assign a user to a profile via their User record.

In the Enhanced Profile view, the permissions and settings of a profile are searchable via the Find Settings search box located at the top-left of the screen. You can also access functional areas directly via their links, which I will now walk you through.

Assigned Apps

This section controls which applications users assigned to the profile can access. Clicking Assigned Apps displays the Assigned Apps screen, as shown in Figure 4-5.

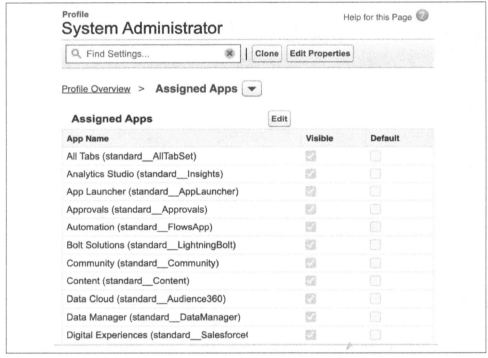

Figure 4-5. Assigned Apps screen

To make changes to the Assigned Apps for a profile, click the Edit button. You can select which apps are visible by checking their applicable checkboxes.

Each profile has a single app assigned as its default app. The default app is the application that users who are assigned to this profile will be automatically navigated to when they first log in to Salesforce.

When you click the Edit button on the Assigned Apps screen, the Default column of checkboxes changes to a single-select column of radio buttons. Simply select which app is to serve as the Profile's default app and click Save.

Navigating to Other Profile Components

There are several ways you can navigate to other areas of a profile, rather than resorting to clicking the Back button in your browser or searching for profiles again in Setup. Notice the various navigation options located at the top of the Profile display screen.

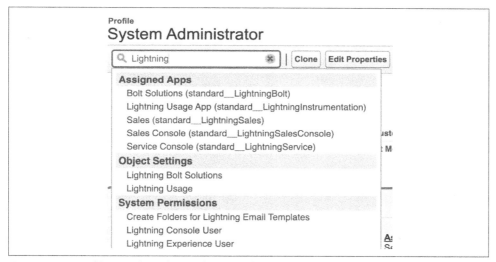

Figure 4-6. Profile search with matching results displayed

You can search for various settings and configuration options by entering a search term in the Find Settings field at the top. A list of matching results appears and narrows as you provide more precise search terms.

Also located at the top of the screen are breadcrumbs that you can click on to go up a level to return to the Profile Overview screen. Additionally, whenever you are in a section of a profile, you can click the down arrow next to it to navigate to other sections (see Figure 4-7).

Figure 4-7. Profile sections drop-down navigation

Notice that from the drop-down menu, the sections are grouped as well by the category of either Apps or System. While the list of sections in the drop-down menu above is extensive, I will cover those that are most commonly accessed and represented on the administrator exam, starting next with Object Settings.

Object Settings

Object Settings display the object permissions for each standard and custom object for a profile, as shown in Figure 4-8.

Each object is listed alphabetically, along with its corresponding API name. The Object Permissions column reveals what actions, if any, the currently selected Profile can perform on records belonging to each object.

You will notice when inspecting the System Administrator Profile that it has generous rights assigned to most objects in your organization. The Object Permissions are often referred to as CRUD rights.

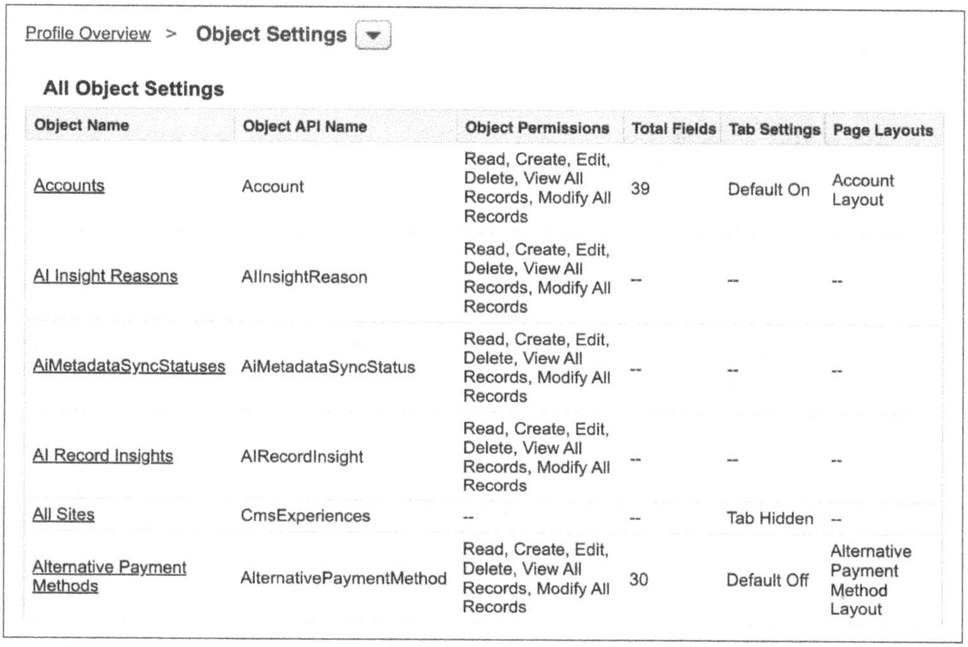

All Object Settings

Object Name	Object API Name	Object Permissions	Total Fields	Tab Settings	Page Layouts
Accounts	Account	Read, Create, Edit, Delete, View All Records, Modify All Records	39	Default On	Account Layout
AI Insight Reasons	AIInsightReason	Read, Create, Edit, Delete, View All Records, Modify All Records	--	--	--
AiMetadataSyncStatuses	AiMetadataSyncStatus	Read, Create, Edit, Delete, View All Records, Modify All Records	--	--	--
AI Record Insights	AIRecordInsight	Read, Create, Edit, Delete, View All Records, Modify All Records	--	--	--
All Sites	CmsExperiences	--	--	Tab Hidden	--
Alternative Payment Methods	AlternativePaymentMethod	Read, Create, Edit, Delete, View All Records, Modify All Records	30	Default Off	Alternative Payment Method Layout

Figure 4-8. Object Settings for the System Administrator Profile

Create, read, update, and delete (CRUD)

CRUD is a common security-related acronym that means create, read, update, and delete. These rights define what actions a user can take on the records of a particular object. CRUD rights are assigned through not only profiles, but also can be further refined via Permission Sets, which I will cover later in this chapter.

Create rights

Create rights allow a user to add new records for an object. For example, a sales representative might need create rights for the Contact object to add new contacts into Salesforce.

Read rights

Read rights allow a user to view existing records. Users with read access to an object can see records but cannot make changes unless additional rights are granted. Support agents often need read access to accounts or cases to understand customer history without necessarily editing sensitive details.

Update rights

Update rights allow a user to modify existing records. This permission is needed for users who are responsible for keeping information current, such as sales teams updating Opportunity Stages or customer success teams updating account information.

Delete rights

Delete rights allow a user to remove records. Since deleting records can affect reporting, analytics, and data history, this option should be reserved for trusted users.

CRUD rights should always be assigned based on the minimum necessary access a user needs to perform their tasks effectively. For example, a marketing user setting up campaigns may need create, read, and update rights on the Campaign object, but should not have delete rights. An analyst building reports may only need read access without the ability to modify or remove records.

Changing Object Settings

To make changes to the Object Settings for a profile, click on the desired object in the list on the Object Settings screen. The Object Settings for that object are displayed (see Figure 4-9).

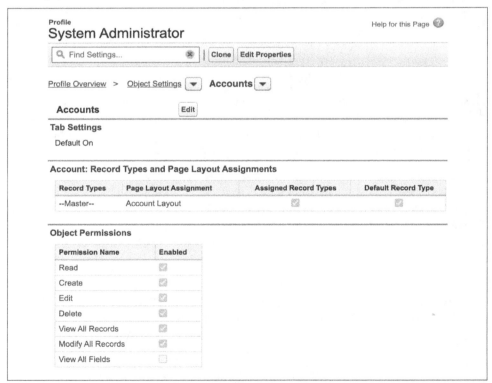

Figure 4-9. Accounts Object Settings for the System Administrator Profile

You can review the current Object Settings on this screen, which includes Tab Settings, "Record Types and Page Layout Assignments," Object Permissions, and Field Permissions. To make changes, click Edit at the top of the screen.

Tab Settings for an object and a profile

Tab Settings control the visibility of individual object tabs in the user interface for the profile you are editing. Tabs provide access points to an object's records. Tabs can be set to Default On, Default Off, or Tab Hidden, depending on what you want the user to see when navigating Salesforce.

Record Type Settings for an object and a profile

Record Type Settings determine which record types are available to profiles when creating new records for the selected object. Record types allow you to offer different business processes, picklist values, and page layouts to different users within the same object.

I'll dive deeper into how to create and configure record types in Chapters 5 and 7. These explain how record types work with business processes and page layouts to support different user experiences within the same object.

Object permissions for an object and a profile

Object permissions define the level of access a profile has to a specific object. These include the CRUD rights. Within a profile, you can enable or disable these permissions by checking or unchecking the corresponding boxes for each object, as shown in Figure 4-10.

One exception is the System Administrator Profile. This profile always retains full CRUD access to all standard and custom objects and cannot be restricted through these settings.

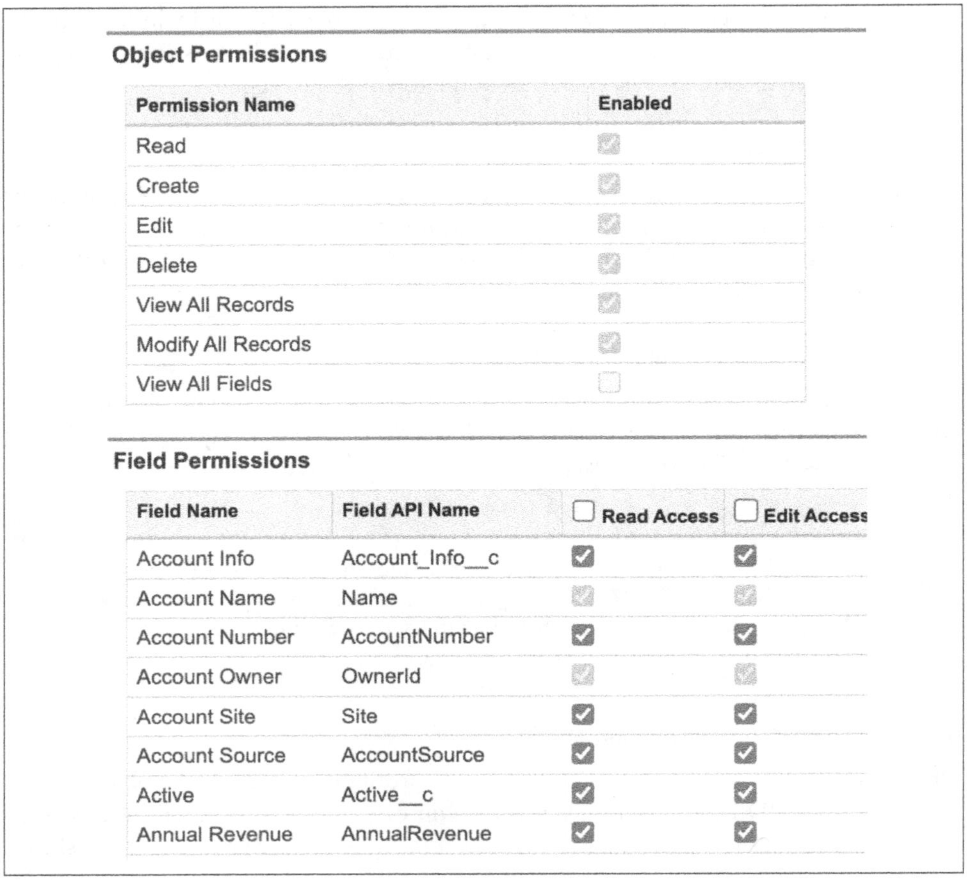

Object Permissions

Permission Name	Enabled
Read	☑
Create	☑
Edit	☑
Delete	☑
View All Records	☑
Modify All Records	☑
View All Fields	☐

Field Permissions

Field Name	Field API Name	Read Access ☐	Edit Access ☐
Account Info	Account_Info__c	☑	☑
Account Name	Name	☑	☑
Account Number	AccountNumber	☑	☑
Account Owner	OwnerId	☑	☑
Account Site	Site	☑	☑
Account Source	AccountSource	☑	☑
Active	Active__c	☑	☑
Annual Revenue	AnnualRevenue	☑	☑

Figure 4-10. Object Permissions and Field Permissions on a profile

Field permissions for an object and a profile

Field permissions determine whether users assigned to a profile can view or edit individual fields on a given object. To make a field read-only, select the Read Access checkbox without enabling Edit Access. To allow users to both view and modify the field, select both Read Access and Edit Access.

These settings provide more granular control than object-level permissions and are useful when certain fields should be visible but not editable for specific users.

System Permissions

System Permissions, as shown in Figure 4-11, control what users can do across Salesforce without being tied to a specific object. Examples include managing activities, using Chatter, or submitting records for approval.

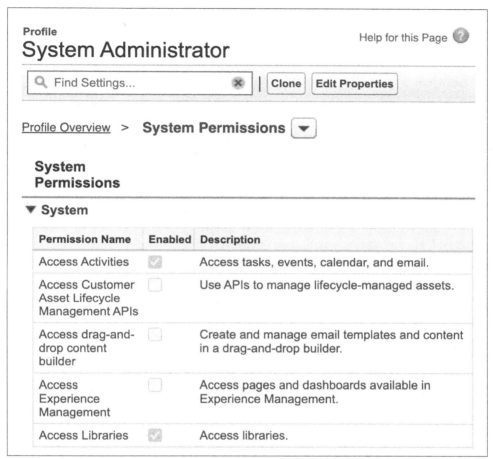

Figure 4-11. System Permissions for the System Administrator Profile

Login Hours

Login hours define the specific times during which users assigned to a profile are permitted to log in to Salesforce. These time-based access controls are configured per day of the week and can be used to enforce working hours, shift schedules, or other access restrictions based on time.

If a user attempts to log in outside the allowed hours for their profile, access will be denied. If a user is already logged in when their permitted login window ends, Salesforce will automatically end their session. This helps reduce the risk of unauthorized access during non-business hours and can be particularly useful in regulated environments or organizations with strict access control requirements.

Each day of the week can be configured individually, and time ranges can be adjusted as needed. By default, profiles allow access at all times unless Login Hours are explicitly set.

IP Ranges

IP ranges define the trusted network locations from which users assigned to a profile can access Salesforce. These ranges are specified as start and end IP addresses, forming a valid address range that functions as a security boundary. Users attempting to log in from outside the defined range will be blocked or challenged, depending on the organization's security settings.

IP ranges are typically used to restrict access to corporate networks, VPNs, or specific regional locations. This feature enhances security by ensuring that only known or approved IP addresses are allowed to access Salesforce, which can help prevent unauthorized login attempts from unknown networks.

IP range settings are configured within the profile. Multiple IP ranges can be defined if users need to access Salesforce from more than one trusted location. When properly configured, IP restrictions provide a strong layer of network-based access control that works in tandem with other user-level permissions.

Session Settings (Profile Level)

Each profile in Salesforce allows you to set session timeout durations that define how long a user session can remain active after inactivity. These settings are helpful in controlling the security exposure for users who might leave their workstations unattended.

Timeout options range from 15 minutes to 24 hours. Selecting a shorter timeout can reduce risk on shared computers or in high-security environments, while longer durations may improve convenience in more controlled settings.

These profile-level settings work in conjunction with the org-wide session settings configured in Setup. When both are defined, the more restrictive of the two will take precedence. For example, if the org-wide timeout is set to 30 minutes and the profile is set to 1 hour, users assigned to that profile will still be logged out after 30 minutes of inactivity. Org-wide settings act as a ceiling that profile-level settings cannot exceed.

Org-wide session management will be covered in more detail later in this chapter.

Password Policies (Profile Level)

Password policies can also be configured at the profile level, allowing you to tailor password behavior for different profiles. These settings include minimum password length, complexity requirements, password expiration periods, and login lockout behavior, as shown in Figure 4-12.

Figure 4-12. Password Policies for the System Administrator Profile

While these options are available at the profile level, they are constrained by the broader password policy defined at the org level. If the org-wide policy is stricter, it will override more permissive settings defined in a user's profile. For example, if a profile allows passwords to last 90 days but the org policy requires expiration every 60 days, the 60-day limit will prevail.

Use profile-level password settings to apply tighter controls where needed, such as for privileged users or high-risk roles. The org-wide policies act as a global standard that all profiles must meet or exceed. You can revise a profile's password policies by clicking Edit and making your desired changes and then clicking Save.

The broader configuration of org-wide password policies will be addressed in "Organization-Wide User Security Features" on page 129.

Creating Custom Profiles

Salesforce provides several standard profiles such as Standard User, Marketing User, and System Administrator. These standard profiles are designed to serve as templates or starting points for creating custom profiles. They offer basic sets of permissions that meet common business needs, but they have limitations.

Limits to Customization

You cannot fully customize a standard profile. Many permission settings, object access levels, and user rights are locked and cannot be changed. Because of this limited flexibility, standard profiles should not be assigned to users in a production environment, with one important exception: the System Administrator Profile is intended to be used as is for users who require full administrative access. Other than the System Administrator, all users should be assigned a custom profile based on a cloned version of a standard profile.

Cloning a Standard Profile

To create a custom profile, you begin by cloning an existing profile. You will find a Clone link beside the Profile Names listed in the All Profiles screen, as shown in Figure 4-13.

Figure 4-13. All Profiles screen with Clone links in the Action column

You will also find a Clone button on a Profile Overview screen, as shown in Figure 4-14.

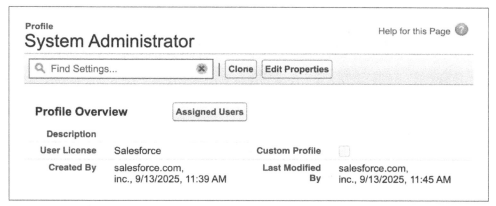

Figure 4-14. Clone button displayed on Profile Overview screen

After clicking Clone, the Clone Profile screen displays, as shown in Figure 4-15.

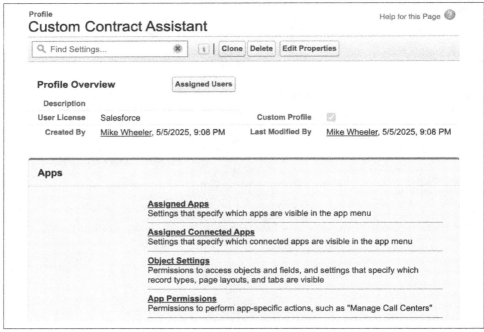

Clone Profile

Help for this Page ⓘ

Enter the name of the new profile.

You must select an existing profile to clone from.   ❘ *= Required Information

Existing Profile	Contract Manager
User License	Salesforce
Profile Name	[ ]

[Save] [Cancel]

Figure 4-15. Clone Profile screen

Enter a Profile Name for your new custom profile that aligns with its intended purpose (for example, a profile for a sales team might be named Custom Sales User). Once you have named your new custom profile, click Save. The new custom Profile Overview screen displays, as shown in Figure 4-16.

Profile
Custom Contract Assistant

Help for this Page ⓘ

🔍 Find Settings...   ✖   ❘ ⓘ ❘   [Clone] [Delete] [Edit Properties]

Profile Overview   [Assigned Users]

Description
User License Salesforce   **Custom Profile** ☑
Created By   Mike Wheeler, 5/5/2025, 9:08 PM   **Last Modified By** Mike Wheeler, 5/5/2025, 9:08 PM

Apps

Assigned Apps
Settings that specify which apps are visible in the app menu

Assigned Connected Apps
Settings that specify which connected apps are visible in the app menu

Object Settings
Permissions to access objects and fields, and settings that specify which record types, page layouts, and tabs are visible

App Permissions
Permissions to perform app-specific actions, such as "Manage Call Centers"

Figure 4-16. Custom Profile Overview screen

You can also add a description to provide internal context about the profile's use case by clicking Edit Properties at the top of the Profile Overview screen. An Edit Properties pop-up window displays, as shown in Figure 4-17.

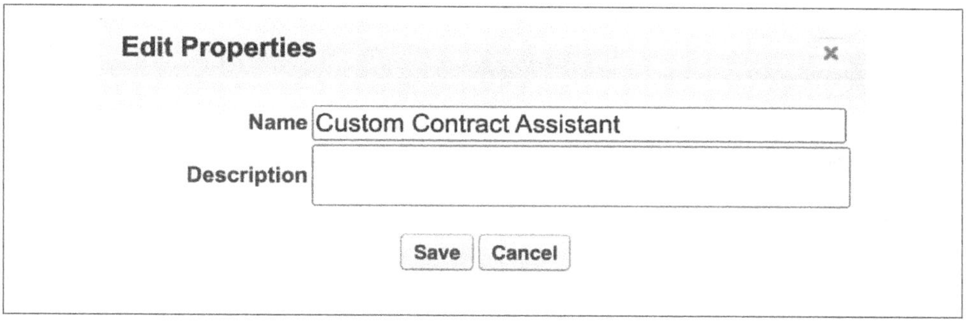

Figure 4-17. Edit Properties window

You can modify app access, object settings, and more, according to the specific requirements of the users who will be assigned this custom profile. Once you have completed your changes, click Save. Your custom profile will now appear in the list of available profiles.

Permission Sets

Profiles establish the baseline permissions for users, but organizations often require more flexibility than profiles alone can provide. As needs change, users may require temporary access to new objects, features, or permissions that go beyond what their profile allows. Rebuilding and managing multiple custom profiles to handle every variation quickly becomes unmanageable. This is where permission sets come in.

A *permission set* is a collection of settings and permissions that can be assigned to users in addition to their profile. While users can only be assigned to a single profile, they can be assigned to a multitude of permission sets.

Permission Sets Grant More Rights

Permission sets add additional permissions and rights on top of what the user already has assigned to them via their profile. Permission sets are always additive. They never remove any permissions.

When a user has multiple permission sets assigned, the combined result is the union of all permissions granted. Salesforce always applies the most permissive access when evaluating user permissions across profiles and permission sets.

A user can be assigned to one or many permission sets at the same time. This flexibility enables you to design modular security models where new rights can be granted without needing to create or edit profiles constantly.

To assign a permission set to a user, navigate to the User record, locate the Permission Set Assignments related list, and click Edit Assignments, as shown in Figure 4-18. From there, you can select one or multiple permission sets to assign to the user.

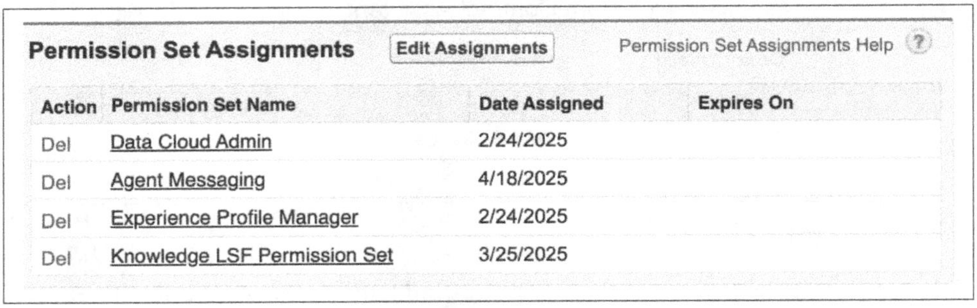

Permission Set Assignments	Edit Assignments	Permission Set Assignments Help ?	
Action	**Permission Set Name**	**Date Assigned**	**Expires On**
Del	Data Cloud Admin	2/24/2025	
Del	Agent Messaging	4/18/2025	
Del	Experience Profile Manager	2/24/2025	
Del	Knowledge LSF Permission Set	3/25/2025	

Figure 4-18. Permission Set Assignments related list

Similarities of Profiles and Permission Sets

Permission sets and profiles are similar in many ways and have a similar look in the user interface. Upon closer inspection, you will find that permission sets have less options on their Permission Set Overview screen, compared to a Profile Overview screen.

The Permission Set Overview screen is divided into sections devoted to apps and system settings. But you will find that the available subsections for these apps and system settings are fewer than those found on a Profile Overview screen.

Because permission sets only add rights and cannot restrict users, they are used for flexibility and extending access. There are certain controls that are only available in profiles and not in permission sets. Profiles serve as the foundation for baseline access and more administrative restrictions.

Creating a Permission Set

Search for and select Permission Sets from Setup and click New to begin the process of creating a new permission set. The Create Permission Set screen displays, as shown in Figure 4-19.

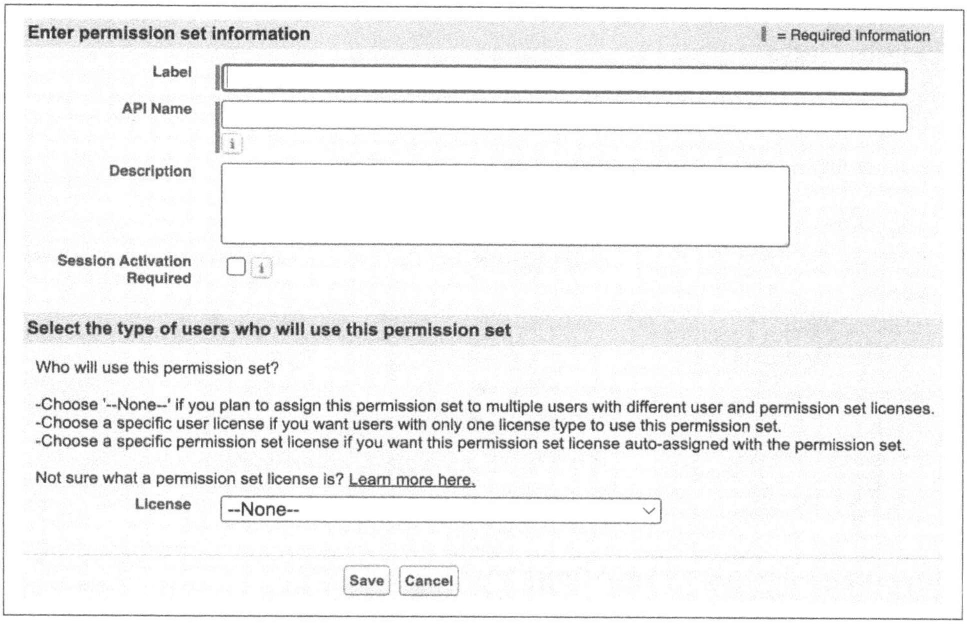

Figure 4-19. Create Permission Set screen

Enter a Label and Description for the new permission set. You can optionally select the type of users who will use this permission set via the License drop-down menu at the bottom of the screen.

Once you have completed the entry of the details of the new permission set, click Save. The Permission Set Overview screen displays. The new permission set is a blank canvas at this point, with no additional rights or permissions granted.

If you were to access the Object Settings of your new permission set, you would notice that all object permissions are set to No Access by default (Figure 4-20).

Remember that permission sets do not take away access previously granted to users via their profile or other permission set assignments. When CRUD rights differ between a profile and a permission set, Salesforce applies the most permissive setting.

You can make any necessary changes to your new permission set so that it fulfills its intended purpose. Once complete, you can assign users via the Manage Assignments button located at the top of the Permission Set Overview screen.

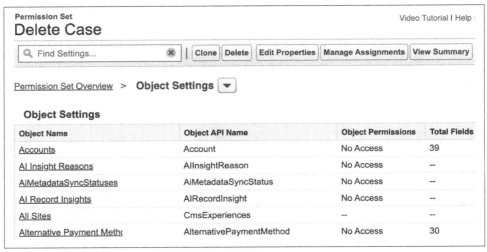

Figure 4-20. No access object permissions on a new permission set

Viewing a Permission Set Summary

It can prove difficult to ascertain what specific rights and permissions are extended via a permission set without clicking through a multitude of links from its Overview screen. This click-inducing headache faded to a bad memory, thanks to the View Summary button.

The Permission Set summary, as shown in Figure 4-21, displays access grouped by category, such as Object Permissions, Field Permissions, System Permissions, App Access, and other assigned capabilities. Each section can be expanded for more detail.

Permission Set Information

See the permissions enabled for this permission set and the permission set groups it's added to.

Related Permission Set Groups   User Permissions   **Object Permissions**   Field Permissions   More ∨

65+ items   Edit   🔍 Search this list...

Label ∨	Object AP... ∨	Read ∨	Create ∨	Edit ∨	Delete ∨
Account	Account	✓	✓	✓	✓
Asset	Asset	✓	✓	✓	✓
Authorization F...	AuthorizationF...	✓	✓	✓	✓

Figure 4-21. Permission Set summary

The Permission Set summary is especially useful when managing complex permission models. It enables you to verify quickly what additional rights a permission set grants without navigating through each individual setting.

Permission Set Groups

A *permission set group* is a container that bundles multiple permission sets together. Instead of assigning several permission sets individually to a user, you can assign the permission set group, which grants the combined permissions of all the included permission sets. This reduces administrative overhead and helps keep user access organized and consistent.

Permission set groups work in the same way as individual permission sets. They add permissions on top of the user's profile. They do not remove any rights, and they do not override existing permissions. If a user already has permissions through another assignment, the most permissive setting will always apply.

Creating a Permission Set Group

To create a permission set group, search for and select Permission Set Groups from Setup. Click New Permission Set Group at the top of the screen, as shown in Figure 4-22.

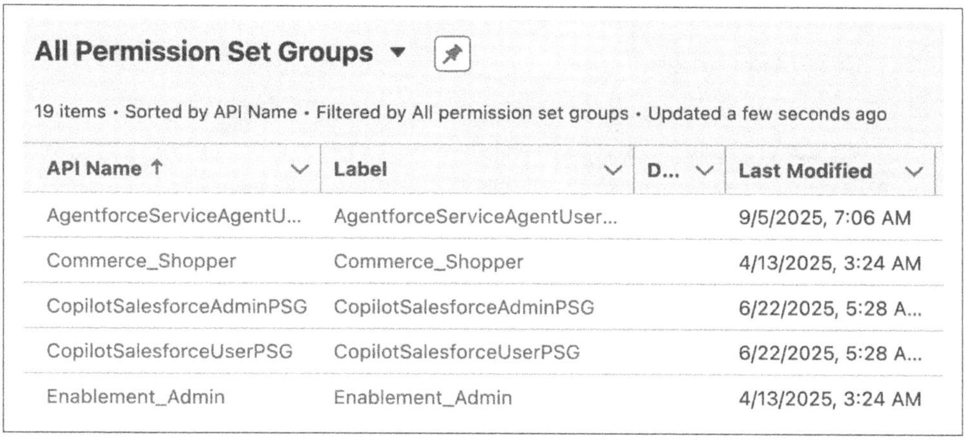

All Permission Set Groups ▼ 📌

19 items · Sorted by API Name · Filtered by All permission set groups · Updated a few seconds ago

API Name ↑	Label	D...	Last Modified
AgentforceServiceAgentU...	AgentforceServiceAgentUser...		9/5/2025, 7:06 AM
Commerce_Shopper	Commerce_Shopper		4/13/2025, 3:24 AM
CopilotSalesforceAdminPSG	CopilotSalesforceAdminPSG		6/22/2025, 5:28 A...
CopilotSalesforceUserPSG	CopilotSalesforceUserPSG		6/22/2025, 5:28 A...
Enablement_Admin	Enablement_Admin		4/13/2025, 3:24 AM

Figure 4-22. Permission Set Groups screen

The "Create a Permission Set Group" pop-up window displays, as shown in Figure 4-23.

Enter a Label and Description for the permission set group and click Save. The Permission Set Group Overview screen displays, as shown in Figure 4-24.

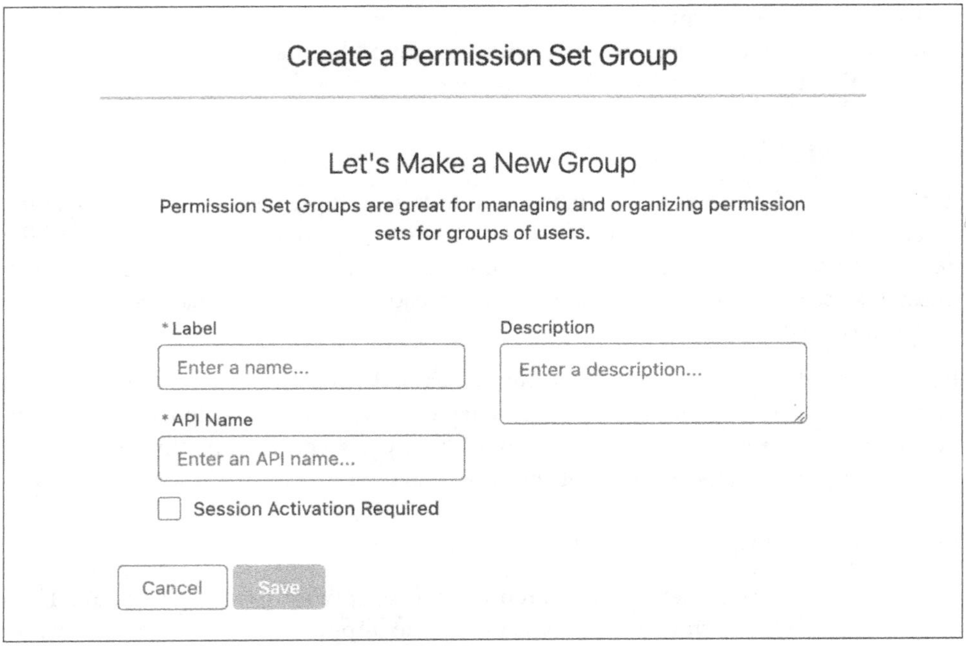

Create a Permission Set Group

Let's Make a New Group

Permission Set Groups are great for managing and organizing permission sets for groups of users.

* Label

Enter a name...

Description

Enter a description...

* API Name

Enter an API name...

☐ Session Activation Required

Cancel   Save

Figure 4-23. Create a Permission Set Group window

Figure 4-24. Permission Set Group Overview screen

You can add existing permission sets to it by clicking "Permission Sets in Group" and using the Add Permission Sets button. Select the desired permission sets to add to the group. Once a permission set group is created, it can be assigned to users via the Manage Assignments button at the top of the screen.

 Permission set groups also offer a feature called *muting permission sets*. Muting gives you the ability to disallow specific permissions from a permission set group without modifying the original permission sets themselves. For example, if one permission set grants the ability to delete records and you want to allow all the other rights but prevent deletions, you can mute the delete permission within the group.

Permission Set Expirations

Salesforce allows you to specify an expiration date when assigning permission sets to users. This provides a way to grant temporary access to additional permissions without the need to manually track and remove them later.

Clicking the Edit Assignments button from the Permission Set Overview screen displays the options for setting an expiration date, as shown in Figure 4-25.

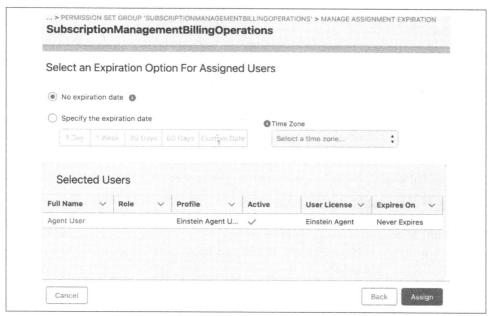

Figure 4-25. Permission Set Group Assignment screen with expiration options for assigned users

You can specify no expiration date, select from a variety of date range options, or set a custom date. The Select Users section of the screen displays when users' assignments end in the Expires On column.

Once an expiration date passes, the permission is automatically removed, reducing the administrative burden and helping maintain tighter security controls.

 You can always view assigned permission sets along with their expiration dates directly from the user's detail page under Permission Set Assignments. Permission set expirations apply only when the assignment is configured to expire at the time of assignment. Existing permission set assignments cannot be retroactively edited to add an expiration date. You must remove and reassign them with the desired expiration, if needed.

Data Sharing and Access

Now that you have learned the baseline access controls of the Salesforce security model via profiles, permission sets, and permission set groups, it is time to traverse through the various additional security mechanisms that can grant wider access. The next step along the way would be considered a basecamp as you attempt to eventually crest the mountaintop of knowledge that encompasses Security and Access on the platform. That basecamp is known as *organization-wide defaults*.

Organization-Wide Defaults

Organization-wide defaults (OWDs) define the baseline level of access users have to records they do not own in Salesforce. Setting the OWD for each object determines how visible and editable records are by default, before any additional sharing rules, role hierarchies, or manual sharing are applied.

To access OWDs, search for and select Sharing Settings in the Setup Quick Find. The Sharing Settings screen displays, as shown in Figure 4-26.

The top of the Sharing Settings screen displays the default sharing settings in the Organization-Wide Defaults section. Each object in your org is listed here, along with the current settings for Default Internal Access, Default External Access, and whether access to individual records for an object can be granted using the role hierarchy feature.

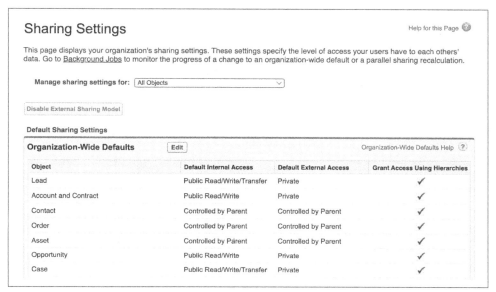

Figure 4-26. Sharing Settings screen

OWD access levels

Common settings for OWDs include Private, Public Read Only, Public Read/Write, and Controlled by Parent, although not all objects support every option:

Private

Setting an object to Private means that only the owner of the record and users above them in the role hierarchy can view and edit the record. All other users will have no access unless other sharing methods are configured.

Public Read Only

Setting an object to Public Read Only allows all users to view records, but only the owner or users higher in the hierarchy can edit them.

Public Read/Write

Setting an object to Public Read/Write allows all users to both view and edit all records of that object, regardless of ownership.

Controlled by Parent

For some child objects, such as Contact or Opportunity, there is also an option for "Controlled by Parent," meaning the access is inherited from the related parent object, such as Account.

Default Internal Access

Default Internal Access defines how users within your Salesforce organization can interact with records they do not own. This setting is configured per object and determines the baseline level of record visibility and editability among internal users. These settings are managed from the Sharing Settings screen in Setup.

For most standard and custom objects, the internal access can be set to Private, Public Read Only, or Public Read/Write. Private restricts access to the record owner and those above them in the role hierarchy. Public Read Only allows all internal users to view records but not make changes unless granted additional access. Public Read/Write permits all users to view and edit all records for that object, regardless of ownership.

Some objects may support the "Controlled by Parent" setting, which derives access from a parent object and is common in master-detail relationships. The internal access configuration acts as the foundation for all subsequent sharing behavior, including sharing rules, role hierarchy visibility, and manual sharing. It is essential that these settings align with your organization's policies on data privacy and collaboration.

Default External Access

Default External Access functions similarly to internal access, but it governs how external users, such as those in an Experience Cloud site, access records in your org. Like internal access, this setting is defined per object and can typically be set to Private, Public Read Only, or Public Read/Write.

Because external users are often customers, partners, or other users outside your company's internal staff, Salesforce recommends beginning with Private for external access. This ensures that no records are exposed to these users by default. From there, additional visibility can be granted using Sharing Rules, Manual Sharing, or Sharing Sets designed specifically for Experience Cloud user profiles.

In objects that support parent-child relationships, such as those with master-detail configurations, "Controlled by Parent" may be available as an option. This means that access to the child object's records depends on the access granted to the parent object's records.

Grant Access Using Hierarchies

In Salesforce, user roles are arranged into a hierarchy that reflects the organizational structure. When Grant Access Using Hierarchies is set for an object, it allows users higher in the role hierarchy to automatically access records owned by users below them. This enables managers and executives to view and interact with records that their direct reports own, even if other sharing mechanisms would otherwise prevent access.

For standard objects, this setting is always enabled and cannot be turned off. It ensures visibility flows upward through the role hierarchy for commonly used objects such as Accounts, Contacts, Opportunities, and Cases.

For custom objects, however, this setting is configurable. When creating or modifying a custom object's sharing settings, you can choose whether to allow access through the role hierarchy.

Disabling Grant Access Using Hierarchies on a custom object breaks this default upward visibility, meaning users higher in the role structure would not automatically inherit access to records owned by users below them. This can be useful in scenarios where compartmentalized access is required, such as when managing records tied to sensitive projects or business units that should remain isolated from one another.

Role Hierarchy

The role hierarchy is accessed via Roles in Setup. Selecting it displays the "Creating the Role Hierarchy" screen, as shown in Figure 4-27.

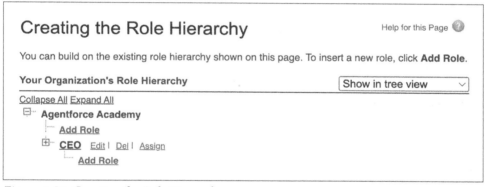

Figure 4-27. Creating the Role Hierarchy screen

You can select to Collapse All or Expand All nodes of the hierarchy via the links at the top of the screen. You can also select different view types for your hierarchy via the drop-down selection at the top-right.

> Salesforce controls vertical access to records based on a user's position in the organization's role hierarchy. It allows users in higher roles to view, and in some cases edit, records owned by users in roles beneath them. This design supports oversight by managers and executives without requiring individual sharing configurations.

Each role can be assigned to one or more users via the Assign link beside it. Users can be assigned to only one role in a Salesforce org.

Sharing Rules

Sharing rules are designed to give users access to records owned by peers or users in other departments who do not report to each other. Sharing rules are created per object from the Sharing Settings screen in Setup. The Sharing Rules screen displays.

The Sharing Rules screen displays the OWDs at the top of the screen (see Figure 4-26). Scrolling down you will eventually locate the Sharing Rules section of the screen, as shown in Figure 4-28.

Figure 4-28. Sharing Rules screen

Sharing rules are appropriate for recurring access needs between departments, such as enabling support agents to view open Cases created by the sales team. They also support complex business models where collaboration between users in unrelated roles is required.

It's important to understand that sharing rules extend access laterally across your organization. This is unlike the role hierarchy, which provides vertical access.

Creating a sharing rule

Sharing rules are created at the object level, by clicking the New button for the desired object. The Lead Sharing Rule screen displays, as shown in Figure 4-29.

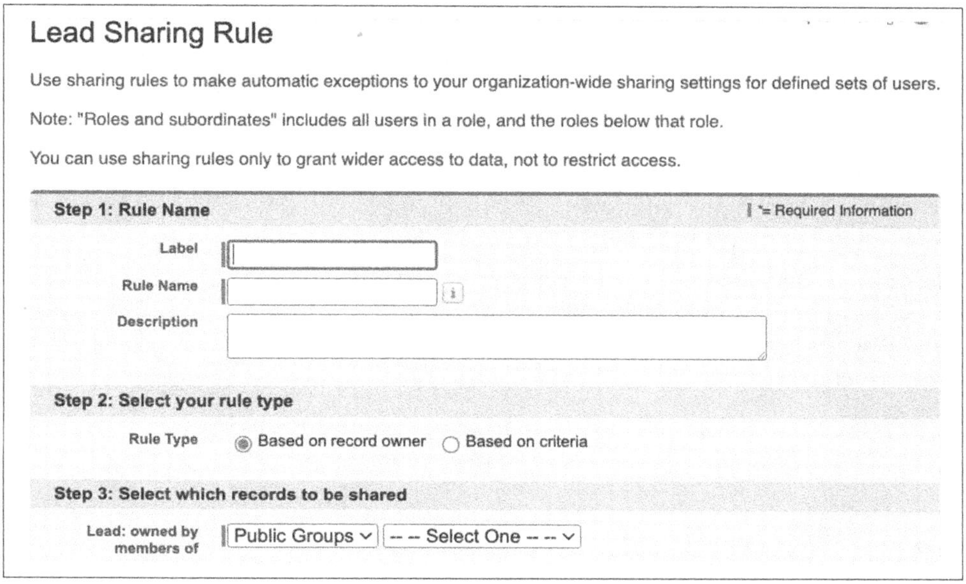

Lead Sharing Rule

Use sharing rules to make automatic exceptions to your organization-wide sharing settings for defined sets of users.

Note: "Roles and subordinates" includes all users in a role, and the roles below that role.

You can use sharing rules only to grant wider access to data, not to restrict access.

Step 1: Rule Name		= Required Information

Label [   ]

Rule Name [   ] ⓘ

Description [   ]

Step 2: Select your rule type

Rule Type ⦿ Based on record owner ◯ Based on criteria

Step 3: Select which records to be shared

Lead: owned by members of [Public Groups ∨] [-- -- Select One -- -- ∨]

Figure 4-29. Lead Sharing Rule screen

Enter a label and description for the new sharing rule in the Step 1 section. In the Step 2 section, select the rule type. Each rule defines either ownership-based or criteria-based access. Ownership-based rules are triggered by the record owner's role or group membership. Criteria-based rules evaluate field values within the record, such as status, region, or record type.

In the Step 3 section, define who the records are shared with and what level of access they should receive, either Read Only or Read/Write. These rules are evaluated after OWDs and role hierarchy access. They cannot reduce visibility and only serve to increase access beyond what has already been granted through other methods.

 When designing your sharing model, use the role hierarchy to manage vertical access and use sharing rules to enable lateral visibility where roles do not intersect. Together, these features form the core of Salesforce's record-level access control system.

Manual Sharing

Manual sharing allows users to grant access to individual records as needed. This method is used in cases where predefined sharing settings do not apply and the access requirement is specific to a particular user or scenario.

Record owners and users with full access to a record can manually share it with other users, roles, or groups. This is done by clicking the Sharing button on the record page. The button is only available when the object's OWD is set to Private or Public Read Only and when the user has the right level of control over the record.

After selecting who to share the record with, the user specifies the access level, either read-only or read and write. The sharing applies only to that individual record and stays in place until manually removed.

Manual sharing is useful for temporary or exceptional access situations, such as providing record access to a colleague covering for someone who is unavailable. It is also helpful when a record needs to be shared with someone outside the usual role or team structure.

This method is best reserved for ad hoc needs and complements broader access models by handling exceptions that fall outside of role-based or rule-based access.

Team Access

Team access in Salesforce provides a way to assign collaborative record access for users working together on Accounts, Opportunities, or Cases. This access model is useful when record visibility needs to reflect teamwork on deals or service issues.

There are separate team features for account teams, opportunity teams, and case teams. Each must be enabled individually in Setup, after which you can configure custom team roles and define the default access levels associated with those roles. These roles have labels such as Account Manager or Support Representative, and they help clarify each user's involvement on a record.

Users with appropriate permissions can manually add other users to a team from an individual record. When a user is added to a team, they are granted access to the record based on the assigned team role. Access can be set to read-only or read and write, depending on what level of involvement is needed.

Users can also define a default team for themselves, which allows them to add the same set of collaborators to every new Account, Opportunity, or Case they create.

Team access offers a repeatable and structured way to grant access without relying on ad hoc sharing or adding users to higher roles. It is best suited to situations where shared responsibility for a record is common and ongoing.

Territory Hierarchy

Territory hierarchy is part of Enterprise Territory Management and supports organizations that organize sales teams based on geographic areas, industry segments, or other criteria. It allows you to assign users to specific segments and automatically grant access to records based on those assignments.

Territories are organized in a hierarchical structure that can reflect national, regional, and local sales boundaries. Each territory can be assigned one or more users and can be linked to Accounts through assignment rules. When a user and an Account are both assigned to the same territory, the user receives access to that Account. This access can also extend to Opportunities and Cases, depending on configuration.

Territory hierarchy provides an alternative to role hierarchy. Instead of using management lines to control access, it uses segment-based ownership. This is particularly useful when sales responsibilities overlap or when users need access to Accounts that do not align with their role in the organization chart.

Users can belong to multiple territories, and territories can be realigned or restructured as business needs change. Territory hierarchy is best used when the access needs of sales or service teams are defined by market segments rather than reporting relationships. It allows for more flexible and scalable access models, especially in complex or matrixed organizations.

Organization-Wide User Security Features

Before concluding this chapter, there are several final security-related settings that are important to understand. These settings do not fit neatly into the object-level or record-level security model, but they influence when and how users can log in, how long their sessions last, and how their credentials are managed. These advanced security features form part of the broader responsibility administrators carry when applying secure and effective access policies.

Setup Audit Trail

The Setup Audit Trail logs administrative changes made within Salesforce, specifically tracking modifications to metadata rather than data records. It records updates to profiles, permission sets, automation configurations, object settings, and other system-level customizations affecting Salesforce operations.

You can access the Setup Audit Trail by searching for and selecting View Setup Audit Trail in Setup. The audit trail details the changes made, including what was changed, who made the change, and the date and time the change occurred. By default, Salesforce displays the 20 most recent setup changes, but you have the option to download the past 180 days of history (see Figure 4-30).

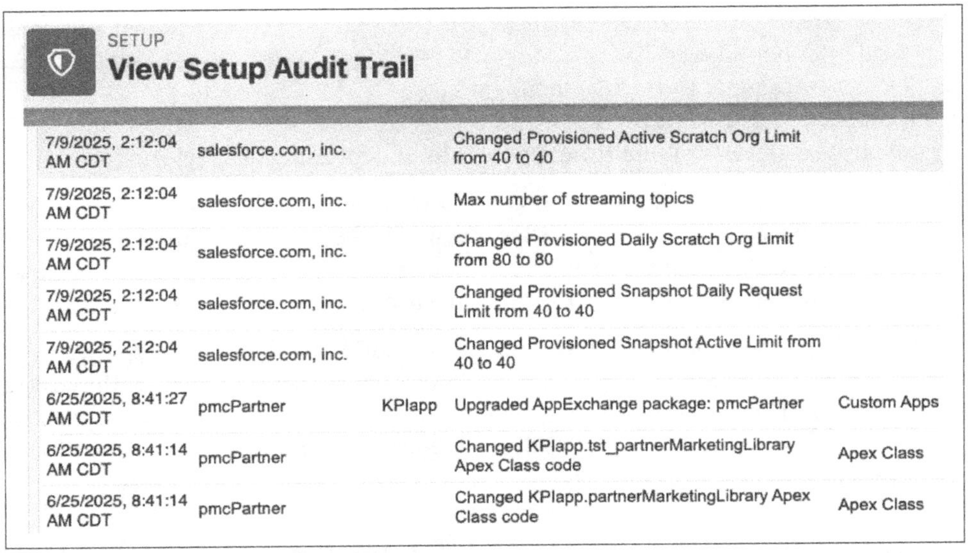

SETUP				
View Setup Audit Trail				
7/9/2025, 2:12:04 AM CDT	salesforce.com, inc.		Changed Provisioned Active Scratch Org Limit from 40 to 40	
7/9/2025, 2:12:04 AM CDT	salesforce.com, inc.		Max number of streaming topics	
7/9/2025, 2:12:04 AM CDT	salesforce.com, inc.		Changed Provisioned Daily Scratch Org Limit from 80 to 80	
7/9/2025, 2:12:04 AM CDT	salesforce.com, inc.		Changed Provisioned Snapshot Daily Request Limit from 40 to 40	
7/9/2025, 2:12:04 AM CDT	salesforce.com, inc.		Changed Provisioned Snapshot Active Limit from 40 to 40	
6/25/2025, 8:41:27 AM CDT	pmcPartner	KPIapp	Upgraded AppExchange package: pmcPartner	Custom Apps
6/25/2025, 8:41:14 AM CDT	pmcPartner		Changed KPIapp.tst_partnerMarketingLibrary Apex Class code	Apex Class
6/25/2025, 8:41:14 AM CDT	pmcPartner		Changed KPIapp.partnerMarketingLibrary Apex Class code	Apex Class

Figure 4-30. View Setup Audit Trail

The Setup Audit Trail is helpful for compliance and governance purposes. It enables you to monitor system-wide changes impacting security, user access, and functionality. Unlike standard history reports, which focus on record-level changes, the Setup Audit Trail provides comprehensive oversight of administrative actions, aiding in troubleshooting and maintaining system integrity.

Session Settings (Org-Wide)

Session settings configured at the org level establish baseline security rules that affect all users. These include how long a session remains active after inactivity, whether reauthentication is required for sensitive operations, and whether IP addresses must remain consistent throughout a session.

Session timeout duration is one of the most frequently adjusted options. Values range from 15 minutes to 24 hours. A shorter session timeout helps reduce risk in unsecured or shared environments, while longer sessions can minimize disruption in secure, internal settings.

Other settings include enabling warnings before timeout, forcing logout confirmations, and determining whether high-assurance security levels are required for certain features. You can also configure whether sessions are invalidated when IP addresses change.

These settings are found under Session Settings in Setup. When both org-wide and profile-level session settings are defined, the more restrictive value takes precedence.

For example, if a user's profile allows a 2-hour session but the org setting is 30 minutes, the 30-minute timeout is enforced.

Profile-level settings were covered earlier in this chapter, and administrators should understand how the two levels interact to design appropriate security policies for their user base.

Password Policies (Org-Wide)

Password policies at the org level establish default security standards for all users. These include requirements such as minimum password length, use of mixed character types, expiration intervals, password reuse prevention, and automatic lockout after failed login attempts.

Salesforce provides a default password policy, but it can be customized to meet industry or organizational standards. For example, an org may require passwords to be at least 12 characters, expire every 60 days, and not be reused for the last five password cycles.

These settings are configured by searching for Password Policies in the Setup menu. They apply to all users, regardless of their assigned profile, and represent the minimum baseline that any profile-level password settings must meet or exceed.

While it is possible to configure stricter policies at the profile level, the org-wide password policy will override any weaker settings. For example, if a profile allows password expiration after 90 days but the org-wide policy requires 60, the 60-day limit will apply.

Earlier in this chapter, I discussed profile-level password configuration. When both levels are in place, administrators should design policies that reinforce rather than contradict each other to maintain consistency and control.

Summary

In Chapter 4, you explored the fundamentals of configuring Security and Access settings within Salesforce. You learned the importance of establishing a secure and efficient environment by defining profiles and permission sets, assigning appropriate permissions, and managing OWDs and sharing rules.

These settings control who has access to specific objects and fields, as well as the actions they can perform. Additionally, you gained insights into Salesforce's layered approach to security, which ensures users see only the data they need, protecting sensitive information and maintaining data integrity. As security and access form the backbone of a well-structured Salesforce environment, mastering these concepts prepares you to confidently manage and secure your organization's data as you proceed into the next chapters.

Chapter 4 Quiz

It's now time to assess your understanding of Security and Access in Salesforce. The following questions will test your comprehension of key features such as OWDs, role hierarchy, sharing rules, manual sharing, restriction rules, team access, and territory hierarchy.

Security and Access controls are central to building a secure and scalable Salesforce environment and are well represented on the Salesforce Platform Administrator certification exam. Take your time with each question. Once you're done, carefully review the answers and explanations in the Appendix to strengthen your understanding of not just the correct answer, but why the other options do not apply.

1. Which Salesforce feature should an administrator use to assign specific page layouts and default record types to a sales team?

   a. User personal customizations

   b. Profile settings

   c. Permission sets

   d. App Launcher

2. A user reports being unable to log in to Salesforce due to IP restrictions. What should the administrator do to resolve the issue?

   a. Adjust the user's profile IP range.

   b. Enable "Log in as Any User."

   c. Freeze the user account.

   d. Reset the user's password.

3. A Salesforce administrator needs to configure strict security settings to prevent unauthorized access. Which combination of actions will best achieve this?

   a. Deactivating inactive users and freezing user accounts

   b. Setting strong password policies and enabling IP restrictions

   c. Activating single sign-on (SSO) and changing page layouts

   d. Adjusting sharing rules and enabling "Log in as Any User"

4. A new employee has been hired to join the customer service team and needs access to Salesforce immediately. What steps should the administrator take to set up the new user?

 a. Reset the user's password and assign them to a profile.

 b. Create a new user account, assign a profile, and configure permissions.

 c. Activate single sign-on (SSO) and provide the credentials.

 d. Freeze the user account and adjust password policies.

5. What is the function of OWDs in Salesforce?

 a. To define required fields during record creation

 b. To enforce password expiration and complexity

 c. To assign tab visibility for users

 d. To set the baseline level of record access for each object

6. What type of access does the role hierarchy provide?

 a. Field-level access for senior management

 b. Lateral access across public groups

 c. Vertical access to records based on user roles

 d. Full access to all records within a profile

7. Which feature is used to grant access to just one record on an as-needed basis?

 a. Sharing rule

 b. Manual sharing

 c. Territory assignment

 d. Profile permission

8. Which feature in Salesforce allows for the tracking of configuration changes over time?

 a. Data Import Wizard

 b. Schema Builder

 c. Audit Trail

 d. Data Loader

Object Manager and Lightning App Builder

The Object Manager and Lightning App Builder knowledge area marks a shift from the foundational Configuration and Setup knowledge area you have explored across the past three chapters. This next knowledge area forms the basis of how you'll structure and present information in Salesforce.

Think of this chapter as your guide to constructing the building blocks that make up any Salesforce implementation. Just as a house needs a solid foundation and framework before adding rooms and furniture, your Salesforce organization needs properly configured objects and user interfaces to function effectively for your users.

At its core, Salesforce organizes everything through objects. I like to think of objects as the nouns of Salesforce. They represent the people, places, and things your organization needs to track and manage. When you first log in to Salesforce, you'll find standard objects like Account and Contact ready to use. These standard objects handle common business scenarios that most organizations need. However, the true power of Salesforce lies in its flexibility to create custom objects that meet your specific business requirements.

In my years working with organizations across different industries, I've seen custom objects created for everything from medical prescriptions to jet engines. This flexibility to create exactly what you need makes Salesforce a versatile platform capable of adapting to virtually any business model.

From the Exam Guide

The Salesforce Certified Platform Administrator Exam Guide outlines the following learning objectives:

- Describe the standard object architecture and relationship model (for example, standard object, parent/child, master detail/lookup/junction relationships, and record types).
- Explain how to create, delete, and customize fields and page layouts on standard and custom objects, and know the implications of deleting fields.
- Given a scenario, determine how to create and assign page layouts, record types, and business processes for custom and standard objects.

Throughout this chapter, we'll explore these concepts in detail, providing practical examples that illustrate how these components work together in real-world situations. By the end, you'll understand how to configure these elements and why certain configurations work better for different scenarios.

Data Versus Metadata: Understanding Salesforce's Building Blocks

Before diving into object creation and customization, it's essential to understand how Salesforce organizes information through two distinct but interrelated concepts: data and metadata.

Think of building a house. The blueprint defines where rooms go, how big they are, and what goes in them. This is your metadata. The actual furniture and people living in those rooms represent your data. In Salesforce, metadata is your structural framework that defines how everything is organized and displayed.

When you work in Setup, you're creating and modifying metadata. This includes everything from defining new objects to configuring fields that determine what kind of information can be stored. Metadata encompasses your page layouts that control how information appears to users, security settings that govern who can see or edit what, and validation rules that ensure data accuracy.

Data, on the other hand, is the actual information that users enter into this framework you've built. When a sales representative enters a customer's name and phone number, that's data. When a service technician logs a vehicle identification number or a support agent creates a case, they're creating data. Each piece of information entered into Salesforce is data that conforms to the structure defined by your metadata.

The interaction between data and metadata becomes clear in everyday Salesforce operations. For example, consider creating a custom field called VIN (vehicle identification number) on a custom Automobile object. That is metadata. When you specify that the VIN must be exactly 17 characters, that is also metadata. But when a user enters a 17-character vehicle identification number into that field, they're creating data that must conform to the rules you've established in your metadata.

Consider metadata as the answer to how information should be stored, displayed, and accessed in Salesforce. Data, meanwhile, answers what the customer's name is, what the Opportunity amount is, and so on. Understanding this how (metadata) versus what (data) distinction helps you make better decisions about structuring your Salesforce environment.

As an administrator, you'll spend considerable time designing and adjusting metadata to ensure users can effectively work with their data. Every decision you make about an object's structure impacts how users enter, view, and work with their information. The Object Manager, which I'll explore next, is where these concepts come together. It is your primary tool for creating and modifying the metadata that defines how your users interact with their data. Understanding this relationship between data and metadata is crucial for making informed decisions about how to structure your Salesforce organization to best serve your users' needs.

The Object Manager: Where Data Meets Metadata

The Object Manager is the primary tool that Salesforce administrators use to manage the structure of data within their Salesforce environment. This structure is defined by metadata, which determines how users interact with data. When you create a custom object or add fields, you're establishing the framework that governs the input, storage, and display of data. This metadata is the backbone of the system, defining not only what information can be collected but also how users interact with it.

To illustrate this, consider the scenario of managing inventory for a car dealership. You would begin by creating a custom Automobile object. This object is an example of metadata. It represents the structure that defines how automobile records will be managed. To capture important details for each vehicle, such as make, model, and year, you would create custom fields. Each of these fields represents metadata that provides a framework for storing and organizing data.

When a user enters a new car into the system, such as specifying the make and model, they are interacting with data, which conforms to the structure set by the metadata. A helpful analogy for understanding this distinction is a spreadsheet. Imagine that you are tracking your automobile inventory using a spreadsheet. The column headers, like Make, Model, and Year, represent metadata, while the rows, each representing a vehicle, contain the actual data.

Navigating the Object Manager

Within the Setup menu in Salesforce, you'll find the Object Manager tab, which gives you direct access to all the customizable objects in your environment, as shown Figure 5-1.

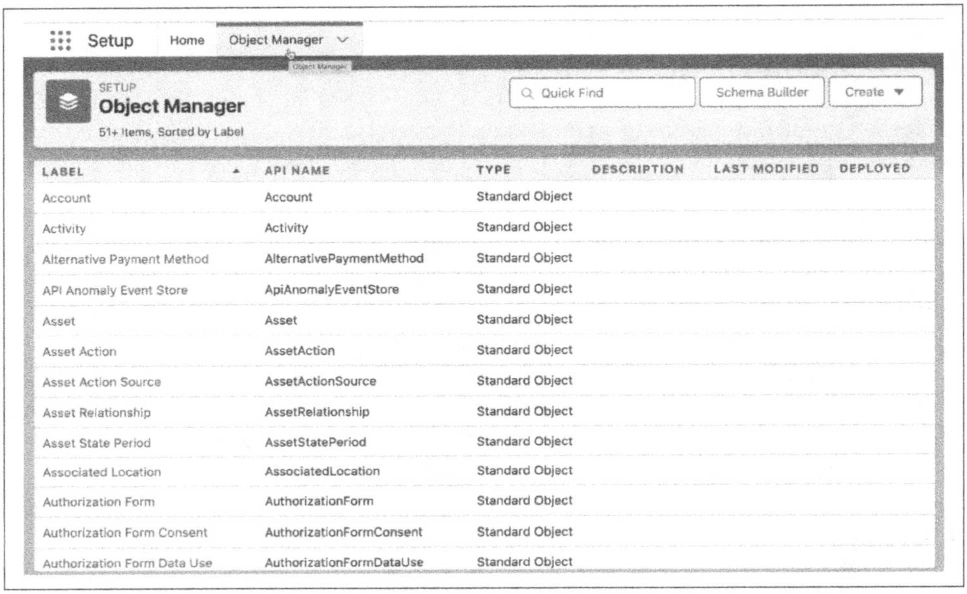

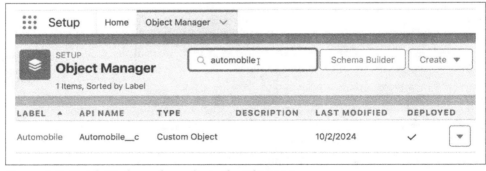

Figure 5-1. Object Manager tab and list of objects displayed

These objects include standard objects like Account, Contact, and Lead, as well as any custom objects you've created to meet your business needs. The Quick Find bar at the top of the Object Manager screen enables you to quickly locate and select specific objects to work with, as shown in Figure 5-2.

Figure 5-2. Quick Find search results in the Object Manager

When you select an object by clicking on it, you are taken to the object's Details screen, as shown in Figure 5-3.

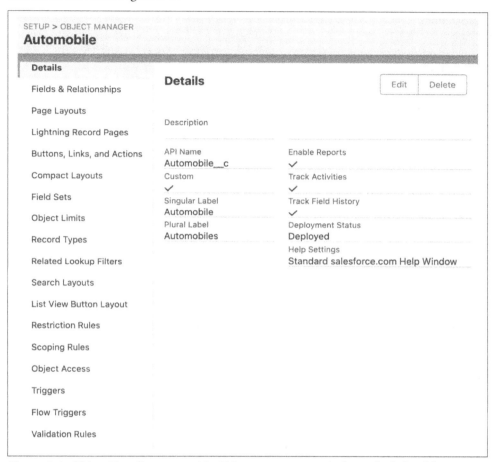

Figure 5-3. Object Details screen with Object management links in the left sidebar

On the left side of the object's Details screen, you'll find links for managing Fields & Relationships, Page Layouts, Lightning Record Pages, and many more object customization options. Each of these aspects allows you to refine how data is captured, displayed, and utilized by users in your organization.

Working with Standard and Custom Objects

Salesforce organizes data through a system of objects, which serve as containers for records. Standard objects, such as Account, Contact, Lead, and Opportunity, come preconfigured in Salesforce and cover common business use cases. They are designed to support typical business functions like managing customers, tracking sales opportunities, and maintaining contact information.

While these objects can be customized to a certain extent, their core structure is defined by Salesforce, and some configurations are limited. Custom objects, on the other hand, are created to support specific business requirements that go beyond what standard objects can accommodate.

Standard Object Architecture

Salesforce's standard object architecture provides a set of predefined objects designed to manage core business processes across various industries. These standard objects represent foundational concepts, such as leads, accounts, and customer interactions, and serve as the building blocks for configuring Salesforce to meet business needs. Understanding these objects and their relationships is essential for implementing a CRM system that supports all stages of customer engagement.

Lead

A Lead represents an individual or organization that has shown interest in your product or service. Leads are typically the first point of interaction in the sales process, captured through various channels like web forms, advertisements, or events. Once qualified, a lead can be converted into an Account, Contact, and Opportunity, transitioning it further along the sales funnel and integrating it into the broader Salesforce ecosystem.

Campaign

A Campaign is used to manage and measure marketing initiatives. This object helps track the performance of marketing activities, whether they involve promotional emails, conferences, or social media advertisements. Campaigns provide metrics such as lead responses and return on investment (ROI), enabling marketing teams to refine their strategies based on measurable outcomes.

Account

Accounts represent companies or organizations with which a business interacts. They are the primary entity around which most business interactions revolve, linking other objects such as Contacts, Opportunities, and Cases. Accounts serve as the anchor for customer relationships, consolidating all associated records to provide a complete view of each organization's history.

Contact

Contacts are the individuals associated with an Account. They typically represent people involved in the sales process, such as decision-makers or key stakeholders. By associating Contacts with Accounts, sales teams can better understand the people they need to engage with at each organization.

Opportunity

Opportunities represent potential revenue-generating deals. This object tracks the details of sales in progress, including their value, closing date, and sales stage. Opportunities are usually linked to Accounts and Contacts, helping sales teams manage the sales pipeline, forecast revenue, and focus efforts on high-priority deals.

Product and Price Book

Products represent the items or services that a company sells. A Price Book is a list of Products, including their prices, allowing sales teams to manage the items included in each Opportunity. By associating Products and Price Books with Opportunities, sales representatives can ensure accurate pricing and tailor offerings to meet customer needs.

Case

Cases are used to track customer service issues, requests, or feedback. Each Case represents a specific customer inquiry, which could be a question, problem, or support request. Cases can be linked to Accounts, Contacts, and even Assets, providing a comprehensive view of a customer's history and support needs.

Knowledge

The Knowledge object allows for the management of articles containing information, such as solutions to common issues, troubleshooting guides, or best practices. Knowledge serves as a centralized content repository for customer service representatives to resolve Cases more efficiently. With the increasing integration of AI into Salesforce, Knowledge articles can also be used as a source for grounding AI-driven service recommendations, enhancing the capabilities of automated tools.

Assets

Assets represent products that customers have purchased, such as equipment or software licenses. These records can track ownership, warranty periods, and maintenance schedules, which is valuable for providing ongoing support. Assets can also be used to track internal items, like office supplies, if needed. Associating Assets with Accounts allows for a full view of each customer's history, including any related service requests.

The Interconnected Nature of Core CRM Objects

Many of these standard objects overlap in functionality across different Salesforce applications. For example, both Sales and Service teams use Accounts and Contacts to manage customer relationships. An Account serves as the central thread linking all interactions, whether they involve closing new deals or handling customer support issues. This interconnected architecture ensures that departments can share a unified view of customer information, promoting collaboration and consistency.

The design of Salesforce's objects allows for a seamless flow of information across different business functions, supporting customer engagement from initial contact through to ongoing service. As an administrator, having a solid understanding of these objects, their relationships, and how they fit within various business processes is essential for building effective and efficient Salesforce solutions.

Salesforce Relationship Model

In Salesforce, relationships between objects define how data points connect and interact with each other. The relationship model allows for the creation of associations that mirror real-world business scenarios, enabling complex data hierarchies and dependencies. Understanding these relationships is fundamental to structuring data in a meaningful way and ensuring that users have a comprehensive view of interconnected information.

Salesforce primarily supports three types of relationships: lookup, master-detail, and many-to-many. Each type serves a distinct purpose based on the requirements of the business process and the level of dependency between the objects.

Lookup Relationships

A *lookup relationship* creates a connection between two objects without enforcing a strong dependency. This type of relationship allows one object to reference another while still existing independently. For example, an Employee object may have a lookup relationship to a Department object, indicating which department the employee belongs to. If the Department record is deleted, the Employee record remains in place, although the link to the department is broken.

In a lookup relationship, you can specify what happens to the child record if the parent is deleted. Options include clearing the lookup field to remove the reference or blocking the deletion to ensure data integrity. This flexibility makes lookup relationships suitable for scenarios where related records need to exist independently and data dependencies are not strictly enforced.

Lookup relationships are commonly used for connecting standard objects such as Opportunities and Contacts to Accounts, where the objects can stand alone, but the relationships enhance data organization and reporting. Refer to Figure 5-4 for more detail.

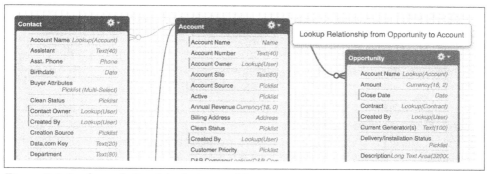

Figure 5-4. Lookup relationships between objects

Master-Detail Relationships

A *master-detail relationship* creates a more tightly bound connection between two objects, establishing a hierarchy where one object is the master and the other is the detail. In this relationship, the detail record is dependent on the master record, meaning that if the master is deleted, all associated detail records are also removed. For example, consider an Invoice object with a master-detail relationship to Invoice Line Items. If the Invoice is deleted, all associated Line Items will be deleted as well, maintaining data consistency.

Unlike lookup relationships, master-detail relationships do not offer options to block deletion or clear the relationship if the master record is deleted; the dependent child records are always deleted along with the master. This type of relationship is ideal for scenarios where records must exist together and reflects a stronger data dependency. Additionally, master-detail relationships enable roll-up summary fields, where calculations such as totals or counts can be performed on the detail records and the results reflected in the master record. For example, you might use a roll-up summary field to sum the total value of all Invoice Line Items and display it on the Invoice.

In certain cases, master-detail relationships allow for reparenting, where the detail record can be reassigned to a different master record. This option is useful for processes where ownership or relationships change, such as transferring an Invoice Line Item to a different Invoice.

Understanding the Differences Between Lookup and Master-Detail Relationships

Choosing the appropriate relationship type is crucial for ensuring data integrity and supporting business processes effectively. Lookup relationships are suitable for scenarios where records need to exist independently of each other, offering flexibility in data management. For instance, an Employee record does not need to be tied to a Department to be meaningful. In contrast, master-detail relationships enforce stronger data dependencies, making them ideal for cases where related records must exist together, such as an Invoice and its associated Line Items.

Another key difference is the ability to perform calculations using roll-up summary fields in master-detail relationships. These fields allow administrators to display aggregated data, such as totals or averages, on the parent record based on the values of related child records. This capability is not available with lookup relationships, making master-detail the preferred choice for scenarios that require summarizing related data.

Deletion behavior also differs between the two types of relationships. In a lookup relationship, administrators can configure what happens to the child record if the parent is deleted, either by clearing the lookup field or blocking the deletion. In master-detail relationships, however, deleting the master record automatically deletes all associated detail records, reflecting the stronger dependency.

 In Salesforce, *parent/child* terminology is often used to refer to hierarchical relationships where one object is linked to another. This term can apply to both lookup and master-detail relationships, although master-detail is more strictly controlled with tighter data dependencies. Understanding these distinctions will help you make informed decisions about which relationship type to use for different scenarios.

Junction Objects (Many-to-Many Relationships)

To create a many-to-many relationship in Salesforce, a Junction object is used. A Junction object acts as an intermediary between two other objects, establishing a many-to-many relationship. For example, in a scenario involving Students and Courses, a third object called Enrollment can be created to serve as the Junction object, allowing each student to enroll in multiple courses and each course to have multiple students.

A Junction object requires two master-detail relationships. This setup ensures that the Junction object maintains interdependencies with both parent objects, making it possible to perform comprehensive data analysis and reporting. However, there are important limitations to consider: an object can have a maximum of two master-detail relationships, and standard objects cannot be used as the detail in a master-detail relationship. Consequently, when creating a new relationship on a standard object, the master-detail option will not be available.

Best Practices for Setting Up Relationships

When setting up relationships in Salesforce, it is important to choose the right type to ensure data integrity and support reporting needs. If data should remain independent, a lookup relationship is generally more appropriate. When you need to enforce dependencies or perform calculations on related data, a master-detail relationship is the better choice.

Avoid excessive complexity when configuring relationships. While it is possible to create intricate data models with multiple relationships, this can lead to data management challenges and impact system performance. Aim to strike a balance between flexibility and simplicity, ensuring that the relationships you create enhance data organization without introducing unnecessary complications.

When setting up master-detail relationships in Salesforce, it's important to be aware of certain limitations. An object can have a maximum of two master-detail relationships. This restriction ensures that data models remain manageable and perform efficiently. Additionally, standard objects cannot be used as the detail in a master-detail relationship. As a result, when creating a new relationship on a standard object, the master-detail field type will not be available. These constraints guide administrators in designing effective data models while maintaining system performance and consistency.

Relationships Between Standard Objects

Salesforce's standard objects, such as Accounts, Contacts, Opportunities, and Cases, often have predefined relationships that reflect typical business scenarios. For example, both Opportunities and Contacts typically have lookup relationships to Accounts, allowing them to be associated with a central customer record. This structure helps consolidate customer data and provides a unified view of interactions across Sales and Service functions. Understanding these standard relationships lays the groundwork for configuring custom relationships that complement existing data structures.

Implications for User Access and CRUD Rights

The type of relationship chosen for an object also affects user access and CRUD rights. In a master-detail relationship, the security settings and ownership of the detail record are determined by the master record. This means that controlling access to the master record effectively governs access to all related detail records. The detail record inherits the sharing and security settings from the master, ensuring consistent access control across related records. This arrangement simplifies management but reduces flexibility, as the detail records cannot have independent security settings.

In contrast, lookup relationships allow for more granular control over data access, as each object can have its own independent sharing and security settings. Administrators can separately configure access based on user roles or profiles for each related object. This flexibility is useful in scenarios where data needs to be managed with distinct security settings or when users should have access to some records but not others, even within the same relationship.

Object Management Best Practices

The importance of maintaining a structured and efficient environment grows exponentially as your Salesforce instance expands. One key best practice is to use clear and descriptive naming conventions when creating custom objects or fields. This approach makes the data model more intuitive and ensures that current and future administrators can easily navigate the system. Consistent naming conventions help everyone involved in managing Salesforce understand the purpose and context of each element, avoiding ambiguity and mismanagement.

Keeping detailed records of changes made within the Object Manager is another valuable practice. Documentation serves multiple purposes: it aids in troubleshooting unexpected issues, facilitates the onboarding of new administrators, and provides a historical record of why specific changes were made. This history can be especially helpful in diagnosing problems or understanding the impact of earlier adjustments.

Providing thorough descriptions for metadata also significantly enhances the platform's usability. As generative AI tools become more integrated into Salesforce, comprehensive metadata details improve the reasoning and decision-making capabilities of AI-driven features. This can make AI tools more effective in offering relevant suggestions, supporting automation, and optimizing system functionality. By adhering to these best practices, administrators maintain a clean, well-documented, and AI-friendly Salesforce environment that supports efficiency and innovation.

Customizing Salesforce with the Object Manager brings many benefits, but there are several common pitfalls that can complicate the environment if not managed carefully. One frequent issue is creating too many custom fields or page layouts. While customization can help tailor Salesforce to specific business needs, excessive customization often leads to clutter, making it difficult for users to navigate effectively. Striking a balance between customization and simplicity is key to maintaining a usable system.

Another common oversight is the misconfiguration of field-level security (FLS). FLS controls user access to specific fields within an object, determining which users can view or edit particular fields. Simply creating a field does not automatically make it accessible to the appropriate users. FLS must be configured to align with business roles and privacy requirements. Improperly configured FLS can either restrict users from accessing important data or expose sensitive information to those without the proper permissions.

By being aware of these pitfalls, administrators can create a more efficient, organized, and secure Salesforce environment that meets business needs without introducing unnecessary complexity.

Object Configuration Options in the Object Manager

Each link in the left-hand menu of the object's Detail screen in Object Manager serves a distinct purpose in configuring an object. There are many links well beyond the scope of the exam, so I will focus on those most relevant to platform administration work.

Fields & Relationships

Click the Fields & Relationships link to display the Fields & Relationships screen, as shown in Figure 5-5.

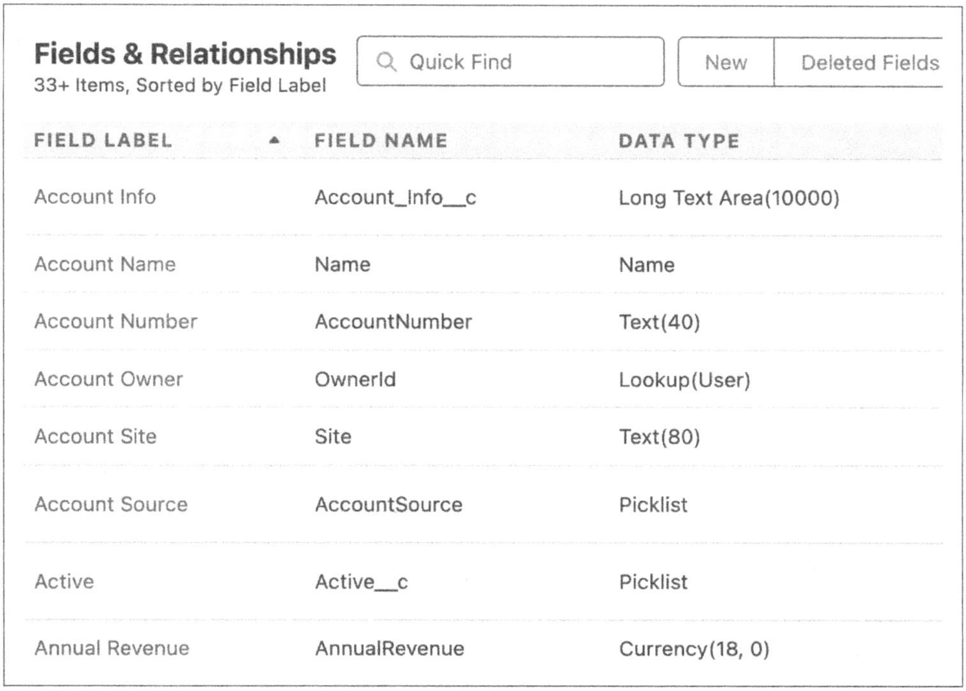

Fields & Relationships 33+ Items, Sorted by Field Label	🔍 Quick Find		New	Deleted Fields
FIELD LABEL ▲	**FIELD NAME**		**DATA TYPE**	
Account Info	Account_Info__c		Long Text Area(10000)	
Account Name	Name		Name	
Account Number	AccountNumber		Text(40)	
Account Owner	OwnerId		Lookup(User)	
Account Site	Site		Text(80)	
Account Source	AccountSource		Picklist	
Active	Active__c		Picklist	
Annual Revenue	AnnualRevenue		Currency(18, 0)	

Figure 5-5. Fields & Relationships screen for the standard Account object

Each field can be customized with various settings, such as data type and help text, which guide users during data entry. Managing relationships determines how data connects across the Salesforce environment.

You will find actions you can take related to Fields & Relationships by way of the New, Deleted Fields, Field Dependencies, and Set History Tracking buttons located at the top-right of the screen, as shown in Figure 5-6.

Figure 5-6. Fields & Relationships action buttons

New custom field. To create a new field on an object, click the New button. The New Custom Field screen displays, as shown in Figure 5-7.

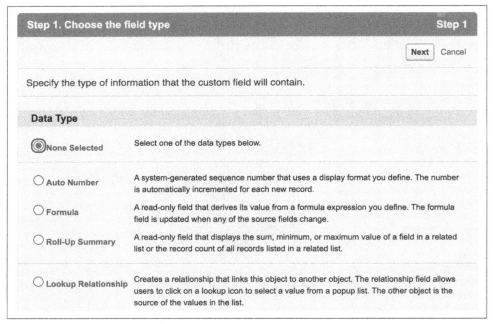

Figure 5-7. New Custom Field screen

Your first step in the creation of a new custom field is to select the Data Type. The Data Type designations are divided into categories. The number of steps involved in creating a new custom field will vary depending on the Data Type you select. You will learn more about creating custom fields and the different data types for fields later in this chapter.

Deleted fields. To view any fields that have recently been deleted on an object, click the Deleted Fields button at the top of the Fields & Relationships screen. The Deleted Fields screen displays, as shown in Figure 5-8.

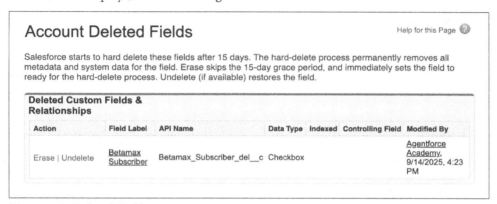

Figure 5-8. Deleted Fields screen

Any fields that have been recently deleted from an object will be listed in the Deleted Fields screen. These fields undergo what is known as a *hard delete* after 15 days, which permanently removes all metadata and system data associated with them.

Before the 15-day period expires, you can either click Undelete to restore the field or click Erase to permanently delete it immediately. Once you choose Erase, the field is permanently removed and can no longer be recovered using the Undelete option.

Field dependencies. You can define dependencies between two fields on an object by clicking the Field Dependencies button at the top-right of the Fields & Relationships screen. The Field Dependencies screen displays for the currently selected object, as shown in Figure 5-9.

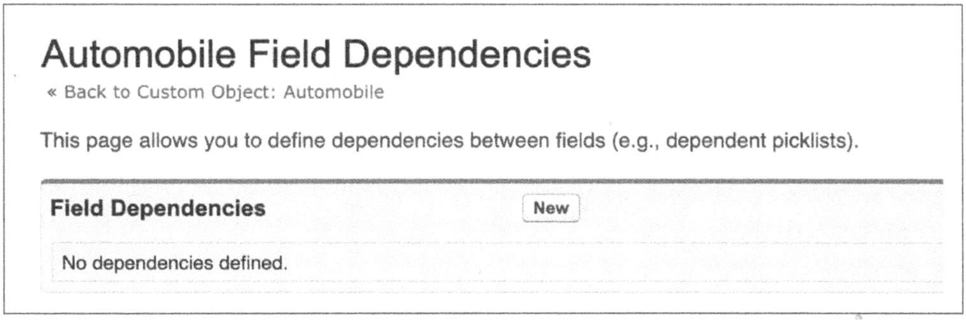

Automobile Field Dependencies
« Back to Custom Object: Automobile

This page allows you to define dependencies between fields (e.g., dependent picklists).

Field Dependencies   [New]

No dependencies defined.

Figure 5-9. Automobile custom object Field Dependencies screen

Field dependencies in Salesforce let you create a dynamic relationship where the values available in one field depend on the selection in another. This relationship isn't limited to picklists; it can also include custom checkboxes as controlling fields, where the user's choice in one field shapes the options available in another. The controlling field can be a standard or custom checkbox or picklist, provided it has at least one option but fewer than 300 values.

To see this in action, consider an inventory of automobiles in Salesforce with picklist fields for Make and Model. Here, the Make field acts as the controlling field, determining which Model options appear based on the selected make.

To establish a dependency between two fields on an object, click the New button on the Field Dependencies screen. The New Field Dependency screen displays, as shown in Figure 5-10.

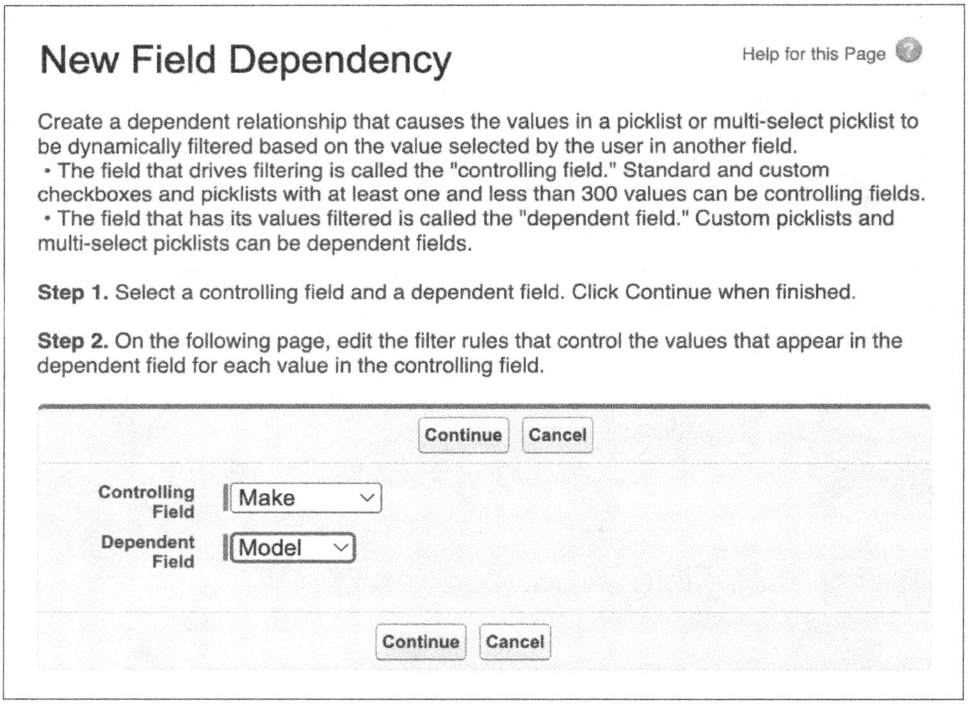

New Field Dependency

Help for this Page

Create a dependent relationship that causes the values in a picklist or multi-select picklist to be dynamically filtered based on the value selected by the user in another field.
  • The field that drives filtering is called the "controlling field." Standard and custom checkboxes and picklists with at least one and less than 300 values can be controlling fields.
  • The field that has its values filtered is called the "dependent field." Custom picklists and multi-select picklists can be dependent fields.

Step 1. Select a controlling field and a dependent field. Click Continue when finished.

Step 2. On the following page, edit the filter rules that control the values that appear in the dependent field for each value in the controlling field.

Continue   Cancel

Controlling Field   Make

Dependent Field   Model

Continue   Cancel

Figure 5-10. New Field Dependency screen

Setting up a field dependency begins with choosing a controlling field and dependent field. Once you have made your selections, click Continue to finish configuring the dependent field's picklist options visibility on the Edit Field Dependency screen, as shown in Figure 5-11.

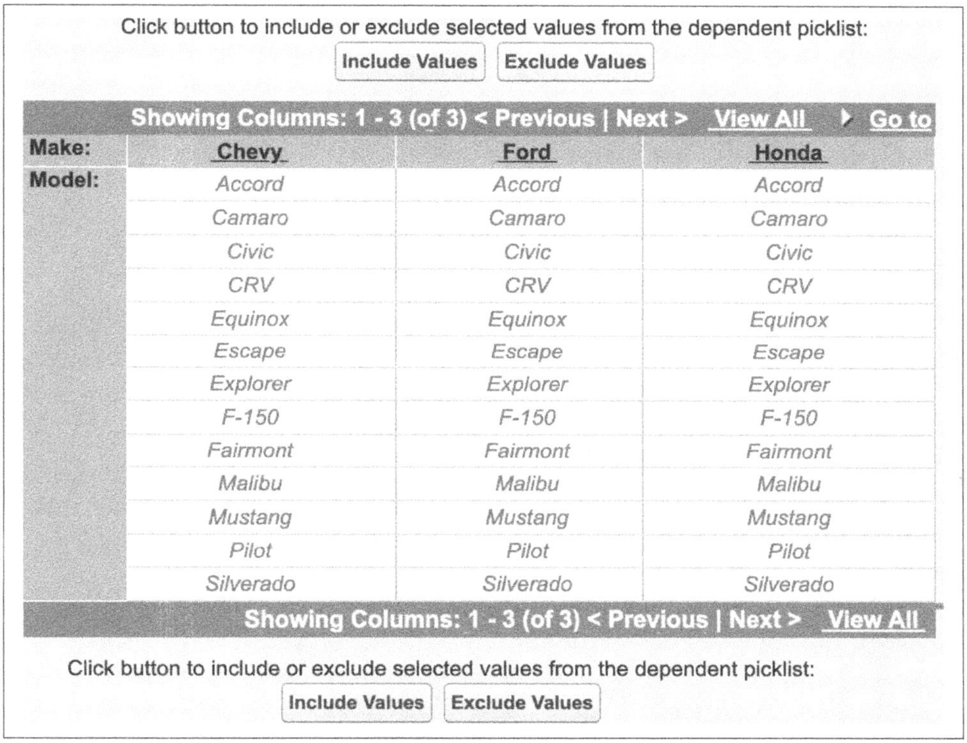

Click button to include or exclude selected values from the dependent picklist:

Include Values | Exclude Values

Showing Columns: 1 - 3 (of 3) < Previous | Next > View All ▶ Go to			
Make:	**Chevy**	**Ford**	**Honda**
Model:	Accord	Accord	Accord
	Camaro	Camaro	Camaro
	Civic	Civic	Civic
	CRV	CRV	CRV
	Equinox	Equinox	Equinox
	Escape	Escape	Escape
	Explorer	Explorer	Explorer
	F-150	F-150	F-150
	Fairmont	Fairmont	Fairmont
	Malibu	Malibu	Malibu
	Mustang	Mustang	Mustang
	Pilot	Pilot	Pilot
	Silverado	Silverado	Silverado
Showing Columns: 1 - 3 (of 3) < Previous | Next > View All			

Click button to include or exclude selected values from the dependent picklist:

Include Values | Exclude Values

Figure 5-11. Edit Field Dependency screen

Here you can specify the available values for each combination. Simply click the appropriate dependent values for each controlling field option and click either the Include Values or Exclude Values buttons as needed. Once all field dependencies have been set, click Save.

Set history tracking. The Set History Tracking button (see Figure 5-6) is used to specify which fields on an object you wish to track. If you have not previously enabled Field History Tracking on an object, you will see the Enable Account History checkbox to do so, as shown in Figure 5-12.

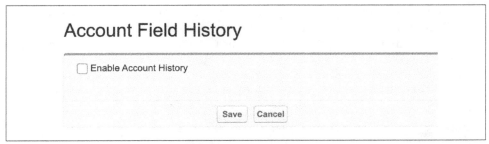

Account Field History

☐ Enable Account History

Save   Cancel

Figure 5-12. Enable Account History checkbox

Checking the Enable Account History checkbox refreshes the screen to display the fields available to track old and new values. Select the fields for which you wish to track history by checking the corresponding checkboxes for each.

After enabling Field History Tracking for an object, it's important to make this historical data visible to users by adding a Field History related list to the page layout. Refer to "Adding a Field History related list to a page layout" on page 157 for more details on adding this list with the Enhanced Page Layout Editor.

You can select up to 20 fields to track history on, per object. If you need to track changes on more than 20 fields, you can track an additional 20 fields via Chatter Feed Tracking, which is covered in Chapter 9.

> While Field History Tracking records both the old and new values for most field types, longer text fields—such as Text Area (Long) or Text Area (Rich)—and multi-select picklists are exceptions. For these fields, Salesforce tracks only that a change occurred, but not what the value was changed from or to. In other words, the Field History related list will show that the field was edited, but it will not display the before and after values.

Page Layouts

The next option available in Object Manager is Page Layouts. This section enables you to control how an object's records are presented to users. Clicking the Page Layouts link in the left sidebar of the Object Manager will display all available page layouts for that object (see Figure 5-13).

To customize the arrangement of fields, related lists, buttons, and other elements on a record's detail page, click a page layout name to open the Enhanced Page Layout Editor for that page layout, as shown in Figure 5-14.

Figure 5-13. Account Page Layouts screen

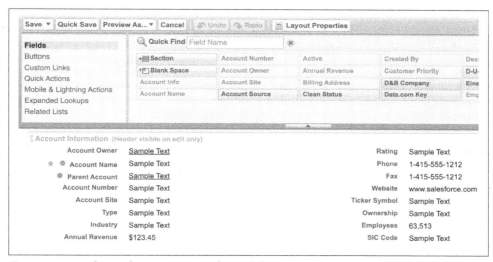

Figure 5-14. Enhanced Page Layout Editor with Account layout displayed

Enhanced Page Layout Editor. The Enhanced Page Layout Editor has its origins in the Salesforce Classic user interface. While Salesforce has long since migrated to the newer Lightning Experience interface, remnants of Classic persist on the platform.

One such example of Classic's persistence is the Enhanced Page Layout Editor. It is here that you can manage the main layout elements and behavior of pages in Salesforce.

The default Lightning pages which are rendered and presented to Lightning users are based on the page layout settings that are set in the Enhanced Page Layout Editor. Later in this chapter, I will go into more depth regarding the newer Lightning Experience interface and the creation and modification of Lightning pages by using the Lightning App Builder.

Real-time preview. The Enhanced Page Layout Editor provides a real-time preview, which shows how the layout will appear to end users. This is particularly helpful when making multiple adjustments, as you can immediately see how the page will look and function. This feature reduces the time needed for trial and error and ensures that the final layout is intuitive and easy to use.

Enhanced Page Layout Editor Customization Options

To better understand the options available in Lightning pages, it is important to first address and understand the foundational aspects of page layouts and design, which are set and maintained in the Enhanced Page Layout Editor. The top-left of the editor contains the various page layout customization options (see Figure 5-15).

These customization options include Fields, Buttons, Custom Links, Quick Actions, Mobile & Lightning Actions, Expanded Lookups, Related Lists, and more. I'll now go through these customization options, starting with Fields.

Fields

The Fields option allows you to add, remove, or rearrange fields on the page layout, customizing the information displayed in records, as shown in Figure 5-15.

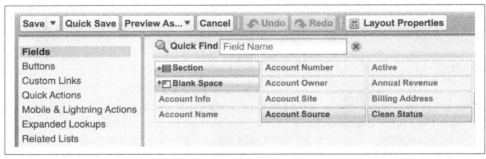

Figure 5-15. Fields available to add or remove from a page layout

Page layouts allow you to arrange fields in a logical order that matches the business process. Fields that are already located on the page layout are grayed out. Fields that are not on the page layout are active and available to be dragged and dropped into place down below on the page layout.

Controlling field visibility and read-only settings

One of the key features of the Enhanced Page Layout Editor is the ability to control field visibility properties at the page level. Hover over a field to display both a Remove and a Properties icon (see Figure 5-16).

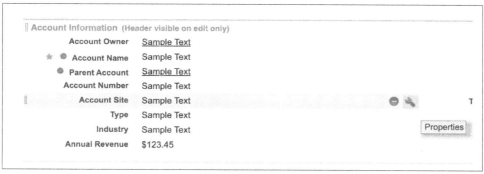

Figure 5-16. Field options in the Editor

Click the Remove icon for a field to remove that field from the page layout. Click the Properties icon to open the Field Properties window, as shown in Figure 5-17.

Figure 5-17. Field Properties window

You can select to make the field read-only or required. Once you have made your selection, click OK to return to the page layout. If you select to make a field read-only, a lock icon will appear next to that field in the editor. If you select to make a field required, a red asterisk will appear next to that field in the editor instead.

Buttons

The Buttons option provides options to add or modify buttons available on the page, as shown in Figure 5-18. Buttons allow users to perform specific actions directly from the record view.

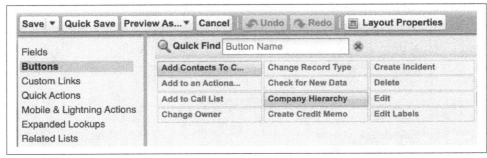

Figure 5-18. Buttons in the Editor

Custom Links

The Custom Links option enables the addition of custom links to external websites or specific Salesforce pages (see Figure 5-19). This helps users quickly access related resources.

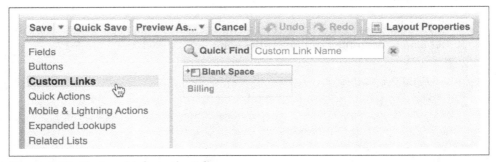

Figure 5-19. Custom Links in the Editor

Quick Actions

The Quick Actions option lets you configure actions, like creating or updating records, that users can perform directly from the layout for enhanced efficiency.

Mobile & Lightning Actions

The Mobile & Lightning Actions option allows customization of actions available in the Salesforce mobile app and Lightning Experience, ensuring consistent user interactions across platforms. The actions in this section are predefined by Salesforce and can be overridden.

Expanded Lookups

The Expanded Lookups option offers settings to define additional information in lookup fields, giving users more context when selecting related records.

Related Lists

The Related Lists option lets you customize related lists to display relevant records associated with the primary record, aiding in comprehensive data visibility (see Figure 5-20).

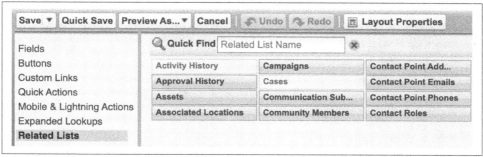

Figure 5-20. Related Lists in the Editor

Related lists are displayed at the bottom of a page layout and provide a quick overview of related records. For instance, on an Account record, you might include related lists for Contacts, Opportunities, and Cases to give users a complete view of the customer relationship.

You can customize which fields are displayed in the related list and adjust the order of related lists to suit the user's needs. Including only the most relevant fields and placing frequently used lists at the top can enhance the efficiency with which users access related data.

Adding a Field History related list to a page layout

If you enable Field History Tracking on an object, you can add the history-related list to the object's page layouts, enabling users to view detailed information about any changes made to the fields.

The history-related list is named based on your object, such as Account History for account records. You can drag and drop the history-related list into the desired position within the Related Lists area of the page layout.

Sections

In addition to placing and rearranging fields on a page layout, you can also create custom sections within a layout. Sections make it easier for users to navigate through a record by logically grouping similar types of information.

You will find a Section element listed first within the Fields options, followed by an option for Blank Space. This appears with the available fields on an object in the Layout Editor, as shown in Figure 5-21.

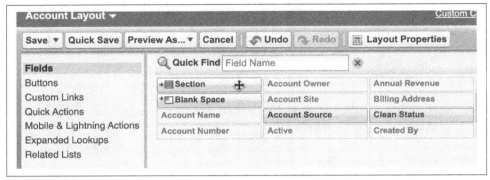

Figure 5-21. Section component

Drag the Section component into the desired position on the page layout to create a new section. Once you have a new section in place, you can specify its columns and Tab key order.

To configure the number of columns in each section of a page layout, hover over a section header in the Enhanced Page Layout Editor to reveal that section's wrench icon. Click the wrench icon to open the Section Properties window, as shown in Figure 5-22.

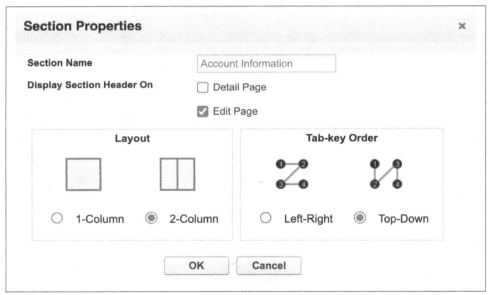

Figure 5-22. Section Properties window

From the Section Properties window, you can select if you want to display the section header on the Detail Page and/or the Edit Page for this page layout.

You can also set the section as either a 1-column or 2-column layout. And finally, you can select Left-Right or Top-Down for the Tab key order. The Tab key order is set for ease of data entry for users who prefer navigating a page layout via the Tab key on their keyboard rather than using a mouse.

Renaming a page layout

The Layout Properties button at the top of the screen in the Enhanced Page Layout Editor enables you to rename a page layout (see Figure 5-23).

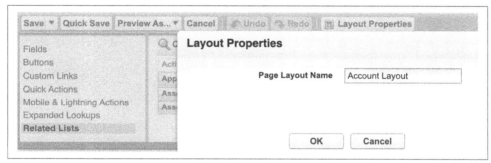

Figure 5-23. Layout Properties window

In addition to renaming your layout, you can also show or hide the Highlights Panel and/or the Interaction Log in console applications by checking the corresponding checkboxes.

Page Layout actions

Returning to the Page Layouts screen (accessible via the link in the left sidebar of the Object Manager), you will find New and Page Layout Assignment buttons at the top-right of your screen, as shown in Figure 5-24.

Page Layouts 4 Items, Sorted by Page Layout Name					Quick Find		New	Page Layout Assignment
PAGE LAYOUT NAME ▲		CREATED BY		MODIFIED BY				
Account (Marketing) Layout		OrgFarm EPIC, 4/13/2025, 3:24 AM		Agentforce Academy, 4/22/2025, 6:13 PM				▼
Account (Sales) Layout		OrgFarm EPIC, 4/13/2025, 3:24 AM		Agentforce Academy, 4/22/2025, 6:13 PM				▼
Account (Support) Layout		OrgFarm EPIC, 4/13/2025, 3:24 AM		Agentforce Academy, 4/22/2025, 6:13 PM				▼
Account Layout		OrgFarm EPIC, 4/13/2025, 3:24 AM		Agentforce Academy, 4/22/2025, 6:13 PM				▼

Figure 5-24. New and Page Layout Assignment buttons

Creating a new page layout.   Clicking the New button on the Page Layouts screen opens the Create New Page Layout screen, as shown in Figure 5-25.

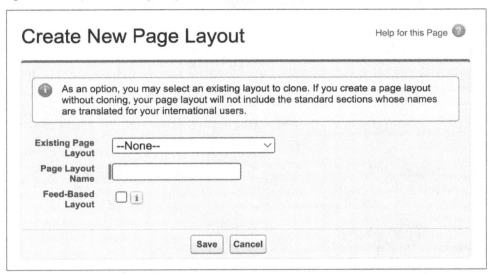

Figure 5-25. *Create New Page Layout screen*

You can select an existing page layout from the drop-down menu to base your new page layout upon, or select None to start from scratch. Enter a Page Layout Name and click Save to save your new page layout. You can then make any additions and adjustments to your new page layout in the Enhanced Page Layout Editor.

Page layout assignments.   Page layouts will not be accessible until you have assigned them to your users.

You can review and adjust which profiles are assigned to which page layouts by clicking the Page Layout Assignment button on the Page Layouts screen.

The Page Layout Assignment screen displays (see Figure 5-26).

Page layouts are assigned by Profile in Salesforce. In the example shown in Figure 5-26, the Account object has not had record types implemented, so there's a single column on this screen. Once record types are introduced on an object, you will see multiple columns on the above screen for each individual record type on the object. You would then need to set Page Layout Assignment by record type and profile.

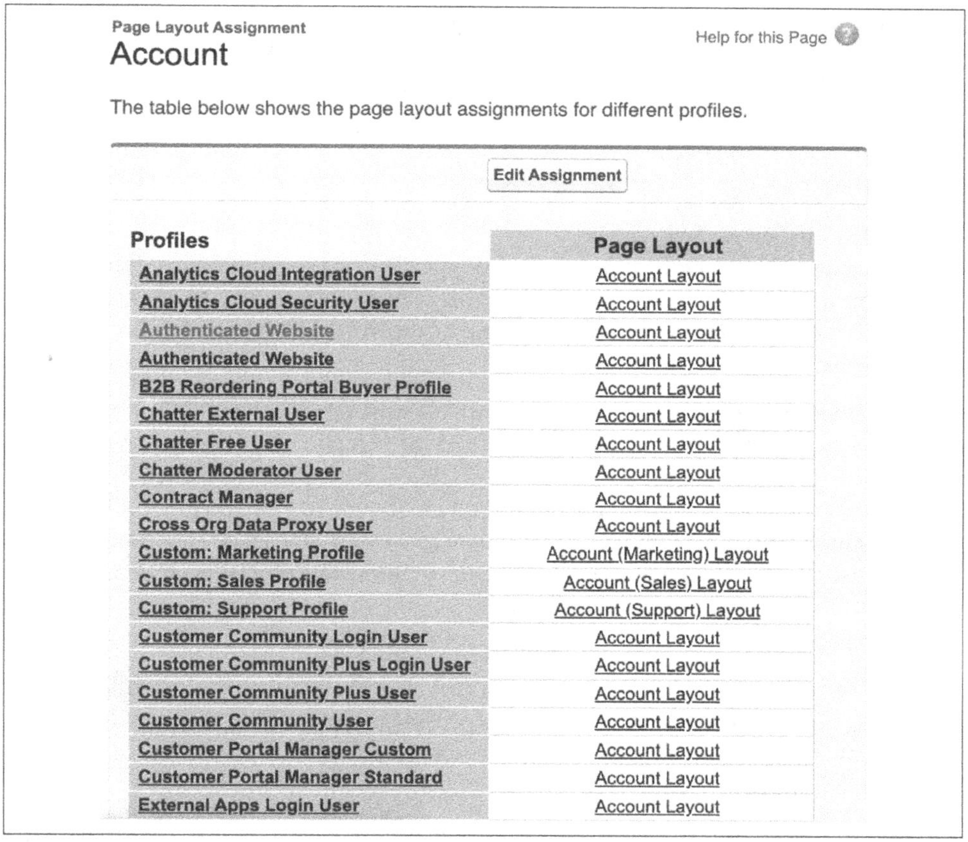

Figure 5-26. Page Layout Assignment screen for the Account object

Record Types—the Adjectives of Salesforce

Record types enable you to create variations of an object's records that reflect different business scenarios. For example, an Opportunity object could have different record types for New Business and Renewal, each with its own unique fields and page layouts. Business processes further enhance customization by defining different stages or workflows for record types, such as separate sales processes for different products.

There are three primary reasons for introducing record types:

Different page layout assignments by record type
> First, they allow for different page layout assignments based on the combination of record type and user profile. This means you can tailor what fields, sections, and related lists are displayed based on the specific type of object.

For example, a Fuel Automobile record type might have a page layout that prominently displays "Miles per Gallon," while an Electric Automobile record type would display fields like "Miles per Full Charge" or Range. This customization ensures that users interacting with these records see only the information that is relevant to that particular type, enhancing the clarity and usability of the interface.

Different picklist options by record type
The second key benefit of using record types is that they allow for different picklist options based on the record type. This feature ensures that the values presented to users are appropriate for the type of record they are working on, reducing errors and improving data consistency.

Consider the scenario where you want to manage different makes of vehicles based on whether the automobile is fuel or electric. The Electric Automobile record type may include manufacturers like Tesla, while the Fuel Automobile record type may need different options like Toyota or Ford. Using record types, you can ensure that only relevant vehicle makes are displayed based on whether the user is creating a record for a fuel or electric vehicle, providing a more streamlined and intuitive experience.

Different Lead, Sales, and Support Processes by record type
The third key benefit is that record types can be connected to standard Lead, Sales, and Support Processes. These processes control which Status field options display on Leads and Cases and which Stage field designations display on Opportunities.

In Chapter 7, you will work through the process of creating both Lead and Sales Processes and Lead and Opportunity record types. You will work through creating a Support Process and Case record types in Chapter 8.

Field Types

When creating a custom field in Salesforce, the first step is to select the appropriate field type. The field type determines the nature of the data you want to store and defines how it interacts with other data within the Salesforce platform (see Figure 5-27).

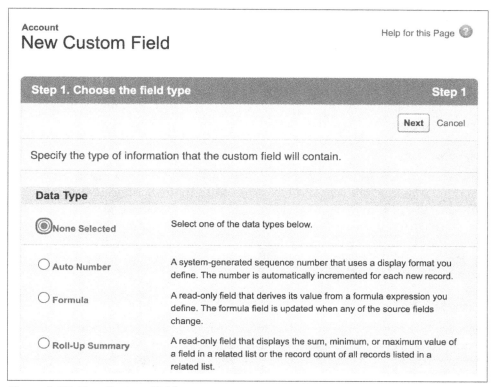

Figure 5-27. New Custom Field screen

Auto Number

This field type is a system-generated sequence number that is automatically assigned to each new record. It is useful when you need to uniquely identify records without relying on user input. For instance, you could use an auto number field to assign unique identifiers to each automobile in an inventory. The format can be customized (for example, AUTO-0001), providing a structured way to track and manage records.

Formula

A formula field derives its value based on other fields. This is a read-only field, meaning users cannot directly enter or modify data. Instead, the value is updated whenever any of the source fields change.

Formula fields are commonly used for calculations, such as determining the age of an automobile based on its manufacturing year or applying a discount percentage on an Opportunity. However, they can also be used for other purposes, such as combining or formatting data. For example, a formula field can combine a Contact's First Name and Last Name fields into a single Full Name field.

Formula fields help automate logic, ensure data consistency, and reduce manual data entry errors across your Salesforce environment.

Roll-Up Summary

This is a read-only field type available only on the master side of a master-detail relationship. A roll-up summary field aggregates data from the related detail records, providing the sum, minimum, maximum, or count of the related records. For example, if you have a master-detail relationship between an Account and its related Orders, you could use a roll-up summary to display the total value of all orders linked to that Account. This field type simplifies data analysis at a summary level without the need for custom code or reports.

Lookup Relationship

A lookup relationship links one object to another, allowing users to associate records without creating strict dependencies. This is useful when you want flexibility. For instance, linking an Automobile record to an Account using a lookup means that even if the Account is deleted, the Automobile can still exist independently. This relationship provides a way to cross-reference data without enforcing ownership or cascading deletions.

Master-Detail Relationship

This relationship type creates a strong dependency between two objects, often referred to as a parent-child relationship, where the master (parent) governs the detail (child). The child record cannot exist without the parent, and actions performed on the master, such as deletion, directly affect the detail. For example, in a scenario where an Automobile object is linked to a Service Record object through a master-detail relationship, deleting the Automobile would also delete all related service records. Roll-up summary fields can be created on the master record to summarize information from the detail records.

External Lookup Relationship

This relationship links a Salesforce object to an external object whose data is stored outside the Salesforce environment. It's especially useful in integrations where data must be referenced or used but not imported directly into Salesforce. This relationship helps in maintaining a connection to external databases or services, expanding the functionality of Salesforce beyond native data storage.

Checkbox

A checkbox is used for capturing true/false information, directly corresponding to a Boolean value in programming. This field type is ideal for tracking straightforward yes/no answers, offering a simple and intuitive way to collect binary information. For example, you might use a checkbox to indicate whether an automobile is available for sale or whether a customer has agreed to the terms of a contract. When set to true, it means the condition is met (such as the automobile being available or the customer agreeing), while false indicates the opposite.

By default, checkboxes are set to unchecked, but you can configure the default value to be checked if that better aligns with your use case. This makes checkboxes an effective tool for capturing key decision points or statuses within your data model, allowing users to easily see and update these attributes as needed.

Currency

The currency field stores financial information, such as the price of an automobile. It automatically formats numbers based on the specified currency and is particularly useful for tracking revenue, costs, and budgets.

Date/time

This allows users to enter or pick a date and time, providing greater granularity than the date field type.

Email

The email field ensures that the information entered follows a valid email format. This helps standardize customer contact details and supports integration with Salesforce's email features. Salesforce does not verify whether the email address itself is real or deliverable. Additional validation would be needed to confirm that the email address actually exists or is in use.

Number

The number field is used for capturing numeric data, such as the mileage of an automobile. It is ideal for situations where only numerical information is required. Leading zeros are removed automatically. You can set constraints, such as minimum and maximum values to ensure data quality, and specify decimal places.

Percent

The percent field allows users to enter a percentage value. This is particularly useful for storing discount rates or progress levels. The system automatically adds the percentage symbol for clarity.

Phone

The phone field is used for capturing phone numbers, and Salesforce automatically formats the data appropriately for better readability based on regional settings. For instance, when entering a number like 1234567890, the field will format it as (123) 456-7890.

Picklist

A picklist allows users to select a value from a predefined list of options. This is useful for maintaining consistency across records, such as specifying the make of an automobile. By limiting the possible inputs, a picklist helps to standardize data entry, making reporting and filtering easier.

Global Value Set

A global value set is a reusable list of picklist values that can be shared across multiple custom picklist fields on different objects, ensuring consistency of values and labels across your Salesforce organization. When you update a value in a global value set, the change is automatically reflected in all picklist fields that reference that global value set, making it easier to maintain standardized options across your org.

Multi-Select Picklist

Multi-select picklists allow users to select multiple values from a list you define. For example, selecting multiple features available in a car, such as sunroof, leather seats, and navigation system. However, they have limitations in reporting and filtering, so it's generally better to consider alternatives like related lists for complex selections.

Text

The text field allows users to enter any combination of letters, numbers, or symbols. It is commonly used for short entries like a vehicle model (for example, Civic or Camry). The maximum length can be defined to ensure the data fits specific business requirements.

> The maximum length of a text field is 255 characters. For longer text entries, Salesforce fortunately provides other text-based variants, as detailed next.

Here are the available text-based variants:

Text Area
> Allows users to enter up to 255 characters, making it ideal for brief descriptions or notes. Changes to this field can be fully tracked in Field History (both old and new values).

Long Text Area
> Stores up to 131,072 characters, suitable for storing detailed information such as notes on an automobile's condition. Field History Tracking will show only that a change occurred, without the actual before and after values.

Rich Text Area
> Offers formatting options, allowing users to add images, links, and formatted text, up to 131,072 characters. This can be used for product descriptions that require more visual detail. Field History Tracking will show only that a change occurred, without the actual before and after values.

Text (Encrypted)
> Stores sensitive information in encrypted form. It is used for data such as Social Security numbers or other personally identifiable information (PII) that need additional security. These fields cannot be tracked with Field History due to encryption.

URL

The URL field allows users to enter a valid website address. This can be useful for linking to online resources, such as a manufacturer's webpage or service schedule. When clicked, the link opens in a separate browser window, making it convenient for users to access additional information.

Geolocation

A geolocation field captures location data in the form of latitude and longitude coordinates. This is useful for mapping physical locations, such as tracking where an automobile is stored or identifying the nearest dealership. While geolocation fields make it easy to store precise location data, Salesforce does not calculate distances automatically out of the box. To calculate distances between two points, you need to use additional tools such as Apex code, formula fields, or external services that can process geospatial data.

Schema Builder

A close companion to the Object Manager is the Schema Builder. It is available via Setup or by clicking the Schema Builder button located at the top of the Object

Manager screen. The Schema Builder is a tool that is helpful in the visualization of objects and their relationships to one another, as exemplified in Figure 5-28.

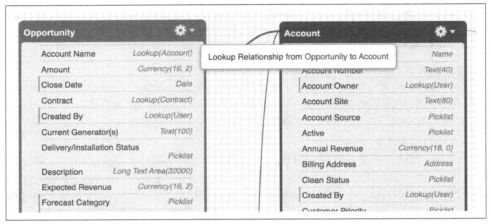

Figure 5-28. Schema Builder with Opportunity and Account displayed

Schema Builder provides a visual map of your Salesforce data architecture, making it easy to see the structure and connections of both standard and custom objects at a glance. It presents objects and their relationships in an interactive interface. Using drag-and-drop functionality, you can identify existing relationships, create new custom objects and fields, and adjust object configurations.

 Schema Builder does not support exporting diagrams.

Another helpful tool to add to your administrative arsenal that also supports drag-and-drop functionality onto a canvas is the Lightning App Builder. It is the second topic of the Object Manager and Lightning App Builder knowledge area this chapter is dedicated to. And now is the time for you to gain expertise with the Lightning App Builder.

Lightning App Builder

The Lightning App Builder enables you to create and customize pages for Lightning Experience and the Salesforce mobile app. It offers a flexible, drag-and-drop interface that simplifies the process of building user-friendly, responsive applications. With the Lightning App Builder, you can create Lightning pages tailored to your organization's unique business needs, whether that involves a custom home page, a record page, or an app page that consolidates important information.

Search for and select Lightning App Builder from Setup to access any Lightning pages currently in your organization, as shown in Figure 5-29. From this screen, you can edit, clone, or delete a Lightning page via the Action links listed to the left of each Lightning page.

Figure 5-29. Lightning Pages screen

You can create a new Lightning page by clicking the New button on the Lightning Pages screen. A window displays the various types of Lightning pages that you can create (see Figure 5-30).

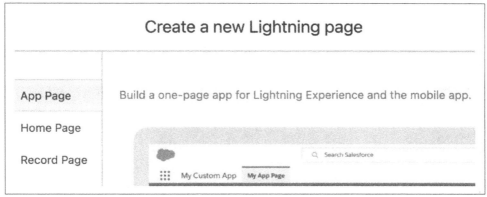

Figure 5-30. "Create a new Lightning page" window

Select the type of Lightning page you wish to create and then click Next. I will detail the different types of pages you can create with the Lightning App Builder in the next sections.

Lightning App Page

An app page aggregates different elements and tools into one place, enabling users to interact with multiple pieces of information without switching between tabs or apps. This can be particularly useful for specific functions, like providing a one-stop overview for sales representatives that includes open Opportunities, recent activities, and performance dashboards.

To create a Lightning app page, click App Page and click Next. You will be prompted to enter a label for your app page. Once you have entered a label and clicked Next, you are tasked with selecting a layout for your app page, as shown in Figure 5-31.

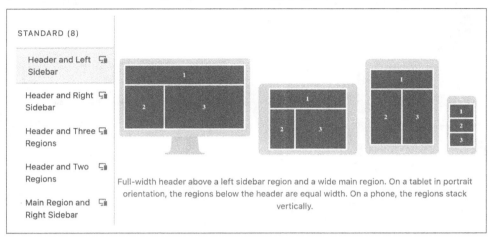

Figure 5-31. App page layout selection

Select a layout and click Done. The Lightning App Builder displays Lightning Components on the left, a drag-and-drop enabled canvas in the middle, and a properties section on the right, as shown in Figure 5-32.

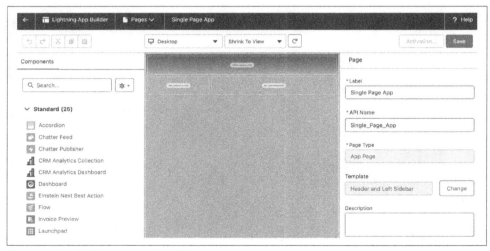

Figure 5-32. Lightning App Builder app page

You can drag and drop Lightning Components from the left side of the screen to the canvas in the middle. You will learn more about Lightning Components and further configuration of Lightning pages later in this chapter.

Lightning Home Page

In addition to app pages, you can create Lightning home pages. A Lightning home page can be customized to deliver information to your users as soon as they log in. This could include dashboards, recent records, or specific tasks that need their attention.

To create a Lightning home page, click Home Page from the "Create a new Lightning page" window. The window updates to display a sample Lightning Experience home page, as shown in Figure 5-33.

Click Next and enter a label for your new Lightning home page, then click Next again. You are presented with the option to choose a page template or clone a Salesforce default home page, as shown in Figure 5-34.

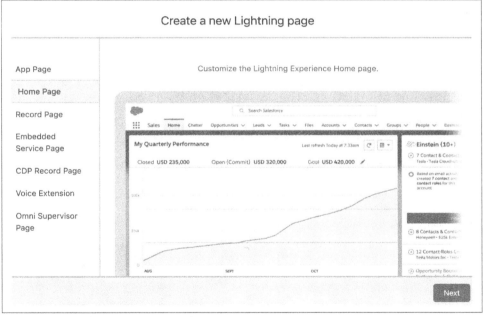

Figure 5-33. Lightning Experience home page preview

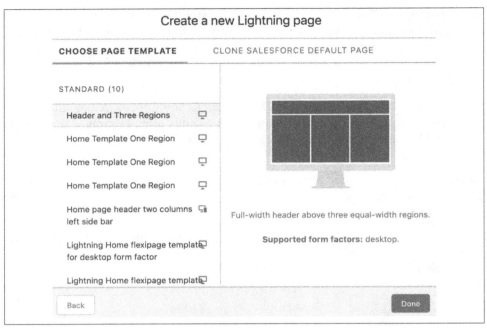

Figure 5-34. New Lightning home page templates and clone options

If you select a page template, a blank canvas displays in the Lightning App Builder, similar to what was shown in Figure 5-32. If you instead select to clone a Salesforce default page, you are presented with page options (see Figure 5-35).

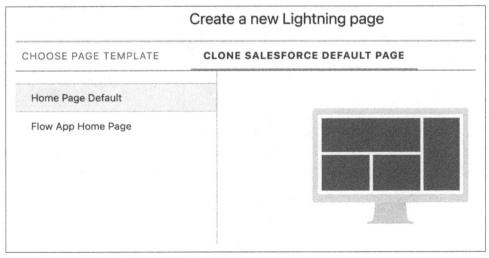

Figure 5-35. New Lightning page clone options

Selecting a standard page to clone from and clicking Done displays the Lightning App Builder with the cloned standard page layout displayed in the canvas. You can make any desired changes to your new Lightning home page. When done, click Save.

Lightning Record Page

You can also create a Lightning record page, which focuses on presenting details about a specific object, such as an Account, Contact, or a custom object like Automobile. These pages are designed to provide all the relevant fields, related records, and actions that users might need when working with a record.

With Lightning App Builder, you can create multiple record pages for different purposes, enhancing the user experience by displaying only the most relevant data. To create a Lightning record page, click Record Page from the "Create a new Lightning page" window.

You will be prompted to enter a label and select an object this new page will be associated with. Once you have specified both, click Next. The window updates with different page template and clone options, as shown in Figure 5-36.

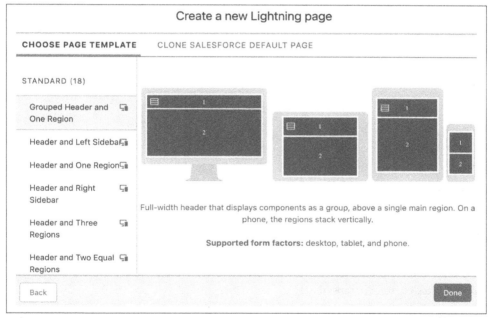

Figure 5-36. New Lightning record page options

Make your selection and click Done. The Lightning App Builder displays your new custom record page. You can drag and drop Lightning Components onto the canvas to lay out the record page to your requirements.

Dynamic Forms

You can also make a record page dynamic, which is known as a *Dynamic Form*. Click in the Details section of the App Builder canvas on a record page. An upgrade notification displays on the right side of the screen (see Figure 5-37).

Dynamic Forms provide a significant improvement in the customization of record pages by allowing individual fields and sections to be placed wherever necessary, without relying solely on traditional page layouts. With Dynamic Forms, you can control field visibility based on certain conditions, making the user interface more dynamic and responsive to the context.

For instance, in the Automobile record page, you could use Dynamic Forms to show only the service history section if the automobile has been marked as used. This ensures that users see only the information they need, based on the status of the record.

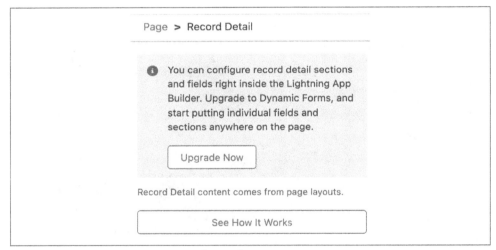

Figure 5-37. Dynamic Form upgrade notification

Lightning Components

Lightning Components are the building blocks of Lightning pages, providing specialized pieces of functionality that can be arranged as needed. There are standard components and custom components.

Standard components are prebuilt by Salesforce and include elements like record details, related lists, activities, and report charts. These components make it easy to add essential functionality without having to write code. For example, you could add a related list component to a record page for the Automobile object, which displays all related service records.

Custom components are created by developers using Lightning Web Components (LWC), Salesforce's modern framework for building fast and responsive UI components. While the older Aura Framework remains supported for legacy compatibility, using LWC is strongly encouraged for new development. For example, if your business requires a real-time visual representation of vehicle diagnostics, a custom LWC could be embedded on the Automobile record page to deliver that functionality.

Lightning Components, whether standard or custom, can be dragged and dropped onto the canvas within the Lightning App Builder to create the desired page layout. You can rearrange components, add or remove them, and customize their properties to ensure that the page meets your specific requirements.

Saving and Activating a Lightning Page

After creating and saving a Lightning page, it needs to be activated to make it available to users. Activation allows you to determine where and how the page is used. There are three levels of activation available in the Lightning App Builder:

- Organization Default
- App Default
- App, Record Type, and Profile

I will detail next each of these three activation options, starting with the most basic and far-reaching: Organization Default.

Organization Default activation

Setting a Lightning page as the Org Default is the broadest level of activation. When you choose this option, your Lightning page becomes the standard layout that all users see when accessing a specific object or feature.

For example, if you create a custom Automobile Record Page and set it as the Org Default, this becomes the standard view for anyone accessing Automobile records in your organization. This activation level works well when you need a consistent interface across all users and don't require specialized layouts for different teams or roles.

App Default activation

The App Default level provides more targeted control over your Lightning pages. Instead of applying the same layout across your entire organization, you can customize pages based on which Salesforce application users are working in.

Consider a scenario where your Vehicle Management app needs an Automobile Record Page focused on maintenance details, while your Sales app requires a different version highlighting pricing and ownership information. App Default activation lets you create these distinct experiences, ensuring users see the most relevant information based on their current context.

App, Record Type, and Profile activation

The most granular control comes from activating Lightning pages based on a combination of App, Record Type, and Profile. This level enables you to create highly specialized experiences tailored to specific user roles and record types, even within the same application.

 When deciding which activation level to use, start by considering whether all users need the same view (Org Default), if views should vary by application (App Default), or if you need role-specific layouts (App, Record Type, and Profile).

The Lightning App Builder provides administrators with the tools to create an engaging, user-centric experience. By taking advantage of features like Lightning Components, Dynamic Forms, and flexible activation options, you can ensure that each user sees what they need, right when they need it.

Summary

In Chapter 5, you explored the foundational aspects of the Salesforce Object Manager and Lightning App Builder, covering a wide range of customization techniques crucial for building and managing Salesforce applications. You learned how to create and customize objects, including both standard and custom objects, and how to use page layouts to control how information is displayed to different users. You delved into more advanced topics, such as creating many-to-many relationships with Junction objects and using record types to tailor records based on specific business needs. You also examined the Lightning App Builder, focusing on creating interactive, user-centric pages using components, Dynamic Forms, and flexible activation options.

These customizations are integral to maximizing the efficiency and usability of Salesforce. They allow you to design pages that reflect the diverse needs of different roles within your organization, enhancing user productivity and ensuring data accuracy.

Chapter 5 Quiz

As you complete this chapter, it's time to assess your understanding of object customization, relationships, record types, and page building within Salesforce. The following quiz is designed to test your knowledge of these key concepts, ensuring that you're well-prepared for the type of questions you may encounter on the Salesforce Certified Platform Administrator exam.

Take your time with each question and carefully consider the answer choices. After selecting your answers, review the answers and explanations in the Appendix to deepen your understanding of why each answer is correct or incorrect. This process will reinforce your knowledge and help you identify areas for further study, ensuring your success in real-world scenarios and on the exam.

1. What is the primary role of the Object Manager in Salesforce?

   a. To manage user permissions and security settings

   b. To provide a visual tool for mapping object relationships and schema design

   c. To create, customize, and manage objects, including defining fields and page layouts

   d. To generate reports and dashboards

2. Which of the following best describes a Junction object?

   a. It links a single record to multiple child records through a lookup.

   b. It enables many-to-many relationships between objects by using two master-detail relationships.

   c. It manages metadata relationships between custom objects.

   d. It is used primarily for storing configuration information.

3. What is a primary purpose of record types in Salesforce?

   a. To control object-level access for different users

   b. To manage data backups and recovery processes

   c. To enable administrators to assign different page layouts by profile and record type

   d. To establish relationships between objects

4. What is a significant benefit of using Dynamic Forms?

   a. To manage lookup relationships between objects

   b. To allow individual fields and sections to be placed directly on a Lightning page and configured with visibility rules

   c. To generate reports on record changes

   d. To create a home page for the Lightning App

5. When should record types be introduced in Salesforce?

   a. When a single master record type is sufficient for all data needs

   b. When different page layouts or picklist values are needed based on the type of record or user profile

   c. When customizing a home page for an app

   d. When creating a new custom object

6. What is the most detailed level of Lightning page activation?

   a. Org Default

   b. App Default

   c. App, Record Type, and Profile

   d. None of these answers

7. Why might you create a different Lightning page for Fuel Automobiles versus Electric Automobiles?

   a. To create dashboards for sales representatives

   b. To display fields like "Miles per Gallon" for Fuel and "Miles per Full Charge" for Electric

   c. To track different permission sets

   d. To manage different home page layouts for users

Attract, Attain, Retain: The Lifecycle of a B2B/B2C Relationship

This chapter is intended to give you background and context for the three fundamentals of not only Salesforce, but of all businesses:

- Sales
- Marketing
- Service

I have elected to devote a chapter to these core business principles in the context of CRM. This background information will be helpful to you if your experience is limited in any or all three of these fundamental business domains.

This chapter will also prove timely to your learning journey, given the next two knowledge areas on the administrator exam and in this book:

- Sales and marketing applications
- Service and support applications

In this chapter, the focus is on marketing principles first, followed by sales principles (I have elected to flip the order here to first cover marketing). These two principles encompass the focus of Chapter 7, I will then round out this chapter with the final principle of service, which will be explored in depth in Chapter 8.

The Lifecycle of Customer Relationships

Marketing, sales, and service represents the full lifecycle of a business-to-business (B2B) or business-to-consumer (B2C) relationship. For any customer relationship, you have to first *attract* their attention, then *attain* them as a customer by closing deals, and then *retain* them by providing excellent service and support. The resulting cadence of any business relationship follows that attract, attain, retain lifecycle.

Think of marketing, sales, and service as the three gears of business, as shown in Figure 6-1. When they are operating in alignment, progress is made and great things happen. When these gears are not aligned, or worse yet, operate as self-contained silos, absent communication and cooperation, breakdowns and failure are inevitable.

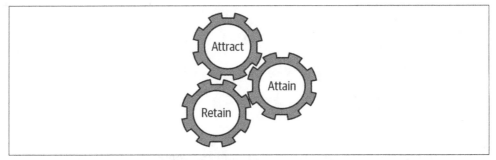

Figure 6-1. The three gears of Salesforce (and business)

It's easy to lose sight of Salesforce's origin story and original primary focus, given its stratospheric growth and maturation. Today, Salesforce offers dozens of cloud offerings. But originally, Salesforce's primary focal point was the management of its namesake—that of a salesforce.

The proper management of a sales team and assisting that team to close more deals in a shorter time frame was the company's goal at the start of a new millennium. The first cloud in Salesforce was the Sales Cloud. Soon to follow were the Marketing Cloud and Service Cloud.

Salesforce didn't invent the tried-and-true principles of successful business. The company just mirrored those principles more efficiently when it came onto the scene. Marketing, sales, and service are the principles of business and baked into Salesforce's DNA. Although Salesforce is highly customizable to virtually any business process or scenario, some areas fall more in their wheelhouse than others.

Salesforce Strengths

Salesforce excels in protracted or complex sales cycles where it's common to have deals measured in months and years. Salesforce shines in the one-size-fits-none business environment of large, complex opportunities.

Marketing serves as one bookend to first feed in leads that convert into potential deals to be closed. Service serves as the other bookend, in which the goal is to retain satisfied customers, especially those who are prone to come back for more.

This virtuous cycle of attract, attain, retain, at large scale, is where Salesforce is able to turn what is typically considered as a cost center of service into a lead generation engine. As those customers are retained through that exceptional customer service experience, effective organizations strive to identify and exploit new opportunities to expand their footprint in an already established customer base.

Salesforce Weaknesses

Salesforce can do a lot of things. And it is highly customizable to fit just about any business requirement or scenario. But just because it can handle certain scenarios doesn't mean it is always the best tool for the job.

There are many instances of a customer relationship lifecycle that open and conclude within the span of a 120-second late-night infomercial. The phenomenon that is "as seen on TV" has spawned many viral hits that lure the masses into impulse buying. This direct response industry is typically a B2C proposition. And the late-night airwaves have been dominated by such hits as the Snuggie, ShamWow, and OxiClean, to name a few.

Salesforce's traditional CRM offering is not geared toward the short lifecycle of direct response marketing relationships. Newer cloud offerings from Salesforce are making great strides in aligning more closely to real-time B2C marketing and sales methodologies, such as Data Cloud and Retail Cloud.

Marketing Overview

Marketing sets the stage for attracting potential customers. In this section, you'll learn how effective marketing strategies are designed not just to attract a broad audience, but to attract the right prospects who are likely to become customers. You will explore marketing in depth in Chapter 7.

Attract—The Goal of Marketing

One of the primary drivers of marketing in Salesforce is *campaigns*. You may be familiar with campaigns in the context of politics. One of the goals of anyone campaigning for office is name recognition. It's very difficult for the unknown to garner votes.

The first goal of marketing or campaigning is to attract attention. In the context of business, that means raising brand awareness and trying to interest potential customers in your brand, product, or service. Let's unfold the basics of the Salesforce marketing application.

Open the marketing application

Click the Marketing CRM Classic app from the App Launcher, as shown in Figure 6-2.

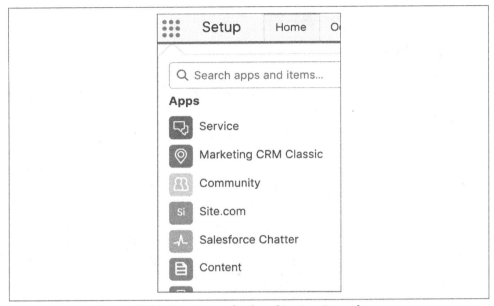

Figure 6-2. Marketing CRM Classic app displayed in App Launcher

Launching the Marketing CRM Classic app opens the Marketing home page.

Marketing home page

The Marketing home page, as shown in Figure 6-3, displays a Quarterly Performance graphic as well as the Home Page Assistant (to the right of the screen, not shown in Figure 6-3). If there are any marketing related items that require your attention, they display on the Home Page Assistant. At the bottom of the Marketing home page, you will find any upcoming events or tasks scheduled for today.

The default tab is the Home tab, which returns you to the Marketing home page, as needed. The Chatter tab is next, where you can access any company highlights happening in Chatter for your organization. You can learn more about Chatter in Chapter 9. The remaining tabs deal with marketing-specific concerns, starting with the Campaigns tab.

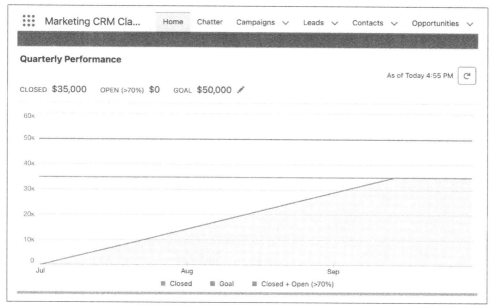

Figure 6-3. Marketing home page

Access the Campaigns tab

If you're using the marketing side of Salesforce, you'll most likely work with Campaigns. Click the Campaigns tab to go to the Campaigns list view screen. If you are visiting the Campaigns tab for the first time, you will see the recently viewed list view. Select the All Active Campaigns list view from the drop-down menu. The screen refreshes to display several marketing campaigns, as shown in Figure 6-4.

Figure 6-4. All Active Campaigns list view

 Depending on the data in your Salesforce instance, you may see woefully out-of-date campaign start and end dates. If that is the case, rest assured that Salesforce will one day update the fake data in these learning accounts they so generously provide. It just won't be today.

You can click on a campaign name to inspect it further. Be sure to click on the Details tab on the campaign to see the types of data points that are tracked (see Figure 6-5).

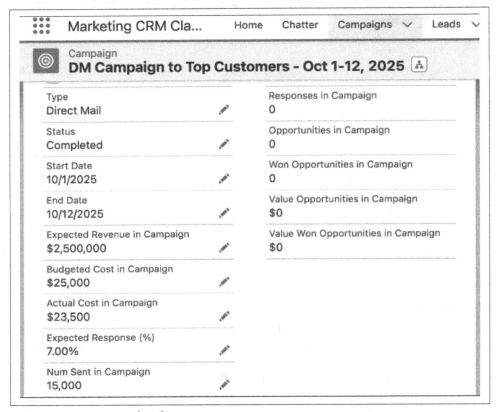

Figure 6-5. Campaign details screen

Beyond the various metrics and data points found in the Details section of a Campaign record, you will also find additional records that are related to a campaign by clicking the Related tab. This displays the related lists for a campaign.

You create campaigns to target your marketing messages to people. You can add people to your campaigns so you can follow them throughout the lifecycle of any potential deals. These targeted individuals are contained within a campaign through the Campaign Members related list.

Campaign members can be either leads or contacts. While it is true that both leads and contacts are people, they carry different distinctions within Salesforce in the context of your marketing efforts. I'll begin with exploring leads.

What Is a Lead?

A lead record in Salesforce represents a potential customer. You can access any leads in your Salesforce organization by clicking the Leads tab from within the Marketing CRM Classic app.

If this is your first time accessing the Leads tab, you'll see the recently viewed list view displayed. You can click the drop-down menu next to the recently viewed list view to select a different list view, such as the All Open Leads list, as shown in Figure 6-6.

		Na... ↑ ⌄	Company ⌄	Stat... ⌄	Email ⌄	Lead Status ⌄
1	☐	Bertha B...	Farmers Coop. of Flori...	Florida	bertha@fcof.net	Working - C...
2	☐	Betty Bair	American Banking Corp.	Pennsy...	bblair@abankingco....	Working - C...
3	☐	Brenda ...	Cadinal Inc.	Illinois	brenda@cardinal.net	Working - C...
4	☐	David M...	Blues Entertainment C...		david@blues.com	Working - C...
5	☐	Jeff Glim...	Jackson Controls		jeffg@jackson.com	Open - Not ...
6	☐	Kathy Sn...	TNR Corp.	Conne...	ksynder@tnr.net	Working - C...
7	☐	Kristen ...	Aethna Home Products	Virginia	kakin@athenahome...	Working - C...

Figure 6-6. All Open Leads list view

What is an open lead?

The concept of an open lead versus a closed lead may cause confusion. An open lead is simply someone who has yet to be converted to a contact. The process by which a lead becomes a contact is known as the *Lead Conversion process*.

The Lead Conversion process is the culmination of a nurturing and qualification process. But before I explore this nurturing, qualification, and conversion cadence of leads, it may be helpful to understand where leads come from and how they find their way into your Salesforce account.

Where do leads come from?

Leads come into your Salesforce instance any number of ways. Some result from inbound marketing efforts, and others result from your outbound efforts.

You can make outbound calls or reach out through LinkedIn to find new leads. You may entice people to visit your website, download a whitepaper, attend a webinar, or enroll in a free course, among other examples. Whatever it may be, you're doing these efforts to bring new people (leads) into your instance of Salesforce.

Lead sources and marketing channels

There are different ways to track your referral sources and how they came to your attention. These different channels need to be thought about strategically and measured so you know which marketing channels bring the greatest return on investment.

You want to think about all the different ways people might become aware of your brand or product or service. You can segment your campaigns by channel to keep track of which channels bring the best results.

Some of these channels include email marketing, which is one of the longest-running marketing mechanisms. Other established marketing channels are advertising on television, print, or radio. You may also find valuable leads at trade shows and conferences.

Leads may also be created through interactions with chatbots on your website.

Web-to-Lead forms.   You can create what are known as *Web-to-Lead forms* and embed them on your website. Then, whenever someone fills out that form, it feeds automatically into your Salesforce instance as a new lead record.

The fine art of gathering lead information.   You will find that it is a balancing act as far as not asking for too much information on your lead forms in the beginning. Your response rates will drop in proportion to the number of fields and requirements you encumber your forms with.

The initial quest of attracting attention means you may have to settle for only an email address or a phone number and, hopefully, the first name of the person filling out your form. You can always follow up and start gathering additional details as part of the lead qualification process. The first order of business is getting the initial lead. Next comes the nurturing of the lead.

Lead nurturing and qualification

If you've ever stepped onto a car lot, you've experienced the nurturing and qualification process firsthand. Salespeople ask qualifying questions about your credit, employment, down payment, trade-in, and time frame for buying a car. Based on your answers, you'll be prioritized.

Those with good credit, a large down payment, or who are paying cash, and who are employed, will receive more attention. Conversely, if you have bad credit, no down payment, are unemployed, and are "just looking," you might just get a business card to reach out later.

Lead qualification questions and the nurturing process help companies prioritize leads based on their likelihood to convert to an eventual sale. As a lead progresses through the various stages of a company's lead qualification process, you will use the Lead Status field to track it.

Lead Status field

You can click on an individual Lead record from the list view to open the Lead Details screen (see Figure 6-7). There you will find the various Lead Status designations displayed in the lead path and also available from the Lead Status field.

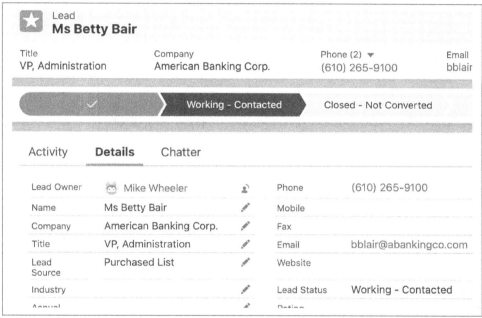

Figure 6-7. Lead path and Lead Status displayed on a lead record

There are two ways you can manually change the Lead Status. You can select a new Lead Status designation from the Lead path by clicking on it and then clicking the "Mark Status as Complete" button. You may also adjust the Lead Status field by clicking the pencil icon next to it. The Lead Status options display, as shown in Figure 6-8.

Once you have selected the updated Lead Status for your lead record, click Save to commit your changes to Salesforce.

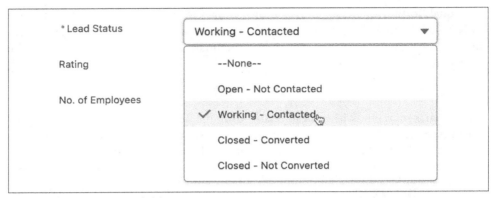

Figure 6-8. Lead Status field options

Closing leads—to convert or not?

Not all leads are created equal. Some leads may prove a dead end for your business. Or the potential deal that the lead is proposing would be unprofitable for your business. Some leads may simply be a bad fit for you to pursue at this time.

There are myriad reasons why you may elect to not pursue a lead further and wish to end the relationship. In these instances, you can set the Lead Status to "Closed - Not Converted" to remove the lead from your All Open Leads list view. This clears up any lead records you are not interested in pursuing so as to focus on those you are.

Once a lead reaches a certain level of qualification, it is handed over to the sales department, whose focus is on closing deals and attaining customers. That handoff is known as the Lead Conversion process.

Introducing the Lead Conversion Process

You can convert a lead record by clicking the Convert button found at the top-right of the Lead record page. The Convert Lead window displays, as shown in Figure 6-9.

The Convert Lead window gives you the option of creating new Account, Contact, and Opportunity records, or choosing from existing records by searching for matches.

If you elect to create new records, you'll get new Account, Contact, and Opportunity records once you click the Convert button at the bottom of the Convert Lead window. The resulting new Account, Contact, and Opportunity records display, as shown in Figure 6-10.

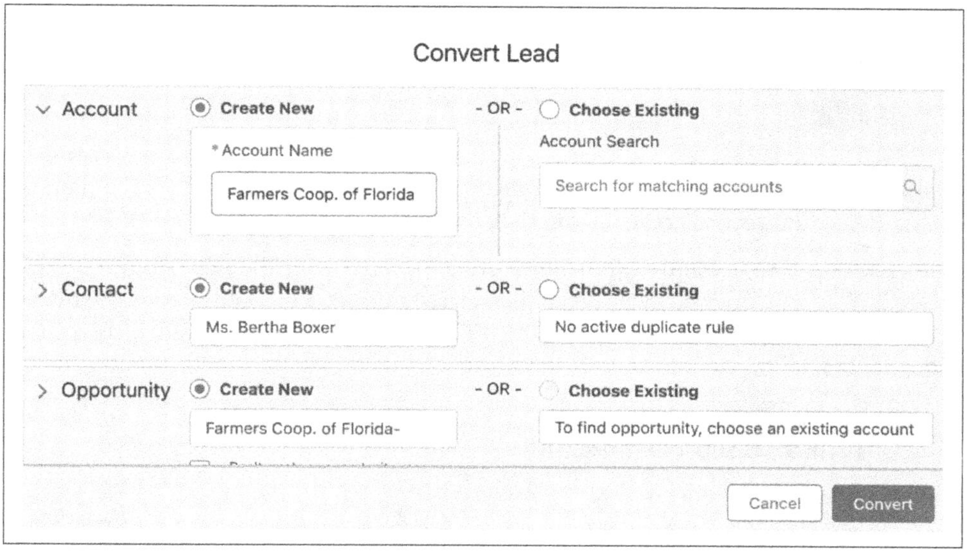

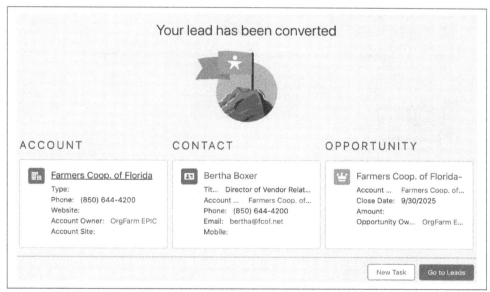

Figure 6-9. Convert Lead window

Figure 6-10. "Your lead has been converted" window

The original details on the Lead record are now populated to the resulting records. The person represented originally as a Lead record is now transformed into a Contact record, and the original Lead record is no longer used in any practical sense by Salesforce.

Previously converted Lead records are still accessible by creating a report on converted leads. You can learn more about converted leads reports in Chapter 10.

The name populated in the Company field on the Lead record becomes the name of the new Account record created from the conversion process.

The resulting Contact and Opportunity are associated with the new Account that is created. You will find them both in the related lists of the new Account, which is accessible by clicking the account name. The Account Details screen displays (see Figure 6-11).

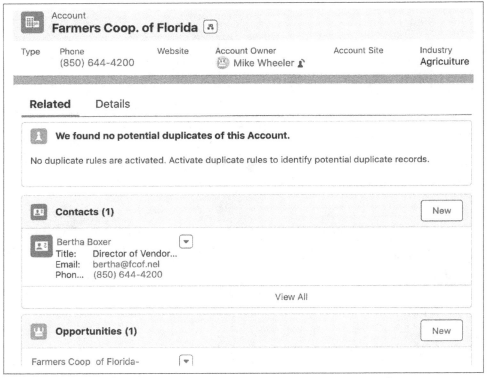

Figure 6-11. Contacts and Opportunities related lists on Account Details screen

The resulting Contact and Opportunity that were created during the conversion process are associated with the Account and can be found in the Related lists section of the Account detail screen, as shown in Figure 6-11.

With the resulting Lead Conversion process and the handoff from Marketing to Sales, your attention on this potential customer's journey will now shift from the attraction (marketing) phase to that of attainment (sales).

Sales Overview

Sales sets the stage for attaining potential customers. Effective sales strategies are designed not just to close deals, but to build lasting relationships with customers.

Attain—The Goal of Sales

The first objective of Sales is to attain commitment from potential customers. In the context of business, that means engaging prospects, addressing their needs, and persuading them that your brand, product, or service is the best solution. To that end, I will next explore the Salesforce Sales application.

Opening the Sales application

To get familiar with Sales in Salesforce, open the Sales application by clicking the Sales app from the App Launcher. The Seller Home screen displays (see Figure 6-12).

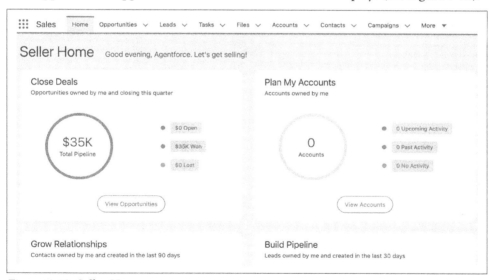

Figure 6-12. Seller Home screen

Seller Home screen

The Seller Home screen is the starting point for sales reps in Salesforce. Seller Home is designed to enhance productivity. By providing more useful information at a glance, it helps salespeople get oriented faster and choose their next steps effectively.

Key features include:

Close Deals
See a snapshot of your current Opportunities, helping you keep track of potential sales.

Plan My Accounts
Have quick access to your active accounts, ensuring you stay updated on client activities.

Grow Relationships
See details about your contacts, facilitating better relationship management.

Build Pipeline
See a summary of your leads, enabling you to prioritize follow-ups.

My Goals
Set and track your sales goals to stay motivated and on target.

Today's Events
View your scheduled events and meetings to plan your day efficiently.

To-Do Items
Manage your tasks and ensure nothing falls through the cracks.

Recent Records
Access your most recent activities for quick reference.

Seller Home is accessible at any time from the Sales application by clicking the Home tab. In addition to the Home tab, you will find a series of other tabs within the Sales application interface. The tabs in the Sales application are the remaining primary Sales objects of Salesforce, including Opportunities, Leads, and more.

Primary Sales Objects

The three records created by the Lead Conversion process are considered the three primary Sales objects you will deal with in Salesforce:

- Accounts
- Contacts
- Opportunities

Of these three objects, Accounts would be considered the parent in an object-oriented principle (OOP) relationship. Contacts and Opportunities would be considered the child records belonging to the parent record of the Account that they are associated with (see Figure 6-13).

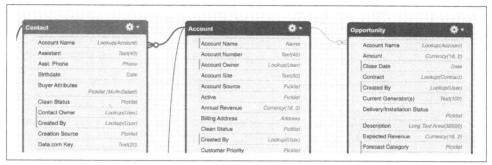

Figure 6-13. Account, Contact, and Opportunity relationship

Accounts Overview

Accounts are typically companies, although Salesforce does support the functionality for what are known as *Person Accounts*. Setting up Person Accounts in Salesforce is an involved process that, once enabled, cannot be reversed.

The primary reason to use Person Accounts is to facilitate more of a B2C Sales focus. While this is a suitable alternative in some instances, B2C/Person Account setup is well beyond the scope of the Salesforce Platform Administrator Certification. For our purposes, moving forward, I will present Accounts in the context of the traditional enterprise approach of B2B.

Accounts are the parent of several related child records, such as the previously mentioned Contacts and Opportunities. Being the three primary sales objects, they work in conjunction to manage customer relationships.

Cases are also related to Accounts and can be found in the related list on an individual Account record.

To begin exploring Accounts records in Salesforce, click the Accounts tab from the Sales app. The Sales home page displays your previously selected or pinned list view for Accounts (see Figure 6-14).

Click on an Account listed in the list view to open the Account Details screen. The default view of the Account record is with the Related tab selected, thus displaying the Related Lists of records that are related to the Account. You can explore the details of an Account by clicking the Details tab to the right of the Related tab. The Account Details display as shown in Figure 6-15.

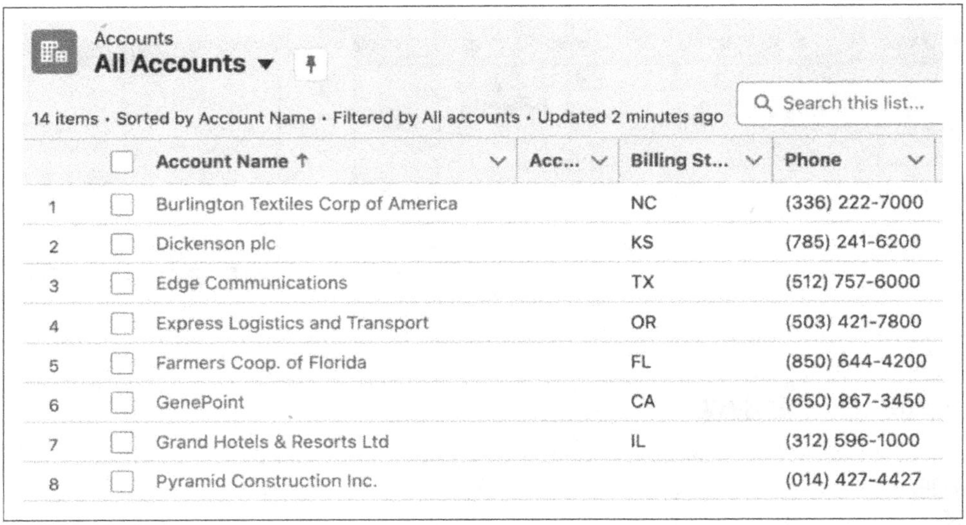

Figure 6-14. All Accounts list view

Figure 6-15. Account Details screen

The Account Details screen provides further information on an account. You can see and change ownership of an account via the Account Owner field.

Over time and through effective account management, the data that is captured on the Account Details screen will become more robust and useful. Your interactions with various Contacts that work for an Account can and will provide you with further insights to further populate your Account records in Salesforce.

Contacts Overview

Contacts are the lifeblood of your business relationships. You can access any related Contacts that work for an Account by way of the Contacts Related list on the Account Details screen.

You can also access Contact records via the Contacts tab from the Sales application, which will display your latest accessed or pinned Contacts list view (see Figure 6-16).

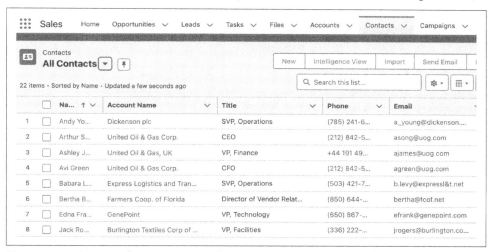

Figure 6-16. Contacts list view accessed via Contacts tab in Sales app

Click a Contact record to display the Contact Details screen with the Related tab selected. The Related lists include any Opportunities or Cases that the Contact is associated with, as shown in Figure 6-17.

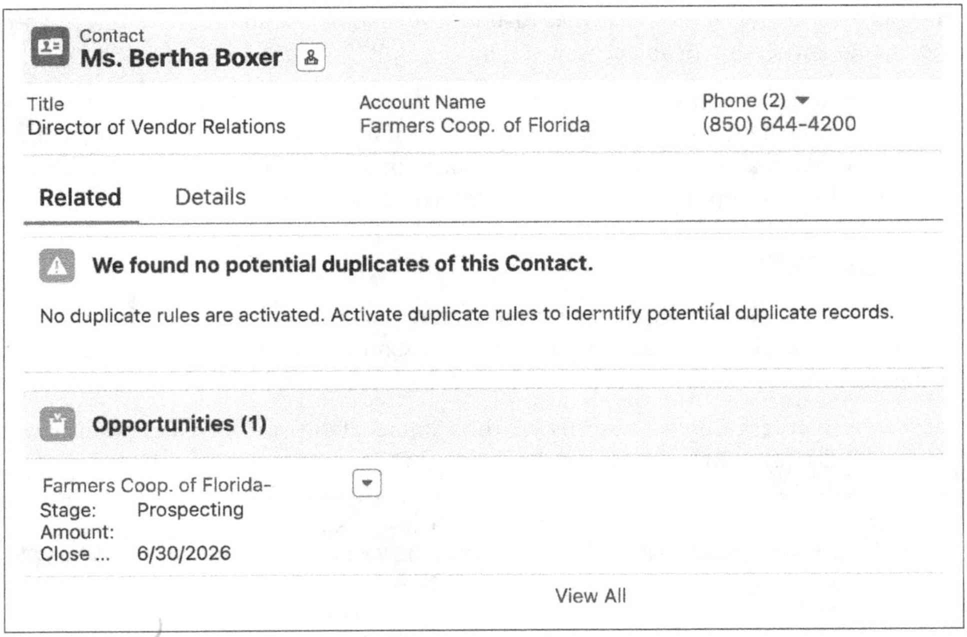

Contact
Ms. Bertha Boxer

Title
Director of Vendor Relations

Account Name
Farmers Coop. of Florida

Phone (2) ▼
(850) 644-4200

Related   Details

⚠ **We found no potential duplicates of this Contact.**

No duplicate rules are activated. Activate duplicate rules to iderntify potentiíal duplicate records.

📇 **Opportunities (1)**

Farmers Coop. of Florida–   ▼
Stage: Prospecting
Amount:
Close ...   6/30/2026

View All

Figure 6-17. Contact Related lists displayed via Related tab

You will also find any Campaigns the currently viewed Contact is a member of in the Campaign History Related list. You can find and adjust any details related to the Contact by clicking the Details tab. The Contact Details display, as shown in Figure 6-18.

You can enter or alter any data related to the Contact by clicking the pencil icon next to the applicable field. You can edit multiple fields at once by clicking the Edit button found at the top of the screen.

You can edit multiple fields on any record in Salesforce by clicking the Edit button on its Details screen. This mass edit functionality is not exclusive to Contact records.

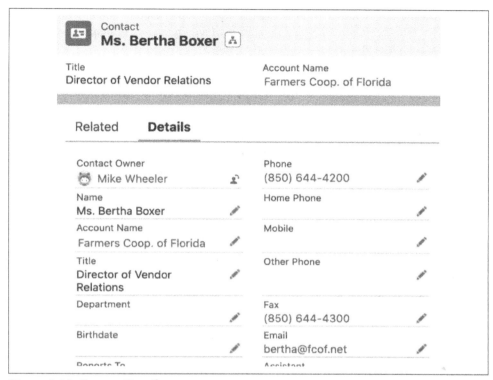

Figure 6-18. Contact Details screen

The Edit Contact window displays. From this window, you can make changes to any editable fields. Once your changes are complete, click Save.

How Are Contacts Related to Opportunities?

If you return to the Related lists for a Contact record, you will find the Opportunities related list. If the Contact you are viewing was created during the Lead Conversion process, and an Opportunity was created as part of that process, the Contact will be associated with that Opportunity.

Clicking on the Opportunity will display the Opportunity Details screen, defaulted to the Activity tab. The Contact Roles Related list (see Figure 6-19) displays a primary contact for the Opportunity.

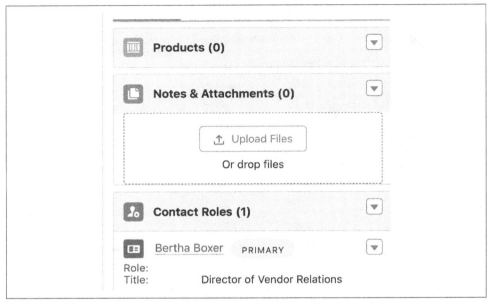

Figure 6-19. Contact Roles Related list on Opportunity Details screen

Contact Roles and Campaign Influence

Contact roles work in conjunction with what is known as *Campaign Influence*. Campaign Influence in Salesforce tracks the impact of marketing campaigns. If a Contact was previously included in a Campaign as a Campaign member, then their association with an Opportunity through a Contact role will help tie any resulting revenue from Close Won Opportunities back to the appropriate Campaign. This helps business owners understand where to allocate their advertising budget effectively.

Opportunities Overview

Opportunities are deals. I like to define a Salesforce Opportunity as an opportunity to do business with another company or individual. Opportunities are divided into various stages as part of the Sales process.

Stages of an Opportunity

Salespeople work in Opportunities, taking them on a journey through various stages. These stages are visually represented at the top of the Opportunity screen in the *Sales Path*, as shown in Figure 6-20.

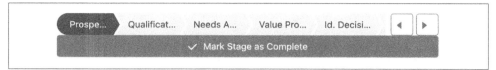

Figure 6-20. Sales Path on an Opportunity record

Sales Path

The first path that Salesforce added to its interface was the Sales Path, exclusive at that time to Opportunities. The Sales Path is a visual representation of the various stages that an Opportunity will go through from its origin stage through the final closed stage.

This Sales Path functionality proved so useful that the collective user base of Salesforce requested that it be added throughout the platform over time. You will work through adding a Case Path to a Case Details page in Chapter 8.

Each stage of an Opportunity increases the underlying probability of its successful closure. These percentages of probability are configured behind the scenes and can be customized based on your own real-world statistical probabilities in the historical data of your business.

In addition to the tight correlation between Opportunity stages and probability of success, there is often a correlation between certain data being captured on the Opportunity Details screen and a salesperson's level of comfort in moving an Opportunity to its next stage. Those data points can be entered on the Details tab.

Opportunity Stages and Probability. The Opportunity shown in Figure 6-21 is currently in the Prospecting Stage with a Probability of 10%, both of which are displayed at the bottom-right. You can change the Stage of the Opportunity either via the Sales Path or the Stage field.

Once you save your Stage changes, notice that the Probability percentage changes. These probability numbers represent the probability for a deal to close successfully and are based on past performance.

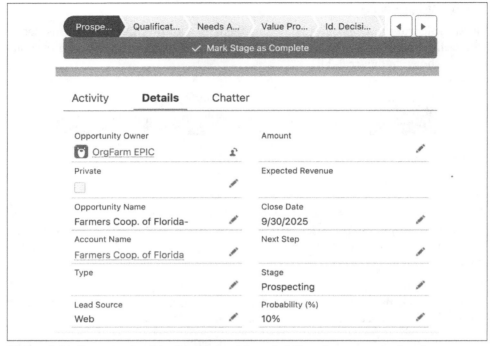

Figure 6-21. Opportunity Details screen with probability of success calculated

These percentages are used to help forecast your pipeline of expected revenue. And as you progress from one stage to the next, each stage gets you progressively closer to a successful Closed Won Opportunity. If you do close an Opportunity successfully, its probability becomes 100%. If you end up losing that deal, the probability drops to 0%.

Opportunity Close Date and forecasting impact.   Entering an anticipated Close Date for an Opportunity has far-reaching implications in Salesforce. You will see in your Sales forecasting the projected amounts for each quarter.

If you change a close date to a different fiscal quarter, the anticipated revenue numbers are updated accordingly in your pipeline. Once you close an Opportunity that is won, its probability goes to 100% and the Close Date field is set to the current date. The expected amount of a Closed Won Opportunity becomes the amount that is realized in whichever quarter you are currently in.

You will learn more about Collaborative Forecasting in Chapter 7.

Closed-lost Opportunities. Sometimes the best decision on a deal is to not pursue it. Effective customer relationship management dictates keeping an eye on profitability and not just closing all deals for the sake of closing deals.

Inversely, there may be times where you do want to close a deal to attain a customer, knowing that this will be what is known as a *loss leader*. You may lose money on an initial deal, but it births a relationship from which you can grow to profitability.

If you select Closed Lost as the final stage for an Opportunity, the Close Date updates to the current date and the Probability is set to 0%. Although you will never close all deals successfully, business is won in the long game through lasting relationships, often strengthened by delivering exceptional customer service.

Service Overview

Service sets the stage for retaining customers. Here, you will see how effective service strategies are designed not just to resolve issues, but to build trust and foster loyalty. Chapter 8 will explore Service in depth.

One of the primary drivers of Service in Salesforce is the Case object. You may be familiar with cases or "trouble tickets" in the context of customer support. The goal of any support team is to resolve customer issues efficiently and enhance customer satisfaction along the way. To that end, I will now explore the Salesforce Service application.

Open the Service Application

Click the Service app from the App Launcher. The Service home page displays, as shown in Figure 6-22.

The Service home page displays a Quarterly Performance dashboard, along with various widgets for Today's Events and Tasks. The tabs in the Service app include Chatter, Accounts, Contacts, Cases, and more.

To dive into Case records, click the Cases tab. Your previously accessed or pinned list view displays, as shown in Figure 6-23.

Figure 6-22. Service home page

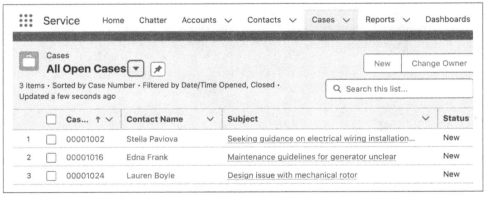

Figure 6-23. All Open Cases list view accessed via Cases tab in Service app

You can explore a Case record by clicking on one from the list view. The Case Details screen for your selected Case is shown in Figure 6-24.

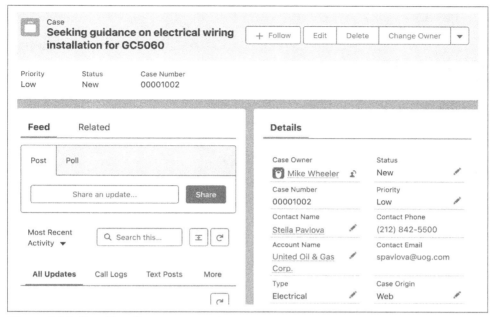

Figure 6-24. Case Details screen

Case Overview and Status Field

The Case Details screen provides various details related to a Case. You will find a Case Number field, which is often given to the customer for their later reference.

Noticeably absent from this screen is a Case Path. Unlike the Lead Details screen and the Opportunity Details screen, the Case Details screen does not have a path on it by default; in Chapter 8, you'll add a path to this screen to visually represent the Case Status field.

The Case Status field is used to track the status of a Case. It behaves in Salesforce similarly to the Status field on Leads and the Stage field on Opportunities.

The default Status options for a Case are New, Working, and Escalated. As with most areas of Salesforce, these options can be configured and adjusted to fit your own unique business scenarios and, in this context, support processes.

Absent from the list of Case Status options is the option to close a Case. I will work you through setting your Salesforce Support Settings to turn on Case closure functionality in Chapter 8.

Although Cases are the primary object from which you provide customer service in Salesforce, the ultimate goal of exceptional customer service is to avoid Cases being created entirely. The preventive steps taken to lessen Case creation in an organization is known as *case deflection.*

Case Deflection

Case deflection refers to strategies aimed at reducing the number of Cases that require human intervention by enabling customers to resolve their issues independently. This alleviates the workload on support teams and empowers customers to find quick solutions.

There are several ways that Case creation may ultimately be deflected. Creating self-service portals, or communities, is a key strategy for case deflection. These portals allow customers to find answers to their questions independently through a comprehensive collection of FAQs and Knowledge articles. By empowering customers to resolve their issues without direct assistance, self-service portals reduce the workload on support teams and enhance customer satisfaction.

Another effective technique is to encourage customer participation in community forums. In these forums, customers can ask questions and share solutions with one another. This fosters a sense of community while enabling customers to benefit from the collective knowledge and experiences of other users, leading to quicker resolutions of common issues.

Additionally, implementing chatbots and virtual assistants can significantly streamline the handling of routine inquiries. These automated tools guide customers to the appropriate resources, providing instant responses and freeing up human agents to focus on more complex issues. By leveraging chatbots, organizations can ensure that customers receive prompt and accurate assistance, further enhancing the efficiency of their support processes.

Experience Cloud: Customer self-service through Digital Experiences

Salesforce's Digital Experiences—formerly known as Portals and later Communities, and now part of the Experience Cloud—serve as an extension of Service in Salesforce. The Experience Cloud enables organizations to build branded spaces where customers, partners, and employees can interact and find information.

User-friendly design makes digital platforms easier to navigate and use, which helps customers quickly find the information and tools they need. Further personalizing interactions significantly enhances Digital Experiences. By leveraging Salesforce's data capabilities, you can tailor a Digital Experience to meet the unique needs and preferences of each customer.

Salesforce Knowledge and Knowledge articles

Knowledge articles are a critical component of Salesforce's Service Cloud, enabling organizations to provide detailed information and solutions to common problems. These articles can be accessed by both support agents and customers, fostering a more informed and efficient service experience.

Effective Knowledge articles should have descriptive and easily searchable titles and provide detailed, step-by-step instructions to resolve specific issues. You can also include screenshots or videos to enhance the clarity of the instructions. You will learn more about Salesforce Knowledge in Chapter 8.

Summary

In this chapter, you explored the lifecycle of customer relationships, focusing on the fundamental principles of marketing, sales, and service within Salesforce. You learned how to attract potential customers using effective marketing strategies and how to utilize the Marketing application to manage campaigns and leads. The chapter also delved into sales, emphasizing the importance of building lasting relationships through efficient sales tactics, and provided an overview of the Sales application, highlighting key features like Accounts, Contacts, and Opportunities.

In "Service Overview" on page 201, you examined how to retain customers by providing exceptional customer service using Salesforce's Service Cloud. This included an introduction to case management, case deflection techniques, and the Experience Cloud for creating digital self-service experiences. The importance of Knowledge articles for empowering both customers and support agents was also discussed. Mastering these core principles of marketing, sales, and service to attract, attain, and retain customers is essential for leveraging Salesforce to manage and enhance your customer relationships effectively. In the next chapter, you'll delve deeper into Salesforce's Sales and Marketing applications, exploring techniques for managing Leads, Opportunities, and Campaigns to further optimize your customer relationship processes.

Chapter 6 Quiz

As you finish Chapter 6, it's time to assess the knowledge you've gathered about the lifecycle of customer relationships in Salesforce, focusing on marketing, sales, and service. This quiz is designed to test your understanding of key concepts, ensuring you're well-prepared for the kind of nuanced questions that may appear on the Salesforce Certified Platform Administrator exam.

Remember, each question is an opportunity to review and strengthen your grasp of essential marketing, sales, and service topics, from lead management to case deflection techniques. Take your time with each question and select the answer that best aligns with the principles you've learned.

After making your choices, carefully review the answers and explanations in the Appendix to solidify your understanding of the correct answers. This process will reinforce your existing knowledge and highlight areas that may require further review, ensuring you're well-prepared for real-world scenarios and exam success.

1. What is the primary goal of the marketing phase in the customer lifecycle?

   a. Retaining customers

   b. Attracting potential customers

   c. Resolving customer issues

   d. Closing sales

2. Which Salesforce feature allows customers to find answers independently, reducing the need for human intervention?

   a. Case Status field

   b. Digital Experiences/Community

   c. Lead Conversion process

   d. Contact roles

3. What is a key benefit of using Salesforce Knowledge articles?

   a. Limiting access to specific IP ranges

   b. Providing detailed information and solutions to common problems

   c. Enabling "Log in as Any User"

   d. Tracking the status of leads

4. How does the Experience Cloud enhance customer service in Salesforce?

   a. By automating the Lead Conversion process

   b. By enabling customers to log in as another user

   c. By providing branded spaces for customers to interact and find information

   d. By managing the Opportunities related to sales

5. What is the primary objective of case deflection strategies in Salesforce?

   a. Converting leads to Opportunities

   b. Reducing the number of cases that require human intervention

   c. Enhancing the lead qualification process

   d. Managing user access and permissions

Sales and Marketing Applications

The Sales and Marketing applications knowledge area encompasses two-thirds of the attract, attain, retain lifecycle. Although the knowledge area name and its learning objectives in the Exam Guide start with Sales-related topics before moving to Marketing topics, I have elected to invert that order in this chapter. Because the lifecycle of a business relationship begins with Marketing and then transitions over to Sales, I have decided to reflect that sequence in this chapter.

By mastering Marketing and Sales applications, you will enable a unified customer experience. This chapter builds upon the foundation laid in the previous chapter, particularly in its introduction to the Lead Conversion process. Here, you will explore how Salesforce tools like Lead and Sales processes, Campaigns, and Opportunities function in real-world scenarios to support the customer lifecycle.

By the end of this chapter, you will have traversed the landscape of implementing and supporting multiple Lead and Sales Processes. This will provide the perfect pivot into the next chapter, where you will complete the triad of attract, attain, and retain by exploring Service and Support applications in Chapter 8.

From the Exam Guide

The Salesforce Certified Platform Administrator Exam Guide outlines the following learning objectives for the Sales and Marketing applications knowledge area:

- Given a scenario, identify the capabilities and implications of the sales process (for example, sales process, Opportunity, path, and forecast impact).

- Given a scenario, apply the appropriate sales productivity features using Opportunity tools (for example, dashboards, lead scoring, Einstein opportunity scoring, and Home Page Assistant).

- Describe the capabilities of lead automation tools and campaign management (for example, leads, lead convert, lead assignment rules, campaigns, and campaign members).

These objectives reflect critical aspects of the Salesforce platform's capabilities in marketing and sales alignment. For example, understanding the sales process involves leveraging tools like Opportunities and paths to streamline deal management, while lead automation and campaign management emphasize optimizing marketing efforts and tracking results.

Throughout this chapter, these learning objectives will guide your exploration of key Salesforce tools and their applications in business scenarios. By mastering these topics, you will develop the skills to support efficient marketing campaigns, seamless lead conversion, and data-driven sales forecasting in Salesforce.

The Customer Journey

The saying, "The more things change, the more they remain the same," perfectly encapsulates the modern marketing landscape. Today's marketers wield powerful tools that enable unprecedented levels of personalization and prioritization. At its core, however, effective marketing still hinges on a compelling value proposition and clear communication.

Salesforce supports this evolution by providing the tools for you to create a 360-degree view of every potential or actual customer within the platform. This customer-centric approach enables marketers to track, analyze, and engage across multiple touchpoints, leveraging features like Campaign Hierarchies and Lead sources to map and enhance the *customer journey*.

The customer journey is a framework that reflects the natural progression of a relationship between businesses and their customers. And you explored this progression in the previous chapter, which covered these three fundamentals of business:

Attract
Capture attention and generate interest using campaigns and landing pages, with Web-to-Lead forms.

Attain
Convert interest into Opportunities through Lead Processes and Lead Conversion.

Retain
Foster long-term relationships via excellent service and post-sale follow-ups.

In this chapter, I will focus on the first two fundamentals, attract and attain, by exploring how Salesforce tools like campaigns, lead automation, and Opportunities support marketing and sales efforts. These tools streamline processes and provide actionable insights that drive effective decision making and customer engagement.

Campaigns: Mapping the Prospect to Customer Journey

Salesforce campaigns serve as the foundation for managing and measuring your marketing efforts. They empower organizations to plan, execute, and analyze their marketing activities with precision, ensuring each initiative contributes to overall business objectives. Whether launching a new product, hosting a webinar, or executing a promotional offer, campaigns enable marketers to track each activity and its impact on customer engagement and revenue generation.

Campaigns Overview

To access campaigns, open the Marketing application from the App Launche and click the Campaigns tab. A Campaign list view displays, from which you can click to open a campaign. The Campaign Details screen displays, as shown in Figure 7-1.

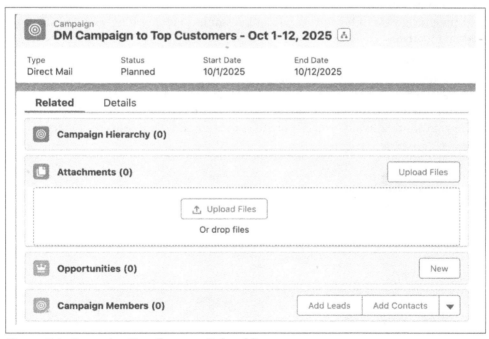

Figure 7-1. Campaign Details screen Related lists

The Campaign Details screen Related lists display any campaigns that are related to the currently viewed campaign in the Campaign Hierarchy related list. You will learn more about related campaigns in "Campaign Hierarchy" on page 216. You may also attach files to relate to this campaign via the Attachments related list.

Any Opportunities that have resulted from the combined efforts and activities of a campaign will be displayed in the Opportunities related list. And any campaign members, whether leads or contacts, will be displayed in that related list.

To create and manage campaigns, users must have the Marketing User checkbox selected on their user record.

Campaign Members

You can associate individual leads and contacts with a campaign as campaign members. These members allow you to track engagement at the granular level, recording interactions such as event attendance, email responses, or completed surveys. As these interactions are logged, campaign members' statuses are updated, providing real-time insights into how prospects and customers are engaging with specific marketing initiatives.

Campaign members are associated with a campaign by way of the Campaign Members related list. Click either the Add Leads or Add Contacts button to add campaign members to the campaign. Depending on which button you select, you'll see either the Add Leads to Campaign window (shown in Figure 7-2) or the Add Contacts to Campaign window, which you can use to search for and select leads or contacts.

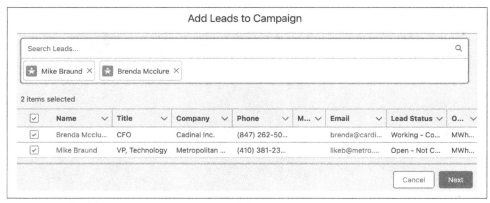

Figure 7-2. "Add Leads to Campaign" window

Select the checkboxes next to the leads or contacts you wish to add to the campaign and then click Next. The Member Status window displays, as shown in Figure 7-3.

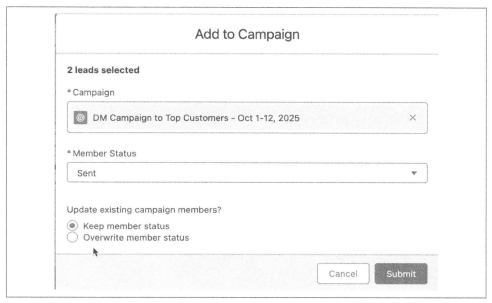

Figure 7-3. Member Status window

You can either keep the campaign members' existing Status field designations or overwrite them by setting the desired Member Status and selecting the "Overwrite member status" radio button. Click Submit to save your selections, which adds the specified individuals to the Campaign Members Related list.

In addition to adding leads and contacts to a campaign, you can also click the down arrow beside the Add Contacts button on the Campaign Members related list to reveal further options (see Figure 7-4).

Figure 7-4. Campaign Members related list with action options displayed

The options Manage Campaign Members and "Import Leads and Contacts" both lead to the Data Import Wizard. This is intentional and correct functionality in Salesforce.

Although both options lead to the Data Import Wizard, they serve slightly different contexts: the first is campaign-specific, while the second is broader. This overlap ensures flexibility, depending on where you access the tool.

Manage Campaign Members

This option allows you to manage campaign participants, including importing them using the Data Import Wizard. This option provides a focused entry point for campaign-related data import tasks.

Import Leads and Contacts

This more general option also uses the Data Import Wizard but is tailored to handle a broader import of leads and contacts, not necessarily linked to a specific campaign.

You will learn how to use the Data Import Wizard in Chapter 11.

Send List Email

This option enables you to send an email to campaign members. The Send List Email window displays, as shown in Figure 7-5.

Draft your message to send to the campaign members by entering the subject and body of the email. Salesforce supports dynamic personalization through merge fields. The "Insert merge field" icon is accessible at the bottom-left of the window, as shown in Figure 7-6.

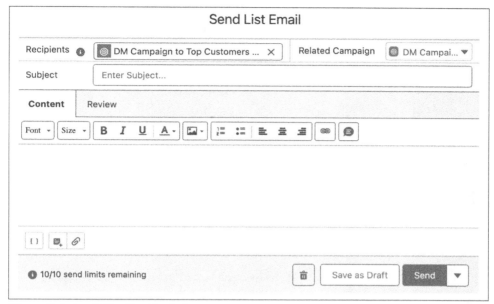

Figure 7-5. Send List Email window

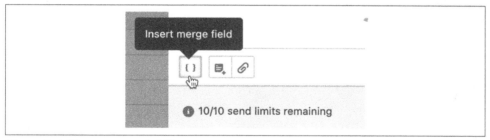

Figure 7-6. "Insert merge field" icon

Clicking the icon displays the Insert Merge Field window, as shown in Figure 7-7.

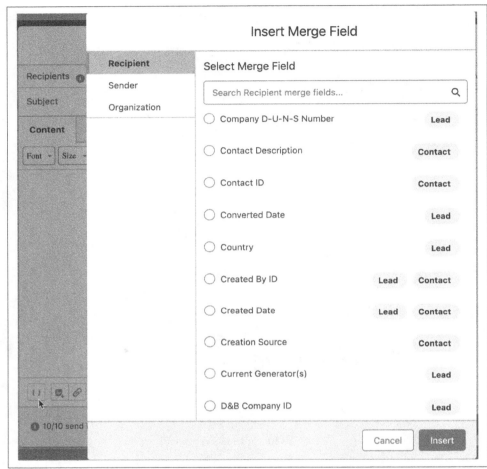

Figure 7-7. Insert Merge Field window

From the Insert Merge Field window you can select merge fields related to the recipient, sender, and/or organization by selecting them and then clicking Insert. For example, you could search for the first name to include in your email body for all Leads and Contacts in your campaign members list, as shown in Figure 7-8.

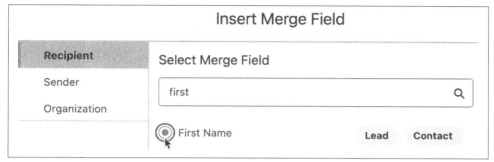

Figure 7-8. Insert Merge Field search and field selection

Once you have selected a field to merge into your email, click the Insert button. The Send List Email window appears with the merge field displayed, as shown in Figure 7-9.

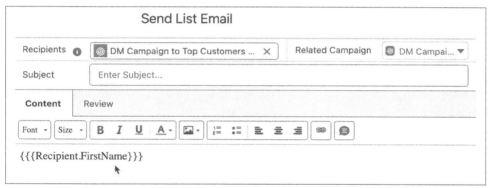

Figure 7-9. Send List Email window with merge field displayed

You can further enhance your email by using the formatting toolbar to add headings, bullet points, hyperlinks, images, and more. You can also attach files to your email by using the "Attach file" button at the bottom of the composer. You can send the email immediately, schedule it for later, or save it as a draft for later completion.

Campaign Details

Click the Details tab on a campaign to display the Campaign Details screen, as shown in Figure 7-10.

Campaign
DM Campaign to Top Customers - Nov 12-23, 2025

Campaign Owner	Leads in Campaign
👤 Mike Wheeler ⟳	2
Campaign Name	Converted Leads in Campaign
DM Campaign to Top ✏	0
Customers - Nov 12-23,	
2025	
Active	Contacts in Campaign
☑ ✏	0
Type	Responses in Campaign
Direct Mail ✏	0
Status	Opportunities in Campaign
Completed ✏	0

Figure 7-10. Campaign Details screen

The Campaign Details screen captures all of the significant details related to a campaign. You can specify the type of campaign it is, such as Direct Mail, Conference, Webinar, Trade Show, and more.

The Status field can be used to segment campaigns into Planned, In Progress, Completed, or Aborted. You can also specify the Start Date and End Date as well as signify various financial considerations, such as expected revenue to result from the campaign and its budgeted cost.

The Campaign Details screen can record the actual cost of a campaign as well as the expected response rate and more. You can also specify a Parent Campaign to establish a Campaign Hierarchy, which I will cover in the next section.

You can track any resulting leads and converted leads and contacts in the campaign, as well as the number of responses and resulting Opportunities. The Campaign Details screen will also keep track of the Opportunities that resulted from this campaign through Closed Won status, and the total value of all resulting Opportunities as well as total amounts from Opportunities that have entered a Closed Won stage.

Campaign Hierarchy

Campaign Hierarchies allow marketers to group related efforts under a single structure, enabling aggregated performance analysis and improved resource allocation. To create a Campaign Hierarchy, navigate to the Details tab of a campaign to display the Campaign Details screen.

You can specify a parent campaign by clicking the pencil icon next to its field. Search for and select the parent campaign and click Save. The parent campaign is saved, and you can click on its hyperlink to navigate to its record.

From the parent campaign record, you will find the child campaign in its Campaign Hierarchy related list. You can also click View All to view the entirety of a Campaign Hierarchy, as shown in Figure 7-11.

Figure 7-11. Campaign Hierarchy related list

The goal of any effective campaign is to generate new prospects for your business. The new people you are targeting in a campaign, or come about as the result of a campaign, are known as leads. I will now explore effective management and automation of leads.

Lead Management and Automation

Salesforce provides administrators with tools to set up lead management processes that fit their organization's strategies. This includes options to customize processes for different business units, create lead record types for various sales situations, and automate lead capture from online forms. These features allow for flexible management and conversion of leads.

Imagine a webinar campaign generating hundreds of leads in a single day. Without a structured process, these leads could fall through the cracks, leaving your team with missed opportunities. By implementing efficient lead management and automation capabilities, every lead can be categorized, prioritized, and routed to the right team members.

Automations throughout these Lead Processes reduce manual effort, enabling your team to focus on what they do best. This optimized workflow bridges the gap between marketing and sales, setting the stage for increased efficiency and higher conversion rates.

Lead Processes

Every organization has unique marketing workflows, often requiring different strategies to manage and qualify leads effectively. A small business might have a straightforward process focused on capturing and nurturing leads, while a larger organization might require more complex workflows to manage leads across multiple teams or regions. Salesforce's Lead Processes enable administrators to configure workflows that align with these varying needs, ensuring that leads are categorized and managed systematically.

Lead Process considerations

It's important to assess whether creating a custom Lead Process is necessary before implementing one. Once you create a custom Lead Process, Salesforce requires that you also create a lead record type and associate the process with it. Introducing record types can add significant complexity to your Salesforce environment and should be done only when an organization has a clear need for multiple distinct lead workflows. For many businesses, the default Standard Lead Process may be sufficient.

Single Lead Process

The built-in process for single leads allows you to configure the Lead Status field to match your marketing team's requirements without the need for custom processes or record types.

For example, a marketing team with a single lead qualification process might only need statuses such as New, Contacted, Nurturing, and Converted. In this scenario, configuring the Standard Lead Process with these status designations is the simplest and most efficient approach. This avoids unnecessary complexity while still enabling the marketing team to track and manage leads effectively.

Multiple Lead Processes

As organizations grow or their marketing strategies become more sophisticated, the need for multiple Lead Processes often arises. For instance, a company with separate workflows for domestic and international marketing efforts might need one Lead Process with statuses like New, Contacted, and "Ready for Sales" for domestic leads, and another with statuses like New, Researching, and Needs Review for international leads. At this point, creating additional Lead Processes and corresponding record types becomes essential to support these distinct workflows.

In the following steps, you'll learn how to configure a Lead Process in Salesforce, starting in the Lead Process Setup screen. These steps should only be followed when you've identified the need for multiple workflows. If a single, unified process is sufficient for your organization, configuring the Standard Lead Process to include all relevant statuses is often the best approach. This ensures a streamlined and efficient system for managing leads without introducing unnecessary complexity.

The Three Salesforce Standard Processes

There are three standard processes in Salesforce, which you can locate by searching for the term "Processes" in the Quick Find box in Setup. The three returned results reside underneath the Marketing, Sales, and Service menus, as shown in Figure 7-12.

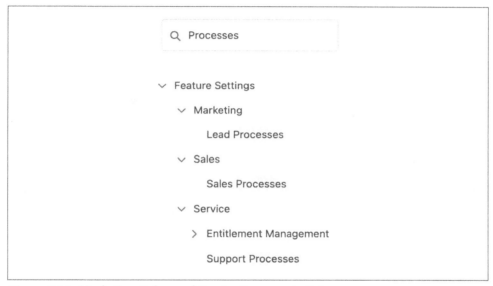

Figure 7-12. Marketing, Sales, and Service Processes in Setup

I will cover Sales Processes later in this chapter. Support Processes will be covered in Chapter 8.

Creating a Lead Process

Click the Lead Processes link in Setup. The Lead Processes screen displays, as shown in Figure 7-13.

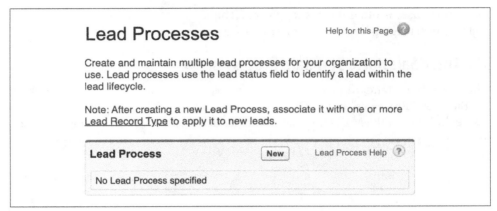

Figure 7-13. Lead Processes screen

Click the New button to create a Lead Process. The New Lead Process screen displays, as shown in Figure 7-14.

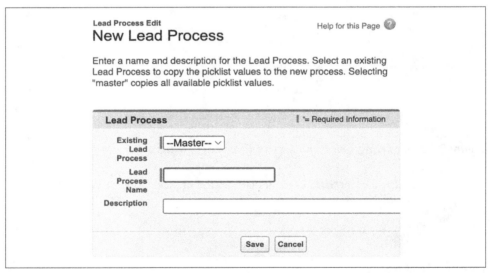

Figure 7-14. New Lead Process screen

Enter the Lead Process Name and Description and click Save. The screen updates for the new Lead Process to select the Lead Status selections for the process, as shown in Figure 7-15.

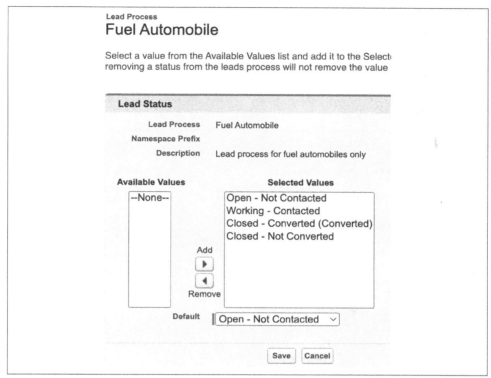

Figure 7-15. Lead Process Status selections screen

The picklist values available for the Lead Status field are displayed in the Selected Values column. To remove values from the picklist, select them and click the Remove button. This moves the value to the Available Values column.

You can also set the Default value for the Lead Status. Once you have adjusted the Selected Values and specified a Default status, click Save. The Lead Processes screen returns and displays your newly created process, as shown in Figure 7-16.

You can repeat these steps to create multiple processes. Once you have created your necessary Lead Processes, you need to create your lead record types in order to see these processes in action. Click the Lead Record Type link on the Lead Processes screen. The Lead Record Type screen displays, as shown in Figure 7-17.

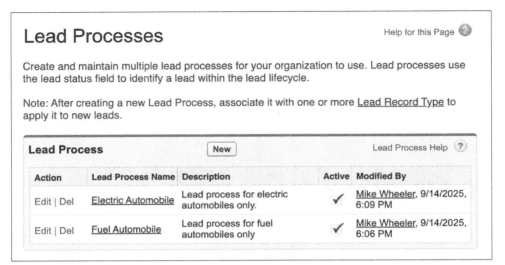

Figure 7-16. Lead Processes screen

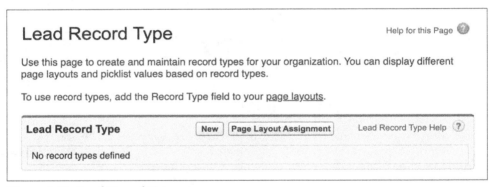

Figure 7-17. Lead Record Type screen

Click New to create a New Lead Record Type. This takes you to the Record Type screen in the Object Manager for the Lead object, as shown in Figure 7-18.

Enter the Record Type Label. It is a good idea to name the record type the same as your Lead Process. You can click the Lead Process drop-down menu to select the appropriate process to associate the new record type with.

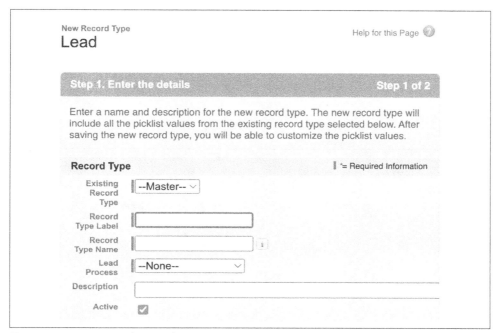

Figure 7-18. New Lead Record Type screen

Although the Description field is not required, it is a good idea to enter a brief description here. The description is displayed to your end users whenever they create a new lead record, helping them to understand which record type to select.

The bottom of the screen is where you can make the new lead record type available by profile. For any profiles that the record type is made available, the Make Default checkbox will be checked and cannot be unchecked. This is because it is the first lead record type; therefore, it will be the default for any profiles to which it is assigned. Subsequent record types created on the Lead object and assigned to a profile will then be adjustable as to which is the default.

Once you have finished your profile assignments, click Next. Step 2 of the New Lead Record Type screen displays, as shown in Figure 7-19.

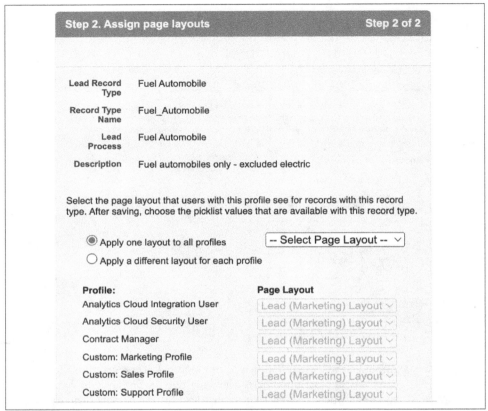

Lead Record Type	Fuel Automobile
Record Type Name	Fuel_Automobile
Lead Process	Fuel Automobile
Description	Fuel automobiles only - excluded electric

Select the page layout that users with this profile see for records with this record type. After saving, choose the picklist values that are available with this record type.

◉ Apply one layout to all profiles   -- Select Page Layout -- ∨

◯ Apply a different layout for each profile

Profile:	Page Layout
Analytics Cloud Integration User	Lead (Marketing) Layout ∨
Analytics Cloud Security User	Lead (Marketing) Layout ∨
Contract Manager	Lead (Marketing) Layout ∨
Custom: Marketing Profile	Lead (Marketing) Layout ∨
Custom: Sales Profile	Lead (Marketing) Layout ∨
Custom: Support Profile	Lead (Marketing) Layout ∨

Figure 7-19. "Step 2. Assign page layouts" screen

The Step 2 screen defaults to the "Apply one layout to all profiles" radio button being selected. You can click the Select Page Layout drop-down menu and select the page layout for all profiles. You also have the option to "Apply a different layout for each profile" via the other radio button and then select specific page layouts by profile.

Once you have completed the page layout assignment(s) for the new lead record type, click the Save & New button to save your new lead record type and begin the process of creating your next one.

Custom-to-Custom Field Mapping During Lead Conversion

During the Lead Conversion process in Salesforce, standard fields automatically map from the Lead object to the corresponding fields on the newly created Account, Contact, and Opportunity records. For example, the standard Lead field Company maps directly to the Account Name field on the resulting Account, while fields such as

Name, Phone, and Email map automatically to the equivalent fields on the newly created Contact.

However, custom fields you create on the Lead object do not automatically map to the new records created upon lead conversion. To ensure these custom details are preserved and accessible after conversion, you must map each custom field from the Lead object to a corresponding custom field on the Account, Contact, or Opportunity objects.

This mapping requires you to create matching custom fields on the destination objects with exactly the same data type. For example, a custom text field on the Lead object that stores a customer's preferred communication method would need to be mapped to a corresponding custom text field on the Contact object; otherwise, that data would be lost upon conversion.

The field length and data type of the source and destination custom fields need to match in order to map correctly. Salesforce does not issue warnings or errors if the destination custom field has a shorter length than the corresponding source field. Instead, data exceeding the defined length of the destination field is truncated, potentially resulting in the loss of important information. For instance, if your Lead field is a 100-character text field and you map it to a Contact custom field of only 50 characters, any characters beyond the 50-character limit are permanently lost upon conversion. Always verify that destination custom fields are of equal or greater length than their source fields to maintain data integrity.

Mapping lead fields

To set up custom-to-custom field mapping, navigate to the Object Manager in Setup and select the Lead object. Click the Fields & Relationships side menu item and then select the Map Lead Fields button at the top-right of the screen. The Custom Fields screen displays, as shown in Figure 7-20.

The Custom Fields screen displays all custom fields on the Lead object on the left side. You will find three tabs across the top of the screen to select either Account, Contact, or Opportunity. As you select a different tab, you will see the right side of the screen change to correspond to the selected object. Select matching fields for Account, Contact, or Opportunity lead fields. Your drop-down field selections persist as you select the different object tabs.

Once you have selected all of the desired custom destination fields to map, click Save. All future lead conversions will now map to the correct fields, preventing data loss. The original lead records are no longer treated as open lead upon conversion. Instead, Salesforce marks it as a converted lead.

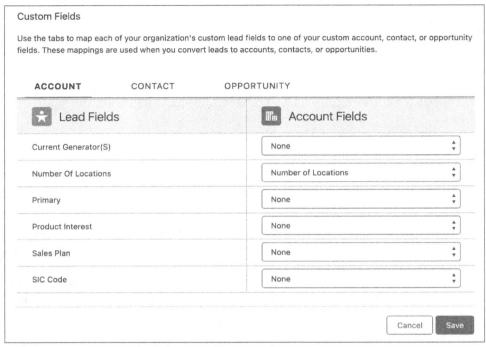

Figure 7-20. Custom Fields screen

At this point, the converted lead record is typically only accessible through a converted lead report. Any future updates to that person's details must be made directly on the resulting Contact record, as the original Lead record is effectively archived.

At the conclusion of a lead conversion, the handoff from marketing to sales is complete. The potential customer journey shifts from marketing's domain to the sales domain. With the marketing side of the journey now complete through the successful conversion of a lead being fully addressed, it's time to turn your attention fully to the sales aspect.

As a result of this Lead Conversion process, three records emerge: an Account, a Contact, and an Opportunity. The next section of this chapter will focus on that resulting Opportunity, as you explore its significance and the ways it supports your sales efforts within Salesforce.

Opportunities in Salesforce

As you learned in Chapter 6, the end result of the Lead Conversion process is the creation of an Account, a Contact, and an Opportunity. During this time of handing off the lead to Sales, or in essence transitioning your focus from attracting attention to attaining a customer, it is the Opportunity that will be the primary focal point moving forward.

Opportunities help businesses track deals through their various stages. The Stage field records each milestone an Opportunity reaches, from initial interest to the ultimate goal of a sales process: its successful closure. They are highly customizable, allowing organizations to align Salesforce with their specific sales processes. By utilizing Opportunities, businesses can forecast revenue, monitor sales performance, and identify trends.

Opportunities are a core part of sales process management in Salesforce, representing potential revenue-generating deals with customers. Each Opportunity provides details such as the account, contacts, and contact roles in relation to these deals, enabling teams to manage sales pipelines effectively.

Opportunity Stages and Probabilities

Opportunity Stages in Salesforce represent the key phases of a sales process, providing a structured way to track deals as they progress toward closure. Each stage is associated with a probability percentage that indicates the likelihood of closing the deal, enabling accurate forecasting and pipeline analysis.

Administrators can define these stages to align with their organization's unique sales process. Common stages include qualification, proposal, negotiation, and closed (won or lost). By using Opportunity Stages and Probabilities, sales teams can prioritize deals, identify bottlenecks, and better understand the health of their pipeline.

The various stages of an Opportunity are visually displayed on the Sales Path, as shown in Figure 7-21.

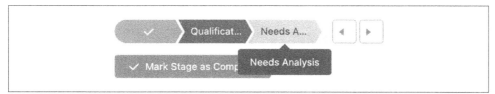

Figure 7-21. Sales Path with stage designations

The Sales Path in Salesforce is a visual tool designed to guide sales representatives through each stage of the sales process. It highlights key fields, steps, and guidance for success, helping teams stay focused and consistent in their approach.

The Sales Path is customizable, allowing organizations to tailor it to their specific sales process and goals. By aligning the Sales Path with Opportunity Stages, businesses can ensure that their teams have clear direction at every step, improving efficiency and outcomes.

Sales Processes

Sales Processes in Salesforce function similarly to Lead Processes, providing a structured way for you to manage and standardize Opportunity Stages. While Lead Processes define the available status options for leads, Sales Processes allow you to control the stages of Opportunities that reflect your specific selling methods.

 The steps involved in setting up the functionality of Sales Processes are the same as those detailed earlier in this chapter for Lead Processes, but instead of selecting different status values for leads, you select stages to be shown for Opportunities. Refer to "Lead Processes" on page 218 for step-by-step details, keeping in mind that during the setup for Sales Processes, you will see Opportunity and Stage instead of Lead and Status.

In Salesforce, each Sales Process is associated with an Opportunity record type. This enables you to customize how different types of sales cycles are handled. You might have one Sales Process for straightforward transactions that move quickly from qualification to closure, and another for complex deals involving stages such as detailed discovery sessions, solution design, and multiple negotiation rounds. By using different Sales Processes, your sales team only sees the stages relevant to their particular sales cycle, helping to keep your processes clear and organized.

To create or adjust a Sales Process, search for and select Sales Processes from Setup (see Figure 7-12). From here, you can set which Opportunity Stages are included for each Sales Process. Once you have set up your Sales Processes, only the selected stages will appear for Opportunities that belong to a specific record type. This ensures each Opportunity follows a logical path tailored to your sales approach, avoiding confusion or unnecessary complexity.

With your Sales Processes clearly defined and implemented, you're now ready to delve deeper into how Opportunities can be measured and forecasted effectively. This understanding begins with key financial metrics such as the Opportunity Amount and Expected Revenue, which play an important role in analyzing your sales pipeline and making accurate revenue projections.

Opportunity Amount and Expected Revenue Fields

In Salesforce Opportunities, the Amount and Expected Revenue fields (see Figure 7-22) serve as key metrics for understanding the potential financial impact of deals. The Amount represents the total monetary value of an Opportunity, offering a straightforward view of the potential revenue if the deal is successfully closed. This value may be derived from the sum of associated products and services or entered manually, providing a clear benchmark for the deal's size.

Amount	
$35,000.00	✎
Expected Revenue	
$21,000.00	
Close Date	
7/8/2025	✎
Next Step	
	✎
Stage	
Id. Decision Makers	✎
Probability (%)	
60%	✎

Figure 7-22. Financial amounts on an Opportunity Detail record

Expected Revenue offers a more nuanced projection by taking into consideration the Amount and the Probability assigned to the Opportunity Stage. For example, if an Opportunity has an Amount of $35,000 and a Probability of 60%, the Expected Revenue is calculated as $21,000. This field incorporates the likelihood of closing the deal, making it a more realistic measure for revenue forecasting.

The Probability percentage associated with each Opportunity Stage can be reviewed and adjusted within Salesforce at the field level. To do this, go to the Object Manager and select the Opportunity object. Click Fields & Relationships, and then click the Stage field. Scroll down to the Opportunity Stage Picklist Values section of the screen, as shown in Figure 7-23.

From here, you can review or edit the Probability values tied to each stage, ensuring they accurately reflect your organization's sales process and historical data.

The Amount field provides a high-level understanding of a deal's potential value and the Expected Revenue field helps sales teams account for uncertainties in the sales process. These figures help salespeople prioritize opportunities and plan strategically. They also play an important role in forecasting. But there are other factors such as Close Date and Forecast Category that also play a central role in projecting financial futures accurately.

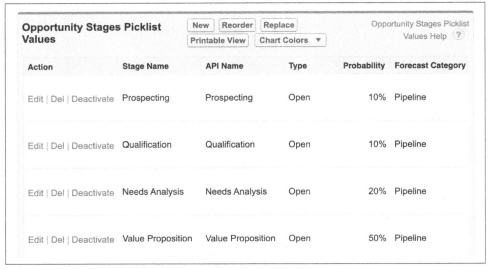

Opportunity Stages Picklist Values					Opportunity Stages Picklist Values Help ⑦
Action	Stage Name	API Name	Type	Probability	Forecast Category
Edit | Del | Deactivate	Prospecting	Prospecting	Open	10%	Pipeline
Edit | Del | Deactivate	Qualification	Qualification	Open	10%	Pipeline
Edit | Del | Deactivate	Needs Analysis	Needs Analysis	Open	20%	Pipeline
Edit | Del | Deactivate	Value Proposition	Value Proposition	Open	50%	Pipeline

Figure 7-23. Opportunity Stages Picklist Values

Close Date and Forecast Category

The Close Date on an Opportunity and Forecast Category both are closely tied to sales forecasting capabilities in Salesforce. They play a central role in pipeline management and revenue projections. Together, they allow you to track the timing and likelihood of deals closing while providing actionable insights for sales planning.

A Close Date on an Opportunity is set to a specific date representing the expected date it will conclude whether as a win or loss. Keeping this date updated is important for maintaining an accurate sales pipeline and ensuring reliable quarterly forecasts. As an Opportunity progresses through different stages, the sales team refines the Close Date to reflect realistic expectations based on ongoing negotiations and customer interactions.

A Forecast Category is directly tied to Opportunity Stages and offers a way to group deals based on their likelihood of closing successfully. Each Opportunity Stage corresponds to a predefined Forecast Category, such as Pipeline, Best Case, Commit, or Closed (Won/Lost).

 Close Date is visible to the user in Figure 7-22, but the Forecast Category is configured behind the scenes in the Opportunity Stages Picklist Values screen, as shown in Figure 7-23.

A Forecast Category provides a standardized framework for evaluating a sales pipeline and typically includes the following:

Pipeline

This includes early-stage Opportunities that are in development but not yet likely to close. These are often exploratory or qualification phases.

Best Case

This represents deals that show promise but still carry some uncertainty. Opportunities in this category have a moderate probability of closing.

Commit

This denotes Opportunities with a high level of confidence and strong potential to close in the current forecast period.

Closed

This categorizes Opportunities that have been completed, either as Won or Lost, marking the end of the sales process for these deals.

By understanding the relationship between Close Dates, Forecast Categories, Opportunity Stages, Probabilities, Amounts, and Expected Revenues, you can vastly improve forecast accuracy, identify pipeline strengths and weaknesses, and align sales efforts with organizational revenue goals.

Utilizing Contact Roles

Contact Roles in Salesforce provide an organized way to identify the individuals associated with an Opportunity and define their specific roles within the sales process. This feature helps sales teams understand the key players involved in a deal, ensuring effective communication and tailored engagement with decision-makers and influencers.

Each Opportunity can have multiple associated Contacts, and their roles can range from decision-maker and influencer to technical buyer or executive sponsor. Assigning Contact Roles ensures clarity about each Contact's contribution to the Opportunity, which is particularly important when managing complex sales cycles involving multiple stakeholders.

To access Contact Roles, search for and select Contact Roles on Opportunities in Setup. The Opportunity Contact Role screen displays, as shown in Figure 7-24.

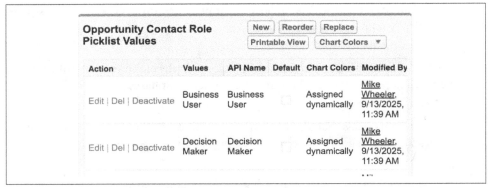

Figure 7-24. Opportunity Contact Role screen

Relevant Contact Roles should be defined to reflect the organization's sales process. You can edit, delete, deactivate, reorder, replace, and create new Contact Roles from the Opportunity Contact Role screen.

Once you have set your necessary Opportunity Contact Roles, you will also want to be sure the Contact Roles related list is displayed on the Opportunity page layout(s). Then you can add Contact records from associated Accounts to the Contact Roles related list on Opportunities, as shown in Figure 7-25.

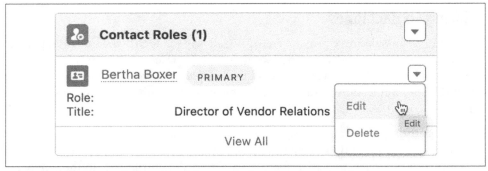

Figure 7-25. Contact Roles related list on an Opportunity record

For each Contact, the appropriate role is selected to indicate their involvement in the deal, as shown in Figure 7-26.

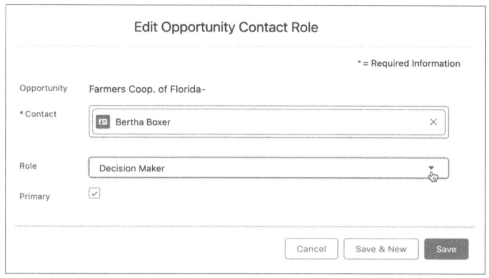

Figure 7-26. Edit Opportunity Contact Role screen

The value of Contact Roles extends beyond just organization. By associating contacts with specific roles, businesses can:

- Improve engagement strategies by tailoring communication to each stakeholder's responsibilities and influence on the deal.
- Enhance reporting and analytics by identifying patterns in stakeholder involvement across successful opportunities.
- Strengthen collaboration among sales teams by providing a shared understanding of who the key players are in each deal, reducing redundancy and improving coordination.

Additionally, Contact Roles play a vital part in Salesforce's Campaign Influence and account-based marketing strategies. By linking Contacts to Opportunities, you can better understand the impact of marketing campaigns on sales outcomes, facilitating data-driven decision making.

Opportunity List View Formats

Salesforce provides a variety of list view formats to help sales reps visualize and interact with their pipeline. These views provide sales professionals with the tools to track and adjust Opportunities dynamically. These list view formats are selectable from the "Select list display" drop-down menu, as shown in Figure 7-27.

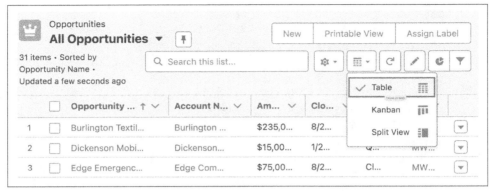

Figure 7-27. "Select list display" drop-down menu

Table view

The table view, as shown in Figure 7-28, resembles a spreadsheet, presenting Opportunities in rows and columns that can be customized to display the most relevant data fields. You can add, remove, or reorder columns to highlight information such as Opportunity owner, probability, expected revenue, or custom fields specific to the organization.

		Opportunity ... ↑ ∨	Account N... ∨	Am... ∨	Clo... ∨	St... ∨	O... ∨	
1	☐	Burlington Textil...	Burlington ...	$235,0...	8/2...	Cl...	MW...	▾
2	☐	Dickenson Mobi...	Dickenson...	$15,00...	1/2...	Q...	MW...	▾
3	☐	Edge Emergenc...	Edge Com...	$75,00...	8/2...	Cl...	MW...	▾
4	☐	Edge Emergenc...	Edge Com...	$35,0...	8/2...	Id...	MW...	▾
5	☐	Edge Installation	Edge Com...	$50,0...	8/2...	Cl...	MW...	▾
6	☐	Edge SLA	Edge Com...	$60,0...	8/2...	Cl...	MW...	▾
7	☐	Express Logisti...	Express Lo...	$80,0...	8/2...	V...	MW...	▾

Figure 7-28. All Opportunities list view in table view

Table view also provides functionality for sorting and filtering. You can sort data by clicking column headers or apply filters to create focused views tailored to your specific needs.

For example, it's easy to isolate Opportunities nearing their close dates or those requiring additional follow-up. Additionally, the table view supports mass updates through inline editing if all of the records in the list are of the same record type. This enables you to make bulk changes, such as reassigning Opportunities, directly from the list. While less visually dynamic than the Kanban view, the table view excels in delivering detailed, actionable insights, making it indispensable for reps and managers seeking comprehensive data analysis.

Kanban view

The Kanban view, shown in Figure 7-29, offers a dynamic, drag-and-drop representation of your sales pipeline. In this format, Opportunities are displayed as cards, grouped by sales process stage, such as Prospecting, Qualification, or Closed Won. Each column in the Kanban view represents a sales stage and provides an overview of the number of Opportunities within that stage as well as their total value. This design enables sales reps and managers to quickly assess the health of the pipeline at a glance.

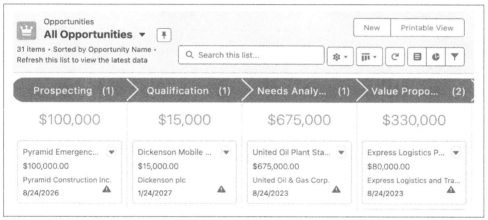

Figure 7-29. All Opportunities list view in Kanban view

A defining feature of the Kanban view is interactivity. Sales reps can move Opportunities through the pipeline simply by dragging a card from one column to another. When this action is performed, Salesforce automatically updates the Opportunity Stage and dynamically recalculates the amounts displayed in each column. This live interaction fosters an intuitive and efficient approach to pipeline management, reducing administrative tasks and encouraging real-time adjustments.

Tailoring Kanban views to your Sales Processes

Kanban views can be customized to match your organization's unique Opportunity Stages and Sales Processes. If your business employs distinct processes for different products, markets, or sales cycles, you can configure separate Kanban views through list views that display only Opportunities relevant to those scenarios. By creating tailored list views, you can represent custom stages specific to different sales workflows or product lines.

Custom filters further enhance the utility of the Kanban view. These filters allow you to refine the display to focus on specific Opportunities, such as those closing in the current month or those owned by a particular sales rep. By offering both a visual overview and interactive controls, the Kanban view has become a favorite tool for many sales teams.

Split view

The split view format, as shown in Figure 7-30, combines the benefits of list views and record detail pages into a single interface, making it a valuable tool for sales reps managing large volumes of Opportunities. In split view, a list of Opportunities appears on the left side of the screen, while the selected record's details are displayed on the right. This dual-pane layout allows you to review, edit, or act on specific Opportunities without losing track of their place in the broader list.

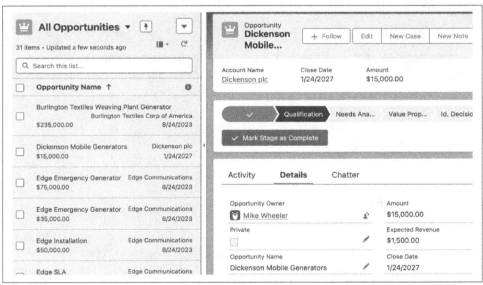

Figure 7-30. All Opportunities list view in split view

This format is beneficial for reps who need to multitask, as it eliminates the need to switch between screens or tabs. By integrating list and record details into a single view, split view enhances efficiency and ensures seamless navigation.

Products, Price Books, and Price Book Entries

Products, price books, and price book entries provide the tools for managing a business's offerings and pricing strategies in Salesforce. Together, they underpin Salesforce's quoting and revenue-tracking capabilities, ensuring consistency and accuracy in sales data.

Products in Salesforce represent the individual items or services a business sells. Each product record includes details such as name, code, description, and unit price, creating a centralized repository for all offerings. This standardized approach ensures that sales teams use consistent product information, reducing errors and streamlining the sales process. Products are directly tied to Opportunities, helping businesses track what is sold and calculate potential revenue.

Price books define pricing structures for different sales scenarios. A price book is a collection of products with specific prices, enabling tailored pricing for customers, markets, or promotions. Salesforce provides standard and custom price books, allowing businesses to maintain default prices or create specialized pricing for specific needs. For example, a custom price book might offer promotional discounts for a seasonal sale or special pricing for key accounts.

Price book entries represent specific listings of products within each price book, capturing both the standard price and any customized pricing. They establish the direct link between products and price books, allowing businesses to define unique pricing scenarios. Price book entries also appear elsewhere in Salesforce as Opportunity products when associated directly with Opportunities. This dual naming convention reflects their context-dependent usage, being referred to as price book entries when related to price books, and as Opportunity products when associated with specific sales Opportunities.

The relationships between products, price books, and price book entries can be clearly visualized using Salesforce's Schema Builder, as shown in Figure 7-31.

Products can be associated with multiple price book entries, reflecting different pricing scenarios across various price books. Price books contain multiple price book entries, supporting diverse pricing structures tailored to different market segments or customer types. Price book entries act as a Junction object linking products and price books, holding specific pricing details such as list price and standard price.

By combining products, price books, and price book entries, Salesforce supports accurate and adaptable pricing, helping businesses manage complex sales scenarios effectively. Administrators ensure these tools are set up and maintained, enabling sales teams to operate efficiently.

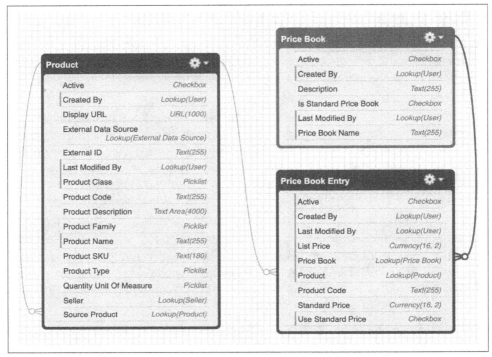

Figure 7-31. Product, Price Book, and Price Book Entry objects in Schema Builder

Adding Products to Opportunities

When adding products to an Opportunity, you select them from the active price book associated with the deal. This ensures that the pricing reflects the appropriate context, whether it's a standard pricing model or a custom arrangement for specific customers or promotions. The Products Related list on an Opportunity is where you can select to Choose Price Book as well as Add Products, as shown in Figure 7-32.

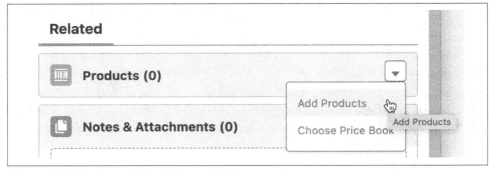

Figure 7-32. Products Related list on an Opportunity

If you click to Add Products without first selecting a price book, the Add Products screen displays and the Standard Price Book is associated with the Opportunity, as shown in Figure 7-33.

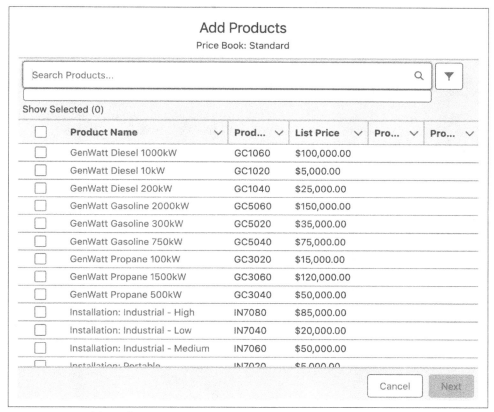

Figure 7-33. Add Products screen

Select the appropriate products and then click Next. The Edit Select Products screen displays, as shown in Figure 7-34.

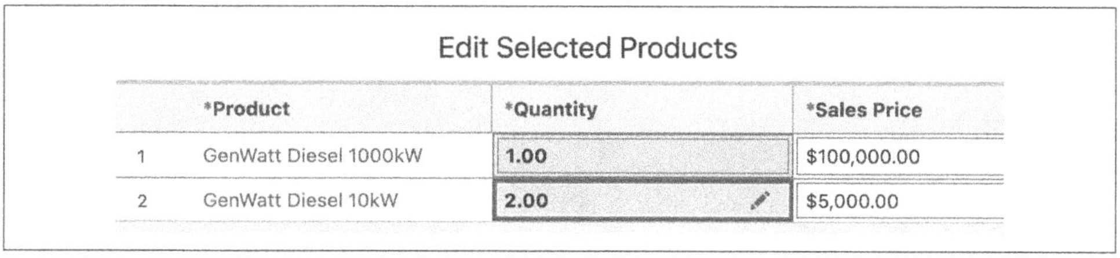

Figure 7-34. Edit Selected Products screen

Here you can specify the Quantity as well as set a date for each line item and provide a description. Any dates, which can be optionally specified on individual product line items, typically indicate when a product or service is expected to be delivered or fulfilled. It helps sales and operations teams plan and manage fulfillment schedules. Click Save to save the selected products to your Opportunity. Based upon the quantities and sales prices for your selected products, the amount of the Opportunity will be calculated.

Adjusting Quantities and Discounts on Opportunity Products

Once products are added to an Opportunity, you can adjust quantities and apply discounts directly within the Opportunity product related list. This flexibility allows sales teams to tailor deals to customer needs while ensuring accurate pricing calculations. Adjustments to quantities automatically update the total Opportunity amount, while discounts are reflected in both the individual product line and the overall deal value.

Price Books

A price book in Salesforce is essentially a catalog that contains a list of products and their corresponding prices. These prices can vary based on the type of customer, promotional offers, or geographic region. For example, a company might use a standard price book for most customers but employ a custom price book for strategic accounts that receive discounted rates.

Price books are accessible via the App Launcher which displays a list of All Price Books in your org (see Figure 7-35).

Figure 7-35. All Price Books list view

Click the Active price book. The Price Book Details screen displays, as shown in Figure 7-36.

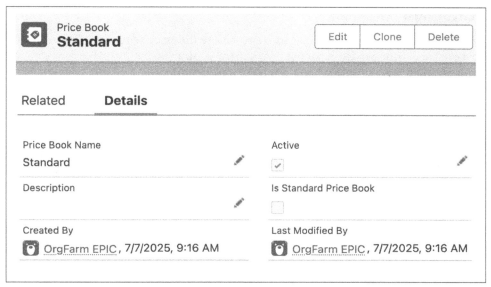

Figure 7-36. Price Book Details screen

To view the products contained in a price book, click the Related tab. The Price Book Entries Related list displays the products contained in the price book (see Figure 7-37).

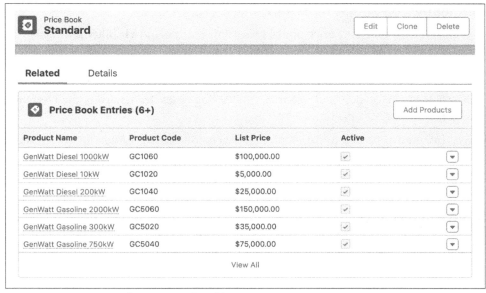

Figure 7-37. Price Book Entries Related list

Activating a Price Book

In Salesforce, price books must be activated before they can be used in Opportunities or associated with products. Activating a price book makes it available for selection by users when managing deals and applying product pricing.

To activate a price book, navigate to the Price Books section in Setup or the App Launcher, select the desired price book, and confirm its status is set to Active. Once activated, the price book becomes available for use in Opportunities.

A standard price book acts as the default repository for all products and their base prices. Every product in Salesforce must first be listed in the standard price book, which serves as the foundation for creating other price books. This ensures that all products have a baseline price available for general use.

Custom price books allow organizations to tailor pricing to specific needs or sales scenarios. For instance, a custom price book might include discounted prices for a limited-time promotion or specialized rates for a key customer segment. Custom price books offer the flexibility to create targeted pricing strategies while maintaining control over how products are priced in different contexts.

By using both standard and custom price books, Salesforce enables businesses to balance consistency with adaptability, ensuring that pricing is aligned with both operational goals and customer expectations.

Managing Access to Price Books

You can control access to price books by setting sharing and visibility settings. Price book access can be managed via sharing rules, manual sharing, and organization-wide defaults. By configuring these settings, you ensure sales representatives see only the price books relevant to their territory, role, or business function. This helps maintain pricing consistency and security, preventing sales teams from inadvertently selecting incorrect or unauthorized pricing.

This structured approach to price book management forms a foundation for accurate sales forecasting. By clearly defining pricing and product offerings, sales teams can confidently utilize Salesforce's Collaborative Forecasting features, which rely heavily on the integrity of Opportunity and pricing data.

Collaborative Forecasting

Collaborative Forecasting in Salesforce enables businesses to predict future revenue, manage sales pipelines, and align organizational goals. It allows tracking of expected revenue from deals at various stages, supporting decision making and strategic planning. It offers flexibility with dynamic forecast types and customization options.

This feature integrates with other Salesforce tools, such as Opportunities and custom objects, providing a view of projected sales. By using Collaborative Forecasting, businesses can improve visibility of sales data, align sales efforts with revenue targets, and adapt to market changes.

Enabling Collaborative Forecasting

To use Collaborative Forecasting in Salesforce, it must be enabled. Search for and choose Forecasts Settings in Setup (see Figure 7-38).

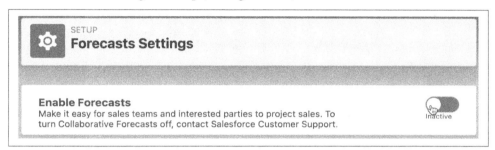

Figure 7-38. Forecasts Settings screen

Click the toggle on the right to enable Forecasts. After a moment, the Sales Forecasts Enabled window displays. Click Done to dismiss the window. The Forecasts Settings screen now displays Available Forecast Types, as shown in Figure 7-39.

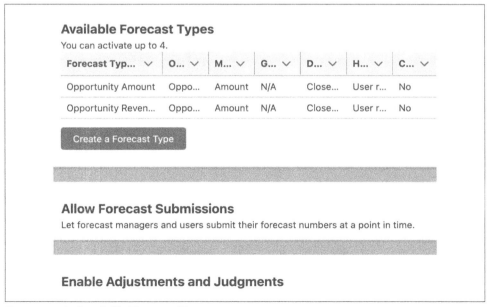

Figure 7-39. Available Forecast Types

Forecast types in Salesforce determine the kind of data included in forecasts and how it is grouped. These types are based on objects such as Opportunities, product schedules, or custom objects, and they allow organizations to align forecasts with their sales processes.

The Opportunity Revenue forecast type focuses on forecast amounts tied to Opportunity Stages. The Opportunity Amount forecast type emphasizes forecasted revenue based on the Total Amount field of Opportunities. This enables organizations to anticipate potential income by directly analyzing the sums attributed to specific sales deals across all stages of the pipeline.

Quantity forecast types focus on forecasting based on the quantity of items or services associated with Opportunities. This type is especially useful for businesses that track product-level forecasts or need to manage inventory and supply chains effectively.

Choosing Forecast Periods

Forecast periods in Salesforce define the time frames used for revenue and pipeline projections. These periods determine how forecast data is grouped, such as by month or quarter, allowing organizations to align forecasting with their reporting and planning cycles.

To configure forecast periods, navigate to Forecasts Settings and scroll down to the "Choose a Default Date Range" section. Click Edit to open the Forecast Period options, as shown in Figure 7-40.

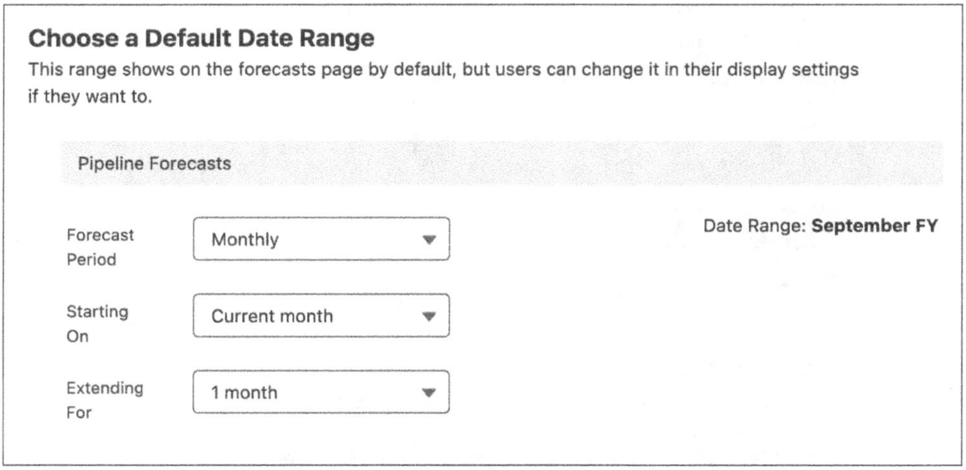

Figure 7-40. "Choose a Default Date Range" window

Salesforce supports flexible options for defining forecast periods, enabling businesses to align these settings with their fiscal calendar or other operational needs.

Adjusting Forecast Data

Adjusting forecast data in Salesforce allows sales teams and managers to refine projections by modifying key inputs such as expected revenue, Opportunity amounts, or forecast overrides. This flexibility ensures that forecasts reflect the most current and accurate information available.

To adjust forecast data, you can access the Forecasts tab and make updates directly to Opportunity amounts or apply overrides to forecast figures at the manager level. Overrides allow managers to modify projections without altering the underlying Opportunity records, maintaining data integrity while ensuring forecasts are realistic and aligned with expectations.

Summary

In Chapter 7, you explored Salesforce's Sales and Marketing applications, focusing on how to effectively manage Campaigns, Leads, Opportunities, and Forecasts. You also learned about setting up Campaign Hierarchies and managing campaign members. The chapter also introduced Lead and Sales Processes, showing how to create workflows that align with your organization's strategies.

You also learned about Opportunities, including their stages, probabilities, and forecasting capabilities. The chapter examined the role of price books, how to associate products with Opportunities, and how Collaborative Forecasting provides visibility into expected revenue.

These tools and processes are important for managing sales and marketing efforts within Salesforce. They help ensure alignment between teams and provide insights into pipeline and revenue tracking.

Chapter 7 Quiz

The following quiz will help you review key topics covered in this chapter. For each question, there is an explanation of the correct and incorrect answers in the Appendix, allowing you to deepen your understanding of these features and prepare for the types of questions you might encounter on the Salesforce Certified Platform Administrator exam.

1. What is the primary purpose of Campaign Influence in Salesforce?

    a. To analyze the performance of email campaigns

    b. To measure the impact of marketing efforts on sales outcomes

c. To identify relationships between marketing campaigns and closed Opportunities

d. To generate leads from web forms

2. Which Opportunity list view format is best suited for visually managing pipeline stages?

   a. Split view

   b. Table view

   c. Kanban view

   d. Compact view

3. What distinguishes custom price books from standard price books?

   a. Custom price books require additional permissions to edit.

   b. Standard price books exclusively support multicurrency.

   c. Custom price books automatically sync with external pricing systems.

   d. Custom price books allow tailored pricing for specific customers or markets.

4. When setting up Collaborative Forecasting, which element must align with Opportunity Stages?

   a. Opportunity names

   b. Record types

   c. Forecast categories

   d. Campaign member status

5. What is the primary function of the Opportunity Product Related list?

   a. To track Opportunity progress through stages

   b. To add and manage products, quantities, and discounts associated with an Opportunity

   c. To define product categories for sales reporting

   d. To assign team roles to an Opportunity

6. What Salesforce functionality allows users to quickly send emails to all members of a campaign?

   a. Mass Emailing

   b. Email-to-Case

   c. Campaign Influence

   d. Send List Email

Service and Support Applications

Customer service plays a pivotal role in any organization's ability to retain customers and build lasting relationships. In Salesforce, the Service and Support applications knowledge area focuses on equipping businesses with tools to streamline support processes and improve customer satisfaction. At its core lies the Case object, a versatile tool for capturing, tracking, and resolving customer issues. By leveraging these tools effectively, businesses can provide prompt and consistent service that fosters loyalty and generates positive brand impressions.

While the service arm of a business is often viewed as a *cost center*—an area that incurs expenses without directly contributing to revenue—it remains an indispensable function. Excellent customer service, although not immediately profitable, has the potential to drive indirect revenue by promoting brand loyalty and positive word-of-mouth. Satisfied customers are more likely to become repeat buyers and advocates, creating new leads and sales opportunities.

This chapter introduces the key components of Salesforce's service features, focusing on how they support different aspects of customer interactions. From foundational case management tools to advanced automation features like Web-to-Case and Email-to-Case, you'll learn how to configure and optimize Salesforce to handle support requests efficiently. Additionally, I will explore advanced service tools such as the Service Console and custom application designs using the Lightning App Builder.

By the end of this chapter, you will have a thorough understanding of the tools and strategies needed to deliver exceptional customer support with Salesforce, ensuring your organization can meet and exceed customer expectations while maintaining operational efficiency.

From the Exam Guide

The Service and Support applications knowledge area of the Exam Guide contains the following learning objectives:

- Describe the capabilities of case management (for example, case, case assignment rules, and queues).
- Given a scenario, identify how to automate case management (for example, support process, case auto-response rules, and case escalation).

Service Cloud User Settings

To leverage Service Cloud functionality in Salesforce, you will want to be sure you have enabled your user account as a Service Cloud User. Search for Users in Setup and select your user account. Your User Detail screen displays, as shown in Figure 8-1.

Figure 8-1. User Detail screen

Check the Service Cloud User checkbox if it is unchecked and click Save. This setting enables or disables key features related to case management and customer support. The Service Cloud User checkbox is tied directly to the number of Service Cloud licenses your organization has available. Each user who has this checkbox selected consumes an available Service Cloud license in your Salesforce org. If you attempt to assign this checkbox to more users than you have licenses, Salesforce will display an error indicating you have exceeded your available licenses.

Accessing the Service Setup Menu

Another important feature of Salesforce related to support is the Service Setup menu, which is accessible by clicking the gear icon at the top-right of the screen. You will see the Service Setup menu option in the resulting drop-down menu (see Figure 8-2).

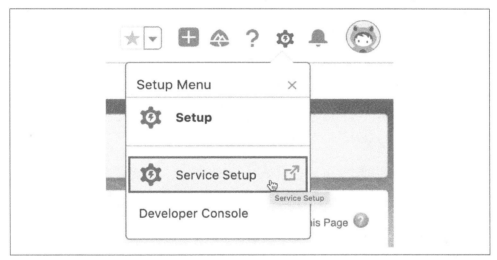

Figure 8-2. Service Setup menu option

If you do not see the Service Setup menu option, the most likely reasons are that you either do not have administrative permissions or have not been assigned a Service Cloud license. Selecting the Service Setup menu option displays the Service Setup Home screen in a new tab in your browser, as shown in Figure 8-3.

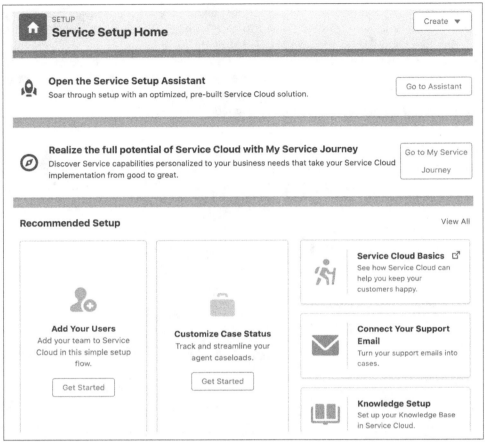

Figure 8-3. Service Setup Home screen

Service Setup Home Screen

The Service Setup Home screen in Salesforce acts as the central hub for configuring and managing service-related features. The interface provides you with access to tools and wizards that simplify the deployment of various service functionalities. By consolidating these resources on a single screen, Salesforce streamlines the process of setting up and optimizing service workflows, making it an attainable starting point for administrators focused on delivering great customer service.

The Service Setup Home screen includes shortcuts to configuring service features such as Email-to-Case and Web-to-Case. These tools enable organizations to capture customer inquiries submitted via email or web forms and automatically convert them into Cases.

This home page also provides a Knowledge Setup Wizard, which allows you to quickly enable and configure Salesforce Knowledge, a centralized repository for creating, managing, and sharing articles. By following the guided steps in the wizard, you can set up Knowledge to provide agents and customers with self-service resources, reducing Case volume and enhancing the service experience. You will learn how to enable and set up these various service-related features throughout this chapter.

Beyond setup wizards, the Service Setup Home screen offers service metrics dashboards that provide a real-time view of key performance indicators (KPIs) such as case volume, average resolution time, and agent workload. These insights enable you to monitor service performance and make data-driven decisions to improve efficiency and customer satisfaction.

Service Setup Sidebar Menu

As you navigate the Service Setup sidebar menu, you'll notice that it is a condensed version of the full Setup menu, containing service and support related links, along with a Quick Find box, as shown in Figure 8-4.

The Service Setup sidebar menu contains additional tools for configuring features like queues and case escalation rules. Each of these service-specific features plays a role in optimizing your customer support efforts, which I will cover in more detail later in this chapter.

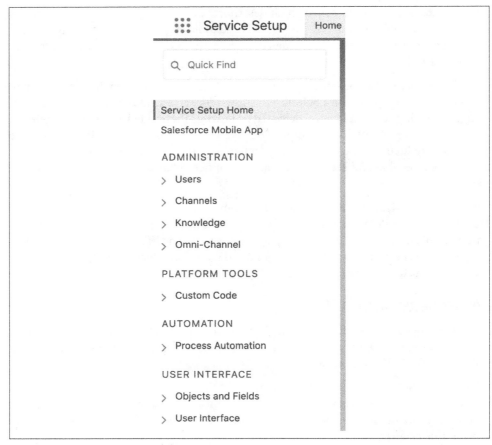

Figure 8-4. Service Setup sidebar menu

Accessing the Service Application

To begin to get familiar with the Case object, it is helpful to experience its nuances in the context of the Service application. Click the App Launcher and select the Service application. The Service home page displays, as shown in Figure 8-5.

The Service application contains a series of tabs spanning the width of the screen. You will find tabs related to Cases, Accounts, Contacts, and more. Click the Cases tab to go to the Cases home page as shown in Figure 8-6.

Figure 8-5. Service home page

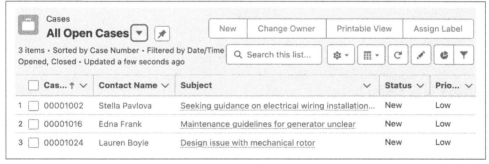

Figure 8-6. Cases home page

The Cases home page contains several list views from which you can select. The sample data in your learner org will contain a variety of Cases, with Case Numbers and Subjects populated. The Status field of Cases is where you track individual Cases through their journey to an eventual (and hopefully successful) resolution.

If you investigate the Case list views available to you, you'll discover that there are list views devoted to all Cases, only open cases (i.e., not resolved), closed Cases, and more. Clicking the hyperlink for a Case number will open the Case Details screen for that case, as shown in Figure 8-7.

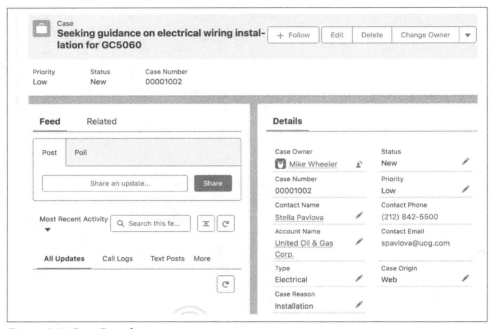

Figure 8-7. Case Details screen

What Is a Case?

A Case represents a customer inquiry, issue, or request for support. Cases are created whenever customers reach out via channels such as email, web forms, or phone. Each Case acts as a record of the customer's concern and serves as a container for tracking its resolution. By effectively tracking Cases, you can generate reports to identify trends and uncover opportunities for creating new Knowledge articles, updating existing documentation, or proactively addressing potential issues.

The Status field on a Case indicates where the Case is in its resolution journey. It is similar in function to the Status field on Leads and the Stage field on Opportunities, providing a way to categorize progress. Open Cases are currently unresolved and require attention. Closed Cases indicate that the issue has been resolved. Closed Cases no longer require action but remain in Salesforce for historical tracking and reporting.

The Status field is also critical for workflow automation and reporting. For example, reports can filter Cases by status, allowing support teams to track open Cases or monitor the resolution rate of closed Cases. Workflows, assignment rules, and escalation rules can also trigger actions based on the Status value, ensuring that Cases are handled in a timely manner.

The Status field on a Case may include values such as New, In Progress, Escalated, and Closed. But in a new Salesforce Developer account, the Closed picklist option for Status may be missing, as shown in Figure 8-8.

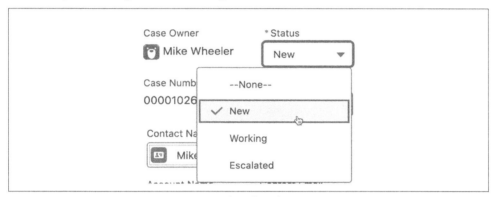

Figure 8-8. Case Status options missing the Closed option

To make Closed available as a selectable Status designation on Cases, you have to add it via Support Settings.

Adding Closed Status via Support Settings

The Status field on the Case object does not include a Closed designation by default; this can confuse new users. You can configure the Status field to include Closed by navigating to Support Settings via the Service Setup. The Support Settings screen displays, as shown in Figure 8-9.

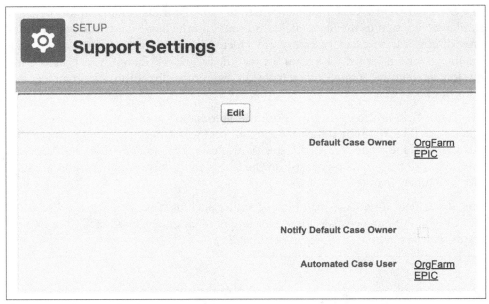

Figure 8-9. Support Settings screen

Click Edit and scroll down and select the Show Closed Statuses in Case Status check-box and then click Save. You will now see Closed as a Status option on Cases.

Additional Support Settings Features

The Support Settings screen includes several other configurations that impact how Cases are managed. The Default Case Owner specifies the user or queue that is assigned ownership of a Case when no criteria from assignment rules are met, for example.

Similarly, the Automated Case User tracks actions performed by automated processes on Cases when no specific user is associated with the activity. This serves as a place-holder, making it easier to audit system-generated changes.

Notifications can be configured in the Support Settings to notify case owners of new or updated cases. You can also enable Case Feed from this screen, which presents case details in a timeline view, organizing interactions, comments, and updates into a clear chronological format.

Case Subject and Description Fields

Other important fields on Case records are the Subject and Description fields. These provide context for the issue being tracked. The Subject field serves as a concise sum-mary of the problem, while the Description field allows for more detailed information. These fields are often populated by customers when Cases originate via Web-to-Case or Email-to-Case. Support agents can use these fields to understand the core issue of a case at a glance.

Standard Service Console Overview

The Service Console in Salesforce is a highly customizable workspace designed to optimize workflows for teams managing complex processes. For example, for an auto dealership's service department, the console can streamline the management of repair requests, customer interactions, and vehicle service histories. By centralizing relevant information and tools, the Service Console helps service agents and managers work more efficiently.

When agents log in to the Service Console, they see a tab-based interface that allows them to handle multiple records simultaneously. Each tab represents an open record, such as a service case, customer profile, or vehicle history. This structure lets agents seamlessly switch between tasks, such as checking a vehicle's maintenance history, updating a repair case, and referencing a customer's contact information. The tabbed navigation enhances multitasking, making it ideal for high-paced service environments.

In the Service Console, navigation is through a drop-down menu located in the upper-left corner. Instead of horizontal tabs seen in standard apps, this drop-down menu provides quick access to key objects like Cases, Contacts, Vehicles, and Knowledge articles. For example, an agent might begin by selecting Cases to manage ongoing repair requests, switch to Vehicles to review service histories, and then move to Knowledge to find warranty documentation or repair guides. This streamlined approach reduces clutter on the screen while ensuring users can quickly locate the information they need.

The layout of the Service Console is designed to highlight critical information. At the top of each record, the Highlights Panel displays essential details such as the customer's name, the vehicle's make and model, the repair priority, and the assigned technician. Below this panel, related lists provide additional context, such as case comments, recent service actions, and any follow-up tasks. This ensures that agents have a comprehensive view of all relevant details without needing to click through multiple screens.

The default configuration of the Service Console offers robust capabilities for managing service operations. For an auto dealership, this could include tracking repair workflows, accessing vehicle service histories, and coordinating with technicians. However, organizations can extend these features further by creating custom console applications tailored to their specific needs.

Case Assignment Rules

Case assignment rules in Salesforce automate the process of routing Cases to the appropriate users or queues based on specific criteria that are defined in advance.

Create Case Assignment Rules

You can search for and select Case Assignment Rules in Service Setup. The Case Assignment Rules screen displays, as shown in Figure 8-10.

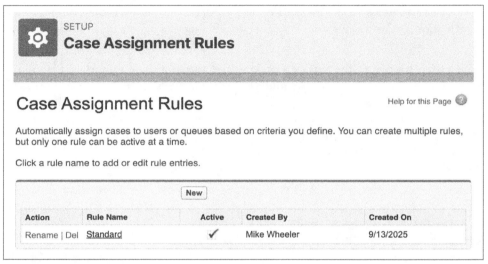

Figure 8-10. Case Assignment Rules screen

A case assignment rule consists of a series of rule entries, which are evaluated in sequence until a matching condition is found. A rule entry includes criteria that determine how Cases are routed. For instance, you can configure a rule entry to assign all high-priority Cases with the Case Origin set to Web to a specific queue for urgent attention.

Assignment rules also support the use of email templates to notify the assigned user or queue of the new Case. Click an assignment rule to view its Rule Entries, as shown in Figure 8-11.

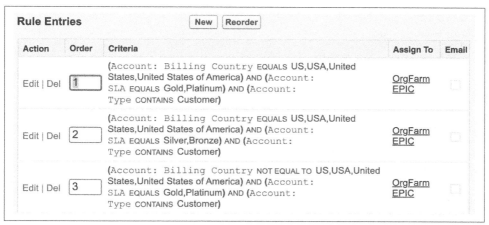

Rule Entries New Reorder

Action	Order	Criteria	Assign To	Email
Edit | Del	1	(Account: Billing Country EQUALS US,USA,United States,United States of America) AND (Account: SLA EQUALS Gold,Platinum) AND (Account: Type CONTAINS Customer)	OrgFarm EPIC	
Edit | Del	2	(Account: Billing Country EQUALS US,USA,United States,United States of America) AND (Account: SLA EQUALS Silver,Bronze) AND (Account: Type CONTAINS Customer)	OrgFarm EPIC	
Edit | Del	3	(Account: Billing Country NOT EQUAL TO US,USA,United States,United States of America) AND (Account: SLA EQUALS Gold,Platinum) AND (Account: Type CONTAINS Customer)	OrgFarm EPIC	

Figure 8-11. Case Assignment Rule Entries

After defining your rule entries, you can test the assignment rule by creating test cases that match your criteria. Verify that cases are routed as expected and that notifications are sent appropriately. Proper testing ensures that assignment rules function correctly and efficiently manage the flow of cases within your organization.

Only one assignment rule can be active at a time, so ensure the desired rule is marked active.

Mass Reassigning of Cases

Mass reassigning of cases in Salesforce enables you to quickly update the ownership of multiple cases at once, minimizing manual effort and ensuring they are handled by the appropriate users or teams. This feature is useful during organizational changes, such as when an agent leaves the company, teams are restructured, or queues are consolidated.

Navigate to the list view of Cases you wish to reassign and ensure your list view filters are set to display only the desired Cases. From the list view, select the Cases by checking the boxes next to each record or use the Select All option for bulk selection (see Figure 8-12).

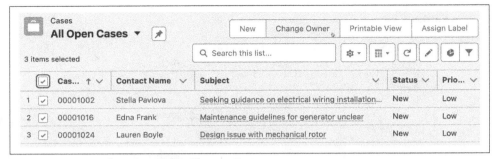

Figure 8-12. *Case list view Mass Change Owner*

Once the Cases are selected, click the Change Owner button, which appears above the list view. This displays the Change Owner pop-up, as shown in Figure 8-13, where you can specify the new owner.

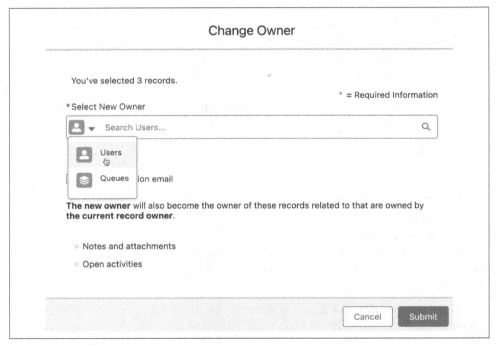

Figure 8-13. *Change Owner pop-up*

You have the option to reassign the Cases to a specific user or to a queue. You will learn about queues in the next section of this chapter.

Enter the name of the desired user or queue in the provided field and confirm the selection. You may choose additional options such as sending a notification email to the new owner. Click Submit to finalize the Case reassignments. Salesforce updates the selected ownership and, if enabled, sends notifications to the new owner.

Case Queues

Case queues in Salesforce provide a powerful way to organize, prioritize, and distribute Cases efficiently across teams. By grouping Cases based on criteria such as priority, type, or geography, queues ensure that no Case is overlooked and the right team members address the right issues promptly.

At their core, case queues act as holding areas for Cases awaiting assignment. When a Case is created, it can be routed directly to a queue rather than immediately assigned to a specific user. This enables team members to take ownership of Cases based on availability, expertise, or current workload. For instance, a support organization might establish separate queues for different product lines, allowing specialized teams to manage Cases that align with their particular skills.

To create a case queue, navigate to Setup, search for and select Queues, and then click the New button. The New Queue screen displays, as shown in Figure 8-14.

Provide a clear and descriptive name for your queue in the Label field. Select the Case from the Available Objects section of the screen and move it over to the Selected Objects section.

Queues are supported on many, but not all, objects in Salesforce. For example, you won't find Account listed as an available object because Account management is not handled through a flexible, ad hoc assignment approach. Queues are best suited for high-volume situations where ownership is not a high-stakes proposition. Cases and Leads are two common queue objects you will find in use in real organizations.

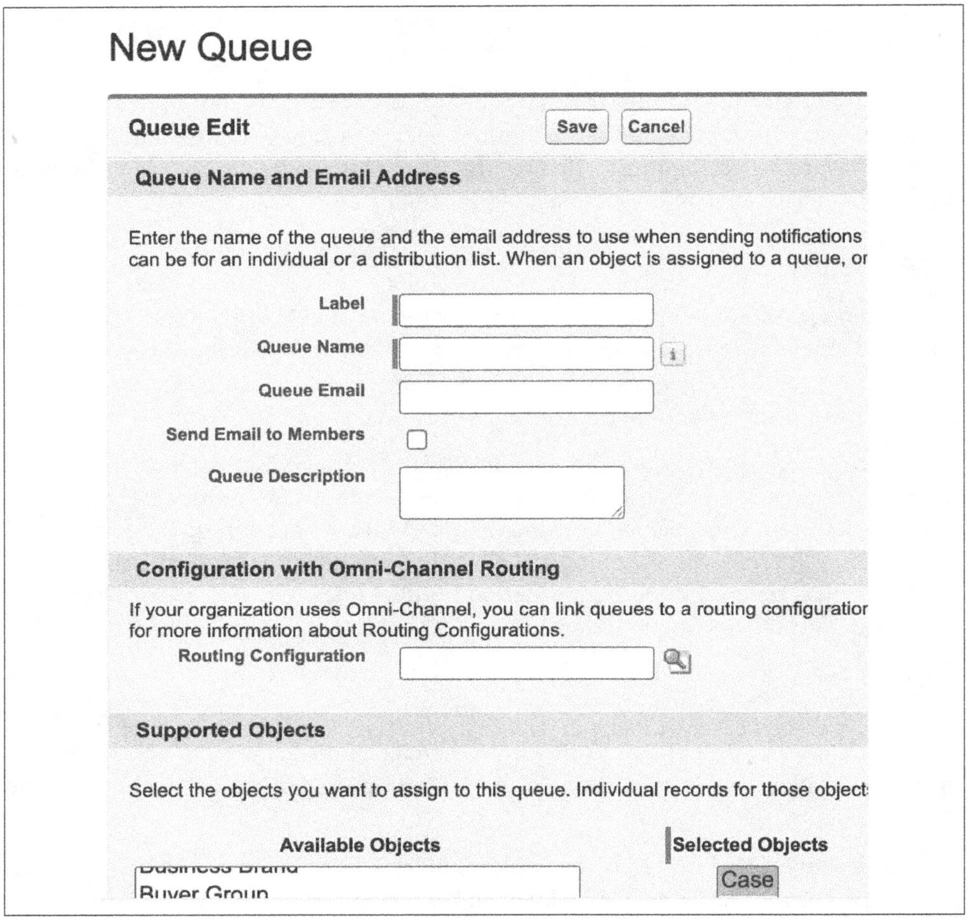

New Queue

Queue Edit   [Save] [Cancel]

Queue Name and Email Address

Enter the name of the queue and the email address to use when sending notifications
can be for an individual or a distribution list. When an object is assigned to a queue, or

Label	[ ]
Queue Name	[ ] [i]
Queue Email	[ ]
Send Email to Members	☐
Queue Description	[ ]

Configuration with Omni-Channel Routing

If your organization uses Omni-Channel, you can link queues to a routing configuration
for more information about Routing Configurations.

Routing Configuration   [   ] 🔍

Supported Objects

Select the objects you want to assign to this queue. Individual records for those object

Available Objects	**Selected Objects**
~~Business Brand~~	Case
Buyer Group	

Figure 8-14. New Queue screen

Next, scroll down to define the members of the queue who can access and manage its
cases, as shown in Figure 8-15.

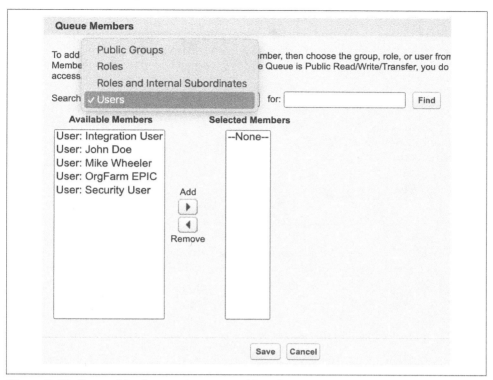

Figure 8-15. Queue Members assignment in New Queue screen

Salesforce allows you to add individual Users, Public Groups, Roles, and "Roles and Internal Subordinates," providing flexibility in managing your queue membership. Users will have visibility into a queue and its assigned Cases only if they are added as members of that queue.

One of the advantages of queues is their seamless integration with case assignment rules and other automation tools. Using Salesforce Flow, you can set routing logic to automatically direct Cases to the appropriate queue based on specified criteria.

From the user's perspective, queues appear as list views within the Cases tab, enabling team members to easily view, claim, or assign Cases. This provides control over workload distribution.

Queues also facilitate effective monitoring and reporting. Metrics such as case volume, average queue time, and resolution rates can offer valuable insights into team performance and workflow efficiency. If a particular queue frequently experiences delays, you can use this data to identify and address potential bottlenecks or resource gaps.

By effectively using case queues, your organization can improve visibility, enhance team productivity, and ensure timely responses to customer inquiries. Next, I will explore how case escalation rules integrate with queues to further automate and refine your case management process.

Case Escalation Rules

Case escalation rules automate the process of ensuring that unresolved or high-priority Cases receive timely attention. By defining specific conditions and actions, these rules help organizations maintain service standards and prevent Cases from being overlooked. Escalation rules are designed to work in tandem with business hours, ensuring that escalations occur only during times when support teams are available to address cases.

Configuring an Escalation Rule

To configure escalation rules in your org, search for and select Escalation Rules from Service Setup. The Case Escalation Rules screen displays, as shown in Figure 8-16.

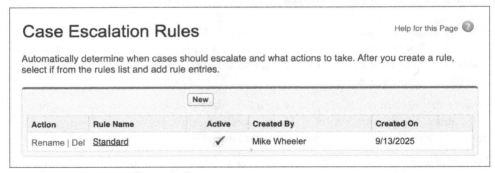

Figure 8-16. Case Escalation Rules screen

As with case assignment rules, there can be only one active case escalation rulein your org.

You can click on the active escalation rule on this screen to inspect it. The Rule Detail screen displays, as shown in Figure 8-17.

Figure 8-17. Rule Detail screen

You will find that an escalation rule consists of a sort order for the rule entry, as entries are evaluated sequentially. The sort order determines which conditions are checked first when the rule is applied. Next, define the criteria that must be met for the case to escalate.

For example, you can set the criteria to escalate Cases with a Priority field value of High or combine multiple conditions using logical operators to create more specific escalation scenarios. You can also decide whether the rule should take business hours into account, ensuring that escalations occur only during your organization's operational hours. Click Edit next to a rule entry to display the Rule Entry Edit screen, as shown in Figure 8-18.

Figure 8-18. Rule Entry Edit screen

Once the conditions are set, configure the actions that should be triggered when the criteria are met. These actions may include reassigning the Case to a specific user or queue to ensure timely handling. Additionally, you can send email notifications to designated recipients, such as team leads or managers, to alert them to the escalation. Using email templates for notifications helps maintain a consistent and professional message across all escalated Cases.

After completing the configuration for the rule entry, save it and return to the rule editor. You can repeat the process to add additional rule entries, each addressing different escalation scenarios.

When all entries are configured, activate the escalation rule by selecting the Active checkbox and saving the rule.

Testing Escalation Rules

It is important to test an escalation rule by creating Cases that match the specified criteria to ensure the escalations and actions occur as expected. Proper testing helps confirm that Cases are being escalated correctly and that notifications are sent to the appropriate recipients, allowing for seamless integration of the rule into support workflows.

Case Status Designations

The Status field on a Case represents where it stands in its lifecycle. It helps agents and automations track progress, prioritize workloads, and drive workflows. While default statuses such as New, In Progress, and Closed cover basic needs, many organizations require additional statuses to reflect their unique processes.

To customize the Status field, navigate to the Case object in Object Manager. Select Fields & Relationships. From there, select the Status field to access the picklist values, as shown in Figure 8-19.

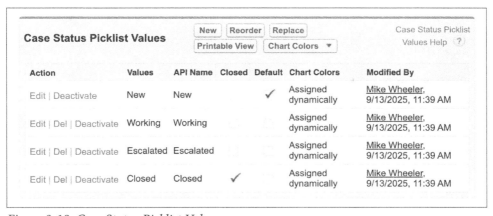

Figure 8-19. Case Status Picklist Values screen

On this screen, you can add new values, reorder existing ones, or deactivate those that no longer apply. For example, if your organization needs a status for when a case is awaiting input from the customer, you can add "Waiting for Customer" to the picklist. Or, if your organization escalates Cases to a different department, a status like Pending Escalation may be appropriate.

To reorder statuses, drag and drop them into a logical sequence that reflects the typical Case lifecycle. For instance, placing New, In Progress, and Escalated before Closed ensures agents can quickly select the appropriate status as they progress through the Case resolution process. After making changes, click Save to finalize the updates.

Support Processes

Support Processes are designed to control which statuses are available for specific types of Cases. This is useful for organizations with multiple teams that handle different types of Cases. For example, a technical support team may need statuses like Diagnosing Issue and Pending Engineering, while a billing team might use Awaiting Payment or Invoice Sent.

Create or Edit Support Process

To create or edit a Support Process, search for and select Support Processes from Setup. The Support Processes screen displays, as shown in Figure 8-20.

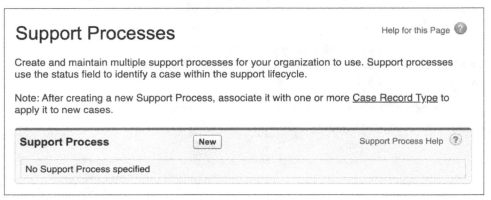

Figure 8-20. Support Processes screen

Click New to create a new process or select an existing process to modify it. When creating a new process, provide a descriptive name, such as Technical Support Workflow, and select an existing Support Process to clone, if applicable. Next, select the statuses that will be available for this process, as shown in Figure 8-21.

After selecting the applicable statuses, save the process.

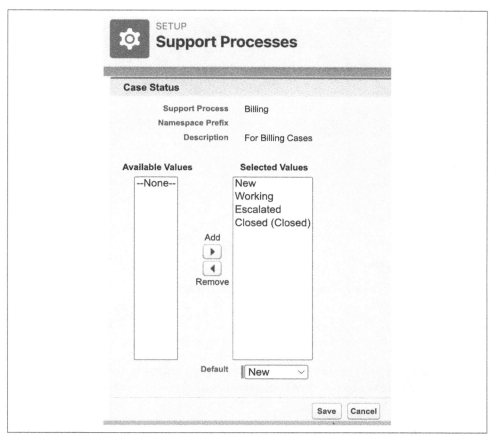

Figure 8-21. Case Status Selected Values for a Support Process

Assigning Support Processes to Case Record Types

Support Processes are assigned to Case record types to ensure that each team sees only the statuses relevant to its workflow. For example, a Case record type for technical support might use the Technical Support Workflow support process, while a record type for billing might use the Billing Workflow support process. This assignment ensures clarity and consistency for agents working on Cases.

To complete the configuration, assign Support Processes to the appropriate Case record types. Navigate to Setup and search for Record Type under the Case object. Select the record type you wish to edit or create a new one. During the setup process, you'll be prompted to assign a Support Process to the record type, as shown in Figure 8-22.

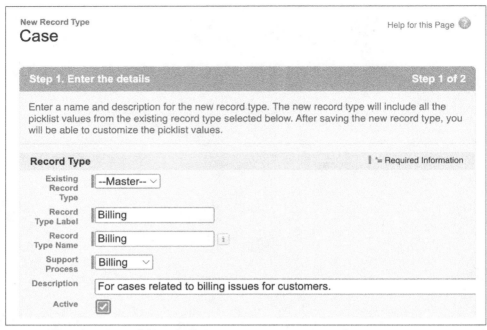

Figure 8-22. Case Record Type with Support Process associated

Choose the appropriate process from the list. After assigning the Support Process, you can customize the record type further by tailoring page layouts or adding custom fields, as needed. Save your changes to complete the setup.

Case Deflection and Self-Service

Case deflection is a core principle of customer support. The aim of deflection is to reduce the number of Cases that require manual intervention. This is accomplished by encouraging customers to find answers to their questions independently. This strategy relies heavily on providing customers with accessible, accurate, and relevant information through various self-service tools. Salesforce facilitates case deflection through features like Knowledge articles, chatbots, and self-service portals.

Knowledge articles are a core component of case deflection. These articles provide detailed information about common issues and their solutions, enabling customers to resolve problems without creating a Case.

For example, a customer experiencing login issues might find a step-by-step guide in the Knowledge base that resolves their problem, eliminating the need to contact support. Chatbots further enhance self-service by guiding customers to relevant articles or suggesting solutions based on their queries. Self-service portals combine these tools into a unified interface, empowering customers to find answers quickly and conveniently.

Setting Up Knowledge Articles

To begin using Knowledge in Salesforce, it must first be enabled. Search for and select Knowledge Settings from Service Setup to display the Knowledge Settings screen, as shown in Figure 8-23.

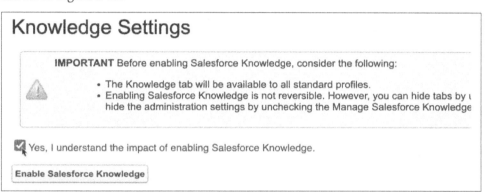

Figure 8-23. Knowledge Settings screen

From this screen, enable Knowledge by selecting the checkbox and clicking Enable Salesforce Knowledge. Once enabled, Salesforce Knowledge becomes accessible as a feature, and you can begin configuring article management options.

> Once you enable Knowledge in an organization, it cannot be disabled

Configuring Knowledge articles

Once you have enabled Salesforce Knowledge, the Knowledge Settings screen updates to display additional settings and information, as shown in Figure 8-24.

You can begin the journey of configuring Salesforce Knowledge from the Knowledge Settings screen. You can optionally set up Knowledge via the Service Setup.

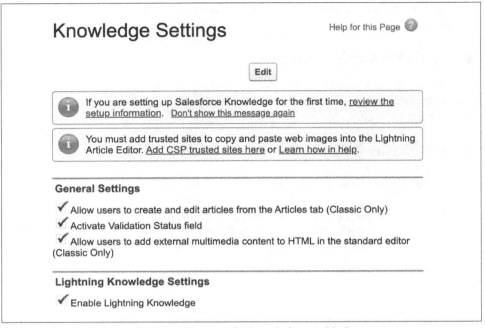

Figure 8-24. Knowledge Settings screen with Knowledge enabled

Knowledge setup via Service Setup

The Service Setup screen, accessible via the Service Setup gear icon at the top-right of the screen, contains a Knowledge Setup card, as shown in Figure 8-25.

Figure 8-25. Knowledge Setup card in Service Setup screen

Clicking the Knowledge Setup card displays the Lightning Knowledge Setup window, as shown in Figure 8-26.

Figure 8-26. Lightning Knowledge Setup window

Click Start to begin the process of enabling Lightning Knowledge. The Choose Your Lightning Knowledge Authors screen displays, as shown in Figure 8-27.

Select your Knowledge authors and then click Next. The final step of the Lightning Knowledge Setup Wizard displays the Get Organized! screen where you enter a Data Category Group and Data Category, as shown in Figure 8-28.

You can enter Data Category Groups and Data Categories to organize your Knowledge articles effectively. Data Category Groups and Data Categories help you classify and structure your Knowledge articles, making it simpler for users to quickly locate relevant information.

For instance, if you are setting up Salesforce Knowledge for an electronics company that sells various products like televisions, speakers, and modems, you might create a Data Category Group named Product Categories. Within that group, you could define individual Data Categories such as Televisions, Speakers, and Modems. By categorizing articles this way, users can easily filter and find knowledge content that is specific to the product they're working with or searching about.

Choose Your Lightning Knowledge Authors
Select from the names below and give your writers permission to drop some knowledge.
You are currently using 2 of 2 available licenses.
Search People...
2 items selected
Full Name
Title
Phone
Email
John Doe
johndoe@fakee...
Mike Wheeler
mike+oreilly@cl...
Back
Next

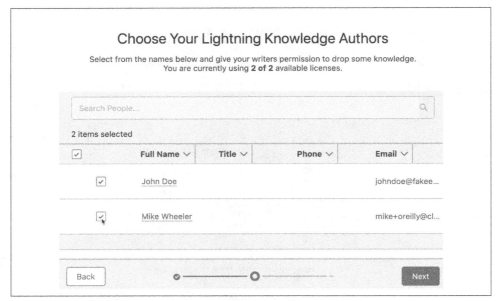

Figure 8-27. Choose Your Lightning Knowledge Authors screen

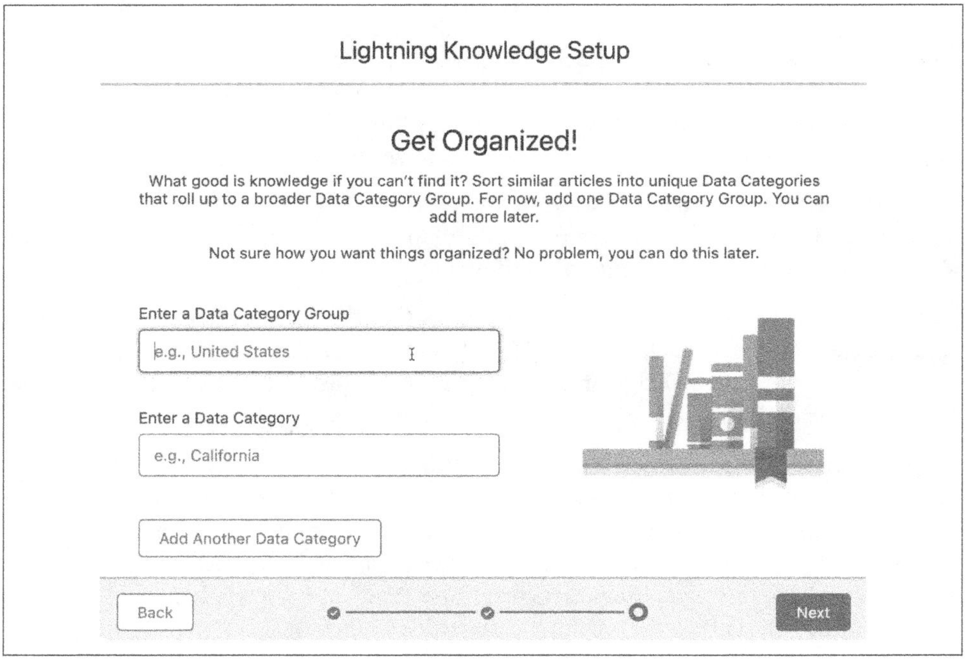

Lightning Knowledge Setup
Get Organized!
What good is knowledge if you can't find it? Sort similar articles into unique Data Categories that roll up to a broader Data Category Group. For now, add one Data Category Group. You can add more later.
Not sure how you want things organized? No problem, you can do this later.
Enter a Data Category Group
e.g., United States
Enter a Data Category
e.g., California
Add Another Data Category
Back
Next

Figure 8-28. Get Organized! Data Category screen

The Data Category Group acts as a broader classification to organize multiple related categories, while individual Data Categories provide a more detailed and targeted way of classifying the Knowledge articles. Together, these categories and groups enhance the user experience by improving search accuracy and allowing users to quickly identify and access the information they need.

After defining your data categories and groups, click next. The Knowledge Setup Wizard updates to display additional options for creating articles or accessing further help topics that provide more detailed setup tips for Lightning Knowledge, as shown in Figure 8-29.

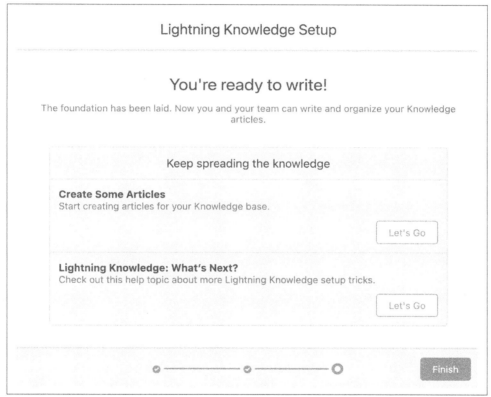

Figure 8-29. Lightning Knowledge Setup Wizard Next Steps screen

Creating record types for Knowledge articles

Record types allow you to categorize articles based on their purpose or audience, making it easier for agents and customers to locate the information they need. For example, you might create separate record types for troubleshooting guides, FAQs, and product documentation. Each record type can have its own page layout, picklist values, and approval process.

To create a record type for Knowledge articles, navigate to Object Manager and select Knowledge. Select Record Types to display any existing Knowledge record types in your org, as shown in Figure 8-30.

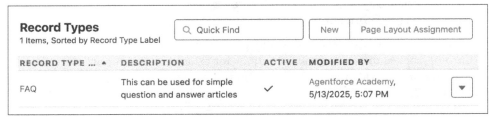

Figure 8-30. Knowledge Record Types screen

From this screen, you can create new record types for Knowledge articles and adjust existing ones as well as revise page layout assignments.

Structuring Knowledge articles

A well-structured article is essential for clarity and usability. Each Knowledge article consists of fields such as Title, Summary, and Content. The Title should be concise and descriptive, making it easy for users to identify the article's purpose. The Summary provides a brief overview of the content, while the Content field contains the detailed information or instructions. Additional fields, such as Keywords, can enhance searchability and ensure articles are easy to find.

When structuring articles, use clear headings, bullet points, and visuals where appropriate. For example, a troubleshooting guide might include step-by-step instructions, screenshots, and links to related articles. Consistent formatting across articles improves the user experience and makes the Knowledge base more professional and effective.

Publishing and Managing Knowledge Articles

Once articles are created, they must be published for use by agents and customers. Salesforce provides workflows and approval processes to ensure articles meet quality standards before they are published.

Knowledge articles begin with a Publication Status of Draft. You will find buttons at the top-right of a Knowledge article to perform various actions for an article, such as Edit, Delete Draft, Publish, and Change Record Type, if enabled, as shown in Figure 8-31.

Figure 8-31. Knowledge article action options, including Publish

Published articles can be assigned to specific audiences, such as internal agents or customers accessing a self-service portal. Using categories, data categories, and visibility settings, you can control who sees which articles, tailoring the experience to the needs of different user groups.

Once Knowledge articles are set up, they can be directly integrated with case management. Agents can search for articles from within the Service and Service Console applications, link them to Cases, and share them with customers. This integration streamlines the resolution process by providing agents with quick access to relevant solutions and allowing them to address customer issues more effectively.

Web-to-Case

Web-to-Case is a Salesforce feature that enables organizations to capture customer inquiries submitted through their website and automatically create Cases in Salesforce. This functionality streamlines the process of collecting, tracking, and managing customer support requests by eliminating the need for manual data entry.

With Web-to-Case, customer issues are routed directly into Salesforce as Cases, where they can be assigned to the appropriate team members and handled using predefined workflows. This ensures that inquiries are addressed consistently and efficiently, helping organizations maintain high standards of customer service.

Enabling Web-to-Case

To enable Web-to-Case, search for and select Web-to-Case from Setup. The Web-to-Case Settings screen displays, as shown in Figure 8-32.

Activate the Web-to-Case functionality if it hasn't already been enabled. This step allows Salesforce to process customer inquiries submitted through your web form. From this screen, you can also set the Default Case Origin and the Default Response Template fields.

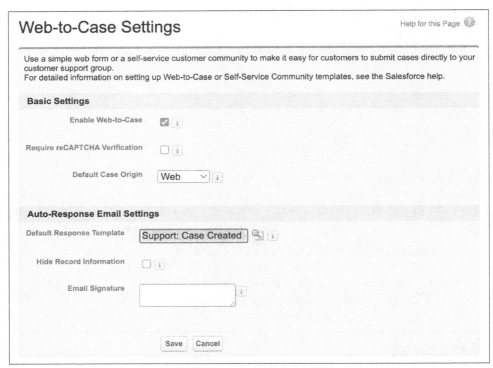

Figure 8-32. Web-to-Case Settings screen

Generating HTML for a Web-to-Case Page

To create a Web-to-Case form to embed on a web page, you will need to generate the HTML code for it. Fortunately, Salesforce provides the Web-to-Case HTML Generator that you can search for and select from Setup. Doing so displays the "Capturing Case Information from Your Website" screen, as shown in Figure 8-33.

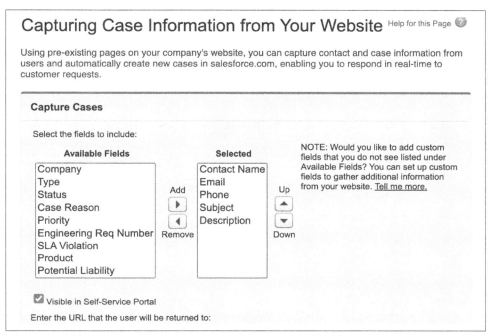

Capturing Case Information from Your Website _{Help for this Page} 🌐

Using pre-existing pages on your company's website, you can capture contact and case information from users and automatically create new cases in salesforce.com, enabling you to respond in real-time to customer requests.

Capture Cases

Select the fields to include:

Available Fields		Selected		NOTE: Would you like to add custom fields that you do not see listed under Available Fields? You can set up custom fields to gather additional information from your website. Tell me more.
Company		Contact Name		
Type		Email		
Status	Add	Phone	Up	
Case Reason	▶	Subject	▲	
Priority	◀	Description	▼	
Engineering Req Number	Remove		Down	
SLA Violation				
Product				
Potential Liability				

☑ Visible in Self-Service Portal

Enter the URL that the user will be returned to:

Figure 8-33. "Capturing Case Information from Your Website" screen

From this screen, you can generate the HTML code for a Web-to-Case form. Customize the form by selecting fields such as Contact Name, Email, Phone, Subject, and Description.

If your organization requires specific information, such as a product serial number or order ID, you can include custom fields in the form. Specify a return URL to direct customers to a confirmation page after submission.

Once your form specifications are complete, click Generate. Salesforce generates the HTML code for your form, as shown in Figure 8-34.

Capture Cases

Copy and paste the sample HTML below and send it to your webmaster.

```
<!--  NOTE: Please add the following <META> element to your page <HEAD>.   -->
<!--  If necessary, please modify the charset parameter to specify the     -->
<!--  character set of your HTML page.                                      -->
<!--  ------------------------------------------------------------------   -->

<META HTTP-EQUIV="Content-type" CONTENT="text/html; charset=UTF-8">

<!--  ------------------------------------------------------------------   -->
<!--  NOTE: Please add the following <FORM> element to your page.          -->
<!--  ------------------------------------------------------------------   -->

<form action="https://webto.salesforce.com/servlet/servlet.WebToCase?encoding=UTF-
8&orgId=00DgK000002Vd8Q" method="POST">

<input type=hidden name="orgid" value="00DgK000002Vd8Q">
<input type=hidden name="retURL" value="https://agentforceacademy.com">
```

Figure 8-34. Generated code for Web-to-Case form

This code can be copied and pasted into your website using a content management system or by collaborating with your website development team. Be sure to validate the placement and design of the form to ensure it aligns with your website's branding and functionality. Any resulting form submissions from your website will route into your Salesforce instance as Cases.

Email-to-Case

Email-to-Case enables organizations to efficiently capture and manage customer inquiries sent via email. When customers reach out through email, their messages are automatically converted into Cases within Salesforce. This seamless integration ensures that support teams can promptly address inquiries, track them systematically, and maintain a comprehensive record of customer interactions.

Unlike Web-to-Case, where inquiries are submitted through a structured web form, Email-to-Case allows for greater flexibility, catering to customers who prefer the convenience of composing an email. This approach accommodates varied communication styles but may require support teams to gather additional details if emails lack structured information. For organizations where email is a primary communication channel, Email-to-Case is an indispensable tool.

Setting Up Email-to-Case

To configure Email-to-Case, start by searching for and selecting Email-to-Case from Setup. The Email-to-Case overview screen displays, as shown in Figure 8-35.

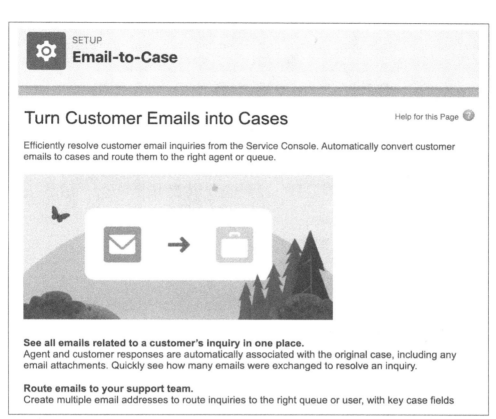

SETUP
Email-to-Case

Turn Customer Emails into Cases

Help for this Page

Efficiently resolve customer email inquiries from the Service Console. Automatically convert customer emails to cases and route them to the right agent or queue.

See all emails related to a customer's inquiry in one place.
Agent and customer responses are automatically associated with the original case, including any email attachments. Quickly see how many emails were exchanged to resolve an inquiry.

Route emails to your support team.
Create multiple email addresses to route inquiries to the right queue or user, with key case fields

Figure 8-35. Email-to-Case overview screen

Click Continue on the overview screen. The Email-to-Case Settings screen will then display. You can enable Email-to-Case by clicking Edit and then checking the Enable Email-to-Case checkbox.

Once you enable Email-to-Case, it cannot be disabled.

Salesforce supports the On-Demand Email-to-Case service, which operates entirely within the cloud. This approach simplifies configuration and avoids the need for additional infrastructure, making it the recommended solution for most organizations.

To complete setup, you will establish the email routing addresses to redirect Case submission to the email services address provided by Salesforce. Locate the Routing

Addresses section at the bottom of the Email-to-Case Settings screen and click New. The Email-to-Case Routing Address Edit screen displays, as shown in Figure 8-36.

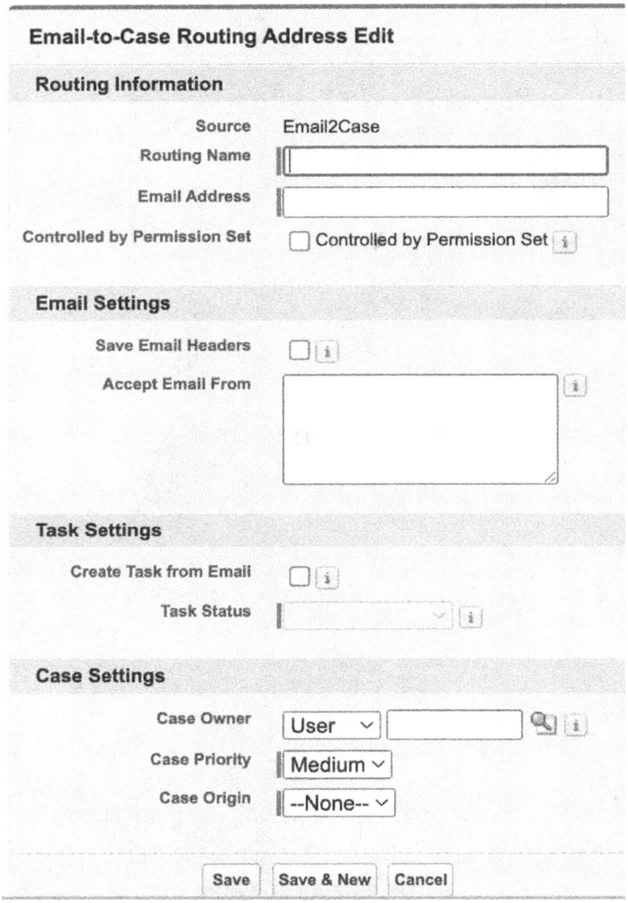

Figure 8-36. Email-to-Case Routing Address Edit screen

For each customer-facing address, Salesforce generates a unique service address. You will then configure your external email client, whether it is Gmail, Outlook, or another provider, to forward emails sent to your customer-facing address to Salesforce's service address. This setup enables Salesforce to capture emails seamlessly and generate Cases without any manual intervention.

Define the default settings for newly created Cases that originate via email. These include specifying the Case Origin as Email, and setting a default Case Priority. Once you have completed the routing address configuration, click Save.

Case Auto-Response Rules

To configure auto-response rules for Email-to-Case, search for and select Case Auto-Response Rules from Setup. The Case Auto-Response Rule Entry screen displays any previously created rules in your org.

You can create a new auto-response rule by clicking New to enter the rule name and mark it as Active via the checkbox. Click Save. Your newly created rule displays in the Rule Entries list. You can then click your rule to further edit it. The Rule Entries screen displays for your new rule. Click the New button in the Rule Entries section of the Rule Detail screen. The Rule Entry Edit screen displays, as shown in Figure 8-37.

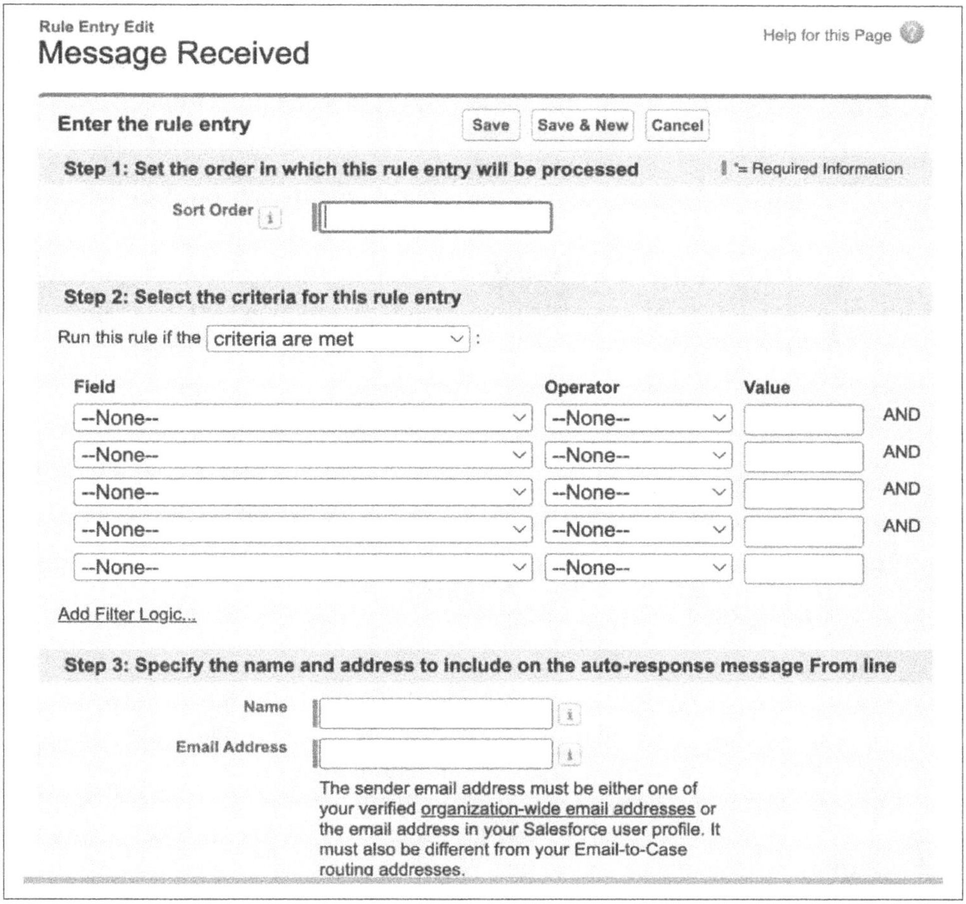

Figure 8-37. Rule Entry Edit screen

The process of creating a rule entry involves several sequential steps to ensure proper configuration. Initially, you must set the order in which the rule will be processed, establishing its priority among other rules.

Define the criteria that this specific rule will evaluate. The next step is to specify the sender's name and address that will appear on the auto-response message. Next, select an appropriate email template that aligns with the purpose of the rule. Additionally, you need to determine whether all recipients in the To and Cc fields should receive copies of the auto-response message.

Testing and Refining Email-to-Case

Thorough testing is essential to ensure that Email-to-Case is configured correctly. Send test emails to verify that Cases are created in Salesforce with the expected attributes, such as origin, status, and priority. Test the integration with routing rules and auto-response rules to ensure that Cases are routed appropriately and acknowledgment emails are sent. Additionally, test the threading feature by replying to an acknowledgment email and confirming that the response is appended to the correct Case.

Periodic review of Email-to-Case settings is recommended. As your organization's needs evolve, you may need to update routing rules, email templates, or custom field mappings to ensure continued alignment with your support processes.

Case Teams

Case teams in Salesforce enable collaboration by bringing together the right people to resolve customer issues efficiently. Whether a Case involves complex troubleshooting, escalations requiring managerial oversight, or input from different departments, case teams provide a structured way to manage roles and responsibilities. By defining specific roles and granting access based on those roles, organizations can ensure that team members have the right permissions to contribute meaningfully to Case resolution.

This feature supports transparency and accountability, making it clear who is involved in a Case and what their responsibilities are. For example, a technical support representative may need full access to edit Case details, while a customer service manager may only require read access to monitor progress. Case teams ensure that such distinctions are enforced consistently, reducing the risk of unauthorized changes and fostering a collaborative environment.

In addition to user access, Salesforce allows the inclusion of external contacts as case team members. While these contacts do not gain functional CRUD rights to the Case, their involvement is captured for documentation purposes. This can be invaluable for maintaining historical records or fulfilling compliance requirements. However, you should carefully consider whether external members' visibility is appropriate in customer portals or communities, as this determines whether their participation is visible to customers.

Salesforce further simplifies the management of case teams through predefined case teams. These are preconfigured groups of users and roles that can be applied to Cases automatically or manually, based on specific criteria. This saves time and ensures that consistent team configurations are applied, particularly for recurring scenarios like high-priority escalations or Cases tied to specific products or services. For instance, a high-priority Case might automatically include a product specialist, a customer service representative, and a support manager as predefined team members.

The ability to add the case team related list to page layouts enhances visibility and accessibility. By including this related list on the Case page layout, users can quickly see who is involved and what roles they hold. This feature streamlines Case collaboration and empowers team members to take ownership of their specific responsibilities.

As organizations scale their customer service operations, the role of case teams becomes even more critical. Ensuring the right people are involved, with the right access levels, is central to delivering exceptional service. By leveraging case teams effectively, businesses can turn even the most complex customer interactions into seamless and well-coordinated resolutions.

Case Team Roles and Predefined Case Teams

A central feature of case teams is the ability to assign roles that dictate each team member's level of access to a Case. Case team roles provide granular control over what team members can view, edit, or manage within the Case. This customization ensures that everyone on the team has the permissions they need to perform their specific tasks while safeguarding the Case data from unauthorized changes.

Case team roles are configured in Salesforce to align with organizational workflows. For example, a Case Manager role might have full access to edit Case fields, update statuses, and close Cases, while a Customer Representative role might be limited to commenting on Cases or updating specific related records. These role-based permissions apply not just to users within the organization but also extend to external contributors added as team members for documentation or compliance purposes.

Predefined case teams enhance the efficiency of this feature by enabling you to create reusable templates of team members and roles. These predefined teams can be automatically applied to Cases based on specific criteria, such as Case type or priority, or they can be manually added as needed. This is particularly useful for recurring scenarios, where the same group of individuals needs to collaborate on similar cases. For instance, a high-priority case involving a product defect might always require a technical lead, a quality assurance manager, and a customer success representative.

Predefined case teams ensure that these roles are consistently assigned, reducing administrative overhead and improving response times.

When configuring predefined case teams, you must consider the roles and access levels as well as how these teams integrate with automated processes. For example, an assignment rule might trigger the addition of a predefined team when a Case is flagged as urgent. This automation ensures that the Case receives immediate attention from the right stakeholders, minimizing delays in resolution.

The visibility of case teams on the Case page is critical for collaboration. By adding the case team related list to the page layout, team members can easily identify who is involved in resolving the Case and what their roles are. This transparency promotes accountability and enables smoother communication, especially in high-stakes scenarios where multiple departments are involved.

A unique aspect of Salesforce's case teams is the inclusion of external contacts as members. While contacts do not have functional CRUD rights, their involvement is recorded for historical and compliance purposes. This practice ensures that all contributors to the Case are documented, providing a clear trail of participation. If your organization is using Digital Experiences (i.e., customer portals or communities), you should review visibility settings carefully to determine whether external members should be visible to end customers.

As roles and predefined configurations become integrated into case workflows, the focus shifts to understanding the impact of these roles on access rights and operational efficiency. Let's explore how case team membership shapes CRUD permissions and what that means for collaborative case management.

Team Access Management and Permissions

Case team membership does more than assign roles; it directly influences the level of access a user has to the Case object. This is governed by CRUD rights defined at the role level. These permissions ensure that each team member's access is appropriate to their responsibilities.

When a user is added to a case team, their access is determined by the case team role assigned to them. For example, a Case Specialist role might have read and update access to modify case details, while a Case Viewer role could be limited to read-only access. This distinction ensures that sensitive case data can be altered only by users with appropriate privileges, while still providing visibility to other stakeholders who need to stay informed.

These role-based permissions intersect with Salesforce's broader sharing model. A team member's ability to perform actions on a case may also depend on their profile permissions or OWDs. For example, if the OWD for Cases is set to private, a user outside the team may have no access to the Case, while a case team member with a role granting read access will be able to view Case details.

In scenarios where collaboration spans departments or external stakeholders, the inclusion of contacts in case teams introduces an important nuance. While contacts do not receive CRUD rights, their inclusion serves as a historical and compliance-focused feature. Documenting external contributors, such as a client's technical lead or a vendor's service representative, provides a comprehensive record of everyone involved in the Case resolution. This practice ensures clarity and avoids gaps in accountability.

A practical example of CRUD rights in action involves an urgent Case escalated to the technical support team. A support agent with update rights assigned through their case team role can modify the Case status and provide updates. Meanwhile, a customer success manager with read-only access can monitor the Case without risk of inadvertently altering details. This balance of access ensures that actions are performed by the right team members while maintaining the integrity of the Case record.

You must also account for visibility settings in customer-facing portals or communities. In these environments, the visibility of case team members can be customized to either expose or hide internal participants. For example, a support agent may be visible to the customer for transparency, while backend contributors, such as a legal advisor, remain hidden to protect sensitive internal operations.

The relationship between case teams, roles, and permissions exemplifies the flexibility of Salesforce's security model. As workflows grow more complex, ensuring proper configuration of these elements becomes critical to maintaining both efficiency and security in case management. From here, I turn to the practical implementation of these concepts, focusing on adding and managing the case team related list in page layouts.

Adding the Case Team Related List to Page Layouts

To add the case team related list to a Case page layout, navigate to the Object Manager and select the Case object. From there, the Enhanced Page Layout Editor allows for customization, enabling the addition of the case team related list. By dragging this related list into the layout, you make it possible for users to immediately view all case team members directly on a Case record.

The case team related list displays the names of the users or contacts, their assigned roles, and the level of access each role grants. This helps users quickly understand each team member's responsibilities and capabilities.

When a case is exposed through a customer portal or community, the case team related list's visibility settings determine whether portal users can view team members. Enabling visibility for external members, such as customer-facing agents, fosters transparency and builds trust. You must weigh these benefits against the need for confidentiality regarding internal contributors.

Parent-Child Cases

Parent-child cases in Salesforce offer a practical solution for managing complex issues that involve multiple, related problems. Cases can be linked together, establishing a hierarchical relationship between a primary, or parent, case and its associated child cases. This allows teams to track and manage interconnected issues while maintaining clear oversight of the broader resolution process.

You can enable parent-child case relationships in the Case Settings within Salesforce Setup. Once it's activated, you can associate child cases with a parent case by linking them in the case hierarchy or by using the Parent Case field on the Case record. This relationship is visually represented in the case hierarchy view, providing a clear, at-a-glance representation of how cases are connected.

This structure improves reporting and accountability by consolidating data from all related cases under the Parent Case. Parent-child cases also play a critical role in customer communication. Updates to the Parent Case can be used to inform customers about the overall progress, while internal teams continue working on child cases, without overwhelming customers with unnecessary details. This distinction between internal workflows and customer-facing updates ensures transparency and clarity.

Another practical application of parent-child cases involves recurring issues that require consistent resolution across multiple stakeholders. For example, a manufacturing defect might generate a parent case documenting the overall issue, with child cases created for each affected customer. By linking these cases, teams can track progress and ensure consistent handling across all impacted parties.

Summary

In this chapter, you've explored Salesforce's Service and Support applications, learning how organizations effectively manage customer support processes. You delved into the lifecycle and functionality of Cases, including setting up and customizing case statuses and Support Processes. Features such as case assignment rules and case escalation rules were detailed, emphasizing their role in automating the routing and timely resolution of customer inquiries.

Additionally, you learned to configure key self-service tools like Web-to-Case and Email-to-Case, enabling efficient capture and handling of customer requests. Salesforce Knowledge was also introduced, demonstrating how to create, structure, and integrate Knowledge articles to empower customers with self-service resources and enhance agent productivity.

You gained practical insights into configuring the Salesforce Service Console. The chapter also highlighted essential collaboration features like case teams, allowing you to manage team roles, permissions, and effectively coordinate efforts on customer cases.

Now, it's time to assess your understanding of these essential service and support concepts through the quiz below.

Chapter 8 Quiz

As you finish Chapter 8, it's time to test your understanding of key concepts related to Service and Support applications in Salesforce. This chapter focused on critical features such as case teams, case queues, Knowledge articles, and parent-child cases for case management. This quiz is designed to ensure you're well-prepared for nuanced questions you may encounter on the Salesforce Certified Platform Administrator exam.

Each question offers an opportunity to review and reinforce your grasp of essential topics. After making your choices, carefully read through the answers and explanations in the Appendix to solidify your understanding. This exercise will highlight areas for review and deepen your confidence in applying these concepts in both exam and real-world scenarios.

1. Which Salesforce feature allows multiple team members to collaborate on a case while defining their roles and access levels?

    a. Parent-child cases

    b. Case queues

    c. Case teams

    d. Experience Cloud

2. Which Salesforce feature provides a hierarchical view of related cases to manage complex issues?

    a. Parent-child cases

    b. Case queues

    c. Case teams

    d. Experience Cloud

3. Which of the following is *not* a benefit of using parent-child cases?

   a. Enabling roll-up reporting for related cases

   b. Establishing a clear hierarchy for linked cases

   c. Automating case assignment to team members

   d. Tracking resolution times across related cases

4. What is the primary use of case escalation rules in Salesforce?

   a. Automatically assigning new cases to users or queues

   b. Escalating unresolved cases based on predefined time criteria

   c. Allowing customers to create cases from the web

   d. Defining the roles of team members working on a case

5. What is the main purpose of Salesforce Knowledge in customer support?

   a. Managing customer contacts and Opportunities

   b. Tracking customer service agreements

   c. Assigning cases automatically to support agents

   d. Providing articles to help resolve customer inquiries quickly

6. When configuring Web-to-Case in Salesforce, what is required to generate cases automatically from your website?

   a. An HTML form generated in Salesforce Setup

   b. JavaScript code created by a developer

   c. Custom-built API integration

   d. External email client configuration

7. Which Salesforce feature can be used to automatically send acknowledgment emails to customers when a new case is submitted?

   a. Case escalation rules

   b. Case auto-response rules

   c. Case assignment rules

   d. Web-to-Case

8. How can Salesforce users create and manage multiple cases related to one primary customer issue?

   a. Parent-child cases

   b. Case queues

   c. Case teams

   d. Escalation rules

9. Which feature would you use to assign incoming cases to specific queues or agents automatically?

   a. Email-to-Case

   b. Case assignment rules

   c. Escalation rules

   d. Auto-response rules

10. Which Salesforce feature helps ensure support cases are addressed within defined time frames?

    a. Case assignment rules

    b. Web-to-Case

    c. Escalation rules

    d. Campaign Influence

Productivity and Collaboration

The Productivity and Collaboration knowledge area of the exam spans a wide variety of topics. This variety of coverage is reflected in the disparate topics found in the Salesforce Certified Platform Administrator Exam Guide.

From the Exam Guide

The Productivity and Collaboration knowledge area consists of four learning objectives:

- Describe the capabilities of activity management
- Describe the features of Chatter
- Describe the capabilities of the Salesforce mobile app
- Identify use cases for AppExchange applications

Here you will learn all about enhancing team collaboration and individual efficiency. I will begin by introducing you to the inner workings of activity management, which is a powerful, productivity enhancing feature set of Salesforce. You will next learn how to facilitate team collaboration in Salesforce via Chatter.

You will then learn the capabilities of the Salesforce mobile app. Finally, I will walk you through the use cases for applications available to be installed in your own org via AppExchange, the Salesforce app store.

And as in previous chapters, you can test your knowledge with a quiz as you conclude. Now it's time for you to begin your Productivity and Collaboration learning journey with activity management.

Activity Management

Activity management in Salesforce is an important mechanism for tracking the activities of sales and service representatives. The end goal is to be able to measure and associate positive outcomes with the various activities that contributed to the successful closure of an Opportunity or successful resolution of a Case, for example.

The primary activities that can be created and measured or reported on in Salesforce are tasks, events, and emails. Some would argue that logged phone calls would be a fourth type of activity. Although there is a dedicated button in the interface to log a call, in actuality a logged call is simply a subtype of a task.

I will begin by exploring activity management in the user interface, along with the Activity Timeline. Once you are familiar with how to access activity management, I will address tasks in their various forms, followed by events and emails.

Accessing Activity Management in the User Interface

To access activity management in Salesforce, navigate to any record detail page, such as an account, contact, or Opportunity. In the record detail view, you will find the Activity tab, usually located next to the Chatter tab, as shown in Figure 9-1.

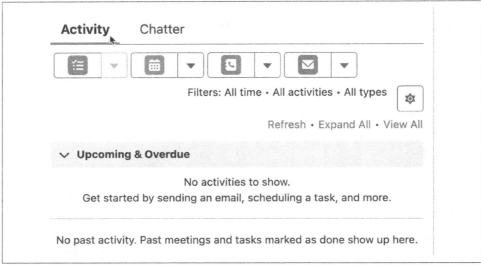

Figure 9-1. Activity tab on a record detail page displaying the Activity Timeline

The Activity tab contains action icons for creating tasks, scheduling events, logging calls, and sending emails. The Activity Timeline appears beneath the action buttons and displays any upcoming and overdue activities along with any past activities related to the record you are displaying.

Task Management in Salesforce

In Salesforce, a task is a to-do item or an action that needs to be completed and serves as a practical reminder to ensure important activities are not overlooked. Tasks can be assigned to yourself or others, and linked to specific records such as accounts, contacts, Opportunities, or Cases. This linkage helps maintain context and relevance, making it easier to keep track of related activities. Tasks include important details such as due dates, priorities, and statuses, which aid in effective time management and accountability.

Tasks in Salesforce are versatile and can be used to remind users of both online and offline activities. For example, tasks can serve as reminders to mail a letter, follow up with a client by phone, or prepare a physical contract for a signature. By setting these reminders, users can ensure that important offline activities are associated with specific records and completed on time.

Creating a new task

To create a new task, click the New Task button from the Activity tab on a record detail page. The New Task window displays, as shown in Figure 9-2.

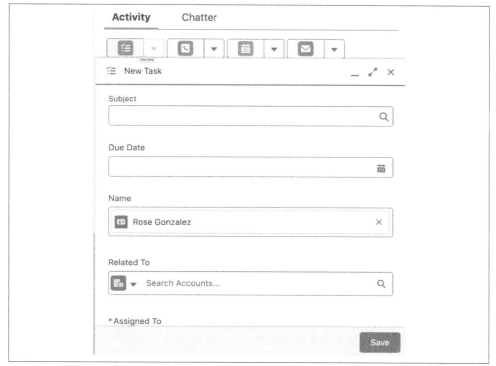

Figure 9-2. New Task window launched via the New Task button

The New Task window is where you can enter the details of the task. You can type in a Subject for the task or click in the field to select one of the prepopulated options. The Related To field denotes which record this task is related to. It automatically populates with the record from which the New Task button was clicked. The Assigned To field defaults to the current user and denotes whom you are assigning the task to.

You can change the Related To and/or the Assigned To automatic designations by clicking the "x" in either of these fields and entering any necessary changes.

Expanding the New Task window

You can expand the New Task window by clicking the maximize icon located at the top-right of the window (see Figure 9-3).

Figure 9-3. New Task window maximize icon

When you maximize the New Task window, it expands to reveal all of the fields, as shown in Figure 9-4.

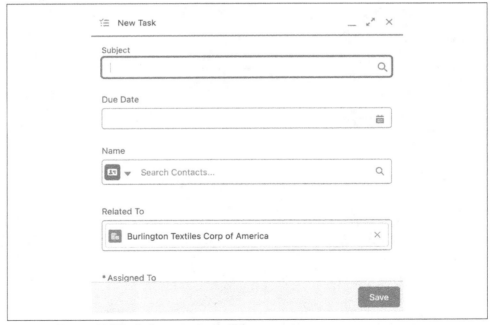

Figure 9-4. New Task window maximized

The Status of the task can be selected from the drop-down menu. Options include Not Started, In Progress, Deferred, and Completed.

Once you have completed entering the details of the new task, click Save. The New Task window closes and you are returned to the record detail page. You will find your newly created task located in the Activity Timeline under the Upcoming & Overdue section, as shown in Figure 9-5.

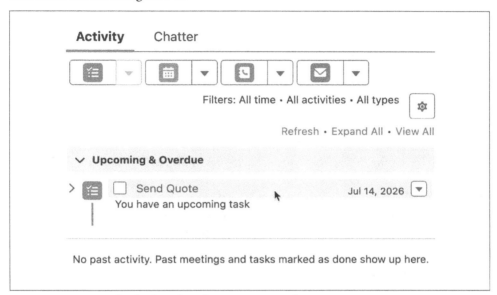

Figure 9-5. New tasks displayed in the Activity Timeline

Activity Timeline

The Activity Timeline provides a comprehensive view of all past and upcoming activities related to a specific record. This timeline is divided into two main sections: Upcoming & Overdue and Past Activities (see Figure 9-6):

Upcoming & Overdue
    This section displays tasks, events, and calls that are scheduled for the future or are past their due date but have not yet been completed. Each entry includes key details such as the subject, due date, and status, allowing users to quickly see what actions are pending and prioritize their workload.

Past activities
    This section lists all completed tasks, past events, and logged calls. It provides a historical record of interactions and activities, which can be useful for tracking progress and maintaining context around customer engagements. Each activity entry includes the date, subject, and any relevant notes or details.

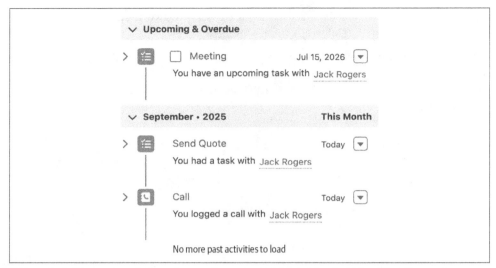

Figure 9-6. Upcoming & Overdue and past activities in the Activity Timeline

Completing a task

When you've finished the action associated with a task, you can mark it as complete by checking the checkbox next to it. This changes the status of the task to Completed.

To do this, open the task and change its status to Completed. You can also add any final comments or details about the completed action.

Once a task is marked as complete, it moves from the Open Activities related list to the Activity History related list on the associated record. This transition helps maintain a clear record of completed actions while keeping your active task list manageable.

Where else do tasks appear in Salesforce?

Tasks appear in several other locations within Salesforce in addition to the Activity Timeline and Activity Related lists. Those additional access points include task list views, home pages, and Salesforce mobile app:

Accessing tasks through list views
> You can access a list of all your tasks by navigating to the Tasks tab, if available in a specific application, or via the App Launcher. Select the Tasks tab to display the Recently Viewed list view for tasks, as shown in Figure 9-7.

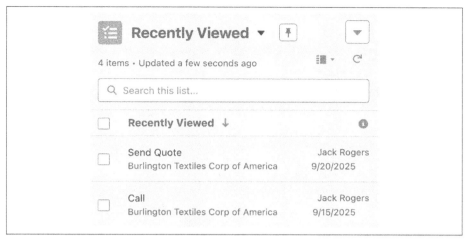

Figure 9-7. Recently Viewed tasks related list

Here, you can create custom list views to sort and filter tasks based on various criteria.

Accessing tasks from home pages

Depending on your org's setup, you might see a task component on your Salesforce home page, displaying your upcoming tasks.

Accessing tasks from the Salesforce mobile app

Tasks are accessible through the mobile app, allowing you to manage your to-do list on the go. Refer to "Salesforce Mobile App" on page 313 for more on mobile task management.

Logging Calls

As I mentioned earlier in this chapter, a logged call is a type of task. There is a "Log a Call" button in the interface that, when clicked, opens the New Task window with the subject of Call already selected. While you could log a call by selecting to create a new task and then selecting Call as the subject, it is quicker to click Log a Call.

You can enter your notes related to the call and click Save. The logged call then appears as a completed task in your Activity Timeline.

Enabling Activity Related Lists

As an alternative to the centralized view of the Activity Timeline, you can display the upcoming and past activities as Activity Related Lists.

To provide a different view of activities for all users in your org, you can enable Activity Related Lists on your Salesforce records, which displays Upcoming & Overdue and past activities as separate lists instead of using the Activity Timeline.

To enable Activity Related Lists, search for and select Record Page Settings in Setup. The Record Page Settings screen displays.

Scroll down until you locate the "Default Activities View (desktop only)" section, as shown in Figure 9-8.

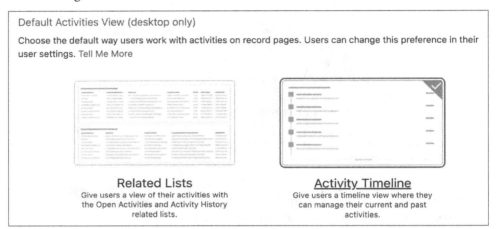

Figure 9-8. Default Activities View for Related Lists or Activity Timeline

This setting is for desktop use only.

Once you are in the Default Activities View settings, you can enable the option to switch from the Activity Timeline to Activity Related Lists. By enabling this setting, the Activity Timeline will no longer display on your records. Instead, you will see two separate related lists: Open Activities and Activity History (see Figure 9-9).

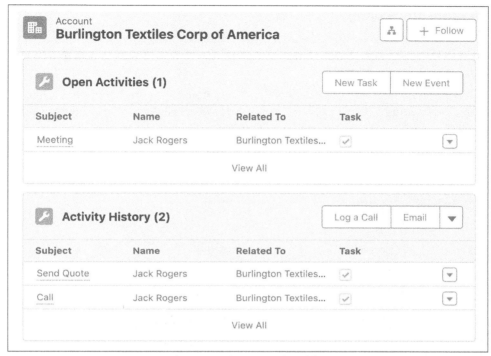

Figure 9-9. Open Activities and Activity History related lists

Open Activities related list.   The Open Activities related list displays tasks and events that are scheduled for the future or are past their due date but not yet completed.

Activity History related list.   The Activity History related list displays all completed tasks, past events, and logged calls.

Users can interact with these lists by clicking on individual entries to view or edit details, similar to how they would with the Activity Timeline.

Enabling Activity Related Lists provides a different way to manage and view activities, allowing users to choose the format that best fits their workflow and preferences. This setup can be particularly useful for those who prefer a clear separation between upcoming and past activities.

 You can always change the default display behavior of activities back to the Activity Timeline by returning to the Record Page Settings menu inside Setup.

Creating and Managing Events

Events in Salesforce are time-based activities, such as meetings, phone calls, or any other scheduled engagement. They help you keep track of important appointments and commitments.

To create an event, you can click the New Event icon in the Activity tab of a record, similar to creating a task. The New Event window displays, as shown in Figure 9-10.

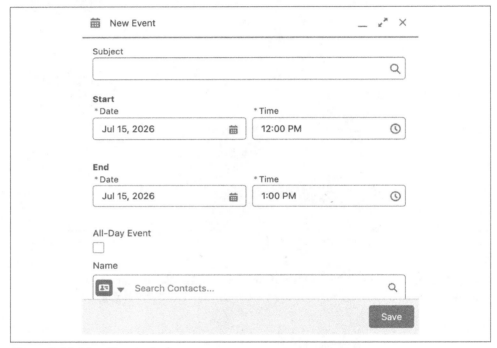

Figure 9-10. New Event window

The New Event window allows you to enter or select the event's Subject, Start and End times, location, and attendees. You can also link the event to relevant records and add a description or notes.

Events can be recurring, enabling you to set up regular meetings or check-ins without creating multiple individual events. You can specify the frequency (daily, weekly, monthly, etc.) and set an end date for the recurring series.

Once created, events appear in your Salesforce calendar, the Activity Timeline of related records, and potentially on your home page, depending on your org's configuration. They're also visible and manageable through the Salesforce mobile app, enabling on-the-go schedule management.

Sending Emails from Salesforce

Salesforce enables you to send emails directly from within the platform. This ensures all communication is captured and associated with the relevant records, maintaining a comprehensive history of interactions.

To send an email from Salesforce, click the email button found in the Activity tab of a record, as shown in Figure 9-11.

Figure 9-11. Email button

This opens an email composition window where you can craft your message, add attachments, and select recipients. The email will automatically be linked to the record you're working from, but you can also manually relate it to other records if needed.

Salesforce offers email templates, which can significantly boost your efficiency by providing preformatted messages for common scenarios. You can create and manage these templates, personalizing them with merge fields that automatically pull in relevant data from Salesforce records.

When you send an email through Salesforce, it's logged as an activity on the related records. This logging ensures that all team members with access to the record can see the communication history, promoting transparency and collaboration.

Email logs

Email logs in Salesforce record all emails sent through the platform for your organization. These logs help identify the status of email deliveries and provide information about your org's email communications.

To access email logs, go to Setup and search for "email log files" in the Quick Find box. Click on the result to see a list of available log files. These are CSV files containing details about your organization's emails.

Each log file includes:

- Email addresses of senders and recipients
- Date and time each email was sent
- Error codes associated with each email

Logs are available for the past 30 days. Regularly reviewing these logs allows you to audit and troubleshoot email communications as needed. When investigating email-related issues, these logs can confirm if an email was sent and show any delivery problems. Error codes in the logs help you understand why an email wasn't delivered successfully, which can help maintain accurate contact lists.

By using these email logs, you can monitor your organization's email communications and address any issues that arise. This contributes to maintaining an effective Salesforce org and supports your team's email operations.

Email deliverability

The email Deliverability settings in Salesforce enable you to configure options that affect your organization's email deliverability. To access these settings, go to Setup and search for "Deliverability" in the Quick Find box. The Deliverability screen displays.

By configuring these settings appropriately, you can enhance your email deliverability and maintain compliance with your organization's email policies. Regular review of these settings helps address any delivery issues that may arise over time.

The Deliverability screen enables you to do the following:

Control who sends emails from Salesforce
You can control who can send emails from Salesforce by selecting one of the following three options from the "Access to Send Email (All Email Services)" drop-down menu. You have three options:

No access
Prevents sending email

System email only
Allows only system-generated emails

All email
Permits sending all types of email

The "System email only" setting is particularly useful for controlling emails sent from sandboxes, preventing test emails from reaching real users during development and testing phases.

Set email bounce management
When activated, bounce management prevents users from sending emails to invalid addresses. If an email bounces, Salesforce blocks further attempts to that address until it's validated. You can also choose to return bounced emails to the sender.

Enable email security compliance

Enabling compliance with standard email security mechanisms improves email deliverability to recipients using email security and authentication tools.

Set Transport Layer Security (TLS)

TLS settings configure encryption for outbound emails. TLS is a security protocol designed to provide communication privacy and data integrity between two communicating applications. In Salesforce, TLS ensures that emails sent from the platform are securely transmitted to the recipient's email server, protecting sensitive information during transit.

The TLS configuration options include:

Preferred

Attempts TLS connection, but sends unencrypted if unavailable

Required

Only sends if TLS connection is established

Preferred Verify

Attempts TLS connection with domain verification

Required Verify

Only sends with verified TLS connection

You can also restrict TLS to specific domains if needed.

Verify ownership of email-sending domains

This option enables you to verify the ownership of email-sending domains using DomainKeys Identified Mail (DKIM). DKIM is an email authentication method designed to detect forged sender addresses in emails, a technique often used in phishing and email spam. With DKIM, the receiver can check that an email claiming to have come from a specific domain was indeed authorized by the owner of that domain.

Salesforce Calendars

Salesforce Calendars provide a visual representation of your schedule, including both events and tasks with due dates. You can view your calendar by day, week, or month, and even overlay it with other users' calendars (if you have the necessary permissions) to facilitate scheduling.

The calendar in Salesforce is deeply integrated with the rest of the platform, allowing you to create records, log calls, or complete tasks directly from calendar entries. This integration streamlines your workflow, letting you manage your activities without navigating away from your schedule view.

You can also create calendar views based on standard or custom objects in Salesforce. For example, you might create a calendar showing upcoming contract renewal dates or project milestones. These object-specific calendars provide valuable visualizations of your data, helping you stay on top of important dates and deadlines.

Chatter for Collaboration

Chatter is a corporate network that enables users to collaborate, communicate, and share information in real time. Enabling Chatter can enhance productivity by fostering a collaborative environment where team members can share updates, ask questions, and work on projects.

To enable Chatter in your Salesforce organization, search for Chatter Settings in the Setup Quick Find box. Select the Chatter Settings menu option to display the Chatter Settings screen, as shown in Figure 9-12.

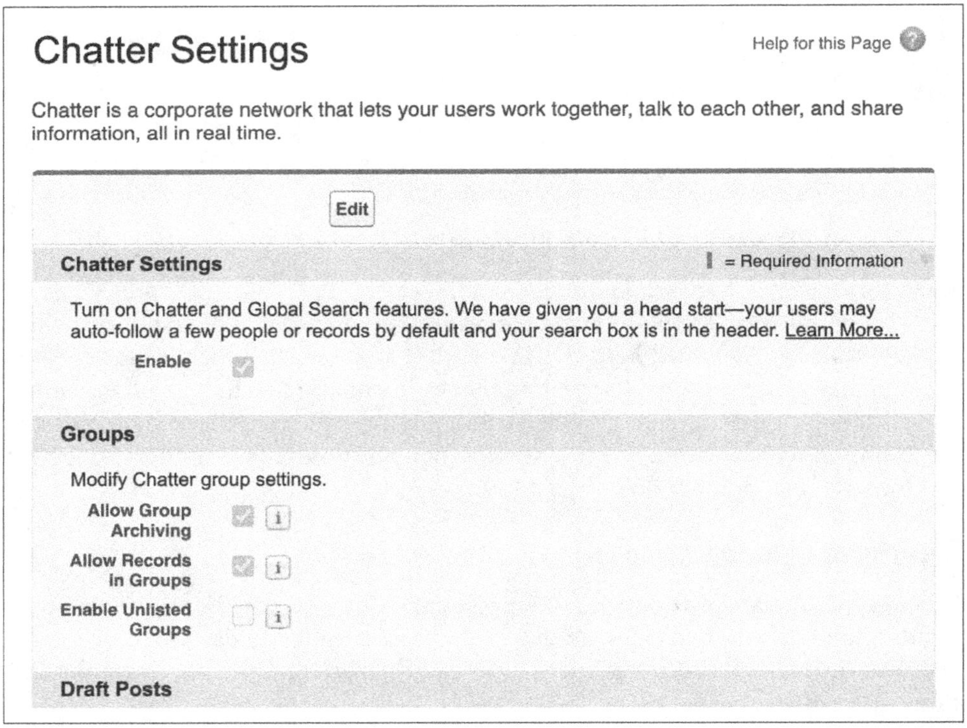

Figure 9-12. Chatter Settings screen

Chatter is enabled by default in both the free Trailhead and Developer learner accounts from Salesforce. You can check or uncheck the Enable checkbox on the Chatter Settings screen to enable or disable Chatter in your organization.

The usability of Chatter is similar in nature to the social network X (formerly Twitter). Chatter enables you to follow any record in your Salesforce instance—not just people. You will find Follow buttons on record detail pages. Once you click to follow a record, the button changes to display Following. You can simply click it again to unfollow the record.

Launching the Salesforce Chatter App

Updates to records you follow are accessible from the Chatter app in Salesforce, which you can launch from the App Launcher.

Once you launch Salesforce Chatter, the Chatter home page displays. To access updates on records you follow and to see company highlights, click the Chatter tab in the Salesforce Chatter app.

Any recent posts or important updates made to records that you follow in Chatter will appear in the What I Follow feed, as shown in Figure 9-13. You can sort by Most Recent Activity or Latest Posts, or use "Search this feed" to find a specific post.

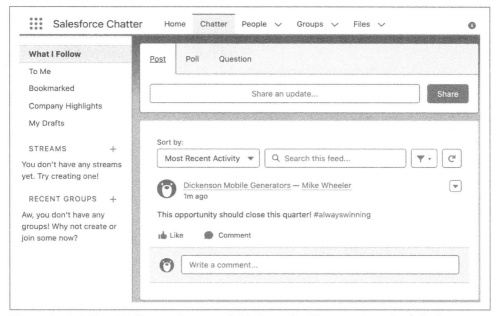

Figure 9-13. What I Follow updates available from the Chatter tab in the Salesforce Chatter app

Additional links along the left will display any Chatter posts made to you, Chatter posts you have previously bookmarked, Company Highlights, and draft posts that you have yet to publish.

Bookmarking Chatter Posts

You can bookmark any Chatter post for later reference by clicking the down arrow located at the upper-right corner of the post and selecting Bookmark. Once you have bookmarked a post, it is accessible from the Bookmarked link on the left.

You can receive alerts whenever any important updates or conversations are happening in a Salesforce record. You can also @mention other users to alert them and, in essence, bring them into a conversation related to a record.

Chatter also supports hashtags, which are called *topics* in Salesforce. You can use topics as a means of categorization for the various conversations underway in Chatter. Any topic is then accessible to users to explore and peruse.

As a Chatter user, you can bookmark your favorite chats for later reference. And you can create custom streams that can consist of updates, topics, and more.

Automatically following records you create

In Chatter settings, you can choose to automatically follow records you create. Navigate to Setup, then search for and select "chatter settings" in the Quick Find box. Within the Email Notifications section, enable Automatically Follow Records I Create to ensure that any new records you create are automatically followed, keeping you updated on any changes or activities related to those records via email notifications.

Salesforce sets a limit on the number of records and users you can follow, with a default cap of 500. If necessary, you can increase this limit by logging a case with Salesforce support. To request an increase, navigate to the Help & Training section in Salesforce and follow the prompts to create a new case, specifying the need for an increased follow limit.

By optimizing your Chatter email notifications and following settings, you can stay informed and connected within your Salesforce environment, ensuring efficient collaboration and timely updates.

Managing what content appears in your feeds is essential for maintaining relevance in your notifications. Go to Settings, select My Feeds, and customize your preferences. These settings allow you to specify which types of records and activities you wish to follow, ensuring your feed is tailored to your needs.

Chatter groups

Chatter groups enable teams to collaborate more effectively by creating dedicated spaces for discussion, project coordination, and information sharing. These groups can be used for a variety of purposes, including project management, departmental collaboration, or even social interactions within the organization.

To create a Chatter group, navigate to the Chatter tab in Salesforce. Click on the Groups subtab and then click New. You will be prompted to enter details such as the group name, description, and the type of group you want to create.

Salesforce offers three types of Chatter groups:

- Public
- Private
- Unlisted

Public groups are visible to all users in the organization, and anyone can join. Private groups require an invitation to join, and a private group's discussions are visible only to members. Unlisted groups are similar to private groups, but the groups' names and details are not visible in group searches or lists.

Once the group is created, you can customize its settings to suit the needs of your team. This includes adding a group photo, setting up email notifications for group activity, and managing membership. You can invite users to join the group by sending them an invitation directly through the group page or by sharing the group link.

Chatter groups also support a variety of collaboration features. Members can post updates, share files, and create polls to gather input from the group. Additionally, you can use @mentions to draw specific members' attention to a post, ensuring that important updates are seen by the right people.

Users have additional actions such as inviting members, managing group settings, and creating events. These actions help manage group activities and ensure that the right members are engaged and informed.

Using Chatter groups effectively can streamline communication and improve collaboration within your organization. By creating focused spaces for discussion and project management, Chatter groups help keep everyone on the same page and foster a more connected and efficient working environment.

Chatter streams

Chatter streams allow users to consolidate updates from multiple Chatter feeds into a single, customizable stream. This enables users to stay informed about the most relevant information without navigating through numerous individual feeds.

To create a Chatter stream, navigate to the Chatter tab in Salesforce and click the "+" icon next to Streams in the left-hand sidebar. Select New Stream. The New Stream window displays, as shown in Figure 9-14.

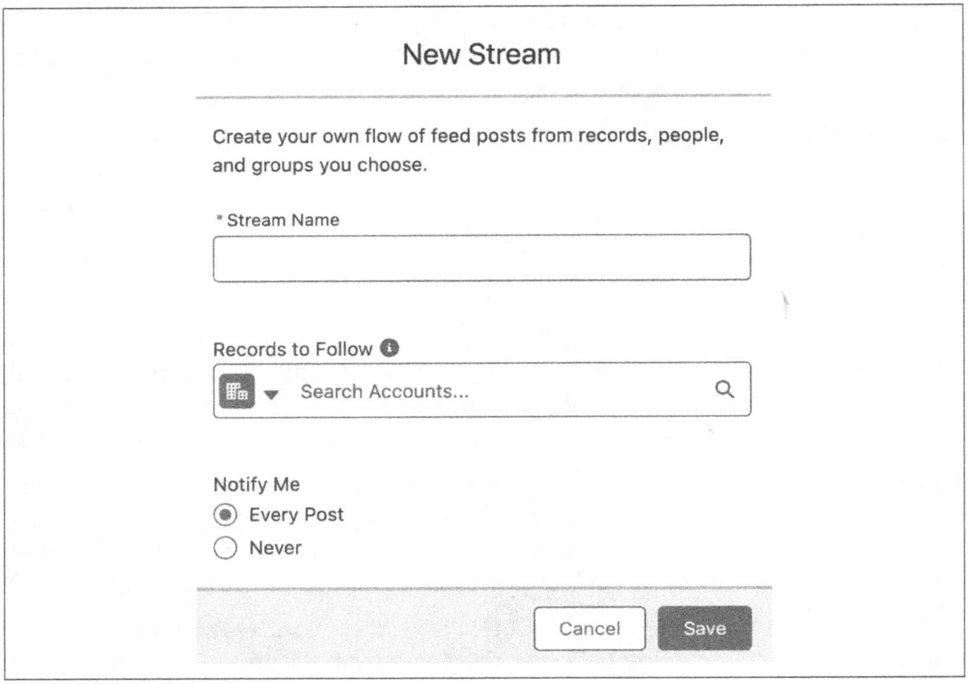

Figure 9-14. New Stream window

Enter the Stream Name and select which type of records you wish to follow in this stream. You can customize notification settings for each stream, choosing to receive alerts to ensure you're always aware of important updates.

Once you complete setting up your Chatter stream, click Save. The new Chatter stream displays any recent updates that fit the criteria you specified.

You can tailor a Chatter stream to focus on specific projects, departments, or areas of interest. For example, you might create a stream that consolidates updates from all groups and records related to a major project or one that includes posts from key executives and company announcements.

Using Chatter streams can enhance productivity. Users can create and manage their own Chatter streams tailored to their specific needs and roles within an organization.

Enabling Chatter Feed Tracking

Chatter Feed Tracking provides a way to stay updated on changes and activities within Salesforce. By enabling feed tracking, you can receive real-time updates about specific records, fields, and objects, making it easier to monitor key changes and collaborate effectively.

Feed tracking is useful for recording changes to fields. When changes are made to tracked fields, they appear as updates in the Chatter feed, allowing you to see what has changed and when. This is particularly beneficial if you have previously set up Field History Tracking on an object. While Field History Tracking allows you to monitor changes on up to 20 fields, enabling Chatter Feed Tracking gives you the ability to track changes on an additional 20 fields, effectively doubling your tracking capacity.

To set up Chatter Feed Tracking, search for and select Feed Tracking from the Quick Find box in Setup. The Feed Tracking screen displays, as shown in Figure 9-15.

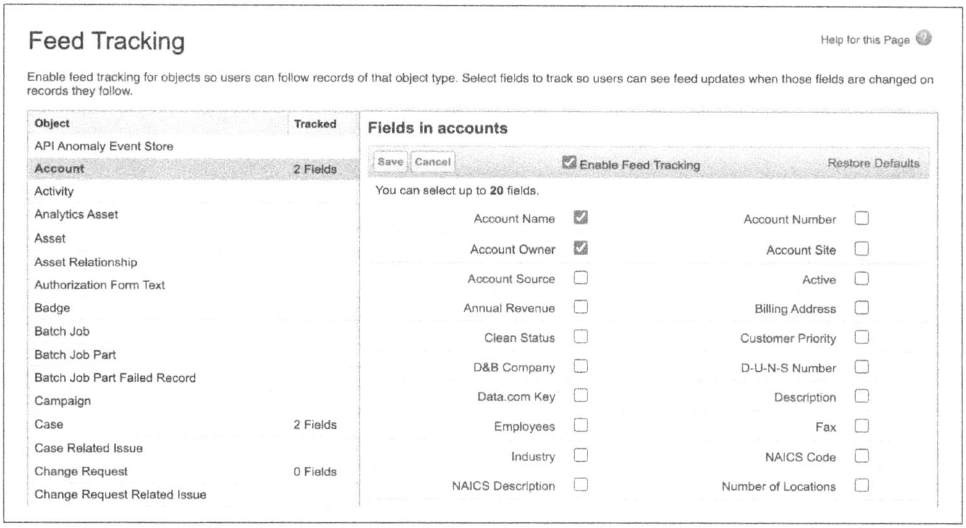

Figure 9-15. Chatter Feed Tracking screen

Choose the object for which you want to enable feed tracking. You will see a list of standard and custom objects available in your Salesforce instance. Check the box to enable feed tracking for the selected object. You can then select the specific fields you want to track.

Remember, you can select up to 20 fields per object for feed tracking. After choosing the fields to track, click Save to apply the changes.

Once feed tracking is enabled and configured, any changes to the tracked fields will appear as updates in the Chatter feed for the relevant records. These updates include information about what was changed, the previous value, the new value, and the user who made the change. This makes it easy to stay informed about important changes and facilitates better collaboration and communication within your team.

In the Chatter feed, tracked changes are displayed in a clear and organized manner, ensuring that you can quickly access and review the information you need (see Figure 9-16).

Figure 9-16. Chatter feed displaying Account Owner change

This visibility helps team members stay aligned and aware of key updates, enhancing overall productivity and transparency.

Salesforce Mobile App

The Exam Guide states that you will need to be able to describe the capabilities of the Salesforce mobile app. There is no better way to get familiar with those capabilities than to download it onto a mobile device of your own. This will enable you to get hands on with the Salesforce mobile app.

Downloading and Installing the Salesforce Mobile App

The Salesforce mobile app is available on the App Store for iOS devices, as well as on Google Play for Android devices. Simply search for "Salesforce" in your device's app store and look for the official Salesforce app.

Logging In to the Salesforce Mobile App

Once you've downloaded the Salesforce app, open it on your mobile device. You will be prompted to log in with your Salesforce credentials. Enter your username and password and tap Log In. The Mobile Welcome screen displays.

Mobile Welcome Screen

The Salesforce Mobile Welcome screen is your starting point when first logging into the Salesforce mobile app. You can return to this screen by tapping the Welcome icon located at the lower-left of the screen.

Notice the additional links along the bottom of the mobile interface, which enable you to install a package as well as get your login details.

You will also find the mobile navigation menu accessible via the Menu icon located at the bottom-right of the screen. Tapping Menu displays the Salesforce Mobile Navigation Menu.

Salesforce Mobile Navigation Menu

The Salesforce Mobile Navigation Menu provides access to the App Launcher, All Items, and the various tabs available to you in the mobile interface, as shown in Figure 9-17.

You can tap on any of these items to go to the home screen for that item. You will also find dedicated tabs along the bottom of the screen for Chatter, Today, Dashboards, and Tasks, in addition to the Menu icon.

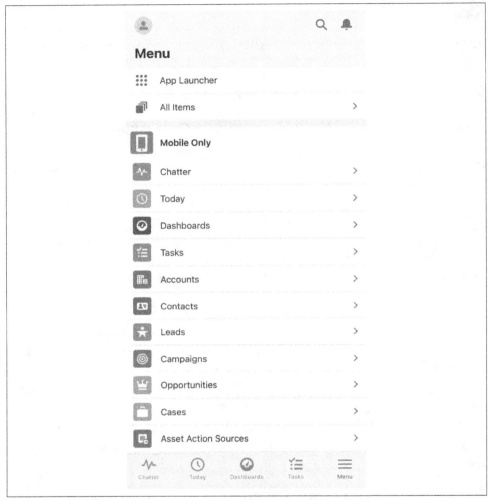

Figure 9-17. Mobile app navigation menu

Chatter in Mobile

Tapping the Chatter button at the bottom of the screen opens the Chatter app on your mobile device. The Chatter home page displays, as shown in Figure 9-18.

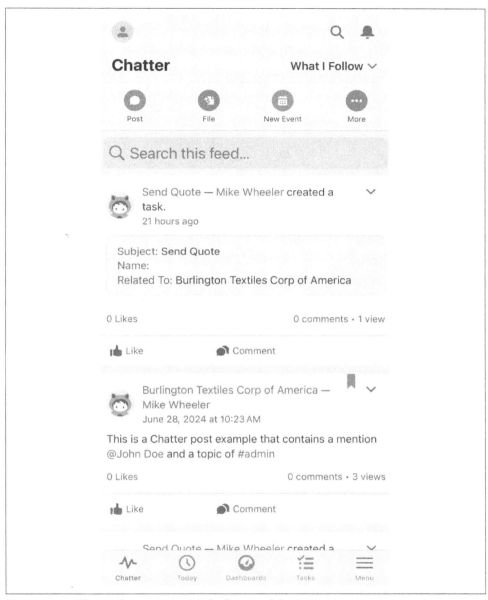

Figure 9-18. Chatter home page in Salesforce mobile app

The Chatter home page displays any updates on items that you follow. You can search this feed as well as perform various Chatter functions via the icons at the top of the screen for creating a new post, sharing a file, creating a new event, and more.

Today Page in the Salesforce Mobile App

The Today page automatically curates your most important data for you. When you first access it, you may receive a notice that access to your calendars is turned off, along with instructions on how to enable calendar access on your mobile device.

Salesforce Mobile Home Page

The home page eventually updates in the mobile app with a series of autogenerated cards that you may find useful, as shown in Figure 9-19.

Select Yes or No to signify whether you find cards useful. These cards will then display whenever you tap the Home icon at the bottom of the mobile app screen.

The mobile app's navigation is designed to be intuitive and efficient. The home page typically shows your most important information at a glance, such as upcoming tasks or key performance metrics.

The Recent section gives you quick access to records you've recently viewed or edited. The search function allows you to find any record in your Salesforce org quickly. The More menu provides access to all available objects and apps, mirroring the functionality of the App Launcher in the desktop version of Salesforce.

You can customize the mobile navigation to prioritize the items most important to you. This customization ensures that you can quickly access the data and functions you use most frequently, maximizing your productivity when working on mobile.

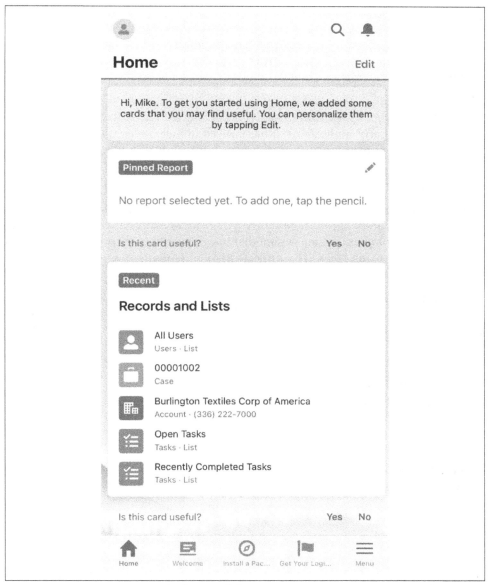

Figure 9-19. Home page in Salesforce mobile app

AppExchange

The Exam Guide specifically mentions that you will need to "identify use cases for AppExchange applications." This learning objective tests your ability to recognize scenarios where leveraging prebuilt solutions can be more efficient than custom development.

AppExchange (*http://appexchange.salesforce.com*) started primarily as a place to find and install third-party applications. It has evolved to include Lightning Components, Flows, Agentforce agents, and listings for consultants and job postings.

Use Cases for AppExchange Applications

When considering AppExchange solutions, it's important to evaluate scenarios where they might be the most appropriate choice. For example, say your organization needs to implement a complex quoting system that integrates with your product catalog and applies custom pricing rules. The project deadline is tight, and your development team is already stretched thin.

In this case, searching for a quoting solution on AppExchange could be ideal. Prebuilt applications can often provide sophisticated functionality that would take months to develop in house, allowing for faster implementation and quicker time-to-value (see Figure 9-20).

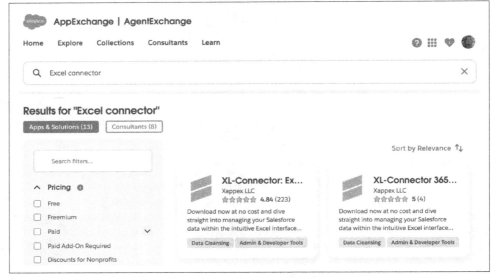

Figure 9-20. "Excel connector" search results on AppExchange

By leveraging AppExchange solutions in scenarios like this, you can often meet complex requirements within short time frames, avoiding the need for extensive custom coding.

Remember, while AppExchange offers many possibilities, it's important to carefully evaluate each solution to see if it fits your organization's specific needs, budget, and security requirements. The exam may present you with scenarios where you'll need to decide if an AppExchange solution is appropriate, or if custom development would be a better choice.

Summary

In Chapter 9, you explored the essential productivity and collaboration tools within Salesforce. You learned about activity management, which is central to organizing tasks, events, and customer interactions. The chapter delved into the power of Chatter for team collaboration and information sharing, highlighting how it can streamline communication within your Salesforce org. You also discovered the capabilities of the Salesforce mobile app, understanding how it enables on-the-go access to your Salesforce data. Finally, you were introduced to AppExchange, Salesforce's marketplace for extending functionality without extensive custom development.

These productivity and collaboration features are fundamental to maximizing the efficiency of your Salesforce implementation. They enable teams to work more cohesively, manage activities more effectively, and extend Salesforce's capabilities to meet specific business needs.

Chapter 9 Quiz

As you finish Chapter 9, it's time to assess the knowledge you've gathered about productivity and collaboration tools in Salesforce. The quiz below is designed to test your understanding of key concepts, ensuring you're well-prepared for the kind of nuanced questions that may appear on the Salesforce Certified Platform Administrator exam.

Remember, each question is an opportunity to review and strengthen your grasp of essential productivity and collaboration topics, from activity management to Chatter functionality and mobile capabilities. Take your time with each question and select the answer that best aligns with the principles you've learned.

After making your choices, carefully review the answers and explanations in the Appendix to solidify your understanding of the correct answers. This process will reinforce your existing knowledge and highlight areas that may require further review, ensuring you're well-prepared for real-world scenarios and exam success.

1. Which of the following best describes the purpose of activity management in Salesforce?

    a. To manage user profiles and permissions

    b. To track sales opportunities and leads

    c. To organize and monitor tasks, events, and customer interactions

    d. To generate reports and dashboards

2. What is the significance of the Activity Timeline in Salesforce?

    a. It shows a user's login history.

    b. It displays the history of field value changes.

    c. It provides a chronological view of past and upcoming activities related to a record.

    d. It tracks the performance of marketing campaigns.

3. Which of the following is *not* a primary type of activity in Salesforce activity management?

    a. Tasks

    b. Events

    c. Emails

    d. Opportunities

4. Which of the following is *not* a function of Chatter in Salesforce?

    a. To facilitate collaboration among team members

    b. To provide a platform for sharing updates and information

    c. To replace email communication entirely

    d. To enable following of records, users, and groups for updates

5. Which of the following statements about the Salesforce mobile app is correct?

    a. It provides exactly the same functionality as the desktop version of Salesforce.

    b. It allows users to access and update Salesforce data on mobile devices.

    c. It can only be used for viewing data, not for making updates.

    d. It requires a separate license from the desktop version of Salesforce.

6. What is a primary benefit of using AppExchange applications?

    a. They always provide free solutions to complex problems.

    b. They eliminate the need for any custom development.

    c. They can extend Salesforce functionality without extensive custom coding.

    d. They are automatically installed in all Salesforce orgs.

7. How does enabling Chatter Feed Tracking for an object benefit users?

   a. It automatically creates new records for the object.

   b. It allows users to see updates and changes to records in their Chatter feed.

   c. It replaces the need for reports on the object.

   d. It restricts access to the object's records.

Data and Analytics Management

The Data and Analytics Management knowledge area of the exam represents two distinct management disciplines. Before you can generate or manage analytics effectively on the Salesforce platform, you must first have quality data. The primary drivers of analytics in Salesforce are reports and dashboards. These both require underlying data before they can be displayed in visually compelling and meaningful ways.

In this chapter, you will start by learning data management principles. Once you have a firm grasp of the underlying data management principles on the platform, you can begin to leverage that data in interesting ways by way of analytics in Salesforce. In the analytics management part of this chapter, you will learn how to create various report formats.

Once you know how to create reports and the available formats, you will be ready to shift your focus to dashboards. Salesforce dashboards display data visually and require an underlying source report from which to draw data.

So in this round-trip learning journey through Data and Analytics Management, you will discover that you must first have quality data, followed by reports that query this quality data effectively, which are then saved into various report formats; those report formats then serve as source reports to then be visually represented in various widgets on dashboards.

From the Exam Guide

The Data and Analytics Management knowledge area of the Exam Guide contains the following learning objectives:

- Describe the considerations when importing, updating, transferring, mass deleting, exporting, and backing up data.

- Describe the capabilities and implications of data validation tools.
- Describe the options available when creating or customizing a report or report type.
- Describe the impact of the sharing model on reports.
- Describe the options available when creating and modifying dashboards (for example, dashboard components, data sources, chart types, subscribing, and running user).

Now that you are familiar with the journey that lies ahead in this knowledge area, it is time to focus on the beginning, or foundation, of great analytics by learning how to ensure quality data in your organization.

Data Management and Quality

Good data management starts with consistent data entry practices. Poorly managed Salesforce organizations are destined to suffer from data quality issues. Key hallmarks of bad data are duplicate records and data points that don't adhere to the intended use cases of individual fields. For example, a phone number field or zip code field may contain myriad different entry conventions that are as diverse as the user base who enters them—each with their own unique preferences.

Salesforce provides many tools and techniques to enforce—or at least encourage—proper data entry. For example, validation rules ensure data is entered in a consistent fashion. Another data quality tool in an administrator's arsenal is *duplicate prevention*, to avoid duplicate records from being entered in the first place.

Data Versus Metadata—A Practical Example

One consistent source of confusion among newer administrators on the Salesforce platform is understanding the differences between data and metadata, which I discussed in Chapter 5. As an administrator, you will deal with both frequently. And if you don't have a solid grasp on the distinctions between the two, you will struggle on the exam and on the job, when it comes to effective data management.

To better understand the differences between data and metadata, consider a car dealership scenario. If you were tasked with managing your auto inventory in Salesforce, you would likely find the need to create an Automobile custom object.

When you create the custom Automobile object, you are defining metadata that outlines the structure and characteristics of the object. To ensure that your system captures all necessary details, you would likely create fields for attributes like year, make, model, VIN, and mileage. These fields are also metadata. They determine what data will be entered by users and how that data will be stored in Salesforce.

As users input new automobile records, such as specifying the year as 2020 or entering the vehicle's mileage, they are interacting with data, but this data is shaped and structured by the metadata you've defined. Without proper metadata configuration, users wouldn't be able to input relevant information correctly, and the data would lack organization and consistency.

Additionally, metadata controls how data is input and how it is displayed to users. For example, modifying page layouts or setting up validation rules within the Object Manager impacts how users view and interact with records. Any changes to metadata, whether adding a new field, modifying a layout, or setting validation rules, can significantly alter the user experience, ensuring that data is entered correctly and displayed in a way that makes sense for your business processes.

Backup and Recovery Considerations

When managing metadata and data, backup and recovery strategies need to be approached differently. Data backups focus on preserving records, ensuring that all the information entered into Salesforce is saved. Metadata backups, however, are aimed at saving the configurations, such as custom objects, fields, page layouts, and validation rules that administrators have created. Both types of backups are critical, but they serve distinct purposes. A solid backup strategy ensures that in case of system failure or unintended changes, you can restore both the data and the framework that governs it.

Data Import Preparation

Before you import data into Salesforce, it's essential to configure the relevant metadata first. Fields, object definitions, and relationships need to be properly set up to ensure that the data you import maps correctly to your customizations. For example, if you are importing vehicle data into an Automobile object, all the necessary fields such as make, model, and VIN must already be in place. Proper metadata setup prevents errors during data import, ensuring that each piece of information lands in the right spot and maintains data integrity.

Data Import Wizard

The Data Import Wizard provides a straightforward interface for importing data into Salesforce. While more limited than other import tools, it serves as an efficient solution for importing records into standard objects like Accounts, Contacts, Leads, and Solutions, as well as into custom objects.

Accessing the Data Import Wizard

To access the Data Import Wizard, search for and select Data Import Wizard in Setup. The Data Import Wizard screen displays, as shown in Figure 10-1.

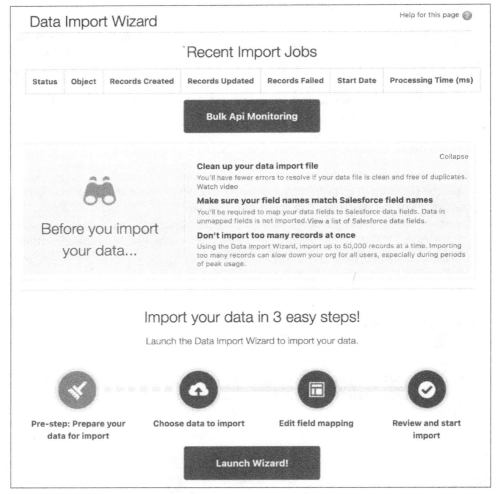

Figure 10-1. Data Import Wizard

Click Launch Wizard! to navigate from the intro screen into the Data Import Wizard, as shown in Figure 10-2.

The top of the screen reveals the three steps involved in importing data: first choose your data, edit field mappings, and start the import.

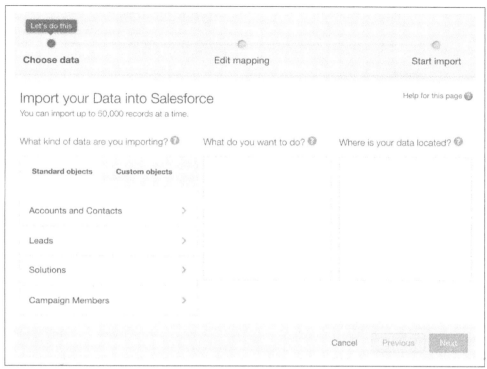

Figure 10-2. "Choose data" in the Data Import Wizard

Starting the Data Import Process

The "Choose data" import options available are for a limited number of standard objects, which include Accounts and Contacts, Leads, Solutions, Campaign Members, and Person Accounts (when enabled in your org). You can also select to import records for custom objects by selecting the "Custom objects" tab instead. After selecting the desired object to import records for, the "What do you want to do?" section populates in the middle of the screen, as shown in Figure 10-3.

Figure 10-3. "What do you want to do?" section in the Data Import Wizard

Your three options here are to introduce new records, update existing records, or do both. As you make your selection, you will see the screen update with further options.

Once you have completed your selections for this section of the screen, the "Where is your data located?" section updates to provide various options for your source data file, which needs to be a comma-separated value (CSV) file, as shown in Figure 10-4.

Figure 10-4. "Where is your data located?" screen showing CSV selection

You can drag and drop your source CSV file into the top section. Alternatively, you can click on the type of CSV file to navigate to the source file on your computer. You can select a plain CSV file, or you can select Outlook, ACT!, or Gmail CSV if you are wanting to import your contacts that you have exported out of one of those systems.

Once you specified the source file, click Next to proceed to the field mapping stage. The "Edit mapping" screen displays, where you can configure field mappings for your data import (see Figure 10-5).

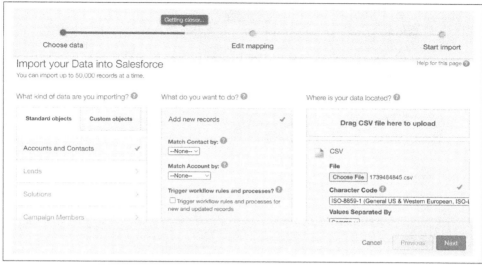

Figure 10-5. Data Import Wizard first step completed

Configuring Field Mappings

To configure field mappings, use the "Edit mapping" screen shown in Figure 10-6. It displays your CSV column headers alongside corresponding Salesforce fields, some of which may be automatically mapped.

Salesforce attempts to match fields automatically based on similar names. For fields it is unable to map, you will see an Unmapped designation.

You can manually map any unmapped fields, by clicking the Map link to the left of the field. For any field mappings that are incorrect, you can click Change to manually change the field mappings.

The screen also provides three sample records pulled from your source CSV file to provide a reference as to what data is actually being mapped. Take time to review these mappings before clicking Next to go to the final step of the Data Import Wizard, which is "Start import," as shown in Figure 10-7.

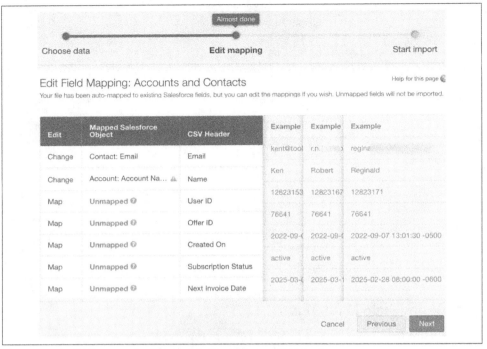

Figure 10-6. "Edit mapping" screen in Data Import Wizard

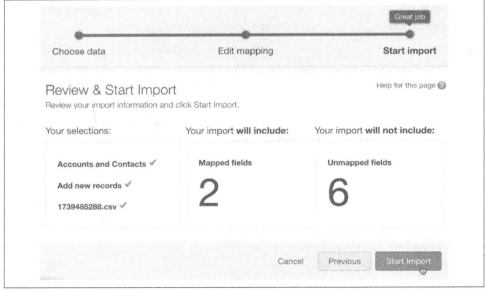

Figure 10-7. "Start import" screen in the Data Import Wizard

The "Start import" screen provides an overview of your selections as well as the number of mapped and unmapped fields for your import. Click Start Import when you're ready to proceed. Salesforce displays a confirmation screen containing your import job details.

Tracking Import Progress

To monitor the status of data imports, navigate to Bulk Data Load Jobs in Setup. This tool provides real-time visibility into import progress, including the number of records processed and any errors encountered. Upon completion of an import, Salesforce sends an email notification detailing the number of successfully imported records, failed imports, and any errors encountered.

The Data Import Wizard efficiently handles smaller imports and basic requirements. However, as your organization grows or import needs become more complex, you'll likely need to leverage the advanced capabilities of Data Loader, which we'll explore next.

Data Loader

While the Data Import Wizard provides a user-friendly interface for importing data into Salesforce, organizations often require more robust tools for handling large datasets or automating data operations. Data Loader is a Salesforce client application that offers advanced capabilities for importing and exporting data, supporting both Windows and Mac operating systems.

Data Loader is helpful in situations where the number of records to be loaded exceeds the 50,000 record limit of the Data Import Wizard. You would also use Data Loader in situations where you need to load standard object records beyond the few that are supported by the Data Import Wizard. Additionally, you can edit and delete records using Data Loader, which cannot be accomplished with the Data Import Wizard.

Installing and Configuring Data Loader

To begin using Data Loader, search for and select Data Loader in Setup. The Data Loader screen displays Downloads and User Guide options, as shown in Figure 10-8.

Clicking Downloads takes you to an external web page, where you can learn more about Data Loader as well as access download links for both Windows and macOS. After downloading and installing Data Loader, you can then launch it. The Data Loader application displays, as shown in Figure 10-9.

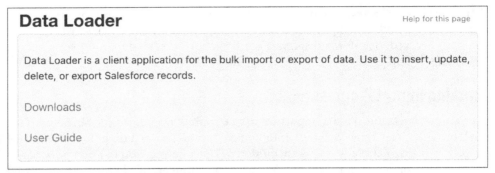

Figure 10-8. Data Loader screen

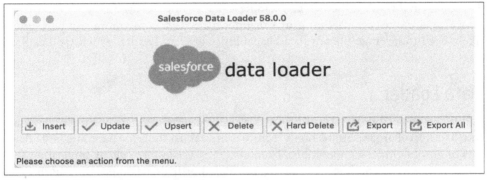

Figure 10-9. Data Loader user interface

Working with Data Loader

Data Loader contains buttons for the various operations you can perform with your data. There are three options related to importing data into Salesforce.

Insert
> Import new data into Salesforce.

Update
> Update existing data in Salesforce.

Upsert
> Import new and update existing data in Salesforce.

Insert

To insert records into Salesforce using a CSV file, start by clicking Insert. You will be prompted to log in to your Salesforce instance with Data Loader, if you haven't already done so. The Log In screen displays, as shown in Figure 10-10.

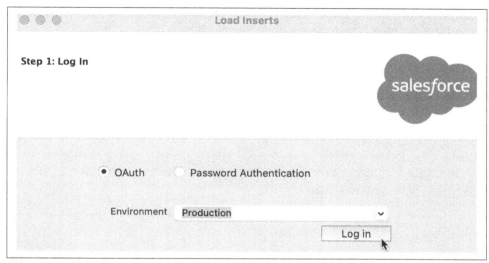

Figure 10-10. Data Loader Log In screen

You have two options for logging into Data Loader; OAuth or Password Authentication. You also need to specify the type of Environment you wish to connect to: Production or Sandbox.

If you select Password Authentication, you will be prompted to enter your username and password. If you select OAuth and click Log In, you will be asked to verify that you wish to allow Data Loader to connect to your instance, as shown in Figure 10-11.

Allow Access?

Dataloader Partner is asking to:

- Access the identity URL service
- Manage user data via APIs

Do you want to allow access for mike@
(Not you?)

Deny	Allow

Allow

To revoke access at any time, go to your personal settings.

Figure 10-11. Data Loader Allow Access? screen

Click Allow to connect Data Loader to your org. Data Loader then proceeds to the second step for Load Inserts, as shown in Figure 10-12.

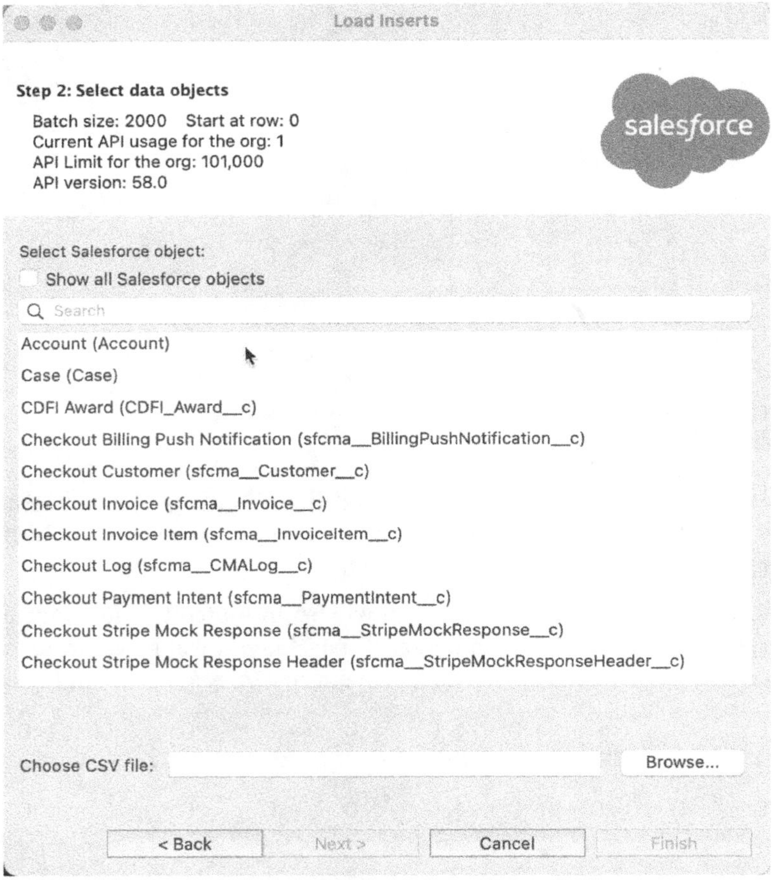

Figure 10-12. Data Loader Load Inserts screen

Select the Salesforce object you want to import records for. You then can click Browse to choose the CSV file that contains the new records you wish to insert. After selecting your import file, click Next to map the CSV columns to the corresponding Salesforce fields to ensure data is correctly assigned, as shown in Figure 10-13.

Click "Choose an Existing Map" or "Create or Edit a Map" to map the column headers in your CSV file with the corresponding Salesforce field names. Finally, review the mapped data for accuracy and click Finish to complete the record insertion process.

Figure 10-13. Data Loader field mapping

 Ensure your CSV file uses consistent date formats and includes all required fields for the target object. Data Loader will fail to insert records if required fields are missing or improperly formatted.

Update

Updates modify existing records in Salesforce using a unique identifier, typically the Salesforce ID or a custom external ID field. The process follows steps similar to Insert, but requires the inclusion of the external ID field in your CSV file.

External ID fields must be marked as unique in Salesforce and properly indexed for optimal performance. Consider creating custom external ID fields if standard unique identifiers don't meet your needs.

Upsert

Upsert operations offer flexibility by combining insert and update functions. To perform an upsert, begin by selecting a unique external ID field that will determine whether a record should be inserted or updated.

Ensure your CSV file includes this external ID field so Salesforce can properly match existing records. Next, map the fields in your file to the corresponding Salesforce fields, just as you would with other data operations. Once everything is set up, run the operation to process the records accordingly.

Delete Versus Hard Delete

In Data Loader, the Delete operation removes records from Salesforce and moves them to the Recycle Bin, allowing for potential recovery. These deleted records remain in the Recycle Bin until they are manually restored or automatically purged after a retention period, which depends on your Salesforce edition and storage limits.

To delete records using Data Loader, select the Delete option, and choose the object from which records will be removed. After uploading a CSV file containing the record IDs, Data Loader processes the deletion, ensuring the records are no longer active but still retrievable from the Recycle Bin.

The Hard Delete operation permanently removes records from Salesforce without sending them to the Recycle Bin, making the deletion irreversible. To enable this option in Data Loader, you must check the Use Bulk API option in the Settings menu of Data Loader. Without this setting enabled, the Hard Delete option will not be available.

Once Use Bulk API is enabled, selecting Hard Delete in Data Loader will completely erase the specified records from the system.

 Because this action cannot be undone, it is vital to create a data backup before performing any mass deletions.

Salesforce tracks deleted records using the IsDeleted Boolean field. When a record is deleted, but not hard deleted, the IsDeleted record is set to True, indicating that the record still exists in the Recycle Bin and can be restored. However, if a record has been hard deleted, it is completely removed from Salesforce, and `IsDeleted` is no longer applicable. Given the permanent nature of a hard delete, administrators should use this function sparingly and only when absolutely necessary.

Export Versus Export All

To prevent unintended data loss, Data Loader provides two export options: Export and Export All. The Export function retrieves only active, nondeleted records from Salesforce, making it ideal for backups, reporting, and data migrations. In contrast, the Export All function includes both active records and those in the Recycle Bin, allowing for recovery of recently deleted data.

The process for both export types is the same. Users select an object, specify the fields to include, and apply filters as needed. However, when using Export All, deleted records that are still in the Recycle Bin will also be included in the output.

Before performing a hard delete, it is strongly recommended that you create a backup using the Export function in Data Loader. This ensures that records can be recovered if they are deleted by mistake.

Automating Data Loader Processing

For recurring data operations, Data Loader offers command-line functionality that enables automation through batch files or scripts. This capability proves invaluable for scheduled data maintenance tasks or regular data synchronization requirements. Refer to the Data Loader User Guide available from the Setup menu for more information on automating Data Loader.

Restoring Deleted Data Using the Recycle Bin

Data that is deleted, whether via Data Loader or manually, can be restored by using the Recycle Bin. Restoring records from the Recycle Bin allows you to recover data with its original state and relationships intact. Once you have identified the record to restore, select it and use the Restore option provided. The record will be returned to its original state and location within Salesforce, reinstating any associations it had with related records such as accounts, contacts, Opportunities, or Cases.

The restoration process is seamless for most use cases, as Salesforce automatically reconnects restored records with their prior data hierarchy. For example, restoring an Opportunity will also restore its related contact roles and associated activities, ensuring the record remains fully functional.

When restoring records, ensure there have been no significant updates to the system that might conflict with the restored record. For instance, if a related account or user has been deactivated since the deletion, the restored record may require adjustments to maintain data integrity.

Records that were deleted more than 15 days ago are not available in the Recycle Bin; they have been permanently removed by Salesforce's retention policy. If the record cannot be restored from the Recycle Bin, you will need to rely on a previously exported backup or Salesforce's Data Recovery Service for retrieval. This underscores the importance of implementing a robust data backup strategy.

Automations such as flows or triggers may execute if they are configured to run when records are created or updated. Be mindful of these scenarios to avoid unintended consequences during restoration.

Data Export Service

Salesforce provides a scheduled Data Export service from the Setup menu. This Data Export function enables organizations to back up their data at regular intervals. Search for and select Data Export from Setup to display the Data Export screen, as shown in Figure 10-14.

Figure 10-14. Data Export Service screen

Data Export aids data security and compliance, offering a comprehensive snapshot of an organization's records. Unlike the export function available through Data Loader, which operates at the object level and requires selecting specific objects individually, the Data Export service is org-wide. This means it captures data from across the entire Salesforce environment rather than from just one object at a time.

It is important to note that this service exports data records, not metadata. While the exported data includes records from objects like Accounts, Contacts, and Opportunities, it does not include metadata elements such as page layouts or validation rules.

You can select to either Export Now or Schedule Export via the buttons at the bottom of the Data Export screen. When initiating or scheduling a data export, you can choose which specific objects to include or select all available objects for a full backup. Once selections are made, the export can either be run immediately or scheduled for a future date.

 If you select All Objects during the export configuration, remember to periodically review and update the selection to include any new objects that may have been created since your initial setup. Objects are not automatically added to the list of objects to be exported in previously configured data exports.

The frequency of the Data Export functionality varies based on organization type but is typically available either weekly or monthly. Once the export process is complete, Salesforce delivers the data as a downloadable link to a ZIP file, which is sent via email.

This ZIP file contains individual CSV files for each selected object, with all records listed row by row. Each CSV file has column headers that correspond to the fields on the object, making it a useful way to view the full structure of an object's data.

For organizations that require more frequent or robust backup solutions, the Data Export service may not provide the level of automation or flexibility needed. In these cases, setting up automated backups using Data Loader or leveraging a third-party backup application from the Salesforce AppExchange can be a more effective approach. These options allow for more granular scheduling and control, ensuring critical business data is consistently preserved.

DataLoader.io

DataLoader.io is a cloud-based application that simplifies data management in Salesforce, offering administrators an intuitive way to import, export, and delete data directly from within a browser. DataLoader.io is similar to the installed Data Loader application, but offers the advantages of being web based and not requiring the installation of separate software on your computer.

Originally developed by MuleSoft, DataLoader.io became part of the ecosystem through Salesforce's acquisition of MuleSoft. As a Salesforce product, DataLoader.io integrates seamlessly with the platform, providing a reliable and efficient solution for managing Salesforce records.

Accessing DataLoader.io

You can access DataLoader.io through its website (*http://DataLoader.io*) or via the Salesforce Setup menu by searching for DataLoader.io (see Figure 10-15).

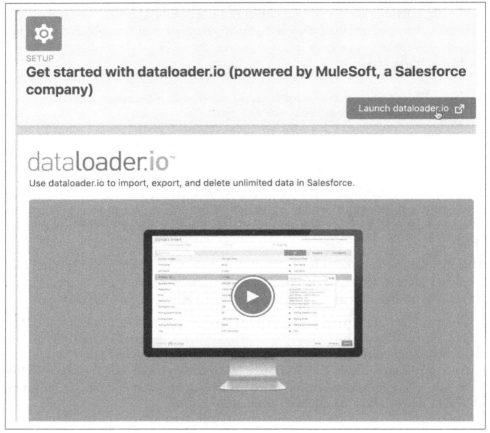

Figure 10-15. DataLoader.io launch screen from inside the Setup menu

DataLoader.io offers the ability to upload data from CSV files and map file columns to Salesforce fields, much like the locally installed Data Loader. You can also export and delete data using DataLoader.io.

Duplicate Rules

I want to transition back to a broader discussion of data management. An important component of data management and quality is *duplicate rules*. These rules are designed to prevent and manage duplicate records in your organization. They work in tandem with *matching rules* to identify potential duplicates and specify actions

Salesforce should take when duplicates are found. This functionality helps maintain data quality, improve reporting accuracy, and enhance the overall efficiency of your Salesforce environment.

Default Duplicate Rules and Matching Rules

Salesforce provides several standard duplicate rules out of the box, which are preconfigured to work with standard objects like Accounts, Contacts, and Leads (see Figure 10-16).

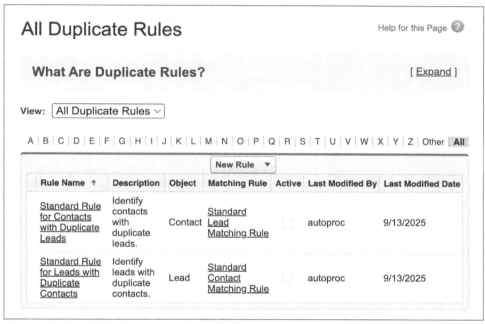

Figure 10-16. All Duplicate Rules screen

These rules are designed to identify duplicates during record creation or updates. For example, the default duplicate rule for Contacts compares a combination of first name, last name, and email address, while the rule for Accounts considers matches based on account name and billing address. These default rules are ready to use but can be customized or disabled as needed to align with your organization's specific requirements.

Matching rules define the criteria used to identify duplicate records. These rules use logic to compare field values and determine whether two or more records are duplicates. Salesforce allows for both simple exact matches, such as ensuring that email addresses are identical, and more advanced matching techniques that account for variations in data. For example, matching rules can detect duplicates with slight spelling differences, such as "Johnathan" and "Jonathan," ensuring a broader capture of potential duplicates.

Customizing Duplicate Rules

While the standard duplicate rules provide a good starting point, you can create custom duplicate rules to handle unique scenarios within your organization. Custom duplicate rules enable you to specify which fields to evaluate and define conditions tailored to your business needs. For instance, if your organization frequently deals with records that share common names but differ in location, you might create a rule that checks for matching names combined with matching city or state fields.

Custom duplicate rules also let you define actions that Salesforce should take when a duplicate is found. For example, you can choose to alert users with a message about the potential duplicate, allow users to proceed but flag the record for review, or block the creation or update of the duplicate entirely. These options provide flexibility in managing duplicate records according to your data policies.

Duplicate Record Sets

When duplicate rules identify potential duplicates, Salesforce creates a duplicate record set to group these records for review. Duplicate record sets are accessible through the Duplicate Record Sets tab, where you can analyze grouped records and take corrective actions, such as merging duplicates or updating fields. These sets provide a centralized way to manage potential duplicates and ensure that records are reviewed and resolved systematically.

This grouping of duplicates helps with immediate data management but also allows for later analysis. Duplicate record sets can be included in reports to track trends in duplicate creation, helping administrators understand underlying issues and refine duplicate rules or data entry processes.

Analytics Management

Effective analytics management in Salesforce begins and ends with quality data. Once you have effectively cleansed the data in your organization, you can then start leveraging and representing that data in reports and dashboards.

You must gain a firm understanding of how to create reports in Salesforce, as well as the different report formats that you can create. These different report formats dictate which widgets are available for use in your dashboards.

Report Formats

In this section of the knowledge area, you will begin with the creation of reports. You will start with the most basic of report formats, which is a Tabular report.

Tabular report format

> The Tabular report format is the most basic of the four. It most closely resembles a basic table or spreadsheet. Its core characteristic is that it contains no groupings of data.

Summary report format

> The Summary report format contains a row grouping and is useful for summarizing records. An example of a Summary report is a list of all accounts, grouped by owner.

Matrix report format

> The Matrix report format is a more complex report format. It contains two groupings of data. An example of a Matrix report is a list of all accounts, grouped by owner and also grouped by state/province.

Joined report format

> The Joined report format provides a way to compare and analyze data from multiple report types within a single report view. It is similar to Joined reports you might create in a spreadsheet tool such as Microsoft Excel.

Accessing Reports in Salesforce

Reports in Salesforce provide insights into your organization's data through customizable analyses and visualizations. The Reports tab is typically available in most standard Salesforce applications, including Sales, Service, and Marketing. You can also access Reports through the App Launcher by selecting it from the All Items section or using the Quick Find box.

Reports home page overview

Search for and select Reports from the App Launcher or click the Reports tab in your current application. The Reports home page displays, showing your recently accessed reports and providing tools to create and manage reports, as shown in Figure 10-17.

The Reports home page is organized to provide quick access to frequently used reports while enabling you to create new reports or access report folders. The page displays your recently viewed reports at the top, followed by private and public report folders below.

Figure 10-17. Reports home page

Report folders and organization

Report folders in Salesforce help organize and control access to reports across your organization. Folders can be public, providing broad access to specified groups, or private, restricting access to specific users. This folder structure ensures reports are both organized and secure.

Public folders.   Public folders make reports available to multiple users based on sharing settings. Administrators can control access to public folders through folder sharing rules, allowing specific groups or roles to view and edit reports within these folders.

Private folders.   Private folders contain reports accessible only to their creators and users granted explicit sharing access. These folders are ideal for storing personal reports or works in progress that aren't ready for broader organizational access.

Creating New Reports

To create a new report, click the New Report button at the top of the Reports home page. The Report Type selection screen displays, as shown in Figure 10-18.

Figure 10-18. Report Type selection screen

The Report Type selection screen organizes available report types by category, such as Accounts & Contacts, Opportunities, Cases, and other standard or custom objects. Each report type determines which objects and fields will be available for your report.

Use the Quick Find box at the top of the Report Type selection screen to quickly locate specific report types, especially in organizations with many custom report types.

After selecting a report type, click Start Report. The Report Builder opens in a new tab, where you can customize your report's fields, filters, and format (see Figure 10-19).

The Report Builder provides a dynamic interface for creating and modifying reports. You will learn the Report Builder in detail in subsequent sections related to the four report formats you can build (and will be tested on in the exam). As described earlier, these four report formats are:

- Tabular
- Summary
- Matrix
- Joined

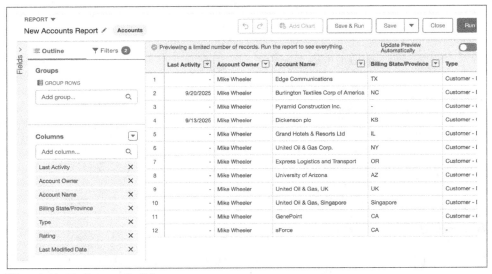

Figure 10-19. Report Builder

Creating Tabular Reports

Tabular reports represent the most straightforward report format in Salesforce, displaying data in simple rows and columns similar to a spreadsheet. While they lack the grouping capabilities of more advanced report formats, such as Summary and Matrix, Tabular reports provide detailed record-level data and are ideal for exporting lists of records. To create a Tabular report, you will need to apply filters and add or remove fields, as needed.

Applying filters

Filters refine your report to show only relevant data. From the Filters panel, you can define criteria using several standard filter options, as shown in Figure 10-20.

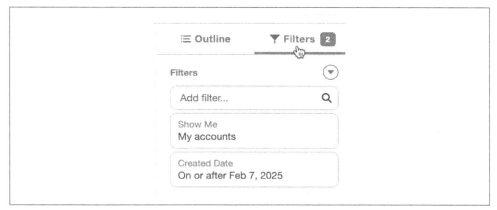

Figure 10-20. Filters options in Report Builder

While Tabular reports can include filters, they cannot display subtotals or groupings. For these features, you'll need to use Summary or Matrix report formats.

Adding fields to your report

In the Fields panel, you'll find the available fields organized by object. To add a field to your report, locate the desired field in the Fields panel and drag it into the Preview panel. You can arrange columns by dragging them left or right to achieve your preferred order.

Hold the Ctrl (Windows) or Command (Mac) key while clicking to select multiple fields simultaneously, and then drag them as a group into your report.

Customizing report column display options

The Report Builder provides several customization options for your Tabular report's data display. By clicking the drop-down menu on any column header, you can access various options for that column, such as sorting data ascending or descending and moving the column left or right (see Figure 10-21).

Figure 10-21. Report column options

Saving and running reports

When your Tabular report configuration is complete, click Save. The Save Report window displays (see Figure 10-22).

Enter a Report Name, select a folder location, and optionally add a Report Description. After saving, you can click "Save and Run" to execute the report and view it as an end user does, outside of the Report Builder.

> The Report Builder provides a limited preview of records, which can be updated automatically by activating the toggle at the top-right of the report preview area. "Save and Run" provides the full list of records instead of a limited preview.

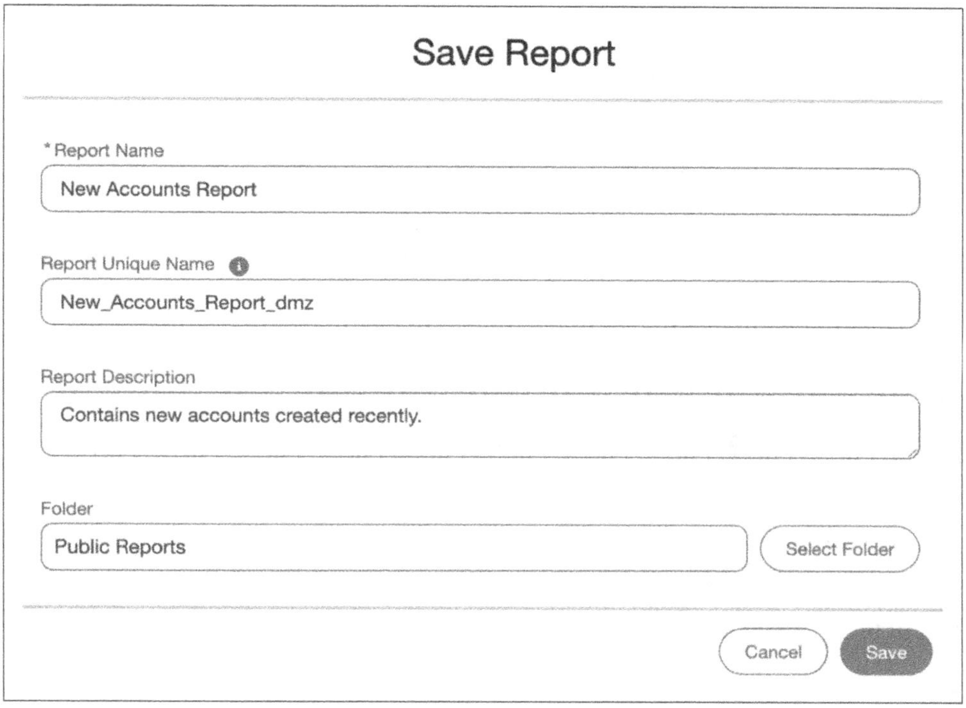

Figure 10-22. Save Report window

Creating Summary Reports

Summary reports extend beyond Tabular reports by allowing you to group records and calculate subtotals based on those groupings. This format enables data analysis across different categories or levels while maintaining the ability to drill down to individual records.

Once you have started a report in the Report Builder, to create a Summary report, you need to add a row grouping. The Report Builder provides an Add Group option in the Outline sidebar. This enables you to group rows of data by selecting a field to group by. For example, you could group Accounts by billing state (see Figure 10-23).

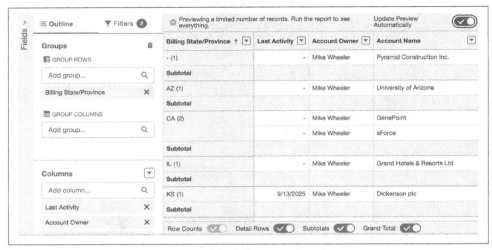

Figure 10-23. Account report grouped by billing state/province

Whenever you add a row grouping to a report, it is considered a Summary report, and the Report Builder reorganizes your data to show records grouped by the values in that field.

Adding charts to Summary reports

Since Summary reports include a grouping of data, that data can then be visually represented through charts that can be added to the report.

The Add Chart button, as shown in Figure 10-24, adds a chart to your report, which you can configure to be a different chart type by clicking the gear icon located at the top-right and selecting a chart type from the Chart Properties overlay.

Figure 10-24. Add Chart button in Report Builder

Chart availability and report formats

Chart options available in Salesforce reports depend on the report format. Tabular reports do not support charts due to their lack of groupings. Summary reports with a single grouping support basic chart types such as bar charts, line charts, pie charts, donut charts, funnel charts, and scatterplot charts.

Summary report toggle options

At the bottom of Summary reports, the interface provides several toggle options that control data display and calculation behavior (see Figure 10-25). These toggles appear as checkboxes and influence how the report processes and presents information:

Figure 10-25. Summary Report toggles

Row Counts
> The Row Counts toggle adds a running count of records to each grouping level. This feature proves particularly useful when analyzing data distribution across groups or verifying record inclusion in specific categories.

Detail Rows
> The Detail Rows toggle determines whether individual record rows appear beneath each grouping. When enabled, users can view every record contributing to group totals. Disabling this option presents only summary-level information, creating a more concise report focused on aggregate data.

Subtotals
> The Subtotals toggle activates or deactivates subtotal rows for each grouping level. These subtotal rows are highlighted and display summary calculations for their respective groups. The subtotals persist even when detail rows are hidden, providing quick insights into group-level metrics.

Grand Total
> The Grand Total toggle controls the display of overall totals at the report level. These calculations appear at the bottom of the report and aggregate data across all groups. When using multiple summary calculations, the grand totals reflect each calculation type separately.

Percentage Calculations
> For numeric fields with summary calculations, an additional toggle enables percentage calculations relative to grand totals. These percentages automatically update as filters change, providing dynamic insights into data composition.

Creating Matrix Reports

Matrix reports differ from Summary reports in that they contain two groupings of data instead of one. The two groupings of data in a Matrix report can be grouped by either row or row and column. You can create a Matrix report by first creating a Summary report that contains one row grouping and then adding a secondary row grouping or a column grouping to further dissect your data.

Once you have created a Matrix report all of the chart optionswill be available and can be added to the report. Whereas a Summary report cannot have a stacked bar or stacked column chart, due to having only one row grouping, a Matrix report can support these stacked chart options. These stacked chart options allow you to see the composition of each primary grouping broken down by a secondary grouping.

Creating Joined Reports

The fourth and final report format you can create in Salesforce is a Joined report. Joined reports provide a way to compare and analyze data from multiple report types within a single report view. This powerful functionality allows administrators and users to consolidate information from different objects while maintaining distinct groupings for meaningful comparisons. Similar to how Excel can combine and display data from different sheets or sources while preserving their distinct structures, Salesforce Joined reports enable side-by-side analysis of related data sets within a unified format.

A Joined report consists of multiple report blocks, with each block representing an individual report that functions independently but shares a common structure with the others. You can create up to five report blocks in a single Joined report, allowing you to display different data sets together in a single view.

Each block must be configured, just like a standard Salesforce report, meaning you can add or remove columns, apply filters, and adjust sorting as needed. This flexibility makes Joined reports particularly useful for scenarios such as comparing sales performance across different regions, analyzing support cases by product category alongside customer feedback, or tracking Opportunities alongside related campaign activity.

Click the Report drop-down menu at the top-left of the Report Builder to display the Choose Format options available. Change the selection from the default Report format to the Joined Report option, then click Apply (see Figure 10-26).

Figure 10-26. Joined Report format selected

Selecting the Joined Report format enables the ability to add additional report blocks. Click Add Block and select another report type that contains the data you want to compare. Repeat this process to add up to five blocks as needed.

Each report block functions independently, allowing you to customize it just like in a standalone report. You can add or remove columns, adjust filters, and even apply sorting criteria unique to each block. To make the Joined report more readable, you can define grouping criteria that organize data across the different report blocks. Groupings in a Joined report can be applied at the row level based on common fields that exist across multiple report types, such as Account Name, Opportunity Owner, and Case Status. This ensures that related records are aligned for meaningful comparisons.

As you refine your report, consider adjusting the column layouts to ensure clarity. Since Joined reports do not merge data into a single data set but rather display data in separate, structured blocks, it's important to arrange information logically. Once you're satisfied with the structure, click Save & Run to generate the final report, where you can analyze side-by-side comparisons and extract key insights.

Exporting Reports

Salesforce allows users to export report data for offline analysis, sharing, or record-keeping. This feature is useful for working with Salesforce data in spreadsheet applications, integrating it with other systems, or maintaining external backups.

To export a report, navigate to the Reports tab, open the desired report, and click the Export button. You will be prompted to choose between two export formats: Formatted Report or Details Only, as shown in Figure 10-27.

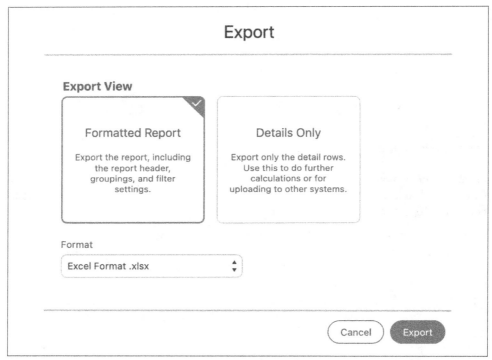

Figure 10-27. Report Export window

Selecting Formatted Report generates an Excel (*.xlsx*) file that preserves the report's structure, including groupings, summary fields, and subtotals. Choosing Details Only exports the raw data as a CSV (*.csv*) file, making it ideal for further manipulation or importing into other systems.

Unlike report subscriptions, exports do not support conditional delivery. When exporting a report, you must manually initiate the export each time updated data is needed. If you require recurring access to exported data, configure a scheduled report subscription to send reports to specified recipients at set intervals, though the export itself will always contain the most recent data available at the time of execution.

Subscribing to Reports

Subscribing to reports in Salesforce enables users to receive scheduled email notifications containing report data. This feature ensures that key stakeholders stay informed about important business metrics without needing to manually run reports each time they require updates. By automating report delivery, users can stay on top of critical changes and make data-driven decisions efficiently.

How to subscribe

To subscribe to a report, navigate to the Reports tab and locate the report you wish to receive updates on. Open the report, then click the Subscribe button at the top of the report screen. This action opens the Edit Subscription window (see Figure 10-28), where you can configure your subscription preferences.

The Edit Subscription window provides options to customize the delivery schedule, recipients, and conditions that trigger the report email. You can choose to receive the report on a daily, weekly, or monthly basis, ensuring that data is delivered at the most relevant intervals for your workflow.

Additionally, if the report includes time-sensitive data, you can choose "Add conditions to this report" to set up conditional delivery only when conditions are met and define specific criteria for the report's results. This means that the report will only be sent if the specified conditions are met, helping reduce unnecessary emails while ensuring alerts for significant changes.

Multiple recipients can be added to a report subscription by selecting users, roles, or public groups. However, only users with the necessary permissions to view the report data will receive the subscription email.

Once the subscription is configured, Salesforce automatically sends an email with the latest report results based on the selected schedule or conditions.

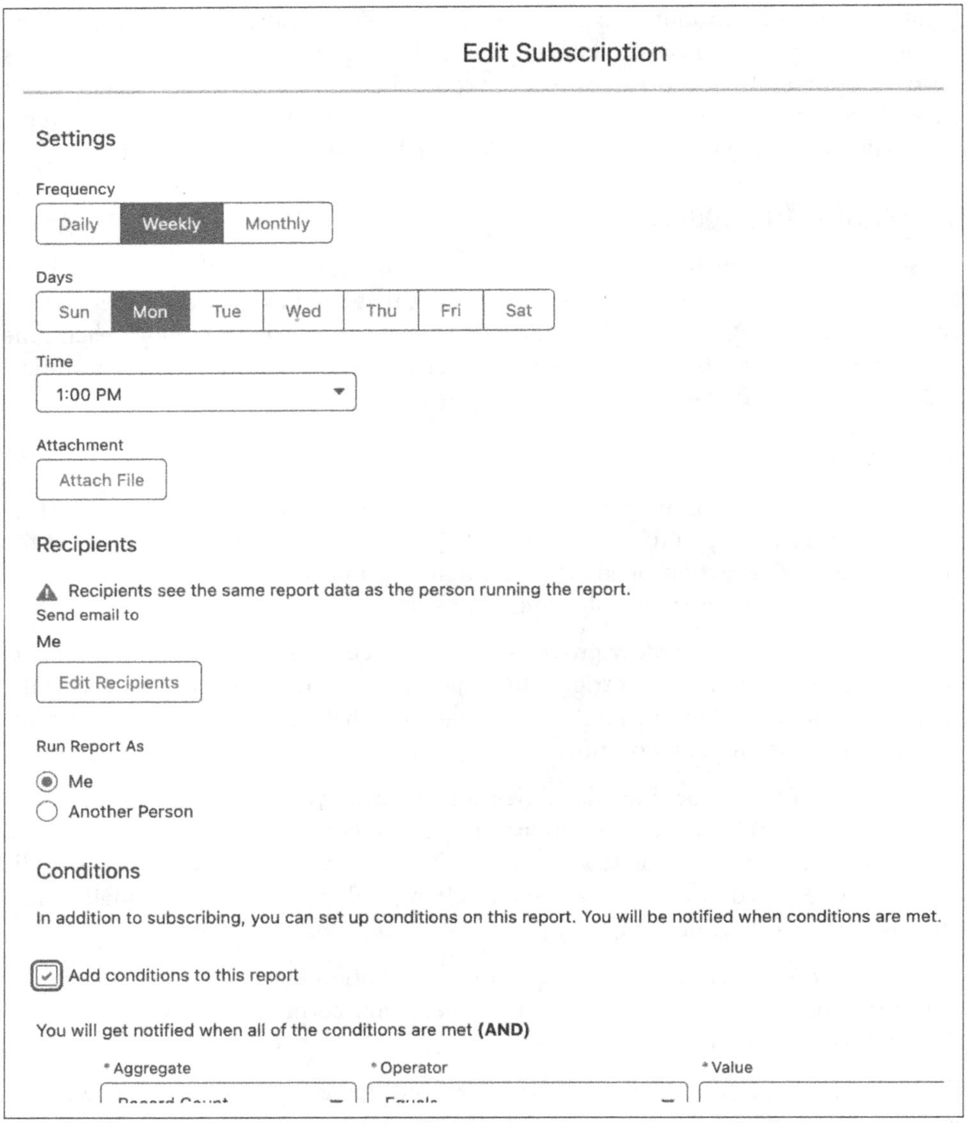

Figure 10-28. Edit Subscription window

Using conditional report subscriptions for proactive monitoring

Beyond scheduled updates, report subscriptions with conditional delivery can serve as a proactive tool for system monitoring and preventive maintenance. You can set up subscriptions to track key operational metrics and receive alerts when anomalies occur.

For example, if an unusually high number of Cases are created overnight, this could indicate a widespread issue affecting customers. By configuring a subscription with an acceptable threshold of new Cases, you can ensure that an email alert is triggered when that threshold is exceeded. This allows you to investigate and address the problem before it impacts a larger audience.

This same approach can be applied across various scenarios, such as monitoring inactive users, identifying duplicate records, or tracking unexpected revenue fluctuations. By leveraging report subscriptions in this way, administrators can stay ahead of potential issues, proactively manage system health, and provide early warnings to their teams. Rather than waiting for end users or executives to report a problem, these automated alerts enable you to take swift action, reinforcing your role as a proactive Salesforce administrator.

Custom Report Types

Custom Report Types in Salesforce provide users with greater control over the data available in reports. Unlike standard report types, which are predefined by Salesforce and often limited in their object relationships, custom report types allow administrators to tailor reports to specific business needs. This flexibility ensures that users can access and analyze the precise data they require without the restrictions of standard reporting options.

Using Custom Report Types in the Report Builder

Custom report types, once created and deployed, appear alongside standard report types when users create a new report in Salesforce. When navigating to the Reports tab and selecting New Report, users are presented with a list of available report types. This list includes both standard report types, which are predefined by Salesforce, and any custom report types that have been configured by administrators. The presence of custom report types in this selection allows users to build reports tailored to their organization's specific data structures and reporting needs.

Creating Custom Report Types

To create a custom report type, search for and select Report Types from Setup. The Custom Report Types splash screen displays (see Figure 10-29).

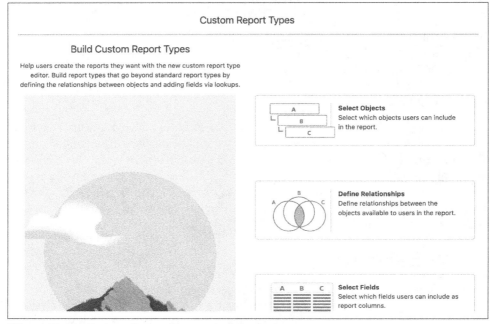

Figure 10-29. Custom Report Types splash screen

The Custom Report Types splash screen provides an overview of the steps involved in creating a custom report type: select objects, define the relationships between those objects, and then select the fields to include as report columns. You can check the "Don't show me this page again" checkbox at the bottom left to not have the splash screen appear in the future.

After you click Continue, the Custom Report Types screen displays All Custom Report Types currently residing in your organization, as shown in Figure 10-30.

To create a new custom report type, click the New Custom Report Type button located at the top-right of the screen. The New Custom Report Type screen displays (see Figure 10-31).

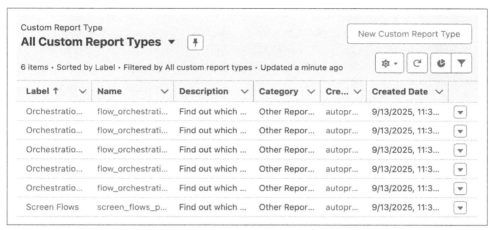

Figure 10-30. All Custom Report Types screen

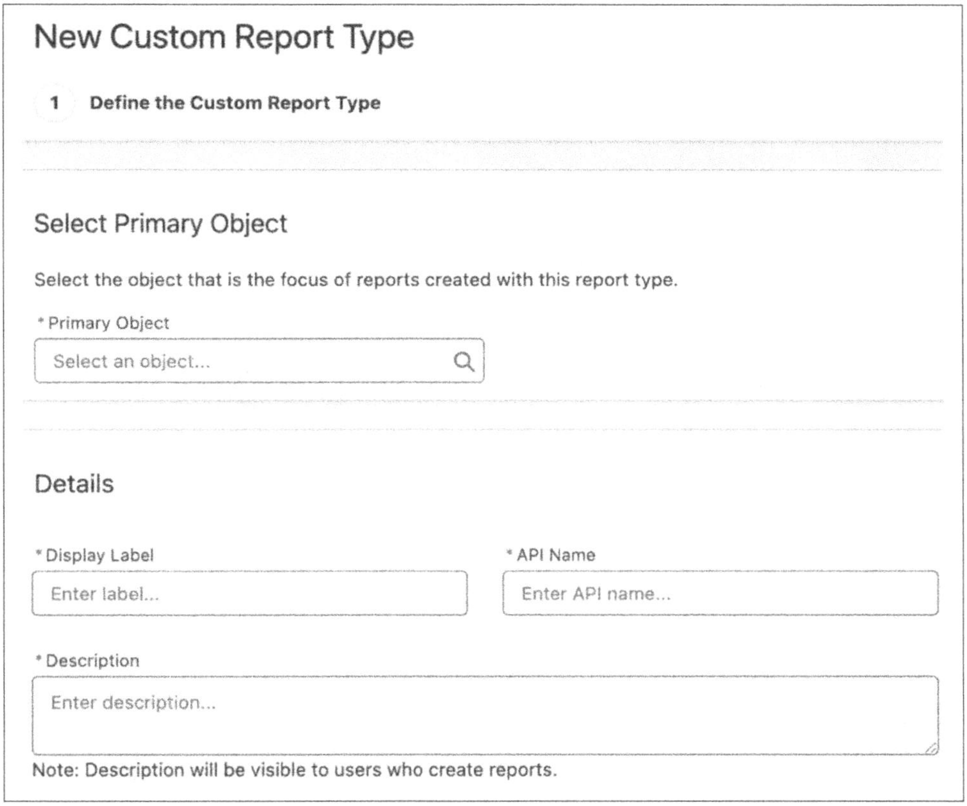

New Custom Report Type

1   **Define the Custom Report Type**

Select Primary Object

Select the object that is the focus of reports created with this report type.

* Primary Object

Select an object...   🔍

Details

* Display Label

Enter label...

* API Name

Enter API name...

* Description

Enter description...

Note: Description will be visible to users who create reports.

Figure 10-31. New Custom Report Type screen

When creating a custom report type, you begin by selecting a Primary Object, such as Account, Opportunity, or Case. Once you have selected the primary object, you will next enter the details for your new custom report type, including the Display Label and Description, which will be visible to users who create reports.

You will also need to select a Category to store your new custom report type in. And finally, set the Availability to either In Development or Deployed.

 An in-development report type is visible only to users with the Manage Custom Report Types permission. A deployed report type is available to all users.

Once you have made your initial entries on the New Custom Report Type screen, click Next to move to the second screen (Figure 10-32), where you select related objects to define which records are included in reports using this report type. You will see your previously selected primary object and can relate another object by clicking the button below your primary object.

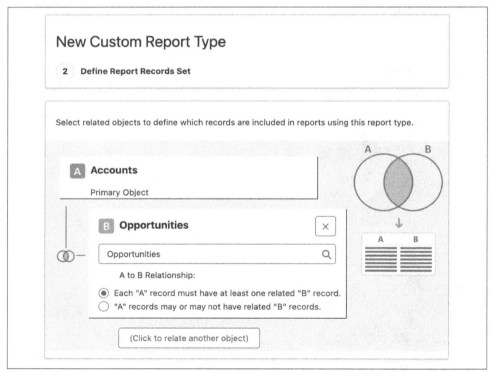

Figure 10-32. Define Report Records Set screen

Here you define the relationship between this primary object and any related objects, determining whether to include only records with related data or to allow records from the primary object even if no related record exists.

The diagram on the right of the screen shown in Figure 10-32 helps visualize the relationships between the specified objects. As you toggle between the two options, you will notice the diagram changing to convey the difference between the first option, in which each object record has at least one related record, and the second option, in which records may or may not have a related record (see Figure 10-33).

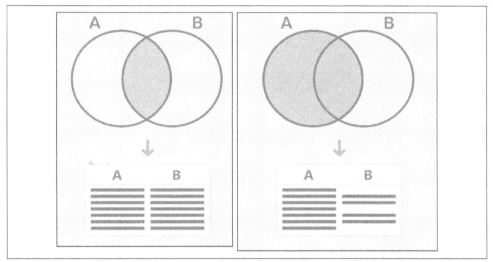

Figure 10-33. Each record must have a related record (left) or each record may or may not have a related record (right)

You can repeat this process to add additional related objects. You can select up to four objects; you'll see an Object Limit Reached message if you attempt to add a fifth (see Figure 10-34).

Once you have defined your objects and their related record designations, click Save. An Overview screen displays information related to your new Custom Report Type, as shown in Figure 10-35.

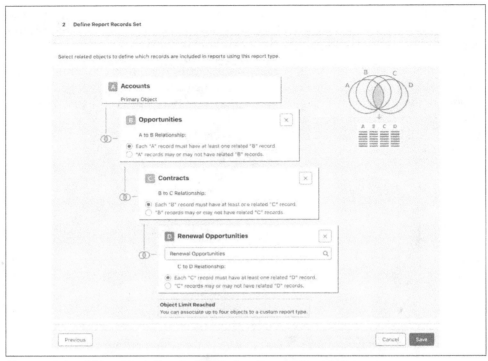

Figure 10-34. Object Limit Reached in Define Report Records Set screen

Figure 10-35. Custom Report Type Overview screen

On the Custom Report Type Overview screen, there are several action buttons available at the top-right. These buttons enable you to preview and edit the layout of your new custom report type.

The Preview Layout button displays the objects in order, along with all of the fields that are included in the new custom report type. You will notice that all fields on all of the previously selected objects are displayed.

Editing a Custom Report Type Layout

You can further refine your new custom report type by specifying which fields are included by default and which fields are available for users to add whenever they build subsequent reports using this custom report type. To do so, click Edit Layout. The Overview screen displays the Custom Report Type Layout screen, as shown in Figure 10-36.

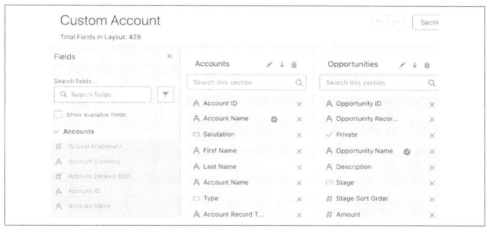

Figure 10-36. Custom Report Type Layout screen

The Custom Report Type Layout screen displays each of the previously selected objects and all of their fields that are included by default in a newly created custom report type. You can remove fields by clicking the × to the right of the field name.

A legend appears at the bottom of the screen that shows the default column designations as well as any fields that were added via Lookup. Default columns will be added automatically to any new reports that are built using your custom report type.

You can specify any field on the screen as a default column for your custom report by selecting it and then clicking the pencil icon which appears. This displays a Field Information pop-up, from which you can check (or uncheck) the Default Column checkbox located at the bottom, as shown in Figure 10-37.

Figure 10-37. Default Column selection on Account Name field

You can further rearrange the layout of your custom report type by including or excluding sections via the drop-down button at the top right. You can also add new sections and lookup fields by clicking their respective buttons.

Once you have completed all necessary adjustments, click Save. Your new custom report type is saved. If you previously set its status to Deployed, it is made available for users to create reports based on your defined structure.

History Reports

History reports in Salesforce provide a way to track changes made to records over time. These reports help administrators and users monitor data modifications, ensuring accountability and transparency in record updates. By using history reports, organizations can track field value changes, identify trends, and audit modifications made by different users.

Field History Reports

Field history reports track changes to specific fields on standard or custom objects where Field History Tracking has been enabled. These reports show old and new values, who made the change, and when the update occurred. For example, an Opportunity field history report can track changes to the Opportunity Stage, allowing sales managers to monitor pipeline progression and identify deals that may be stalling. These reports are useful for understanding how data evolves over time and ensuring that key updates are being made appropriately.

Case History Reports

Case history reports track changes to Case records, including updates to status, priority, or ownership. These reports allow support teams to monitor how Cases progress through the service process, ensuring that customer issues are handled efficiently and identifying trends in resolution times. By reviewing Case history, service managers can evaluate response effectiveness and optimize Case handling workflows.

Campaign Influence Reports

Salesforce's Collaborative Campaign Influence model provides a structured and automated approach to attributing Opportunity revenue across multiple campaigns. By leveraging Campaign Influence reports, organizations gain deeper insight into how marketing efforts contribute to revenue generation and pipeline growth. These reports enable teams to analyze which campaigns are most effective in driving sales and optimizing marketing investments.

Salesforce includes several standard reports designed to assess Campaign Influence. The campaigns with influenced Opportunities reports help marketing teams identify which campaigns have successfully influenced Opportunities, whether they are still active or have closed. This report provides a clear view of how marketing activities contribute to business growth by allowing users to filter data by date range, campaign type, or Opportunity status. Another key report, the Campaign ROI Analysis Report, measures return on investment by comparing the revenue influenced by a campaign against its cost. Since Collaborative Campaign Influence distributes attribution across multiple campaigns, Salesforce calculates ROI based on assigned influence percentages, ensuring a more accurate representation of marketing impact. In addition to these standard reports, Salesforce users can create custom Campaign Influence reports tailored to their business needs. Reports can be customized to analyze influence by industry, region, Lead source, or any other segmentation relevant to the organization.

To ensure Campaign Influence reports provide meaningful and reliable insights, proper data management is essential. Opportunities must have accurately assigned contact roles, and campaigns should be consistently linked to the correct leads and contacts. Organizations should review their Campaign Influence settings to confirm that auto-association rules align with their business model and that both marketing and sales teams follow best practices for maintaining data integrity. Rather than relying solely on default reports, teams can refine their analysis through customized reporting that aligns with their strategic objectives. For setting up Campaigns, refer to Chapter 7.

Converted Leads Reports

By default, converted leads do not appear in standard lead reports, because once they are converted Salesforce considers them part of the Contact, Account, and Opportunity objects. However, Salesforce provides a way to generate reports on converted leads.

Navigate to the Reports tab, select New Report, search for and select "Leads with converted lead information," and then click Start Report. The Report Builder opens with the beginnings of your converted leads report (see Figure 10-38).

Figure 10-38. Lead Conversion Report

You may have to adjust the filters to pull in all converted lead information. To extract meaningful insights, you can customize the report by adding fields related to the conversion process, such as Converted Date.

Further grouping the report by the Converted Date allows for trend analysis, showing how lead conversion rates fluctuate over time. Filtering by owner or Lead source can provide additional insights into individual or campaign-level performance. If Opportunities are created upon conversion, comparing the number of converted leads to the number of resulting Opportunities can help assess the efficiency of the sales process.

While the converted leads report is useful for historical tracking, it does not include lead activity postconversion, as the lead record itself is no longer active. If further tracking of a converted contact's journey is needed, reports on Contacts, Opportunities, or Accounts should be used in conjunction with lead conversion data.

Collaborative Forecast Reports

Collaborative Forecast reports in Salesforce provide sales teams and leadership with critical visibility into projected revenue, pipeline health, and quota attainment. These reports enable organizations to track how forecasted revenue aligns with actual sales performance, helping teams identify trends and make informed business decisions.

Administrators play a key role in ensuring that forecast reporting is properly configured to align with business goals and that sales teams have access to accurate, up-to-date insights. For a deeper understanding of how forecasting is structured within Salesforce, refer to Chapter 7.

Salesforce includes several standard reports designed to help organizations analyze forecasts. The Forecast versus Quota report compares projected sales to assigned quotas, allowing sales leaders to monitor whether teams are on track to meet their targets. This report highlights trends in performance, making it easier to identify areas that require additional focus. The Pipeline Inspection report provides a breakdown of Opportunities across forecast categories such as Pipeline, Best Case, Commit, and Closed. By analyzing this report, sales managers can assess deal movement within the pipeline and pinpoint potential risks that could impact revenue. The Forecast Trends report tracks changes in forecasts over time, allowing organizations to monitor shifts in projected revenue and adjust strategies as needed to stay aligned with business goals.

In addition to standard reports, organizations can create custom reports using the Collaborative Forecasting data model. Custom reports can be tailored to track specific forecast metrics, such as performance by region, product line, or sales representative, providing more granular insights into revenue trends. These customized reports enable teams to refine their forecasting analysis to better fit their business needs.

Dashboards

Dashboards in Salesforce transform raw data into visually compelling insights, enabling users to monitor key performance metrics at a glance. While reports provide detailed, row-level data, dashboards consolidate and summarize this information into charts, graphs, and tables that offer a high-level view of business performance. By leveraging dashboards, administrators, sales teams, service managers, and executives can track trends, measure progress toward goals, and make informed decisions more efficiently.

Dashboards are built using underlying reports, meaning that every dashboard component, or widget, is powered by a report. This enables users to view data dynamically, with real-time updates ensuring that the most current business information is always accessible. Whether tracking sales pipeline health, monitoring customer service case volume, or assessing marketing campaign effectiveness, dashboards provide a centralized view of the metrics that matter most.

A well-designed dashboard enhances productivity by reducing the time spent digging through reports to find relevant insights. Instead of running multiple reports separately, users can interact with a single dashboard to analyze business performance from multiple angles. With customizable filters, different teams can tailor dashboards to their needs, ensuring that each user sees the data most relevant to their role.

This section will cover the fundamental components that make up a dashboard, how to create and customize dashboards for different use cases, and best practices for optimizing dashboard design. By understanding how to leverage dashboards effectively, you can maximize Salesforce's analytics capabilities, making data-driven decision and make more intuitive and efficient.

Dashboard Tab and Folders Overview

The Dashboards tab serves as the central location for accessing, managing, and organizing dashboards in Salesforce. Whether you are reviewing an existing dashboard or creating a new one, understanding how to navigate the Dashboards tab and its folder structure is essential for efficiently working with Salesforce analytics.

When you click the Dashboards tab, you are taken to the Dashboards landing page, as shown in Figure 10-39, where you can search for existing dashboards, browse through folders, or create a new dashboard.

Figure 10-39. All Dashboards selected on Dashboards home screen

Dashboard folders and organization

Salesforce dashboards are stored in folders, which help users organize and control access to them. This allows dashboards to be categorized based on department, function, or specific business needs.

Folders can be set to public or private. Public folders allow all users with the necessary permissions to view the dashboards inside, while private folders restrict access to specific individuals or groups.

Finding and accessing existing dashboards

To open an existing dashboard, navigate to the Dashboards tab and either search for a dashboard by name or browse through the available folders. Once a dashboard is located, clicking on its name will open it in the Dashboard Viewer, where users can review data visualizations, apply filters, and refresh the displayed data if necessary.

Impact on dashboards when source reports are deleted

Since every dashboard widget is powered by an underlying report, deleting a report directly impacts any dashboard that relies on it. If a report used in a dashboard is deleted, the affected widget will display an error message indicating that the report is missing. The rest of the dashboard will remain intact, but any widgets linked to the deleted report will no longer function properly.

Administrators should be mindful of this behavior when managing reports, especially in shared dashboard environments. Before deleting a report, it is good practice to verify whether it is being used in a dashboard. This can be done by checking report usage or communicating with dashboard users to ensure critical visualizations are not disrupted. If a report must be deleted, consider replacing it with an updated version and updating the affected widgets accordingly.

Creating a Dashboard

From the Dashboards home screen, click New Dashboard. The New Dashboard window opens, as shown in Figure 10-40.

Enter the dashboard Name, Description, and select a Folder where the Dashboard will be stored. Once the initial setup is complete, click Create to open the Dashboard Builder to build out your new dashboard.

Figure 10-40. New Dashboard window

Adding widgets to a dashboard

The Dashboard Builder allows you to add various components (widgets) to display report data in various visual formats, such as charts, tables, metrics, and gauges. Click the "+ Widget" button to add a widget to the blank dashboard canvas. The Widget options pop-up opens, as shown in Figure 10-41.

Figure 10-41. Widget options for a dashboard

You can add a chart or table widget, plain text, or insert an image on your dashboard.

Dashboard widgets overview

Dashboard widgets are added to the canvas of a dashboard. Each chart or table widget requires an underlying source report from which to draw its data. These source reports in effect serve as a query to bring in the data needed for the widget.

The widgets that you can select vary based on the underlying source report, or more specifically, the format of the underlying source report. For example, a Tabular report format supports only a table dashboard widget option, as shown in Figure 10-42.

Figure 10-42. Add Widget window with table widget selected

Summary source report dashboard widget options

If you select a source report with at least one row grouping, which is a Summary report, then you have a much larger selection of available dashboard widgets to choose from; the only options not available are stacked bar charts, both horizontal and vertical.

Matrix source report dashboard widget options

If your selected source report contains multiple groupings, meaning that it is a Matrix report, then all available dashboard widget options become available for you to choose from. The overall report format to dashboard widget availability is intertwined, and once you understand the correlations, you will be well prepared to approach any number of dashboard scenarios, both on the exam and on the job.

Dashboard data visibility: Running user versus dynamic dashboards

The *running user* setting determines whose data permissions are applied when a static dashboard is viewed. You can specify the running user during the dashboard creation process, or, if you're working with an existing dashboard, you can change the running user by opening the dashboard Properties window via the gear icon, as shown in Figure 10-43.

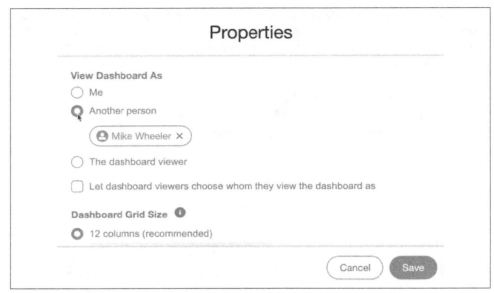

Figure 10-43. View Dashboard As in dashboard Properties window

Static dashboards

In a static dashboard, you assign a specific user as the running user, and every viewer sees data as though they were that user. This choice is made in the dashboard properties when you set the running user. Dynamic dashboards, on the other hand, are designed to provide individualized views of data without the need for creating separate dashboards or folders for different users.

Dynamic dashboards

In a dynamic dashboard, the data is shown based on the privileges of the currently logged-in user. Although the running user setting is still present, the system automatically uses each viewer's own permissions to determine which data is displayed. This ensures that each user sees only the data they have access to, offering personalized insights while still using a single dashboard layout.

It's important to note that while every dynamic dashboard relies on the running user setting, not every dashboard with a running user is dynamic. In static dashboards, you control the data view by specifying a fixed running user, whereas dynamic dashboards allow the running user to be determined at runtime based on who is logged in by selecting the dashboard viewer.

Limits of dynamic dashboards

There are specific limitations and considerations associated with dynamic dashboards. They cannot be saved in private folders or scheduled for automatic refresh; instead, they must be refreshed manually. Additionally, there are limits on the number of dynamic dashboards you can create, depending on your Salesforce edition.

Adding Filters to a Dashboard

Filters enhance dashboards by allowing users to adjust the displayed data dynamically without modifying the underlying reports. This flexibility makes dashboards more versatile by enabling users to analyze data from multiple perspectives within a single view.

To add a filter to a dashboard, open an existing dashboard in the Dashboard Builder and click "+ Filter." Choose a field that exists in the underlying reports, such as Region, Opportunity Stage, or Account Type. Filters apply across all widgets that include the selected field, ensuring consistency in data filtering.

After selecting a field, define the filter values that users can choose from when viewing the dashboard. For example, if filtering by Region, you might include values such as North America, Europe, and Asia-Pacific.

Users can then select a region from a drop-down menu to adjust the dashboard display accordingly. If a widget's report does not contain the filtered field, that widget will display No Data when the filter is applied.

Once the filter is configured, click Save to apply it to the dashboard. Users can now interact with the filter when viewing the dashboard, allowing for more customized data analysis without altering the original reports.

Dashboard Refresh and Limits

Salesforce dashboards do not update in real time. Instead, they display cached data from the last refresh. Users can manually refresh a dashboard or set up scheduled refreshes to ensure data remains up-to-date.

To refresh a dashboard, click Refresh in the top-right corner. This pulls the latest data from the underlying reports. However, frequent manual refreshes are not always practical, so Salesforce allows administrators to schedule dashboard refreshes at regular intervals.

To schedule a refresh, click Subscribe, then select how often the dashboard should refresh. Options include daily, weekly, or monthly. You can also specify recipients who should receive an email notification when the dashboard refreshes. This ensures that key stakeholders always have access to the most up-to-date metrics.

Subscribing to Dashboards

By subscribing to a dashboard in Salesforce, users can receive scheduled email updates containing the latest dashboard data. This feature ensures that key stakeholders have access to refreshed business insights without needing to manually open and refresh the dashboard.

Unlike report subscriptions, which can be configured with conditional delivery to act as a preventive monitoring tool, dashboard subscriptions do not offer conditional triggers. They are purely time-based and will send updates regardless of changes in data.

How to subscribe to a dashboard

To subscribe to a dashboard, navigate to the Dashboards tab and open the desired dashboard. Click the Subscribe button, typically located in the top-right corner of the dashboard screen. The Edit Subscription window displays.

Configure the frequency of updates. Users can choose to receive dashboard updates daily, weekly, or monthly, depending on their reporting needs. Additionally, users can add other recipients, ensuring that the right team members receive the emailed dashboard snapshot. However, recipients must have access to the dashboard in Salesforce to view the email content.

How subscribed dashboards are delivered

Subscribed dashboards are sent via email as an embedded snapshot of the dashboard's latest data. The email contains an image of the dashboard at the time of the scheduled refresh, along with a link to open the live version in Salesforce. Unlike report subscriptions, which can be configured to include exported CSV files, dashboards are always delivered as a visual snapshot rather than an interactive data set.

Best practices for dashboard subscriptions

Since dashboard subscriptions do not offer conditional triggers, they should be used for regular data monitoring rather than proactive alerting. For preventive monitoring, where an alert should only be sent when certain conditions are met (such as a spike in case volume), report subscriptions with conditional delivery should be used instead. Dashboards, on the other hand, are best suited for scheduled executive updates, performance tracking, and general visibility into key business metrics.

Downloading dashboards

Downloading a dashboard in Salesforce allows users to save a static version of the dashboard for offline reference, sharing outside of Salesforce, or inclusion in presentations and reports. Unlike report exports, which generate structured CSV files containing raw data, exported dashboards are purely visual snapshots and do not include underlying data in a downloadable format.

To download a dashboard, click the Download drop-down option from the top-right of the selected dashboard. A *.png* image file of the Dashboard downloads to your computer.

Summary

As you conclude Chapter 10, it's time to assess the knowledge you've gained about data and analytics management in Salesforce. This chapter has provided essential insights into managing data quality, importing and exporting data effectively, and leveraging analytics through reports and dashboards.

Salesforce's data and analytics tools allow businesses to organize, analyze, and visualize their data for better decision-making. In this chapter, you explored how reports, dashboards, snapshots, and forecasting tools provide valuable insights into business performance.

Chapter 10 Quiz

This quiz is designed to test your understanding of key concepts, ensuring you're prepared for the types of questions that may appear on the Salesforce Certified Administrator exam.

Remember, each question is an opportunity to review and reinforce your understanding of important topics, from using the Data Import Wizard and Data Loader, to creating custom reports and dashboards.

Each question challenges you to recall and apply what you've learned. Take your time with each question and select the answer that best aligns with the principles you've learned. After making your choices, carefully review the answers and explanations in the Appendix to solidify your understanding of the correct answers. This process will reinforce your existing knowledge and highlight areas that may require further review, helping ensure you're fully prepared for real-world scenarios and exam success.

1. What is the primary purpose of the Salesforce Data Export service?

    a. To export metadata for system configuration backup

    b. To allow users to manually export individual records to Excel

    c. To provide scheduled or on-demand exports of data records in an organization

    d. To enable real-time data synchronization with third-party applications

2. When using the Data Export service, how is the exported data delivered?

    a. As a downloadable link sent via email, containing a ZIP file of CSV files

    b. As an Excel file attached directly to an email

    c. As a JSON file stored in a Salesforce custom object

    d. As a real-time feed to an external data warehouse

3. What is a key difference between exporting reports and exporting data via the Data Export service?

    a. Reports can be scheduled for export with conditional delivery, while Data Export does not allow scheduling.

    b. Data Export provides data backup, whereas report exports are based on predefined report filters.

    c. Reports are exported as JSON files, while Data Export provides CSV files.

    d. The Data Export service only supports exporting custom objects, while reports include both standard and custom objects.

4. Why would an administrator use a converted leads report?

    a. To track leads that have been deleted from the system

    b. To analyze which marketing campaigns resulted in the most lead conversions

    c. To find leads that have been reassigned to a different owner

    d. To measure the average response time for new leads

5. Which of the following history reports is *not* available in Salesforce?

    a. Case history reports

    b. Login history reports

    c. Chatter Feed Tracking reports

    d. Setup Audit Trail reports

6. Which of the following best describes the difference between report subscriptions and data exports?

    a. Both allow conditional delivery based on data thresholds.

    b. Report subscriptions support conditional delivery, while data exports do not.

    c. Data exports are limited to reports only, while report subscriptions allow full object exports.

    d. Both require administrative privileges to configure.

7. What determines the data a user sees when viewing a dashboard?

    a. The user's personal security settings

    b. The filters applied within each widget

    c. The running user assigned to the dashboard

    d. The underlying reports used in each widget

8. When editing a Salesforce dashboard, what is required for each widget to display data?

    a. The dashboard must be set to refresh every hour.

    b. The user must have administrator permissions.

    c. The underlying report must be saved and accessible to the user.

    d. The widget must be linked to a report.

9. What is the purpose of a dashboard filter?

    a. To modify the underlying report's data permanently

    b. To allow users to adjust the displayed data without changing the underlying report

    c. To restrict access to certain reports based on security settings

    d. To enable scheduled email delivery of dashboards

10. What happens when a user deletes a report that is linked to a dashboard widget?

    a. The dashboard automatically generates a new report to replace it.

    b. The widget remains unchanged but no longer updates.

    c. The widget displays an error message indicating the report is missing.

    d. The dashboard is deleted along with the report.

11. Which report format must you use to visually compare two different field groupings, such as this quarter's revenue versus last quarter's revenue?

    a. Tabular

    b. Summary

    c. Matrix

    d. Joined

Workflow/Process Automation

Throughout the preceding chapters, you've built a solid Salesforce foundation. You're now ready to take the next step: learning how to automate business processes in Salesforce to save time and reduce the manual steps required for repetitive tasks.

In this chapter, we'll explore the powerful automation capabilities that Salesforce provides. While the platform now revolves around Flow as the primary automation tool, we'll begin with a simpler, but still essential, automation feature: *approval processes*.

Why start here?

Approval processes are structured and easier to configurethan Flows, making them a great introduction to the automation mindset. They provide a guided experience that helps you get comfortable with concepts like automation triggers, record locking, and email notifications before diving into the more advanced, logic-driven world of Flows.

Historically, Salesforce offered three primary tools for automation: workflow rules, Process Builder, and Flow. Salesforce has since retired workflow rules and Process Builder from active use. While you can no longer create new automations with them, you may still encounter these legacy tools in existing Salesforce implementations.

 You should not expect questions specifically about workflow rules or Process Builder on the Salesforce Platform Administrator certification exam. However, it's still useful to understand what they are in case you encounter them on the job.

Currently, Salesforce Flow is the platform's most robust and flexible declarative automation tool. With Flow, you can automate nearly every use case once handled by the legacy tools, plus many more. You'll learn how Flow functions as a visual programming environment, enabling you to create sophisticated automations without writing code. Each Flow element maps to a programming concept, but remains accessible through a visual, drag-and-drop interface.

Beyond building automations, you'll develop essential skills for keeping them reliable, like building fault paths for graceful error handling and using Flow Builder's debug tools to test your automations before deploying them. These practical skills ensure your automations stay strong, even when faced with unexpected real-world scenarios.

From the Exam Guide

The Workflow/Process Automation knowledge area of the Exam Guide contains the following learning objectives:

- Given a scenario, identify the appropriate automation solution based on the capabilities of the tool.
- Describe capabilities and use cases for Flow.
- Describe capabilities and use cases for the approval process.

Automation Home

Automation in Salesforce refers to configuring processes that streamline repetitive tasks and business logic, allowing users to work more efficiently and consistently within the platform. To see a consolidated view of your declarative (i.e., noncode) automations, search for and select Automation Home in Setup. The Automation Home screen displays, as shown in Figure 11-1.

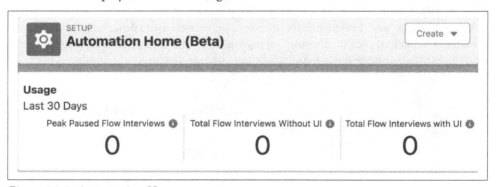

Figure 11-1. Automation Home screen

The Automation Home screen in Salesforce provides a centralized view of your organization's automation processes, primarily focused on Flows. It includes key automation metrics and performance insights into your automations. If you're visiting Automation Home for the first time and haven't yet deployed any Flows, you'll see all analytics display zero. These figures will update as automations are activated and begin running in your organization.

Approval Processes

Approval processes in Salesforce provide a structured method for automating how records are approved in your organization. From expense approvals and discount authorizations to content reviews and time-off requests, approval processes ensure that important decisions follow your organization's established protocols while maintaining proper documentation directly within Salesforce.

Automated approval processes offer significant advantages over manual approval methods. They provide consistent enforcement of your organization's approval policies, automated record locking through the approval cycle, and comprehensive audit trails of all approval activities. This structured approach reduces errors, increases accountability, and accelerates decision making across your organization.

When designing approval processes, it's important to account for potential bottlenecks. Approvers should be carefully selected and not overburdened. Consider alternative approval paths or additional notifications to address delays and ensure the approval workflow remains efficient and responsive.

Planning Your Approval Process

Before creating an approval process, thorough planning is essential. The approval process structure varies based on your organization's business requirements, but most approval workflows share common elements that require careful consideration.

When you search for and select Approval Processes from Setup, you see a list of recommended steps to take, as shown in Figure 11-2.

The list of recommended steps starts with reading the help topic, which is linked to from the list. You can click it to open the topic in a new browser window.

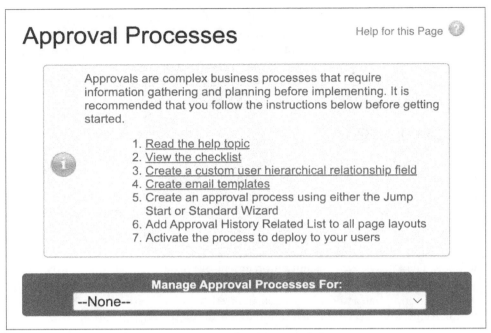

Figure 11-2. Approval Processes screen with recommended steps

Approval process checklist

The next step in Salesforce's recommended list of steps is to view the checklist for creating an approval process. The checklist provides a high-level overview of preplanning steps that should be undertaken before building out your approval process. You can review those steps by clicking the "View the checklist" link in step 2 of Figure 11-2.

Creating a custom user hierarchical field

The third step is to optionally create a custom user hierarchical field. This type of field allows you to define a user-to-user relationship beyond the standard Manager field that exists on user records. It's useful in cases where approval routing needs to go to someone other than a user's direct manager, such as a department lead, regional coordinator, or another designated reviewer.

Once this field is created, you can reference it when assigning approvers in your process. This option complements the standard methods available for specifying an approver in Salesforce, which include assigning to a specific user, a user's manager, a role, a queue, or even allowing the submitter to manually select an approver at runtime.

Creating email templates for approval processes

The fourth step is to create email templates to be used in your approval process. When a record is submitted for approval, Salesforce can send notifications to assigned approvers using your specified email template.

The templates you build and use in your approval process should provide approvers with essential information about the record requiring approval and clear instructions for responding to the request. You can also include a direct link to the record to be approved as part of the email template, allowing for quick navigation for approvers who receive email alerts as part of the approval process.

Click the "Create email templates" link in the list to display the New Template screen, as shown in Figure 11-3.

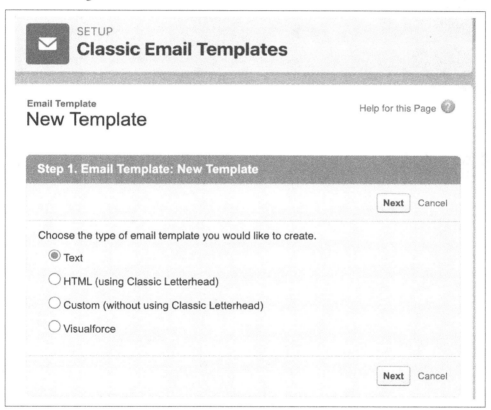

Figure 11-3. New Template screen

Approval processes use Classic Email Templates, not Lightning Email Templates. Despite this limitation, you can still create effective and professional-looking notifications.

The New Template screen begins with you first selecting the type of email template you wish to create. Your selection will dictate how many steps are involved after you click Next.

Text email templates. The Text option is the most basic of the available template types. It supports plain text only and does not support images, colors, or formatting. This is ideal for simple communications or when email deliverability is a top concern. Selecting Text and clicking Next displays the new Text Email Template window, as shown in Figure 11-4.

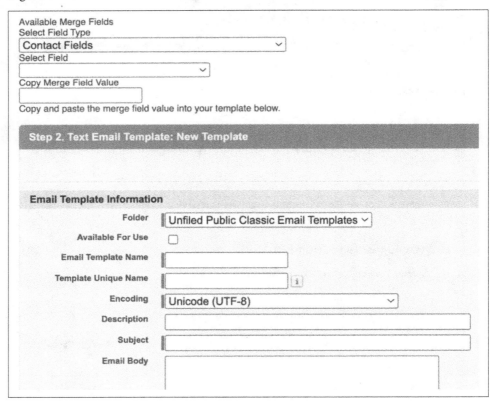

Figure 11-4. New Text Email Template window

The Available Merge Fields selector at the top enables you to personalize your message by inserting dynamic fields from Salesforce records. After selecting a merge field, copy and paste it into the Subject or Email Body fields, as needed. Check the Available For Use checkbox to make it available to select in approval processes.

HTML email templates (using Classic Letterhead). This template type allows for branded, formatted emails that use a predefined Classic Letterhead. The letterhead defines elements like your logo, colors, and header layout. After selecting this option, you'll complete the rest of the template by adding merge fields, a subject line, and the email body.

HTML templates support open tracking if Enhanced Email is enabled in your org, making this a strong option when email engagement needs to be monitored in approval processes.

Custom email templates (without Classic Letterhead). Despite not including HTML in the name, Custom Email Templates are another type of HTML email. The key difference is that you're not required to use a letterhead. This gives you full control to define your own structure and style using HTML.

When creating this type of template, you'll enter the HTML code directly into the editor. If your template includes images, you must first upload those files into the Salesforce Documents tab or as public files in the Files tab. The images must be referenced using their file URLs in your HTML code. This ensures that they render correctly in the final email.

Like the Classic HTML option, Custom Email Templates also support open tracking when Enhanced Email is enabled in your org.

Visualforce email templates. Visualforce templates offer the highest level of customization for email templates in Salesforce. Visualforce is a Salesforce framework that uses a tag-based markup language similar to HTML, allowing for dynamic, data-driven content. While Visualforce templates don't directly contain Apex code, they can leverage Visualforce components and merge fields to dynamically pull data from Salesforce records and related objects, enabling more tailored and personalized messaging than standard templates.

For example, a Visualforce email template could dynamically display a customer's recent orders or a table summarizing multiple related records, such as outstanding invoices or purchased products, directly within the email.

However, Visualforce templates typically require assistance from developers or more advanced Salesforce administrators for initial creation and ongoing maintenance. They do not support open tracking functionality natively. Additionally, detailed

Visualforce development is beyond the scope of the Salesforce Platform Administrator certification exam.

Creating an Approval Process

The fifth step in the approval process is to create the approval process using either the Jump Start or Standard Setup Wizard. As you begin building an approval process, you'll quickly recognize the value of having your email templates ready to go beforehand. That is because you will find that many of the configuration steps you work through in the approval process wizards involve selecting email templates for various notifications.

Let's walk through how to create an approval process. To begin, select the object the process will apply to from the Manage Approval Processes For drop-down field on the Approval Processes screen Figure 11-2. The object can be any standard or custom object, such as an Account or a Reimbursement Request, for example.

Once the object is selected, the screen refreshes to display any active or inactive approval processes currently in your org for that object. Click Create New Approval Process and choose either the Jump Start Wizard or the Standard Setup Wizard.

Choosing a Wizard

Salesforce offers two guided paths for creating an approval process. The Jump Start Wizard is designed for quick, single-step approvals and takes care of many configuration details behind the scenes. Use this option when the approval path is straightforward and does not require conditional logic or multiple steps.

The Standard Setup Wizard gives you more control over the approval process structure. Use it when your scenario involves parallel approvals or complex routing logic. Begin with the Jump Start Wizard if your requirements are simple and you want to get a basic approval process up and running quickly.

The Jump Start Wizard

Once you select Use Jump Start Wizard, the screen prompts you to configure several key areas. The first area to fill out this information section, as shown in Figure 11-5.

Start by entering a concise name that reflects the purpose of the process. You can also select an email template to notify the approver.

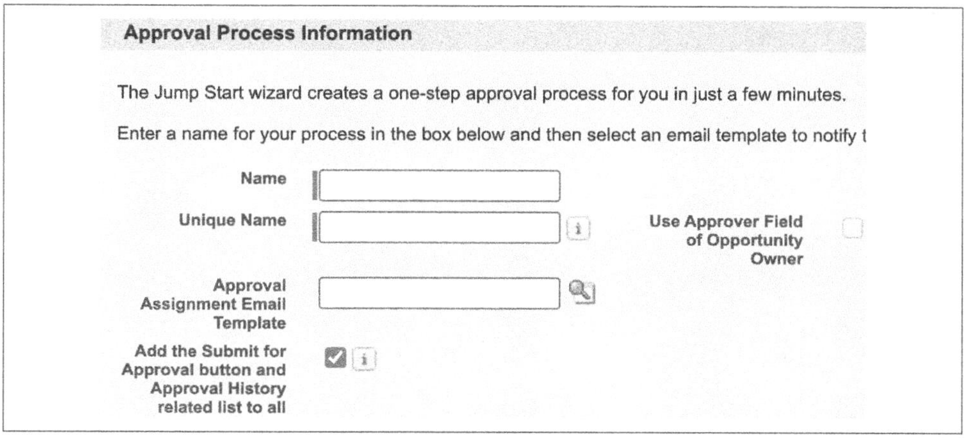

Figure 11-5. Approval Process Information section of an approval process

Once you have entered the Approval Process Information, scroll down to the Specify Entry Criteria section (see Figure 11-6).

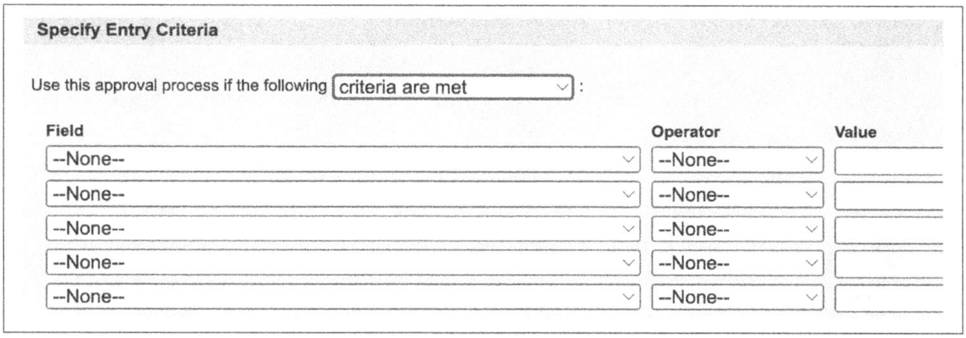

Figure 11-6. Specify Entry Criteria section for the Jump Start Wizard

Define the entry criteria that determine which records should trigger the approval process. This is typically based on field values, such as Status, Amount, or Owner, on the selected object. You can select either the default option of "criteria are met" or "formula evaluates to true" from the drop-down list.

Selecting formula evaluation updates the screen to display the Formula editor, as shown in Figure 11-7.

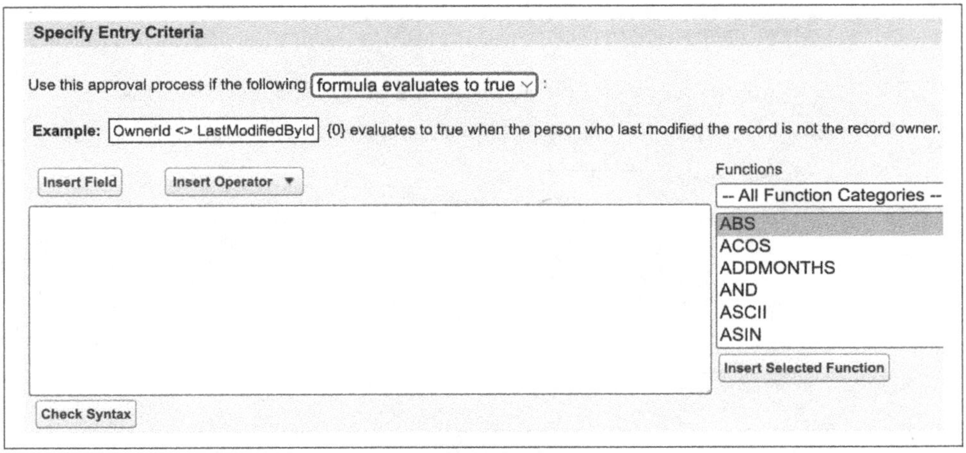

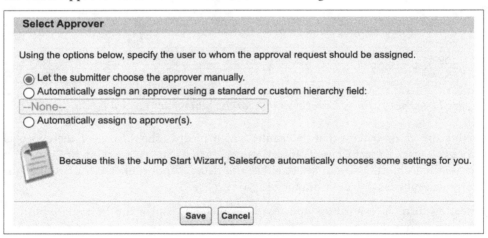

Specify Entry Criteria

Use this approval process if the following [formula evaluates to true ∨] :

Example: [OwnerId <> LastModifiedById] {0} evaluates to true when the person who last modified the record is not the record owner.

[Insert Field]   [Insert Operator ▼]

Functions
-- All Function Categories --
ABS
ACOS
ADDMONTHS
AND
ASCII
ASIN

[Insert Selected Function]

[Check Syntax]

Figure 11-7. Formula editor in Specify Entry Criteria section

The Formula editor facilitates entering fields, operators, and functions by way of their corresponding buttons. Once you have entered your entry criteria formula, click Check Syntax to verify that your formula is structured correctly and no syntax errors are found.

Once you have specified your entry criteria for the approval process, scroll down to the Select Approver section of the screen, as shown in Figure 11-8.

Select Approver

Using the options below, specify the user to whom the approval request should be assigned.

⦿ Let the submitter choose the approver manually.
◯ Automatically assign an approver using a standard or custom hierarchy field:
[--None--   ∨]
◯ Automatically assign to approver(s).

Because this is the Jump Start Wizard, Salesforce automatically chooses some settings for you.

[Save] [Cancel]

Figure 11-8. Select Approver section of an approval process

There are multiple options available for the approver assignment:

Let the submitter choose the approver manually
> The first option provides flexibility by allowing the user who submits the record to select the appropriate approver at submission time. This works well when the appropriate approver varies based on contextual factors, your organization has a complex approval structure, or you want to give submitters discretion over the approval routing. When this option is selected, the submitter will see a lookup field during the submission process where they can select any user with appropriate permissions.

Automatically assign an approver using a standard or custom hierarchy field
> The second option leverages your existing organizational hierarchy in Salesforce to determine approvers. You can choose the standard Manager field on the User object or any custom hierarchy field you've previously created on the User object. The system then automatically routes the approval request to the submitter's manager (or the value in your custom hierarchy field).

Automatically assign to approver(s)
> The third option allows you to designate specific users or related users as approvers. When choosing this option, you can select a specific user in your Salesforce org who will always be the approver for these requests. Alternatively, you can designate a user from a related record, such as the record owner, Opportunity owner, or account manager. This approach works best when you have dedicated individuals for specific types of approvals or when certain roles always handle approvals regardless of the record's other attributes.

After you complete these steps, Salesforce automatically configures several default settings. It creates a single approval step, sets up automatic record locking when records are submitted, and generates basic approval and rejection actions. While these defaults work well for simple processes, they may not accommodate more complex approval requirements.

The Jump Start Wizard offers speed and simplicity at the expense of flexibility. For multistep approvals or processes requiring advanced logic, the Standard Setup Wizard provides a more suitable approach with comprehensive configuration options.

The Standard Setup Wizard

When you click the Create New Approval Process button and choose Use Standard Setup Wizard from the drop-down menu, the wizard begins with the same basic information as the Jump Start Wizard, requiring a process name and description. From there, it expands into detailed configuration sections, starting with specifying entry criteria (see Figure 11-9).

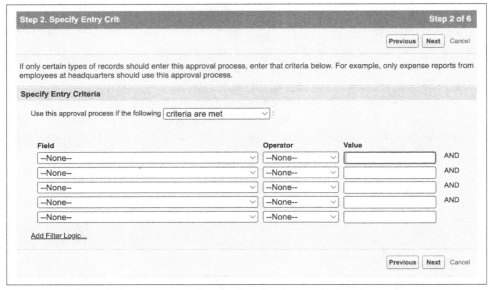

Figure 11-9. Specify Entry Criteria for the Standard Setup Wizard

You'll define entry criteria with additional options for formula-based conditions. Next, you'll specify how to handle records that don't meet the entry criteria. They can be automatically approved, automatically rejected, or routed to bypass the process entirely.

A significant advantage of the Standard Setup Wizard is its support for multistep approval paths. For each step, you define entry criteria, approver assignments, and rejection handling. This allows for complex approval hierarchies where, for example, first-level managers approve smaller amounts while executives approve larger transactions.

The Standard Setup Wizard also provides granular control over automated actions. You can configure actions to occur at different points, such as during initial submission, and for approval, rejection, recall, or final approval. For each point, you can add multiple action types including email alerts, field updates, tasks, and outbound messages.

Adding an approval process related list

After configuring your approval process, the final steps involve preparing for deployment and activating the process. Add the approval history related list to your object's page layouts to provide users with visibility into approval status and history. This related list displays important information including current status, submitter, approvers, and approval dates.

Testing an approval process

Always test before deploying an approval process. In a sandbox or developer organization, simulate various scenarios to verify that your process behaves as expected. Test both positive paths where records are approved and negative paths where records are rejected or recalled. Confirm that all automated actions execute correctly and that the appropriate users receive the correct notification emails.

Activating an Approval Process

After testing confirms your approval process functions correctly, you're ready for activation. Navigate to your Approval Process detail page and click the Activate button. Activation makes your approval process immediately available to users who have permission to submit records for approval. While approval processes are useful for structured, multistep record review, they don't offer the flexibility of Flow for broader logic or interactivity. It's time to go with the Flow!

Go with the Flow

Flow is the primary declarative automation tool available on the Salesforce platform. It enables you to automate complex business logic and streamline user interactions without writing code. Common examples of Flow in action include automatically assigning incoming support cases to the appropriate team based on specific criteria, guiding customer service agents through step-by-step troubleshooting processes, and updating related records when key values change, such as updating an account's status when an Opportunity closes.

Using Flow, you can automate routine tasks, enforce consistent business rules, and reduce manual effort, significantly increasing efficiency and accuracy across your organization.

Flow Builder

Flow Builder is the visual, drag-and-drop interface used to create and manage Flows. Behind the scenes, every Flow you create is XML code that Salesforce interprets and executes. This XML code defines everything from the logic paths to variable assignments and record operations.

To access Flow Builder, search for and select Flows in Setup. The All Flows screen displays (see Figure 11-10).

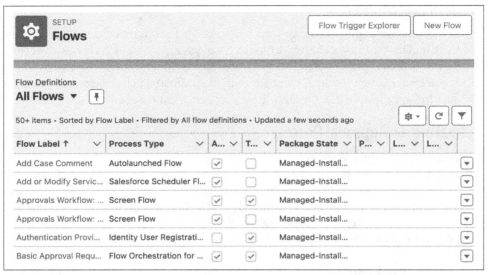

Figure 11-10. All Flows screen

The All Flows screen displays a list of existing Flows in your organization. To create a new Flow, click the New Flow button at the top of the screen. The New Automation window displays options for creating a Flow, as shown in Figure 11-11.

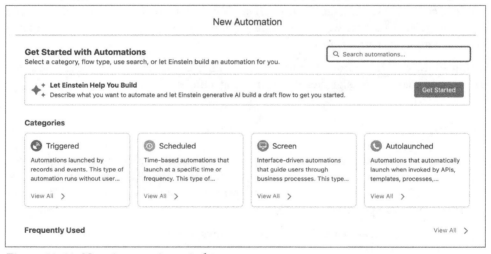

Figure 11-11. New Automation window

When creating a new Flow, you can select Let Einstein Help You Build (select from different Categories or Frequently Used Flow types). When you select a Category, the selection screen updates, enabling you to filter by one or multiple categories. You can then select from the available types, as shown in Figure 11-12.

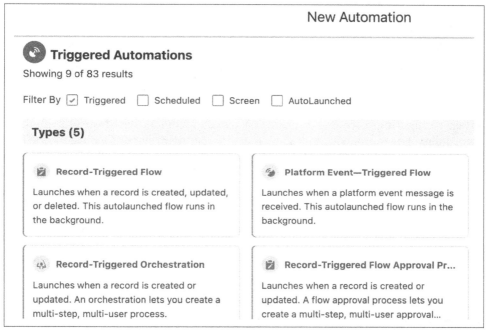

Figure 11-12. Automations Selection screen

The Flow Builder currently supports many types of Flows; I'll provide an overview of the most commonly used types.

Record-Triggered Flows

Record-triggered Flows automatically execute whenever a Salesforce record is created, updated, or deleted. For example, you could use a record-triggered Flow to automatically update related records when an Opportunity is marked as Closed Won.

Screen Flows

Screen Flows guide your users through interactive screens to collect input or display information. These Flows provide a visual user interface and can help simplify data entry for complex, multistep processes.

Unlike record-triggered Flows that run in the background, screen Flows create interactive, guided experiences for users by presenting a series of screens that collect information, display data, or guide users through complex processes.

To create a screen Flow, navigate to the Flows screen in Setup and click New Flow. Select Screen Flow from the Flow type options. The Flow Builder canvas displays, ready for you to add screens and logic.

The primary building block of a screen Flow is the Screen element, which you can add to your canvas. Each screen can contain various components, such as text display, input fields, choice components, and display components that guide users through a process.

When configuring a screen, you can add dynamic content based on user input or record data. For example, you might show different fields based on a user's previous selections or display record information from Salesforce. You can also customize the appearance of your screens with headers, footers, and help text to guide users effectively.

Screen Flows are particularly useful for guided data entry, multistep approval processes, or complex decision trees where user input is required. They can be embedded into Lightning pages, launched from buttons or links, or even invoked from other automation tools. This flexibility makes them suitable for a wide range of business scenarios.

For example, you might create a screen Flow to guide sales representatives through a quote-creation process, ensuring they capture all required information while dynamically calculating pricing based on selections. Or you could build a customer service Flow that walks agents through troubleshooting steps, adapting the process based on customer responses.

When building screen Flows, you'll typically combine Screen elements with Decision elements to create branching logic and with Assignment elements to store and manipulate variables based on user input. You might also include record operations to create, update, or retrieve Salesforce data during the Flow.

Schedule-Triggered Flows

Schedule-triggered Flows run automatically at specified times without user intervention. They allow you to automate tasks that need to occur regularly or at specific times, making them ideal for data maintenance, periodic notifications, or timed business processes.

When configuring a scheduled Flow, you first define when and how often it should run. You can schedule a Flow to run:

- Once at a specific date and time
- Daily at a designated time
- Weekly on selected days of the week
- Monthly on specific dates or relative days (e.g., the first Monday)
- Yearly on specific dates

After setting the schedule, you define which records the Flow should process. Unlike record-triggered Flows that operate on a single record, scheduled Flows typically work with collections of records that match specific criteria. For example, you might select all Opportunities that have been open for more than 30 days or all Cases that haven't been updated in a week.

Scheduled Flows are particularly useful for automating routine maintenance tasks, such as updating record statuses, sending reminders, or cleaning up old data. For instance, you might create a scheduled Flow that runs nightly to identify stale leads and either update their status or assign them to a queue for review.

You can also use scheduled Flows for time-sensitive business processes. For example, a scheduled Flow could send customers renewal reminders 30, 15, and 7 days before their contract expires, helping your sales team stay ahead of potential churn.

When building a scheduled Flow, you'll typically use Get Records elements to retrieve the records you want to process, followed by Loop elements to iterate through them and perform the necessary actions. You might also include Decision elements to apply different logic based on record attributes.

Autolaunched Flows

Autolaunched Flows run in the background without user interaction when called by another process. Unlike screen Flows that require user input, autolaunched Flows execute automatically when invoked, making them ideal for backend processes.

Autolaunched Flows are similar to record-triggered Flows in that they run without user interaction, but they differ in how they're initiated. While record-triggered Flows respond to data changes, autolaunched Flows are explicitly called by:

- Other Flows
- REST API calls
- Custom buttons or links
- Apex code

This flexibility makes autolaunched Flows a versatile tool for building reusable components for your automation strategy. For example, you might create an autolaunched Flow that calculates pricing based on complex rules, then call that Flow from multiple screen Flows and record-triggered Flows to ensure consistent calculations across your organization.

Autolaunched Flows can also serve as integration points with external systems. By exposing an autolaunched Flow through a Representational State Transfer (REST) API, you enable external applications to communicate with Salesforce using standard web protocols. This allows other systems to trigger Salesforce automations, creating a seamless connection between your CRM system and various business applications.

A common use case for autolaunched Flows is to encapsulate complex business logic that needs to be reused across multiple processes. For instance, you might create an autolaunched Flow that determines customer discounts based on their purchase history, account status, and current promotions. This Flow could then be called from Opportunity-related processes, quote generation screens, and order processing systems to ensure consistent discount application.

Building a Flow

Once you've selected the type of Flow you wish to create, Salesforce displays the Flow Builder canvas, which is the main workspace for building automations visually, as shown in Figure 11-13.

From this Flow Builder canvas, you'll add and configure Flow elements to define your business logic. As you add each element, you'll establish how your Flow responds to various scenarios, ensuring each step clearly aligns with your business requirements.

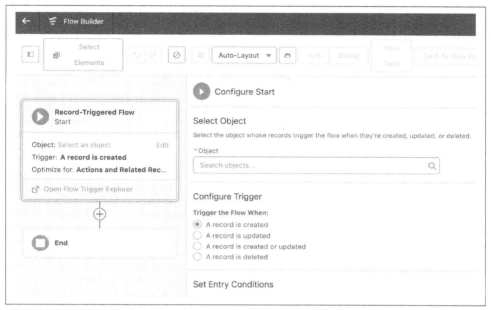

Figure 11-13. Flow Builder interface

Flow Resources

Flow Resources are used to store and manage values that your Flow will reference or manipulate as it runs. These values can include user inputs, calculated results, record data, static text, and more. Resources are essential building blocks that allow your Flow to operate with flexibility and logic. Whether you are updating a field, comparing a number, displaying a message, or calculating a value, you will often work with Flow Resources to store and pass data between elements.

To access Flow Resources, click the manager icon on the left side of the Flow Builder screen. This displays a list of all Resources currently available in your Flow, as shown in Figure 11-14.

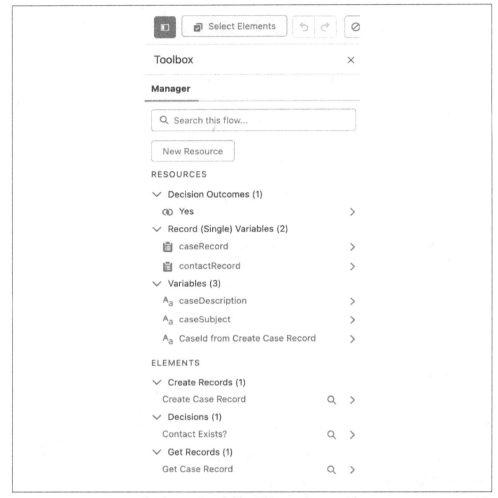

Figure 11-14. Manager displaying available resources in your Flow

From there, you can click New Resource to create one. You'll be prompted to choose the type of resource you want to create: Variable, Constant, Formula, Text Template, or Stage. Each resource type serves a different purpose.

Variable resource

The Variable resource type is used to store a value that can change as the Flow progresses. This is one of the most commonly used resource types. Variables can hold a single value, like a number or a text string, or a collection of values, such as a list of records. Variables are often used in assignment steps or passed between elements to retain and update information.

Constant resource

A Constant is similar to a variable, but the value you define at creation cannot be changed during the Flow. Constants are helpful when you need a fixed reference value, such as a discount rate or a region code, that is reused in multiple places.

Formula resource

Formulas are used to calculate values based on logic and expressions. A Formula resource can combine text, perform math, or evaluate conditions using field values, variables, and functions. The result is calculated dynamically when the Flow runs, and the value can then be used wherever needed within the Flow.

Text Template resource

Text Templates allow you to define and reuse blocks of text that include merge fields or variables. These are commonly used to display messages to users in Screen elements or to generate dynamic content in email alerts or confirmation messages.

Stage resource

Stage is a specialized resource used in screen Flows to track where a user is in a multistep process. It allows you to visually represent progress and guide users through structured steps, making it easier for them to complete a sequence of actions.

Working with Flow Resources

These resources can be selected and referenced throughout your Flow wherever needed. By using them effectively, you gain more control over how data moves and changes within your automation, allowing for clearer logic and a more dynamic experience.

Resources are what hold the data your Flow will work with. These values may come from user input, be calculated in real time, or be retrieved from the Salesforce database. But not all values need to be created manually. Salesforce also provides built-in global variables that allow you to reference system-level information without extra configuration.

Global Variables

Global variables provide system-defined values that are always available to your Flow. These are not created manually like other resources, but can be selected and referenced in many Flow elements, such as formulas, conditions, assignments, and filters. They offer context about the current user, the record being processed, the running Flow itself, and even the current date and time.

You can access global variables from fields where values are selected or formulas are defined.

Some commonly used global variables include:

$User
> This references data about the user running the Flow, such as their ID, name, email, or role. This is useful when routing records or sending notifications.

$Record
> Available only in record-triggered Flows, this variable refers to the record that caused the Flow to launch. You can access its fields without needing a Get Records element.

$Flow
> This provides Flow-level information, like whether the Flow is being debugged, or stores the system-generated fault message if an error occurs.

$System
> This provides access to the current date and time as well as other system-level values.

$Profile
> This allows you to check against the user's profile name or ID to drive decisions or apply filters.

Global variables are often used in conditions for Decision elements, filters for Get Records, default values in input fields, and calculations inside formulas. They make your Flows more dynamic and responsive to real-time context, without requiring hard-coded logic or extra steps.

By becoming familiar with these system-level values, you will be able to build smarter Flows that react differently depending on the user, the data, or the environment they are operating in.

When working in Flow Builder, global variables may appear under slightly different names depending on the context. For example, when setting values in formulas or conditions, you may refer to $User.Id, $Record.Name, or $Flow.FaultMessage. However, when accessing global values from the New Resource dialog or selecting resources directly from the UI, you will see these same variables presented with friendlier labels such as Running Flow Interview, Running Org, and Running User, as shown in Figure 11-15. These are simply alternate labels for the same global context values used in your Flow logic.

Figure 11-15. Global variables in the All Resources panel

Now that you've seen how both resources and global variables support your Flow behind the scenes, it's time to shift focus to the other half of building Flows: the elements themselves.

Elements are the actions your Flow performs, whether it's gathering input, making decisions, or updating records. Elements you place on your Flow canvas often rely on Resources or global variables to function, which is why understanding both is key to building smart, effective automation.

Flow Elements

Elements are the building blocks of Flows in Salesforce. They work together to create your automations. Each element serves a specific purpose in your Flow, from making decisions and assigning values to retrieving and manipulating records. Clicking the "+" sign in the Flow Builder opens the Add Element pop-up, as shown in Figure 11-16.

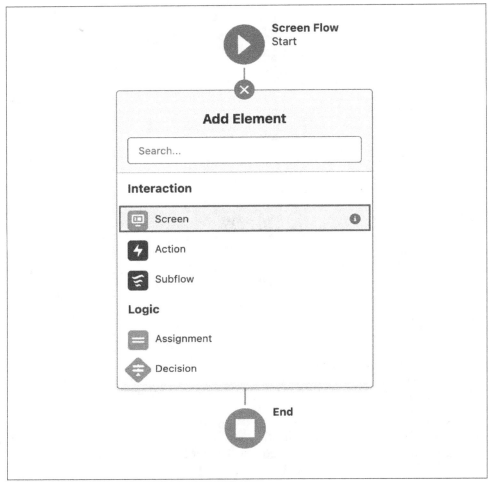

Figure 11-16. Add Element pop-up

Flow Element Types

You can scroll down the Add Element pop-up to see that the available elements are grouped into three categories: Interaction, Logic, and Data.

Flow Interaction elements

Flow Interaction elements are used to either engage users directly or to invoke related processes and actions behind the scenes. These elements are foundational to how a Flow gathers input, performs tasks, or connects with other Flows. The Flow Interaction elements include Screen, Action, and Subflow:

Screen

> The Screen element is what introduces interactivity to a Flow. When used in a screen Flow, it allows you to guide users through a series of steps, presenting fields where they can enter or select information. These fields might include text inputs, checkboxes, picklists, or display text. Screen elements are useful when you want to capture data from a user or walk users through a process, such as submitting a request or updating a record.

Action

> The Action element is used when you want the Flow to perform a specific task automatically. Actions can include sending an email, creating a task, or invoking a Quick Action. These are system-level tasks that do not require user input but execute as part of the Flow logic to carry out predefined actions. Action elements are especially helpful for automating follow-ups or triggering processes that would otherwise require manual steps.

Subflow

> The Subflow element allows one Flow to call another. This is useful for keeping your Flows modular and maintainable. For example, if multiple Flows across your organization all require the same logic, like applying a discount rule or performing a credit check, you can build that logic once in its own Flow, then reference it from other Flows using a Subflow element. Subflows pass data in and out through variables, and when used effectively, they help avoid duplication and reduce maintenance. We'll revisit Subflows later in the chapter, once you've seen how Flows are structured and how reusable components can simplify more complex automations.

Flow Logic element

Logic elements in Flow are used to control the behavior of the automation by evaluating conditions, manipulating data, and determining how a Flow progresses. These elements focus entirely on the internal decision making and data handling within the Flow. The Flow Logic elements include Assignment, Decision, Loop, Transform, Collection Sort, Collection Filter, and Pause:

Assignment

> The Assignment element is used to set or update the values of variables in a Flow. This can include assigning a static value to a variable, copying a value from a field, or adjusting a number. For example, you might use Assignment to update a variable with the total number of Cases tied to an account, or to format a string value based on user input. You can perform several assignments within a single element, which makes it useful for grouping related updates together as the Flow moves forward.

Decision

The Decision element introduces conditional logic into your Flow. It checks one or more conditions and then guides the Flow along different paths depending on whether those conditions are true. Each outcome path has its own criteria, and you can also define a default outcome that handles anything that doesn't match the earlier conditions. For example, you might route a record down different paths depending on its status or priority. The Decision element allows you to create branches in your logic so the Flow behaves differently based on what is happening at that moment.

Loop

The Loop element allows you to cycle through a group of records or values one at a time. This is especially helpful when you are working with collections, such as a list of Cases or contacts. Within a loop, you can reference the current item and perform actions such as updating fields, checking conditions, or assigning new values. Loops help you apply the same logic to each item in a group without having to repeat your Flow steps for every individual record.

Transform

The Transform element lets you map and restructure data between different objects or data structures within a Flow. Rather than simply filtering or sorting records, the Transform element allows you to map fields from one object type to another, such as mapping fields from Opportunity records into Task records. For example, you can quickly create tasks using data from Opportunities, automatically transferring fields like Opportunity Name and Close Date into corresponding Task fields. This helps streamline data management and reduces the need for additional assignment steps or loops within your Flow.

Collection Sort

Collection Sort is used to order a collection of records by a specific field. You can choose whether to sort in ascending or descending order. This is helpful when your Flow needs to look at the first or last item in a list or when the order of records matters for the logic that follows. For instance, you might sort Opportunities by close date to find the next deal expected to close.

Collection Filter

Collection Filter allows you to take a collection and remove any records that do not meet certain conditions. This changes the contents of the collection, leaving only the records that match your criteria. For example, if your Flow gathers all contacts for an account, you could use Collection Filter to keep only the ones marked as active. This is a useful way to narrow down large data sets before making decisions or updates.

Pause

The Pause element is used to temporarily stop a Flow until a specified time or condition is met. This is typically used in scenarios where a delay is required between actions, such as sending a follow-up email a day after a Case is closed or waiting for a record update before continuing. Pause is most often used in conjunction with scheduled paths or time-based automation. A scheduled path is a branch in a record-triggered Flow that runs some actions immediately and schedules other actions to occur a set amount of time after the triggering event. While not as commonly used as other Logic elements, Pause can be helpful in approval processes, escalation scenarios, or when spacing out automated actions for a better user experience.

Flow Data elements

Flow Data elements allow your Flow to interact directly with records in the Salesforce database. These elements are responsible for retrieving, creating, updating, and deleting data, as well as rolling back changes when needed. Together, they form the core of how a Flow reads from and writes to the data layer in your org (see Figure 11-17).

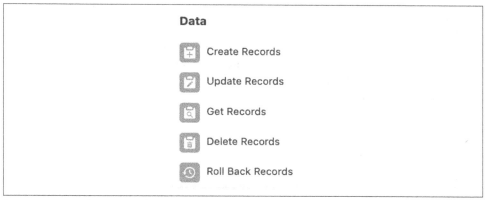

Figure 11-17. Flow Data elements

The Flow Data Elements include Create Records, Update Records, Get Records, Delete Records, and Roll Back Records:

Create Records

The Create Records element is used to insert new records into Salesforce. This is commonly done when capturing user input or when a process requires that new data be added based on other activity in the Flow. For instance, a Flow might create a follow-up task after a Case is closed or generate a new Opportunity when a qualified lead is converted. Records created through this element can be simple, like a single task, or more complex, such as creating multiple related records at once using data stored in a collection variable.

Update Records

The Update Records element modifies existing records in Salesforce. These updates can be based on new information gathered in the Flow or logic that determines a change is needed. An example is setting an Opportunity's stage to Closed Won after contract approval, or updating the status of related Cases when an account is deactivated. The records updated can come from earlier steps in the Flow, from collections, or from conditions that identify them on the fly. This element helps keep record data current and consistent with ongoing automation.

Get Records

The Get Records element retrieves one or more records from Salesforce based on criteria you define. This allows the Flow to look up existing data, such as all contacts for a given account or the highest value Opportunity in a pipeline. The result can be stored as a single record or as a collection. Once retrieved, the data can be used in other Flow elements to inform logic, populate fields, or perform additional actions. Get Records is foundational for Flows that rely on context or need to make decisions based on the current state of your data.

Delete Records

The Delete Records element removes records from the database. This can be used in cleanup processes or when removing data that is no longer needed. For example, a Flow might delete draft tasks if a Case is canceled, or remove outdated records during a scheduled cleanup. Records deleted this way are sent to the Recycle Bin, offering a safeguard against accidental removal. Flows involving deletion often include a confirmation step, especially when initiated by a user, to reduce the risk of unintended data loss.

Roll Back Records

The Roll Back Records element undoes changes that have occurred earlier in the same transaction. This is particularly useful in scenarios where a Flow encounters an error or when a condition is no longer met mid-process. By using this element, the Flow can back out of a partial update and maintain data integrity. For instance, if a Flow attempts to create several records and fails partway through due to a validation rule, Roll Back Records ensures that none of the changes are saved. This element is a safeguard for more complex Flows that span multiple operations and helps maintain clean and reliable data outcomes.

Handling Errors in Flow with Fault Paths

Fault paths fundamentally change the end-user experience when errors occur in Flows. Without fault paths, users encounter generic error messages that provide little context or guidance when a Flow fails. These technical errors often reference system components unfamiliar to the average user, creating frustration and help desk tickets.

With properly implemented fault paths, you can present customized error messages, suggest corrective actions, or even attempt alternative approaches automatically.

Organizations should implement fault paths for any Flow elements that interact with the database, particularly create, update, and delete operations. External system integrations represent another critical area for fault handling, as network issues, authentication problems, or API changes can disrupt these connections unexpectedly.

To add a fault path to a Flow element, locate the fault connector on elements that support fault handling. When you click this connector, you can draw a path to another element that should execute when an error occurs, as shown in Figure 11-18.

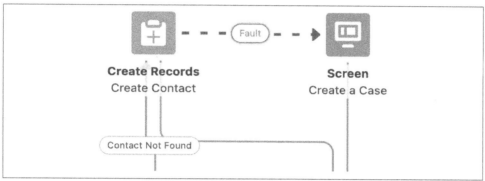

Figure 11-18. Fault path in a Flow

When designing fault paths, consider capturing detailed error information to support troubleshooting. The system variable $Flow.FaultMessage contains valuable information about what went wrong. Assign this value to a text variable in your fault path, then display it to administrative users or log it for later review. For end users, transform this technical message into user-friendly guidance that helps them resolve the issue or contact appropriate support.

A well-designed fault path might include a Screen element displaying a friendly error message, a Decision element that determines whether the user can retry the operation, and actions such as creating a log record or sending an email so administrators can review the error. This approach changes potential system failures into manageable user experiences that maintain confidence in your Salesforce implementation.

Debugging and Testing Flows

Flow Builder includes a built-in debug tool accessible via the Debug button in the top button bar. This allows you to simulate Flow execution with test data, watching each step process in real time. You can provide variable values, record data, and user context information to test various scenarios without affecting your production data.

The Debug console shown in Figure 11-19 displays each element as it executes, showing the values of variables at each step and the path taken through your Flow logic. This visibility helps identify logic errors, incorrect variable assignments, or unexpected branching decisions before they impact your users.

Figure 11-19. Debug Details for a screen Flow

For record-triggered Flows, the debug tool allows you to simulate record creation or updates with specific field values, helping you verify that your automation responds correctly to different data scenarios. You can test where everything works as expected and edge cases that might otherwise cause errors in production.

 Remember that Flows execute in the context of the current user, so testing should verify behavior across different user profiles to ensure appropriate access to records and fields. A Flow that works perfectly for an administrator might fail for another user, due to permission differences.

Flow Version Management and Creating New Versions

Salesforce tracks each saved version of Flows. Whenever you make changes to a Flow, you have the option of either saving as a new version of the existing Flow, or creating a new Flow entirely (see Figure 11-20).

Figure 11-20. Save As New Version and Save As New Flow

It's important to include a clear description for each new version of your Flow, particularly in a shared environment or when collaborating on projects for clients. Including who made the changes and why helps your team quickly understand the purpose and context behind each version, simplifying troubleshooting and ongoing maintenance.

After completing your edits, either activate a new version, which automatically deactivates the previous version, or save as a new Flow.

Flow Trigger Explorer

As your Salesforce organization grows, managing multiple record-triggered Flows can become complex. The Flow Trigger Explorer is a tool designed specifically to help you manage and visualize these record-triggered Flows. Remember that record-triggered Flows are those that run automatically when records are created, updated, or deleted.

To access Flow Trigger Explorer, click the Flow Trigger Explorer button located at the top of the All Flows screen. This provides a centralized, visual representation of all the record-triggered Flows configured in your Salesforce organization (see Figure 11-21). When you select and expand an object in the Flow Trigger Explorer, you'll see detailed information about each Flow triggered by that object.

The sequence shown in Flow Trigger Explorer matters, as it reflects the exact order in which these record-triggered Flows will execute when a record changes. This sequence follows Salesforce's established order of execution.

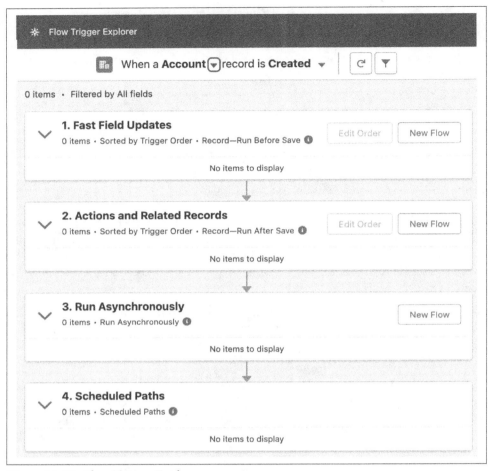

Figure 11-21. Flow Trigger Explorer

Flow Trigger Explorer helps you optimize your automation strategy. You can use it to identify redundant or conflicting Flows, consolidate similar automations, and ensure your record-triggered Flows run in the correct sequence. Additionally, reviewing Flow Trigger Explorer before creating new automations provides clear insight into the existing landscape, helping to prevent overlap or conflicts with existing record-triggered Flows.

Flow Templates

Flow templates in Salesforce provide prebuilt automation solutions for common business scenarios, helping you implement best practices without starting from scratch. These templates serve as excellent starting points that you can customize to fit your specific business requirements.

For example, Salesforce provides templates for automating lead routing, managing approval processes, handling customer support case escalations, and streamlining user onboarding. Using these templates can significantly reduce setup time and ensure you leverage proven methods for common workflows.

To access Flow templates, navigate to the Flows screen in Setup and click New Flow. The New Automation window displays with different Categories to select from, as shown in Figure 11-22.

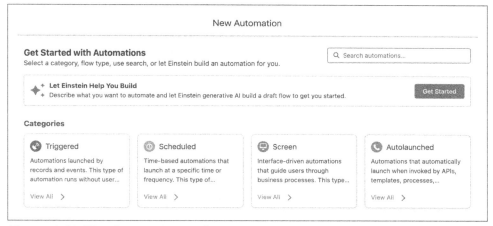

Figure 11-22. New Automation window

Click the View All link under your desired Category. The window updates to display the available Types and Templates, as shown in Figure 11-23.

Figure 11-23. Flow Templates in the New Automation window

The templates screen displays a variety of templates organized by category. Each template includes a description that explains its purpose and functionality, helping you identify the right template for your needs. The Flow templates available cover a variety of common use cases.

Using a Flow template

After selecting a template, click Create to create a new Flow based on the template. The Flow Builder opens, as shown in Figure 11-24, with the template's preconfigured elements and logic, allowing you to customize it for your organization.

You will find that Flow templates make for a great learning tool, as you can inspect the various elements and configuration choices Salesforce has included in them. They provide a gentler learning curve than starting your Flow learning journey from scratch with a blank canvas.

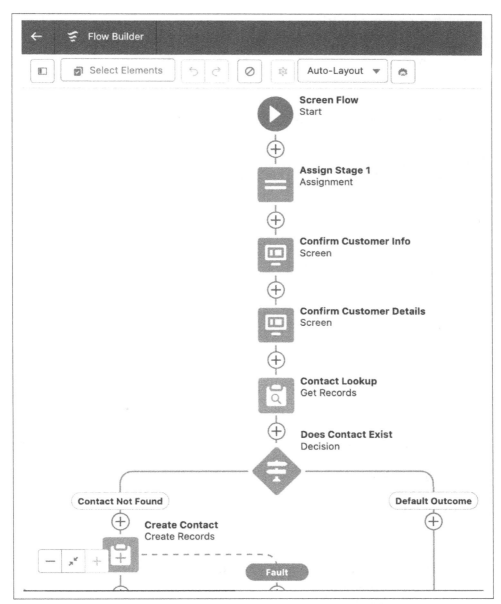

Figure 11-24. "Create a case" Flow template displayed in Flow Builder

AppExchange Flow Solutions

Beyond the built-in templates in Flow Builder, Salesforce's AppExchange, as discussed in Chapter 9, offers a wealth of additional Flow solutions created by Salesforce partners and the broader Salesforce community. These solutions range from simple utility Flows to comprehensive business process automations.

To explore AppExchange Flow solutions, search for and select AppExchange in Setup or go to *https://appexchange.salesforce.com*.

In AppExchange, use the search function to find Flows related to your specific needs, or select the Flow filter by Solution Type, as shown in Figure 11-25.

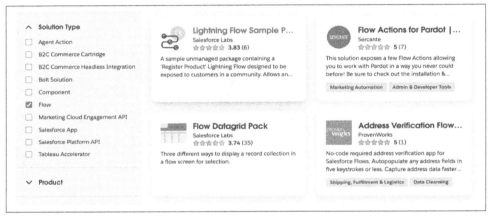

Figure 11-25. AppExchange Flow solutions

The combination of built-in Flow templates and AppExchange solutions provides a rich library of automation patterns and best practices that you can leverage to accelerate your implementation of Salesforce automation.

Migrating Legacy Automations to Flow

As Salesforce phases out workflow rules and Process Builder, organizations must migrate their existing automations to Flow. Salesforce provides dedicated tools to facilitate this transition, helping you preserve business logic while adopting the more powerful Flow framework.

The Automation Migration Process

To access the migration tools, search for and select "Migrate to Flow" in Setup. The "Migrate to Flow" screen displays (see Figure 11-26).

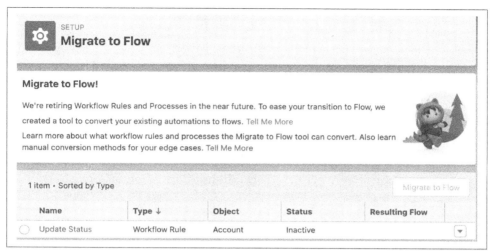

Figure 11-26. "Migrate to Flow" screen

The migration interface presents a list of your existing workflow rules and Process Builder processes. Each item includes details about its objects, and activation status. A Resulting Flow column indicates whether each automation has already been migrated.

To begin migration, select one or more automations from the list and click the "Migrate to Flow" button. Salesforce's migration tool analyzes each selected automation and attempts to create an equivalent Flow. This analysis maps criteria to Flow conditions, actions to Flow elements, and preserves the original logic structure as closely as possible.

After processing, the tool presents a summary screen showing which automations were successfully converted. For each conversion, you can review the resulting Flow before finalizing the migration.

Adding Flow Descriptions with Salesforce Einstein

Salesforce Einstein is Salesforce's original artificial intelligence technology, integrated deeply into the Salesforce platform. Einstein provides predictive analytics, automated insights, and recommendations based on historical data. It helps simplify and enhance productivity by intelligently analyzing existing Salesforce data and processes.

One practical example of Einstein's capabilities in Salesforce Flow is the ability to analyze an existing Flow and generate a clear, human-readable description of its functionality. This feature is particularly useful when reviewing Flows created by another person or revisiting your own Flows after not having looked at them for an extended period. Additionally, having Flows explained by Einstein can significantly reduce the learning curve as you start working with Flows, helping you quickly understand complex logic through clear, step-by-step explanations.

 Agentforce is a newer generation of AI technology designed to leverage generative artificial intelligence and advanced reasoning capabilities. While Einstein initially focused primarily on predictive analytics and recommendations based on past data, Agentforce expands AI capabilities by providing generative and conversational AI experiences. Agentforce powers sophisticated automation in areas such as customer service, enabling dynamic interaction handling, intelligent case management, and real-time conversational capabilities.

Whether labeled as Einstein or Agentforce, Salesforce is clearly signaling its commitment to embedding artificial intelligence throughout the platform. Salesforce continues to move forward rapidly with AI innovation, making it an integral part of how you interact with the platform.

Einstein's Flow explanation feature is available in Salesforce's free developer accounts, but you must enable Einstein via Einstein Setup in your Salesforce org before you can use these AI-enhanced features. While specific Einstein and Agentforce features are not directly covered on the Salesforce Platform Administrator certification exam, understanding these AI trends and capabilities helps you stay current with Salesforce's evolving platform strategies.

Einstein provides a comprehensive summary, as shown in Figure 11-27, that you can review and add to the Flow's description field, making the Flow's purpose clear to anyone who encounters it in the future.

Figure 11-27. *Einstein Flow summary*

Creating Flows with Prompts

Instead of manually constructing a Flow element by element, you can now describe the automation you want to build in natural language prompts. To do this, from the New Automation window, click Let Einstein Help You Build, as shown in Figure 11-28.

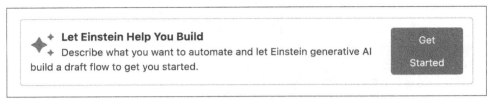

Figure 11-28. Let Einstein Help You Build a New Flow

The New Automation window updates, as shown in Figure 11-29.

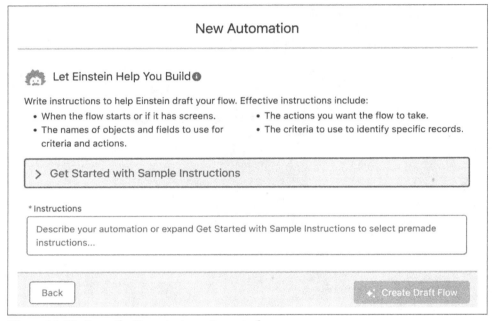

Figure 11-29. Describe Your Automation window

You can enter your instructions for your automation or get started with sample instructions. Once your instructions are crafted to your liking, click the Create Draft Flow button at the bottom right of the screen. The Flow Builder displays your resulting Flow (see Figure 11-30).

You can further refine your Flow instructions as well as have Einstein summarize your Flow, as detailed in the previous section. If necessary, you can extend the functionality of your Flow further by adding additional elements manually.

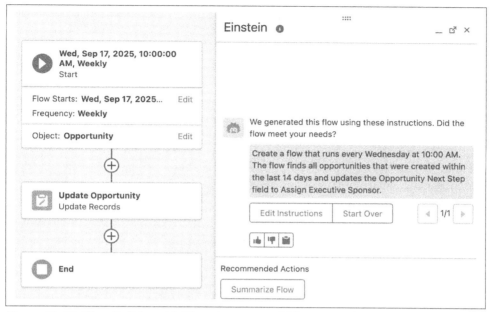

Figure 11-30. Flow Builder with Einstein-generated Flow

The Future of Flow

As Salesforce continues to enhance the Flow Builder with improved user interfaces, expanded capabilities, and deeper AI integration, the line between declarative automation and custom development will continue to blur. These advancements make Flows increasingly approachable while preserving flexibility that developers appreciate.

By understanding that Flows are essentially a visual programming environment generating executable code, you'll gain a deeper appreciation for both their capabilities and constraints as you build automation solutions for your organization.

Summary

In Chapter 11, you've explored Salesforce's process automation capabilities, focusing primarily on approval processes and Flows. You began by learning about approval processes, which provide structured methods for reviewing and approving records based on your organization's business requirements. You discovered how to plan, configure, and deploy approval processes using both the Jump Start and Standard Setup Wizards.

The chapter introduced you to Salesforce Flow as the primary declarative automation tool on the platform. You learned about the different types of Flows. For each type, you explored common use cases and configuration options, understanding when to apply each solution in your organization.

You delved deeply into Flow components, examining how elements like Assignments, Decisions, Loops, and record operations work together to create comprehensive business process automations. You saw how these elements function as visual programming methods, allowing you to build advanced logic without writing code. The introduction of Agentforce and Einstein highlighted how AI is making Flow development more accessible, helping you understand existing Flows and generate new ones from natural language descriptions.

This chapter also covered practical implementation aspects, including using prebuilt templates, creating custom approval processes, and managing Flow versions. You learned essential techniques for error handling through fault paths and debugging Flows, ensuring your automations remain robust even when unexpected scenarios arise.

By mastering declarative automation tools, you will possess the skills to streamline business processes, enforce consistent procedures, and significantly reduce manual effort within your Salesforce organization. These capabilities represent core competencies for Salesforce administrators, empowering you to deliver significant value by translating business requirements into automated solutions without relying on development resources.

As you apply these concepts in your Salesforce implementation, remember that effective automation balances technical capability with clear business process design. The most successful automations execute technical steps correctly and align seamlessly with how users work and how the organization operates.

Chapter 11 Quiz

It's now time to assess your understanding of Workflow/Process Automation in Salesforce. The following questions will test your comprehension of key concepts and ensure you're prepared to implement these tools effectively in your organization.

Remember, the capabilities of process automation are central to the Salesforce Platform Administrator certification exam. Take your time to consider each question carefully, as they're designed to reinforce important concepts and prepare you for similar questions you might encounter on the exam. After answering each question, review the answers and explanations in the Appendix to deepen your understanding of both correct and incorrect options.

1. What is the primary difference between a record-triggered Flow and a schedule-triggered Flow?

   a. Record-triggered Flows can only update records, while schedule-triggered Flows can create new records.

   b. Record-triggered Flows execute when records change, while schedule-triggered Flows run at specified times.

   c. Schedule-triggered Flows can include Screen elements, while record-triggered Flows cannot.

   d. Record-triggered Flows run in the user's context, while schedule-triggered Flows always run as the system user.

2. When using an approval process, what happens to a record by default when it is submitted for approval?

   a. The record is automatically shared with all potential approvers.

   b. The record is locked to prevent edits during the approval process.

   c. The record is cloned to preserve its original state.

   d. The record is assigned to a queue for processing.

3. In a Flow, what element would you use to process each record in a collection one at a time?

   a. Collection process

   b. For Each

   c. Loop

   d. Iterator

4. What is the purpose of a fault path in Flow Builder?

   a. To skip elements when a user has insufficient permissions

   b. To create shortcuts in the Flow for experienced users

   c. To handle errors that occur during Flow execution

   d. To bypass validation rules during record creation

5. Which two wizards are available for creating approval processes in Salesforce? Select two.

   a. Jump Start Wizard

   b. Advanced Configuration Wizard

   c. Standard Setup Wizard

   d. Quick Setup Wizard

6. What happens when you activate a new version of a Flow that is already active?

    a. Both versions run simultaneously until the older version completes all existing executions.

    b. The new version fails to activate until you manually deactivate the current version.

    c. The previous version is automatically deactivated when the new version is activated.

    d. You must schedule a time for the version change to take effect.

7. Which Flow type would you use to create a guided process for sales representatives to qualify leads?

    a. Record-triggered Flow

    b. Screen Flow

    c. Schedule-triggered Flow

    d. Autolaunched Flow

8. In an approval process, what determines the order in which approval steps are executed?

    a. The order in which the approval steps appear in the Setup page

    b. The entry criteria defined for each approval step

    c. The hierarchy level of the assigned approvers

    d. The Priority field value on the approval step

9. What is a key advantage of using Einstein with Flow Builder?

    a. It automatically tests Flows for you with various data scenarios.

    b. It enables Flows to make decisions using machine learning models.

    c. It can analyze existing Flows and generate descriptions of their functionality.

    d. It eliminates the need for administrators to understand Flow concepts.

Preparing for the Salesforce Platform Administrator Certification

You have now successfully worked your way through every knowledge area on the Salesforce Certified Platform Administrator exam, and you are likely anxious to take the exam. Before you rush to register for the exam, I encourage you to take to heart the advice in this chapter.

This advice is born out of my personal experiences and feedback from thousands of students I have helped to pass this certification exam. In this chapter, I share my own first Salesforce certification exam experience. I also address the importance of understanding concepts deeply, as opposed to simply memorizing practice test questions. It is here that you will find the best advice for maximizing your chances of passing the first time and virtually ensuring success on a retake if needed.

As with all things in life, your success will depend on your effort and preparedness. Now is the time to take the next important step in completing your certification journey successfully while eschewing any tempting supposed shortcuts.

I highly encourage you to embrace conceptual learning, which will serve you better than trivia-based learning blitzes. Allow me to now share my own initial Salesforce certification exam experience.

If at First You Don't Succeed

On July 9, 2012, I attempted my first Salesforce certification exam. I had driven roughly two hours from my home in the Nashville, Tennessee, area to the nearest testing center in Bowling Green, Kentucky.

The site was the campus of Southcentral Kentucky Community & Technical College. I parked my car and walked nervously into the testing area, my head swimming with memorized facts and information I had been cramming in for the past weeks.

At the testing location, I had to empty my pockets and lock away all my belongings. There would be no outside resources or help during the exam. They provided me with two blank sheets of paper and a pencil for notes during the exam, but I would not get to keep them afterward.

I entered the testing room and sat at a computer with the test loaded. I clicked to begin, and for the next 90 minutes I progressed through waves of doubt and second thoughts.

There were pockets of confidence as I answered questions I believed I knew, but inevitably, I encountered a valley of despair as question after question stumped me. I began to doubt that I would pass this exam.

I did my best with the knowledge I had. At the conclusion of the exam, I was greeted by a mysterious review screen. Staring back at me was a list of the 60 questions and my multiple-choice and multi-select answers. I reviewed a few but feared changing a correct answer to an incorrect one.

As the seconds ticked down toward zero, I submitted my exam. The computer seemed to consider my fate for the longest second of my life and then revealed my fate:

Fail.

I was devastated.

I have no recollection of leaving the room. I don't recall handing over the two pieces of paper and pencil, nor my personal belongings being returned to me.

My memory returns at some point on my two-hour drive back home from Bowling Green. I called my wife to share the unfortunate news that after months of study and hundreds of hours of preparation, I had come away empty-handed.

As I discussed the experience with my wife, I started to recall a few things that were on the exam. I realized that I should record the conversation to capture the topics I could recall. We agreed my best course of action would be to hang up the call and start a voice memo to myself instead. My future self would thank me for this decision.

As I drove and recorded, I talked to myself, sharing the experience of the exam. I recorded whatever I could remember that was on the test. My spotty recollections of various topics and the answers I selected provided valuable insights to validate my understanding of those topics.

Try, Try Again

The experience of failing and getting back up, coupled with recalling as much as I could from the exam, really helped guide my studies moving forward. I prepared relentlessly for a retake in the coming days. I also decided that rather than driving two hours to a testing center, I would test remotely from home next time.

On July 22, 2012, I attempted the exam a second time. The house was empty and free from distractions, and my internet connection proved stable throughout the test.

As the seconds counted down, I realized I was much more methodical with my test-taking approach. I finally clicked to submit the exam. An agonizing second elapsed as I awaited my fate:

Pass.

I thought I misread the result; I thought I had failed.

The reality sank in. I passed. I was now a certified Salesforce professional and I knew my life had changed.

Within a month of passing that certification, I accepted my first full-time Salesforce position and doubled my salary in the process. Passing that first Salesforce certification exam indeed changed my life. And those life changes have continued up to you and me crossing paths today.

Rest assured that although this path may not be easy, it is attainable. There are no shortcuts! More importantly, it is worth the investment of your time and effort and can change your life. The key to your success is to be resilient, determined, and to put in the work.

Registering for the Exam

To register for any Salesforce certification exam, you begin on Trailhead Academy (*https://trailheadacademy.salesforce.com*) (see Figure 12-1).

From the Trailhead Academy home screen, navigate to the Certifications menu and select "Find a Certification." The Trailhead Academy Catalog of certifications displays. Click the Salesforce Certified Platform Administrator card to display its certification home page.

Click the Register Now button for the Salesforce Certified Platform Administrator exam, as displayed in Figure 12-2.

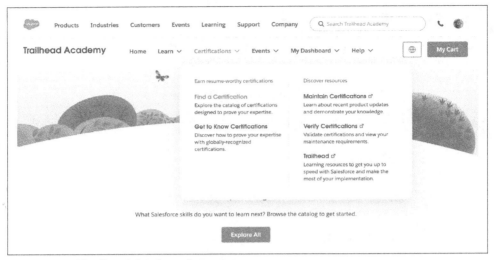

Figure 12-1. Trailhead Academy home screen

Figure 12-2. Register Now button

You will then be redirected to Pearson VUE, Salesforce's certification testing provider, where you can continue the scheduling process.

Creating a Pearson VUE Account

If you are scheduling a Salesforce certification exam for the first time using Pearson VUE, you'll need to create an account on the Pearson VUE platform. Visit *https://home.pearsonvue.com/salesforce* and select the option to create an account. Provide accurate details, including your full name exactly as it appears on your government-issued ID and a valid email address. After completing the form, Pearson VUE will send a verification email. Follow the instructions in the email to activate your account, after which you'll be able to manage and schedule your Salesforce certification exams.

Scheduling your certification exam

With your Pearson VUE account set up, log in and select the Salesforce Certified Platform Administrator exam from the list provided. You can choose either online proctored testing, allowing you to take the exam from home, or onsite testing at a Pearson VUE testing center. Choose a convenient date and time from the available options, provide your payment details, and finalize the scheduling. Your upcoming exam details will be clearly listed under the Upcoming Appointments section of your Pearson VUE dashboard.

Rescheduling your certification exam

Sometimes life presents unexpected challenges, and rescheduling your exam becomes necessary. If you need to change the date or time of your scheduled Salesforce certification exam, you can easily manage this through your Pearson VUE account.

To reschedule, log in to your Pearson VUE account, navigate to the Upcoming Appointments section, and select the exam appointment you wish to adjust. Follow the prompts to choose a new date and time from the available options.

Keep in mind that rescheduling must generally be completed at least 24 hours before the scheduled exam time to avoid forfeiture of your exam fees. Be sure to check Pearson VUE's policies on rescheduling and cancellation when scheduling your exam to stay informed about any deadlines or potential fees.

By planning ahead and using the rescheduling feature responsibly, you can maintain flexibility and manage unexpected situations without stress.

Testing remotely from home with online proctored exams

Choosing the online proctored exam option allows you to take your Salesforce Certified Platform Administrator exam remotely. Before your exam, confirm your computer meets Pearson VUE's technical specifications by running their provided system test. Ensure your testing environment is quiet, private, and free from disruptions. Use a reliable desktop or laptop with a working webcam and microphone; mobile devices are not supported for this type of exam.

On the day of your exam, log in to your Pearson VUE account about 30 minutes before your scheduled time. Follow the prompts for identity verification, which will require a valid government-issued ID. Your online proctor will then check your environment via your webcam to ensure compliance with testing rules. During the exam, maintain visibility on your webcam, avoid leaving the testing area without permission, and ensure no unauthorized materials are accessible. The proctor will continuously monitor your session to maintain exam security.

Salesforce Certification Exam Retake Policies

You can retake a Salesforce certification exam two times for a total of three attempts per release cycle. Your first retake can be one day after your first attempt. If you fail the exam a second time, you can retake the exam one more time 14 days later.

If after three attempts you do not pass the exam, you will have to wait until the next release of the exam. The three annual exams are scheduled for release roughly four months apart in the winter, spring, and summer.

Retakes do have some repeat questions

If you happen to fail the exam the first time and need to retake it again, you will likely encounter some repeat questions. Not all questions will be a repeat from test to test, but there will be more repeated questions if your retake is within the same test version cycle.

Salesforce presumably employs a question bank of more than 60 graded and 5 ungraded questions for their certification exams. Whenever you are taking the exam, these questions will be presented to you in a random order, and the possible answers and their sequencing may also appear differently between attempts.

Testing Onsite at a Pearson VUE Testing Center

If you prefer taking your exam in a traditional testing environment, you can select onsite testing at a Pearson VUE testing center during scheduling. Choose a suitable location, date, and time that fits your needs. On the day of your exam, arrive at the testing center at least 15 minutes before your scheduled exam start time. You will be required to present two forms of identification, including a primary government-issued photo ID such as a driver's license or passport, and a secondary form such as a credit card, debit card, student ID, or employee ID. Both IDs must exactly match the name you used when creating your Pearson VUE account. At the testing center, you will secure your personal items, such as phones or smartwatches, in lockers provided. Once checked in, you will be guided to your testing station, where your exam will be proctored in person.

Certification Verification

Upon successfully passing your Salesforce Certified Platform Administrator exam, your certification becomes publicly verifiable. Through Trailhead, you can choose whether to allow your certifications to be publicly available. By opting in, you enable potential employers or others to verify your certification credentials easily. To verify

Salesforce certifications, individuals can visit the Trailhead verification page and enter a name or email to view the active certifications an individual holds. Only currently active certifications are displayed; retired certifications or scores from previous exams are not included in these verification results.

Obtaining an Exam Voucher or Discount

Salesforce certification exams typically involve a registration fee, but there are ways to reduce or eliminate this cost. If you work for a Salesforce partner, your employer may provide exam vouchers as part of its professional development initiatives.

Salesforce partner organizations have a vested interest in certifying their employees, because the number and type of certifications held by staff are part of the evaluation criteria Salesforce uses for its partner tiering system.

Partners with higher numbers of certified employees typically achieve higher partner tiers. Those tiers are Registered, Ridge, Crest, and Summit (the highest). The higher tiers grant partners greater recognition, better positioning in the Salesforce ecosystem, and access to exclusive resources and opportunities.

Additionally, Salesforce regularly hosts special events called Certification Days, where attendees can obtain vouchers or discounts on certification exams. Participating in these events is an excellent way to gain valuable insights into the certification exams and benefit from reduced registration fees. To keep up-to-date with upcoming Certification Days and other special promotions, regularly check the Trailhead website and Salesforce's official social media channels.

Testing Onsite at a Salesforce-Sponsored Event

If you opt for an onsite proctored exam at a Salesforce-sponsored event, such as Dreamforce or TrailblazerDX, you'll experience a structured environment similar to a traditional testing center. This option is ideal for those who enjoy the energetic atmosphere of Salesforce events and prefer in-person interactions.

When you arrive at the event, identify yourself to the staff as a test taker. As with testing at a designated center, you'll need to bring a government-issued photo ID and a second form of ID, such as a student ID, credit card, or employee ID card. Ensure these IDs match the name on your test taker profile and are not expired. Don't forget the authorization code from your registration confirmation email, which is necessary for verification.

Your personal belongings will be secured in a lockbox or locker to prevent unauthorized access to study aids or electronic devices. Prohibited items include smartwatches, phones, and other electronics, which will be returned upon exam completion.

Testing at a Salesforce event provides the added benefit of networking opportunities and immediate access to resources and support from the Salesforce community. This setting can enhance your overall exam experience and support your success in becoming a certified Salesforce Platform Administrator.

Effective Study Techniques

There are myriad ways that you can improve your odds of passing the certification exam the first time. Although these techniques will never take the place of understanding the topics on the Administrator exam at a conceptual level, they can serve as a force multiplier in setting you up for exam success.

While some of this advice may be readily apparent to you, I encourage you to review this next section carefully as you game-plan your test taking experience. The preparation you put in now may be just the thing to carry you from failing to passing, and every question counts toward that goal!

Importance of Being Well Rested

The best thing you can do during the final few hours before your exam is to relax and to not fixate on what you are about to do. The thought of cramming at the last minute will permeate your mind, but resist that urge.

Rather than staying up excessively late the night before an exam, you will be better served to get rested and not tax your body and mind. That time will come once you begin the actual exam, so why multiply the strain on yourself by pulling a late- or all-nighter?

The fresher your mind, the sharper your reasoning and recall will be. There's a reason why there are limits on the number of hours that truck drivers and airline pilots can perform their jobs. When they push the limits and boundaries of what their bodies are telling them to do, bad things can happen. The same applies to you, me, and everyone. Respect your limits that make you human.

Comprehensive Review of Your Study Materials

If you have worked through this book, chapter by chapter, then you have completed the quizzes at the end of each. It would be a great idea for you to revisit those questions with a fresh perspective.

If there are any questions that you don't feel confident about, revisit that topic and read through the applicable sections in this book. You can also get hands on in your own Salesforce learner account, gaining more hands-on experience to apply what you are learning.

You will find as you revisit concepts that your understanding becomes clearer over time and with experience. I draw an analogy to ironing a shirt.

No one expects a shirt to be free from wrinkles with a single swipe of an iron. But through repeated passes from various angles, the wrinkles become smooth and clear. Our minds work much the same way when trying to retain information and tackle new concepts.

In addition to the now hopefully worn pages of this book, there are other resources you can use to supplement your studies. I will next explore some of those additional options, as well as address how best to incorporate them into your studies and preparation.

Practice Exams

The common temptation in certification preparation is to simply gravitate toward taking practice tests. This can easily become romanticized as a shortcut to passing. But it is easy to fall into the trap of what I like to call trivia-based learning.

If you only study via practice tests, you will begin to memorize the answers and will grow increasingly dependent on the exam questions being worded in a very specific fashion. The reality is that the actual exam contains very detailed, scenario-based questions. If you have been training yourself through a regimented diet of practice test questions, you will struggle to answer the actual exam questions, because you will not understand the underlying concepts the questions are testing.

This is why I always recommend that students not take practice tests early in their studies, but only once they have covered all of the topics represented on the exam. Only then, once all topics and concepts have been addressed, will you be able to approach exam questions—practice or actual—with some semblance of comprehension.

There is a reason that the complete practice test in this book resides in the final chapter, rather than at the beginning. Practice tests are a great barometer for your preparedness for an exam, but not when you are first starting out. There are other resources available that you can avail yourself of earlier in the study process to gauge your knowledge level, topic by topic, such as my Salesforce Certified Administrator Assessment Scorecard (*https://www.rapidreskill.com/admin-scorecard*).

Test-Taking Strategies

You can greatly improve your odds of passing the exam the first time by approaching your initial attempt strategically. Some of the tips in this section are more practical or technical in nature, whereas others have more to do with mindset. Taking the time now to proactively think through strategy will help you to approach the exam with a balanced level of confidence.

Balanced Confidence

It is important to avoid the extremes of the confidence scale when approaching any certification exam. You want to go into it neither too confident nor too pessimistic.

I think the right approach to exam mindset is what I like to call a coin-toss mentality. If you can tell yourself that you have a 50/50 shot of passing, and remind yourself that the sun will come out tomorrow regardless of the outcome, then you will avoid placing undue pressure on yourself.

If you place too much pressure and importance on having to pass right now, you will increase your stress level during the exam and invite doubt to creep in. Taking a reasoned approach that the outcome of success is assured, it is just a matter of time. Whether you pass on the first time, or require a retake, that's going to be OK.

On the flip side of being overly pessimistic is being too confident. If you are absolutely certain that you are going to pass the exam, your confidence will be undermined as soon as you hit a few questions you are unsure of.

The more that you can set your expectations in the middle, expecting full well that there will be challenges during the exam, the better you will handle yourself and manage your time and efforts most effectively. And beyond the internal battles of the mind and the fine balancing act of your confidence, you will also want to be sure you aren't adding additional pressures on yourself by what you say to others in advance of your exam date.

Don't Announce Your Attempt in Advance

Your anticipation and excitement will likely grow as your test date approaches. I want to encourage you to resist the urge to announce your testing intentions to your boss or coworkers in advance of that date.

This is to avoid placing undue pressure on yourself. During the actual test-taking experience, there will be moments of doubt once you hit a few questions in a row that you're less than confident about. In that scenario, if you have announced in your workplace that you are taking the exam, you may start to worry about what your boss or peers will think if you fail.

This can lead to an increasing cycle of stress and pressure, thus affecting your performance on the exam. To avoid this, wait until after you have passed the exam to make any proclamations at work. And if you are hoping to be reimbursed for your exam attempt by your employer, you should be able to broach that after you have safely passed the exam.

Understanding the Exam Structure

Salesforce is continually updating its platform, with three new releases each year. Salesforce updates the Certified Platform Administrator exam three times a year as well.

The number of graded questions on the Certified Platform Administrator exam is 60. You will also have 5 ungraded questions on your exam. There is no differentiation between the graded and ungraded questions.

The newest Salesforce features are not immediately reflected on the current version of the exam. Salesforce takes a few release cycles to work new features into the graded questions on the exam. These questions initially appear as ungraded questions, giving Salesforce the opportunity to hone and perfect them. In this way, Salesforce is using test takers to help figure out which questions are performing ideally in the test taking context.

Salesforce's goal is to write compelling and engaging test questions that test your knowledge and understanding of the various topics it is testing you on. With these ungraded questions, Salesforce is verifying that a desired range of correct answers are being made. Salesforce doesn't want everyone either missing a question or getting it correct, which would point to a question being too hard or too easy. This split testing of test questions during their ungraded phase helps Salesforce to author and perfect good test questions that will eventually make their way into the graded questions bank of the exam.

Types of Questions on the Exam

There are only two types of questions on the Salesforce Certified Platform Administrator exam:

- Multiple choice
- Multiple select

Multiple choice

Multiple choice questions are the more straightforward question and answer type found on the exam. You are presented with multiple options for the correct answer from which you are to select only one.

You will either get the question correct or incorrect based upon your single selection from the multiple-choice answer set. These options are represented as radio buttons, and you can only physically select one answer.

Multiple select

Whenever you are expected to select more than one correct answer from a group of potential answers, you will be told how many you should select. This guidance appears below the questions and tells you to "Select Two" or "Select Three," etc.

To receive credit for a multiple select question, you must select all of the correct answers; partial credit is not given.

Multiple select answers are selectable via checkboxes and you can select any number of combinations. If you select too many or too few answers and then attempt to go to the next question, an error will appear and you will be instructed to select the correct number of answers.

You can mark any question for later review, to make those you are unsure about easier to locate on the final review screen at the end of the exam.

Effective Time Management During the Exam

You are allotted is 105 minutes to complete the exam. This is a long period of time to sit in place and concentrate. Although you can ask the proctor for a break, if needed, you will want to be sure you have attended to any personal needs as much as possible beforehand.

Whether taking the test remotely or in a testing center, you will not be able to use outside resources or help. The proctor will pause your exam if they notice you looking away from your screen very often, or if you are talking. You will also want to be sure your surroundings are free from distractions or noise, which can be construed as you receiving outside help during the exam.

You also cannot have your phone within reach or utilize any sort of recording device. Other forms of electronics, such as tablets or other computers, are also not allowed.

First pass: Quick answering, marking for review, and consistent guesses

As you are beginning the exam, attempt to work through all of the questions quickly as a first pass. Go with your initial impression as to what the correct answers should be.

You will also need to decide what your "letter of the day" is. This is the letter you will consistently guess for any questions you have no clue as to what the correct answer should be.

If you encounter questions where you are unable to rule out any of the potential answers as the correct one, you should consistently select the same letter for your answer, which will statistically improve your chances of at least getting some of these questions correct.

For example, if you were to encounter five such questions and you guessed A, B, C, D, and E respectively, you are spreading your chances across five different answers. This method might seem logical, but it reduces your likelihood of getting any correct. By choosing one letter consistently, such as C, you statistically improve your chances.

When guessing, each option (A, B, C, D, E) has a 20% chance of being correct. By consistently choosing one letter, say C, for five questions, the probability of getting at least one correct increases. Here's the breakdown:

- When you guess, there's an 80% chance of getting a question wrong. This is like rolling a dice and hoping it doesn't land on a certain number.
- If you guess the same wrong answer five times in a row, the chance of being wrong each time multiplies: 80% × 80% × 80% × 80% × 80%, which equals about 33%.
- This means there's a 33% chance you'll get all five wrong if you pick the same letter.
- So, the chance of getting at least one right is the opposite of getting all wrong: 100% −33%, which equals about 67%.

By sticking with one letter, you maximize the chance of hitting at least one correct answer out of multiple guesses. This strategy leverages the law of large numbers, improving your odds (67%) over random selection (20%) for each question.

The only exception to consistently guessing the same letter for questions you don't know the answer to is when you *know* your "letter of the day" answer is incorrect. In this case, select from one of the remaining answers.

For any questions you are unsure of, beyond guessing the same letter consistently, you can also mark them for later review. This will allow you to more easily identify which questions you struggled with and to revisit them on your second pass.

The goal in your first pass on the exam is to get through all questions as quickly as possible. Upon reaching the conclusion of the exam, you are greeted with an Assessment Summary screen where the questions you marked for later review are marked with asterisks. From this screen you can navigate to those specific questions and review them.

Second pass: Reviewing marked questions

You can click on any of the hyperlinked answers in the Assessment Summary screen to go back to that specific question. This gives you a quick way to pinpoint those questions you were unsure of and marked for later review.

This second pass is all about homing in on those questions about which you were unsure. Now is the time to reassess your initial impressions and consider making revisions. When in doubt, it is usually in your best interest not to change your answers from your initial impression.

Reserve any changes of your answers at this stage to only those questions you are sure you initially answered incorrectly. Go through each question you marked for later review, and as you finalize your answers, uncheck the checkbox for later review on each question.

As you work through these questions, you will eventually see that no more asterisks appear next to your answers in the Assessment Summary screen. Once you have no further questions marked for later review, you are ready to move on to your third pass, assuming you have time remaining.

Third pass: Finding like-kind questions and checking for mistakes

Once you have completed your first two passes, this third and final pass is intended to be a final check of all questions, starting with the first. In this pass, it is all about rereading the questions and double-checking your answers.

It is not outside the realm of possibility that you misclicked on an answer. So you want to double-check your work, being mindful that you can make mistakes, and human error can sink an otherwise successful test attempt.

Beyond finding any potential mistakes in your answer selections, you will also want to identify any like-kind questions. As you work your way through the questions, you may recognize the same topic being asked about in multiple questions, in different ways.

You can toggle between these like-kind questions and perhaps gain more insight based on the wording and answer options of each. These added insights may help you to connect the dots and flip your understanding of a key topic, allowing you to correct any misunderstandings along the way.

And if time allows: Memorize, memorize, memorize

If you have moved briskly through the exam and completed your three passes with time to spare, you can now shift your focus to memorizing what is on the exam. Your hope and goal is that this memorization will not be necessary because you are ultimately going to see that you have passed the exam upon submission.

But on the off chance that you fail the exam, the more you can memorize of what was on it will prove invaluable for your retake attempt. This is the same concept that I stumbled upon as I performed my first post-exam recollections into a voice memo on my drive home.

Rather than trying to recall and memorize after the exam, it is optimal to do this during the actual exam—as time allows. As the final minutes tick down, do what you can to memorize as many of the topics as possible, just in case.

Receiving Your Test Results

Once you have signaled that you are done with your exam and click to submit, you will be prompted to verify that you indeed are done taking the exam. Once you have confirmed that, you will be presented with an overall Pass/Fail status, along with individual percentage scores for each knowledge area.

Salesforce does not provide an overall percentage for the entire exam. But you can either do the math or use one of the many online calculators that take into account the percentage weighting of each knowledge area to figure out how many questions you got right or wrong to come to an overall score.

Your test results will also be sent to the email address you used to register for the exam. If you pass, you will also receive your certification as a PDF, which you can share on social media.

Once you pass the certification, I encourage you to share the good news on LinkedIn. You can also connect with me and tag me in your post.

When I am tagged with the news of someone passing a certification exam, I will typically like and comment on their post and also endorse the applicable skill on LinkedIn upon verifying the credential.

Certification Verification

If you opt in to certification verification, your certifications are made publicly verifiable via the Trailhead website.

To verify a Salesforce certification, navigate to the Credentials menu (*https://trailhead.salesforce.com*) and select Verify Certifications. The Verification screen displays, as displayed in Figure 12-3.

Figure 12-3. Certification Verification screen

You can enter the name or email address of anyone to see which Salesforce certifications they currently hold, as well as the date that they attained them. Failed certification exam attempts are not displayed, nor are final scores. Only the name of the certification and the date of attainment are displayed in the verification results.

> Retired certifications do not appear in the verification results. Only active certifications are displayed in the results of a certification verification search on Trailhead.

Certification Maintenance

Once you have attained your Salesforce Platform Administrator credential, you will want to be sure to keep up with the certification maintenance requirements. Salesforce requires certified professionals to maintain their credentials by completing maintenance modules once a year. These maintenance modules ensure that you stay up-to-date with the latest Salesforce features and best practices.

Salesforce will send you email reminders as your applicable certification maintenance deadlines approach. You will be directed to complete the certification maintenance modules on Salesforce Trailhead (*https://trailhead.salesforce.com*).

It is your responsibility to keep track of your certification maintenance due dates, which are displayed for your reference on your Trailhead profile. If you fail to complete your certification maintenance, you will lose your certification and have to pass the exam again to regain it.

The work you do for your maintenance on Trailhead will help you retain your certification and earn points. These points contribute to your overall Trailhead ranking, providing additional incentives and recognition for your continuous learning efforts.

By staying proactive with your certification maintenance, you will ensure that your Salesforce Platform Administrator certification credential remains valid and that your skills stay current.

Summary

In Chapter 12, you received comprehensive guidance to prepare for the Salesforce Platform Administrator certification exam. You learned the importance of persistence and resilience, gaining personal insights into overcoming initial setbacks. The chapter detailed the entire exam registration process, from creating a Pearson VUE account to choosing between remote and onsite proctored exams, ensuring you are well-prepared logistically.

You explored effective study techniques, emphasizing the value of rest, thorough review of study materials, and hands-on practice through Salesforce Trailhead. Test-taking strategies were outlined to help you manage time effectively during the exam, including quick first-pass answering, marking questions for review, and performing multiple review passes for accuracy.

Understanding the exam structure and the types of questions you'll encounter was crucial, with a focus on conceptual understanding over memorization. You also learned about receiving your test results, Salesforce's retake policies, and the importance of certification verification and sharing your success on LinkedIn. By following these strategies, you are well-prepared to approach the Salesforce Platform Administrator certification exam with confidence.

Chapter 12 Quiz

As you finish Chapter 12, it's time to assess the knowledge you've gathered about preparing for the Salesforce Platform Administrator certification exam. This chapter has equipped you with essential strategies for exam registration, effective study techniques, and test-taking strategies.

The quiz below is designed to test your understanding of these key concepts, ensuring you're well-prepared for the types of questions that may appear on the Salesforce Certified Platform Administrator exam.

Remember, each question is an opportunity to review and strengthen your grasp of the preparation process, from registering for the exam to effective time management during the test.

Take your time with each question and select the answer that best aligns with the principles you've learned. After making your choices, carefully review the answers and explanations in the Appendix provided to solidify your understanding of the correct answers. This process will reinforce your existing knowledge and highlight areas that may require further review, ensuring you're well-prepared for real-world scenarios and exam success.

1. What is the primary benefit of using Salesforce Trailhead for exam preparation?
   a. Memorizing answers to practice questions
   b. Gaining hands-on experience with Salesforce
   c. Scheduling the certification exam
   d. Networking with other Salesforce professionals

2. Which of the following is a recommended strategy for managing time effectively during the exam?
   a. Review all questions at the end of the exam.
   b. Make a quick first-pass answer and mark questions for review.
   c. Answer the easiest questions last.
   d. Spend equal time on each question.

3. Why is it important to be well-rested before taking the Salesforce Platform Administrator certification exam?
   a. To reduce the time needed to complete the exam
   b. To ensure sharp reasoning and recall during the exam
   c. To memorize more information the night before
   d. To avoid the need for breaks during the exam

4. What should you do if you fail the Salesforce Platform Administrator certification exam on your first attempt?

   a. Review and study the areas where you were weak.

   b. Retake the exam immediately.

   c. Change your career path.

   d. Take a different certification exam.

5. How can you verify your Salesforce certification after passing the exam?

   a. Print the certification results.

   b. Share the results on social media.

   c. Email Salesforce support.

   d. Use the certification verification feature on Trailhead.

6. Which of the following strategies can help improve your performance on the Salesforce Certified Platform Administrator exam? Select two.

   a. Memorizing questions and answers from practice tests

   b. Understanding the underlying concepts being tested

   c. Taking hands-on practice exams

   d. Skipping difficult questions entirely

Salesforce Certified Platform Administrator Practice Test

At this stage in your learning journey, you've explored every knowledge area required for the Salesforce Certified Platform Administrator exam. Now, it's time to put that knowledge to the test. This chapter presents a full-length practice exam designed to simulate the real exam experience, reinforcing your understanding and helping you identify any areas that may need further review.

This practice test consists of 60 multiple-choice and multiple-select questions, mirroring the structure and scenario-based style of the actual Salesforce Platform Administrator certification exam. The real exam consists of 65 questions in total, but 5 of those are unscored and do not contribute to your final result. Since Salesforce does not indicate which questions are unscored, this practice test provides only 60 graded questions to give you the most accurate measure of your readiness.

Exam Format and Time Allocation

In the actual exam, you will have 105 minutes to complete all 65 questions. However, since this practice test contains only 60 scored questions, you should limit yourself to 90 minutes to more closely reflect your potential exam score.

Question Types and Scoring

This practice test follows the same format as the real Salesforce Platform Administrator exam. Some questions are multiple choice, requiring you to select one correct answer from a list of options. Others are multiple select, meaning you must choose two or more correct answers as specified in the question. The number of correct choices will always be indicated. If a question does not specify the number of answers to select, you should assume that only one is correct.

No Partial Credit

There is no partial credit on multiple-select questions. If a question requires two correct answers and you only choose one, you will not receive any points for that question. There is also no penalty for incorrect answers, so it is always in your best interest to make an educated guess rather than leaving a question blank. Since this practice test excludes the five unscored questions that appear on the real exam, your score on this test will reflect only the 60 graded questions.

Knowledge Area Breakdown

The Salesforce Certified Platform Administrator exam is structured according to specific knowledge areas, each contributing a set percentage to the overall score. Based on the latest Salesforce Platform Administrator Exam Guide, here's how the 60 scored questions will be distributed:

- Configuration and Setup: 20% (12 questions)
- Object Manager and Lightning App Builder: 20% (12 questions)
- Sales and Marketing Applications: 12% (7 questions)
- Service and Support Applications: 11% (7 questions)
- Productivity and Collaboration: 7% (4 questions)
- Data and Analytics Management: 14% (8 questions)
- Workflow/Process Automation: 16% (10 questions)

This distribution ensures that the topics most heavily tested—such as configuration, automation, and data management—are properly weighted, just as they are in the real exam.

How to Use This Practice Test

To get the most out of this practice test, you should aim to complete it in one sitting under exam-like conditions. Set a timer for 90 minutes and do your best to finish within that time frame. Because there is no penalty for incorrect answers, make sure to attempt every question, even if you are unsure. Answering under timed conditions will help you gauge your pacing and build stamina for the actual exam.

After completing the test, review your responses carefully. The answer guide in the Appendix will show the correct answer for each question along with an explanation of why that answer is correct. Each question in the answer guide will also be mapped to its corresponding knowledge area, so you can identify which topics you have mastered and which may require additional study.

Final Notes Before Taking the Exam

As you approach your exam date, take time to review the Exam Guide on Trailhead to ensure you understand all the topics covered. Use hands-on practice in a Salesforce environment to reinforce key concepts and build familiarity with the platform. Taking this practice test under timed conditions will help you develop confidence and improve your pacing. Once you feel prepared, schedule your exam and take the next step toward becoming a Salesforce Certified Platform Administrator.

Full Practice Test

This practice test is designed to give you the most accurate simulation of the Salesforce Certified Platform Administrator exam, allowing you to apply what you've learned across all knowledge areas. By completing this test under timed conditions, you will gain a realistic measure of your readiness and identify any areas where further review may be beneficial.

The following 60 questions reflect the format, structure, and complexity of the real exam. Each question is scenario-based and requires you to apply your understanding of Salesforce functionality, best practices, and system configurations. Some questions are multiple choice, requiring you to select one correct answer, while others are multiple select, requiring you to choose two or more correct answers, as specified in the question. The number of correct responses will always be indicated.

To maximize the effectiveness of this practice test, approach it under exam-like conditions by setting a 90-minute timer and completing it in one sitting. Since there is no penalty for incorrect answers, ensure that you answer every question, even if you are uncertain. If you need guidance on test-taking strategies, refer to Chapter 12 for insights on managing time, making educated guesses, and avoiding common pitfalls.

After completing the test, review the detailed answer explanations to reinforce your understanding. Each explanation includes the correct answer, a rationale for why it is correct, and the corresponding knowledge area it belongs to. This will help you pinpoint your strengths and focus your final review on any areas where you may need additional study.

By taking this test strategically and analyzing your performance, you can refine your understanding, boost your confidence, and ensure you are fully prepared for the actual Salesforce administrator exam.

Question 1

As the Salesforce Platform Administrator, you are invited to a large project kick-off meeting. The project manager has tasked you with setting up a way for the project team members (all of whom are Salesforce users) to collaborate on the project by sharing files and tracking progress on Chatter in Salesforce. The request is that the project team members and you should be the only users able to view the project activity in Chatter. What do you create to fulfill this request?

A. Create a public Chatter group and only invite the project team members.

B. Create a private Chatter group and add the project team members.

C. Install a project management app from AppExchange.

D. Nothing; this cannot be done in Salesforce.

Question 2

A Salesforce administrator needs to create a custom Lightning record page for the Opportunity object. The page should display key Opportunity details, related lists, and a report chart component, while ensuring that users can take quick actions directly from the page. Which tool should the administrator use to configure this layout?

A. Page layouts

B. Compact layouts

C. Lightning App Builder

D. Record types

Question 3

The director of client services has asked you to update a Quarterly Revenue Dashboard component, so that this quarter's revenue is compared to the previous quarter's revenue via a stacked bar chart. Which report format must your source report be in order to fulfill this request?

A. Tabular

B. Matrix

C. Summary

D. Joined

Question 4

A Salesforce administrator needs to create an interactive solution that allows customer service agents to follow a guided step-by-step troubleshooting process when handling support cases. The solution should dynamically adjust based on the agent's selections and require no coding. Which type of Flow should be used?

A. Record-triggered Flow

B. Screen Flow

C. Autolaunched Flow

D. Schedule-triggered Flow

Question 5

The director of client services has asked you to add a new field on all Account records. This new field needs to provide the total amount of all Closed Won Opportunities for each individual account. What type of field should you create to fulfill this requirement?

A. Text

B. Currency

C. Roll-up summary

D. Number

E. Formula

Question 6

The director of IT informs you, late in the day, that another Salesforce administrator in your organization has abruptly left the company. This departing administrator's user account cannot be deactivated because it is tied to several key dashboards as the running user. The account is also associated with several scheduled reports that are delivered daily, and has several other core settings in the system that will take time to reassign to you.

You need to prevent this departing administrator from being able to log in to Salesforce as quickly as possible. What can you do to fulfill this request, without deactivating the departing administrator's user account?

A. Assign a read-only profile to the departing administrator.

B. Freeze the departing administrator's user account.

C. Change the departing administrator's role.

D. Monitor the departing administrator's user account to see if they try to log in.

Question 7

During the Lead Conversion process in Salesforce, which types of records can be created? Select three.

A. Lead

B. Contact

C. Case

D. Opportunity

E. Account

Question 8

A new user requests that their Salesforce user interface display in Spanish instead of English. What can you, as the user's Salesforce administrator, do to fulfill this request?

A. Change the locale of the user.

B. Change the language setting of the user.

C. Nothing. Salesforce does not support other languages and is available in English only.

D. Change the default language setting in the company profile.

Question 9

A Salesforce administrator needs to display key metrics and related lists at the top of the Contact record page for quick reference. Which feature should be used?

A. Page layouts

B. Highlights Panel

C. Compact layout

D. Related list quick links

Question 10

A customer service manager wants to automatically assign incoming Cases to support agents based on the Case's product category. Which feature should the administrator use?

A. Case assignment rules

B. Escalation rules

C. Auto-response rules

Question 11

A sales director wants a private space where sales team members can collaborate, share files, and discuss key deals within Salesforce. The solution should allow only invited users to participate and should not be visible to other employees. Which feature should the administrator use?

A. Private Chatter group

B. Public Chatter group

C. Opportunity teams

Question 12

The IT department requires that certain users have temporary access to modify specific fields on the Account object without making permanent changes to their profile settings. The access should be automatically revoked after a set period. Which feature should the administrator use to grant this access?

A. Permission set with an expiration date

B. Role hierarchy

C. Profile

D. Sharing rules

Question 13

A Salesforce administrator needs to ensure that sales representatives can edit only Opportunities they own, while allowing sales managers to edit all Opportunities owned by their team members. Additionally, support agents should not have access to Opportunities at all. Which security configurations should the administrator use to meet this requirement? Select two.

A. Organization-wide defaults

B. Sharing rules

C. Role hierarchy

D. Permission sets

E. Public groups

Question 14

A Salesforce administrator is building a Flow to automate a process that updates related records when an Account's status changes. The process requires looping through all related Contacts and updating their Status field. Which Flow components should the administrator use to achieve this? Select two.

A. Loop element

B. Decision element

C. Assignment element

D. Screen element

E. Subflow

Question 15

A Salesforce administrator is designing a record-triggered Flow that automatically updates a Case's priority based on the number of days it has been open. The priority should be updated at specific time intervals rather than immediately when the record is edited. Which Flow feature should the administrator use to accomplish this?

A. Scheduled paths

B. Loop

C. Subflow

D. Screen element

Question 16

A Salesforce administrator needs to ensure that users are automatically logged out after 30 minutes of inactivity to enhance security. Which setting should be configured?

A. IP restrictions

B. Single sign-on (SSO)

C. Session timeout

D. Login Hours

Question 23

A sales manager wants to ensure that all Opportunities in the Proposal Stage have an estimated Close Date within 90 days of the Created Date. What is the best way to enforce this?

A. Validation rule

B. Auto-response rule

C. Flow

D. Case assignment rule

Question 24

A Salesforce administrator needs to create a custom dashboard that displays data according to the logged-in user's access level so that each user only sees the data relevant to them. How should this be configured?

A. Report filters

B. Dynamic dashboard

C. Dashboard components

Question 25

A Salesforce administrator needs to ensure that different teams within the sales department only see fields relevant to their specific job responsibilities when viewing Opportunity records. Which feature should be used to accomplish this?

A. Record types

B. Field History Tracking

C. Page layouts

D. Validation rules

Question 26

A Salesforce administrator needs to prevent users from logging in to Salesforce outside of business hours. Which feature should be used to enforce this restriction?

A. Login Hours

B. Session timeout

C. IP restrictions

D. Multi-factor authentication

Question 27

A company wants to ensure that leads from large enterprise companies are automatically assigned to the Enterprise Sales Team when they are created. Which Salesforce feature should be used?

A. Web-to-Lead

B. Lead assignment rules

C. Field mapping

D. Auto-response rules

Question 28

A company needs to ensure that customers can submit Cases through a public-facing form on their website, and that these Cases are automatically created in Salesforce. Which feature should the administrator enable?

A. Web-to-Case

B. Email-to-Case

C. Case assignment rules

Question 29

A Salesforce administrator is creating a custom object called Project and needs to ensure that deleting a related Account record also deletes all associated Project records. Which relationship type should be used?

A. Lookup relationship

B. Master-detail relationship

C. External lookup relationship

D. Many-to-many relationship

Question 30

A Salesforce administrator needs to design a record-triggered Flow on the Contact object that updates a Contact's status only if it meets certain conditions before proceeding with the update. Which Flow elements should be used? Select two.

A. Decision

B. Assignment

C. Get Records

D. Screen

Question 31

A Salesforce administrator needs to create a custom field that calculates the number of days between a Lead's created date and its converted date. Which field type should be used?

A. Roll-up summary

B. Formula field

C. Text field

D. Number field

Question 32

A sales executive wants to track how many leads convert into Closed Won Opportunities. The Salesforce administrator needs to set up a report to measure this lead conversion rate. Which report type should be used?

A. Opportunities with Contacts

B. Leads with Converted Lead Information

C. Sales Pipeline

D. Opportunity History

Question 33

A company wants to ensure that customers receive immediate email confirmations when they submit a new Case through the company's support portal. Which Salesforce feature should be used?

A. Escalation rules

B. Case assignment rules

C. Auto-response rules

D. Web-to-Case

Question 34

A Salesforce administrator needs to display the total number of products added to an Opportunity. What type of custom field should be created?

A. Formula field

B. Roll-up summary field

C. Currency field

D. Number field

Question 35

A Salesforce administrator needs to build a Flow that automatically updates a related Opportunity's close date whenever the Account's contract end date changes. Which Flow elements should be used? Select two.

A. Record-triggered Flow

B. Assignment

C. Update Records

D. Screen

Question 36

A Salesforce administrator is building a Lightning record page for the Account object and wants to display dynamic components that only appear when an Account has a high revenue. Which feature should be used?

A. App Builder filters

B. Component visibility rules

C. Record types

D. Page layouts

Question 37

A company wants to ensure that when an Opportunity is marked as Closed Won, a Contract record is automatically created. How can this be accomplished?

A. Record-triggered Flow

B. Lead assignment rule

C. Approval process

D. Workflow rule

Question 38

Which Salesforce feature automates the creation of cases from customer inquiries submitted via a website?

A. Campaign Influence

B. Web-to-Case

C. Collaborative Forecasting

Question 39

A Salesforce administrator needs to ensure that sales managers can view and compare sales data from different time periods within the same report. Which report feature should be used?

A. Historical trend reporting

B. Summary formula

C. Report filters

D. Custom report type

Question 40

A Salesforce administrator is building a Flow that should run at a scheduled time every night to check for Opportunities that have been open for more than 90 days and update their status. Which Flow elements should be used? Select two.

A. Schedule-triggered Flow

B. Assignment

C. Screen

D. Update Records

Question 41

A Salesforce administrator needs to create multiple new users in Salesforce while ensuring that each user receives a system-generated email with login credentials. What is the most efficient way to accomplish this?

A. Use the Add Multiple Users option in Setup.

B. Manually create each user one at a time.

C. Assign permission sets before creating the users.

D. Use a public Chatter group to add users automatically.

Question 42

A Salesforce administrator needs to ensure that users cannot view or edit specific fields on the Account object unless they have special permissions. Which feature should be used to enforce this?

A. Field-level security
B. Profile
C. Sharing rules
D. Role hierarchy

Question 43

A Salesforce administrator needs to ensure that when a high-priority case is opened, it is assigned to a high-priority support queue, and if it remains unresolved for a set period of time, a notification is sent to the support manager. Which two features should be used?

A. Case assignment rules

B. Escalation rules

C. Case teams

D. Web-to-Case

Question 44

A Salesforce administrator wants to create a single report that compares Opportunities from two different record types, displayed in separate blocks within the same view. What type of report should be used?

A. Summary report

B. Matrix report

C. Joined report

D. Tabular report

Question 45

A Salesforce administrator is building a Flow that must check whether an Account has existing related Contacts before creating a new Contact record. Which Flow elements should be used? Select all that apply.

A. Assignment

B. Get Records

C. Decision

D. Screen

Question 46

A Salesforce administrator needs to enable multicurrency in Salesforce so that international sales teams can track revenue in their respective currencies. Where can this setting be activated?

A. User Personal Customizations

B. Company Information

C. Opportunity settings

D. Currency management

Question 47

A Salesforce administrator needs to ensure that a group of support agents can work together on complex cases that require multiple specialists. Which feature should be used to accomplish this?

A. Case assignment rules

B. Entitlements

C. Escalation rules

D. Case teams

Question 48

A Salesforce administrator wants to ensure that sales users can collaborate on accounts, share files, and communicate in real-time within Salesforce. Which feature should be used?

A. Activity Timeline

B. Chatter

C. Email-to-Case

Question 49

A Salesforce administrator needs to ensure that when a new Opportunity is created, the related Account's custom field "Last Opportunity Created Date" is automatically updated. Which type of Flow should be used?

A. Record-triggered Flow

B. Screen Flow

C. Autolaunched Flow

D. Approval process

Question 50

A Salesforce administrator needs to track vendor contracts and allow each contract to be associated with multiple accounts. Additionally, each account may have multiple contracts. How should the administrator configure this many-to-many relationship?

A. Create a Junction object."

B. Use a lookup relationship between Accounts and Contracts.

C. Use a master-detail relationship between Accounts and Contracts.

D. Enable external sharing.

Question 51

A Salesforce administrator wants to create a report that only includes Opportunities where the Amount is greater than $50,000. Which report feature should be used?

A. Filter

B. Summary formula

C. Cross filter

Question 52

After an acquisition, the acquiring company decides to use the acquired company's Salesforce instance as its system of record. The Salesforce administrator needs to update the company name, default locale, and fiscal year settings to reflect the acquiring company. Where should these changes be made?

A. Company Information

B. Business hours

C. Fiscal year setup

D. Locale settings

Question 53

A Salesforce administrator needs to ensure that only users from the company's office network can access Salesforce, while allowing executives to log in from any location. Which security setting should be used?

A. IP restrictions

B. Login Hours

C. Multi-factor authentication

D. Trusted devices

Question 54

A Salesforce administrator needs to evaluate incoming Cases using complex routing criteria that cannot be handled by assignment rules. The Cases must be routed to the correct queue automatically without requiring user input. Which Flow elements should be used? Select two.

A. Pause

B. Decision

C. Assignment

D. Screen

Question 55

A Salesforce administrator needs to ensure that different teams see different picklist values for the Lead Source field based on their business process. Which feature should be used?

A. Field-level security

B. Record types

C. Validation rules

D. Page layouts

Question 56

A Salesforce administrator wants users to automatically see updates in Chatter when specific fields on the Account object are changed. Which feature should be enabled?

A. Chatter Groups

B. Chatter Feed Tracking

C. Chatter Streams

D. Chatter Publisher Actions

Question 57

A customer support manager wants to track how long it takes for agents to close cases and wants to ensure cases that remain open for over 48 hours are automatically escalated. Which Salesforce feature should be used?

A. Case assignment rules
B. Escalation rules
C. Case teams
D. Support Processes

Question 58

A sales manager wants to ensure that all new Opportunities are assigned to the appropriate sales representative based on the Opportunity's region. The assignment should happen automatically when the Opportunity is created. Which Salesforce feature should be used to meet this requirement?

A. Workflow rule

B. Assignment rule

C. Approval process

D. Sharing rule

Question 59

A Salesforce administrator wants to ensure that certain fields on the Opportunity object are only visible to specific profiles. Which feature should be used?

A. Record types

B. Field-level security

C. Page layouts

D. Role hierarchy

Question 60

The VP of marketing has purchased a list of 60,000 leads that needs to be imported into Salesforce. Which data import tool is best suited for importing these records?

A. Data Import Wizard

B. Data Export

C. Data Loader

Answer Keys

Chapter 2 Answer Key

1. C: Company Settings define the organization's core identity and operational parameters, such as name, contact details, default language, and locale. User interface and application settings, as well as data security and privacy settings, are configured in separate areas of Salesforce. While tracking the fiscal year is a component of Company Settings, it's not its primary function.

2. C: Enabling Multiple Currencies allows for the handling of financial transactions and reporting across different currencies for global business operations. This functionality specifically focuses on financial conversions, not just tracking sales data by country. Translation services and user interface customization for international users are handled through separate language and customization settings, respectively, and are unrelated to currency management.

3. C: Business Hours settings allow administrators to define distinct business hours for different departments. Workflow automation is used for process automation, system auditing tracks system changes, and role hierarchy manages access and permissions. These are all separate features from setting business hours.

4. A: The Default Locale setting establishes the regional formatting for dates, addresses, and names. Login restrictions are managed through security settings, and email templates and interface themes are customized separately from the Default Locale setting.

5. C: Correctly configuring Business Hours affects workflows, service level agreement (SLA) tracking, and customer support operations. This is distinct from customizing the Salesforce mobile app, managing user roles and permissions, or data backup and recovery processes, which are handled in other areas of Salesforce.

6. B: Default organization settings define the default locale, language, and time zone for the entire organization. Record visibility and data sharing rules are part of security settings, while user access to the mobile app is managed through mobile security settings. Automated workflows and approval processes are configured separately.

7. A: The Lightning App Builder is a visual interface that enables users to create and customize Salesforce pages. Managing user licenses, setting up business hours and currency, and configuring data security settings are all handled in separate areas within Salesforce Setup.

8. B: Customizing the App Menu improves navigation efficiency by helping users quickly access applications that are tailored to their specific workflows. This is unrelated to improving system security, managing data storage, or configuring email services, which are all managed in other parts of Salesforce.

Chapter 3 Answer Key

1. B: Enabling "Log in as Any User" is the correct choice because it gives administrators direct access to a user's environment for troubleshooting. Freezing a user account temporarily prevents a user from logging in but doesn't allow direct access. Setting password policies secures accounts but also doesn't provide direct access. While viewing user login history is helpful for troubleshooting, it doesn't provide direct access to the user's environment.

2. C: Unlocking a user's account is the recommended way to resolve a locked user account in Salesforce. Deactivating the user removes all access, which isn't necessary for a locked account. Freezing an account prevents login attempts but doesn't resolve the locked status. Enabling "Log in as Any User" is a troubleshooting feature and doesn't directly unlock the account.

3. B: When you deactivate a user account, the user can no longer log in or access Salesforce. A deactivated user won't receive any notifications, including Chatter. Deactivating a user does not delete their records automatically, and their reports and dashboards remain with their account unless they are manually transferred.

4. C: Setting password policies improves overall security by enforcing strong passwords, expiration periods, and lockout policies. Password policies cannot prevent users from changing their passwords. Enabling "Log in as Any User" is a separate feature. Also, limiting access to specific IP ranges is a different security measure, not part of password policies.

5. C: User login history provides a record of a specific user's login attempts, including unsuccessful ones. User profile settings control permissions, not login monitoring. Login Access Policies apply to the whole organization and don't track

individual attempts. Finally, permission sets provide additional permissions but also do not track login attempts.

Chapter 4 Answer Key

1. B: Profile settings are the correct choice because they let an administrator customize page layouts and set default record types for specific groups of users, such as a sales team. User personal customizations, on the other hand, apply to individual users and cannot be used for team-wide changes. Permission sets provide additional permissions but don't directly change page layouts or record types. Lastly, the App Launcher is used for navigation and doesn't offer customization options.

2. A: To resolve a user's login issue caused by IP restrictions, the administrator should adjust the user's profile IP range. This allows the user to log in from different IP addresses. Enabling "Log in as Any User" is a troubleshooting tool, but it doesn't fix IP restrictions directly. Freezing a user account prevents them from logging in at all, which would make the issue worse, not better. Similarly, resetting the user's password won't solve an IP restriction problem.

3. B: The best way to configure strict security settings is to set strong password policies and enable IP restrictions. This combination is highly effective at preventing unauthorized access. While deactivating inactive users and freezing accounts can improve security, they don't fully prevent unauthorized access on their own. Activating single sign-on (SSO) and changing page layouts are not directly related to preventing unauthorized access. Similarly, adjusting sharing rules and enabling "Log in as Any User" aren't effective as standalone security measures for access.

4. B: To set up a new employee, an administrator must create a new user account, assign a profile, and configure permissions. This is the complete and correct process for a new user. Resetting a password is only for existing accounts. While single sign-on (SSO) is a feature, it doesn't directly create a new user account. Freezing an account is for preventing access and isn't part of the new user setup process.

5. D: Organization-wide defaults are used to set the baseline level of record access for each object across all users in your organization. In contrast, required fields are defined at the field and layout level, not through organization-wide defaults. Password policies are handled in security settings, not here, and tab visibility is configured with apps and profiles.

6. C: The role hierarchy provides vertical access to records based on user roles, allowing users in higher roles to access records owned by users below them. It doesn't grant field-level access, which is handled separately, nor does it provide lateral access across public groups. While profiles grant object-level access, the

role hierarchy provides record visibility, not automatic full access to all records within a profile.

7. B: For providing as-needed access to a specific record, manual sharing is the best feature to use. It's designed for granting ad hoc, case-by-case access. Sharing rules apply broadly to many records, not individual exceptions. Territory assignment is for access based on segmentation models, not for one-off record access. Finally, profiles control object-level access but don't grant record-level permissions.

8. C: The Salesforce Audit Trail feature is used for tracking configuration changes over time, which helps maintain data integrity and security. The Data Import Wizard is a tool for importing data, not for tracking changes. Schema Builder is for visualizing and managing data models, and it doesn't track changes over time. Data Loader is for bulk importing or exporting of data and also doesn't track changes over time.

Chapter 5 Answer Key

1. C: The Object Manager in Salesforce is primarily used by administrators to create, customize, and manage objects, including defining their fields and page layouts. It allows for the modification and maintenance of all aspects of objects. User permissions and security settings are managed through profiles and permission sets, not the Object Manager. The Object Manager does not provide a visual interface for mapping relationships between objects; that functionality is handled separately through the Schema Builder. Reports and dashboards are handled in separate tabs and not through the Object Manager.

2. B: A Junction object is unique in Salesforce because it enables many-to-many relationships by using two master-detail relationships. Other relationships, such as lookup or single master-detail, only allow one-to-many links between records. The Object Manager allows administrators to configure these, but the function itself is specific to Junction objects. It does not serve as a metadata management tool, nor is it used to store configuration information.

3. C: A primary purpose of record types is to allow administrators to assign different page layouts by profile and record type. This provides flexibility so users in different capacities can see the most relevant information for their business process. Object-level access is managed through profiles and permission sets. Backups and recovery are handled through data management tools. Relationships between objects are created using lookup and master-detail relationships.

4. B: A significant benefit of Dynamic Forms is that they allow individual fields and sections to be placed directly on a Lightning page and configured with visibility rules. This provides greater flexibility and a better user experience. Dynamic Forms are not used for managing lookup relationships, which are handled in the

Object Manager. They also don't generate reports on record changes or create home pages for apps; these functions are handled by other Salesforce features, such as the Reports and Dashboards tabs and the Lightning App Builder.

5. B: Record types should be introduced in Salesforce when there is a need to distinguish between different types of records, specifically when different page layouts or picklist values are needed based on the record type or user profile. If a single master record type is sufficient for all data needs, then additional record types are not necessary. Record types are not used for customizing home pages or for creating new custom objects; their purpose is to differentiate records within an existing object.

6. C: The most detailed level of Lightning page activation is the combination of App, Record Type, and Profile, which allows for the most specific customization by tailoring the user experience based on user roles and record characteristics. The Org Default applies to all users without any specific differentiation. App Default applies the page to all users of a specific app but doesn't consider record types or profiles.

7. B: You might create different Lightning pages for Fuel versus Electric Automobiles to display fields like "Miles per Gallon" for Fuel and "Miles per Full Charge" for Electric. This ensures that the fields displayed are relevant to the specific record type. The primary reason is not to create dashboards. Similarly, it is not for tracking different permission sets, which are used for access control. Differentiating home page layouts is also not the reason, as this is a part of record-specific customization.

Chapter 6 Answer Key

1. B: The primary goal of the marketing phase is to attract potential customers. Retaining customers and resolving customer issues are goals of the service phase, while closing sales is the focus of the sales phase.

2. B: Digital Experiences/Community is a Salesforce feature that allows customers to find answers independently, which reduces the need for human intervention. The Case Status field only tracks the progress of a Case, and the Lead Conversion process is for converting leads into Opportunities, not for self-service. Contact roles are used to manage relationships within Opportunities and do not provide self-service capabilities.

3. B: Salesforce Knowledge articles provide detailed information and solutions to common problems. Limiting access by IP range is a security feature, not a benefit of Knowledge articles. Enabling "Log in as Any User" is a troubleshooting feature, and tracking the status of leads is managed through lead records and the Lead Status field.

4. C: The Experience Cloud enhances customer service by providing branded spaces where customers can interact and find information. It does not manage the Lead Conversion process, nor does it enable customers to log in as another user. Managing Opportunities is a sales function, not a primary feature of the Experience Cloud.

5. B: The primary objective of case deflection strategies is to reduce the number of Cases that require human intervention. Converting leads to Opportunities is related to the sales phase, and enhancing the lead qualification process is related to the marketing and sales phases. Managing user access and permissions is an administrative function, not a case deflection strategy.

Chapter 7 Answer Key

1. B: Campaign Influence measures how marketing campaigns contribute to sales success. It is not limited to just email campaigns, as it tracks overall marketing effectiveness. While it does identify relationships between campaigns and closed Opportunities, that is a feature, not its main purpose. Generating leads from web forms is handled by a separate feature called Web-to-Lead, not Campaign Influence.

2. C: The Kanban view is the best for visually managing pipeline stages because it visually represents the stages and allows for easy drag-and-drop management of Opportunities. In contrast, the split view shows records and lists side-by-side but doesn't effectively visualize pipeline stages. The table view presents Opportunities in rows and columns without any visual management of the stages. The compact view is not a valid list view format in Salesforce.

3. D: Custom price books are distinct from standard price books because they allow tailored pricing specific to individual customers or markets. The type of price book does not control editing permissions; those are managed by user profiles and roles. Both standard and custom price books can support multicurrency if the feature is enabled. Custom price books do not automatically sync with external pricing systems; this requires additional integration.

4. C: When setting up Collaborative Forecasting, forecast categories must align directly with Opportunity Stages to ensure accurate forecasting. Other elements like Opportunity names and record types do not directly impact forecasting. Additionally, campaign member status is related to campaigns, not Collaborative Forecasting.

5. B: The primary function of the Opportunity Product Related list is to add and manage the products, quantities, and discounts that are associated with a specific Opportunity. Tracking Opportunity progress through stages is handled by Opportunity Stages, not this related list. Defining product categories is done on

the product records themselves, and assigning team roles to an Opportunity is a function of Contact Roles.

6. D: The Send List Email feature allows users to quickly send emails to all members of a campaign directly from campaign records. The older feature of Mass Emailing is separate and distinct from the campaign member interface. Email-to-Case is used for creating Cases from emails, not for sending emails to campaign members. Campaign Influence measures marketing effectiveness but does not send emails directly.

Chapter 8 Answer Key

1. C: Case teams allow collaboration by assigning roles and permissions to team members on a case. Parent-child cases link related cases but do not assign roles or permissions. Case queues are used to organize cases for assignment but do not define team roles. Experience Cloud is a customer-facing tool and does not manage internal collaboration roles.

2. A: Parent-child Cases link related cases in a hierarchical manner, ideal for complex issue management. Case queues organize Cases for team assignment but do not provide a hierarchical structure. Case teams enable team collaboration but do not define hierarchical Case relationships. Experience Cloud is focused on external customer interactions, not hierarchical internal case management.

3. C: Automating Case assignment to team members is not a benefit of using parent-child cases; case assignment automation is achieved using case assignment rules or queues. Parent-child cases do, however, provide benefits such as enabling roll-up reporting, establishing a clear hierarchy for linked Cases, and tracking resolution times across related Cases.

4. B: The primary purpose of Case escalation rules is to automatically escalate unresolved Cases based on predefined time criteria. The automatic assignment of new Cases to users or queues is handled by case assignment rules. Allowing customers to create cases from the web is the function of Web-to-Case. Defining the roles of team members working on a Case is a feature of case teams.

5. D: The main purpose of Salesforce Knowledge in customer support is to provide a repository of articles that help resolve customer inquiries quickly. Managing customer contacts and Opportunities is done separately, and tracking customer service agreements is managed using Entitlements. Additionally, automatic case assignment is handled by assignment rules, not Knowledge.

6. A: When configuring Web-to-Case, an HTML form generated in Salesforce Setup is required to automatically create Cases from a website. JavaScript code and custom-built API integrations are not necessary for Web-to-Case implemen-

tation. External email client configuration is relevant for Email-to-Case, not Web-to-Case.

7. B: Case auto-response rules are used to automatically send acknowledgment emails to customers when a new Case is submitted. Case escalation rules escalate unresolved Cases but don't send acknowledgments upon case creation. Case assignment rules handle assigning Cases to agents but don't directly manage customer emails. Web-to-Case captures inquiries but does not automatically handle customer acknowledgment emails.

8. A: Parent-child cases are used by Salesforce users to create and manage multiple cases related to one primary issue by hierarchically grouping them. Case queues manage the assignment of cases, not their hierarchical grouping. Case teams manage collaborative roles, not multiple related cases. Escalation rules handle time-based escalation, not the grouping of related Cases.

9. B: Case assignment rules are the feature used to automatically assign incoming Cases to specific queues or agents based on defined criteria. Email-to-Case converts emails into Cases, but it doesn't automatically assign them to specific queues. Escalation rules escalate Cases after a specified time, not immediately upon creation. Auto-response rules send automatic responses to customers but do not handle Case assignments.

10. C: Escalation rules help ensure support Cases are addressed within defined time frames by automatically escalating unresolved cases after a specified period. Case assignment rules assign Cases but do not manage response time frames. Web-to-Case is used to capture Cases, but it does not manage escalation based on time frames. Campaign Influence measures the impact of marketing and is not related to Case handling timelines.

Chapter 9 Answer Key

1. C: Activity management in Salesforce is primarily for organizing and monitoring tasks, events, and customer interactions. It's not mainly about managing user profiles and permissions, which are handled in security settings and user setup. While activities can be connected to Opportunities and leads, the purpose of activity management is broader than just tracking sales. Furthermore, while you can report on activities, its main purpose is not to generate reports and dashboards.

2. C: The Activity Timeline in Salesforce provides a chronological view of past and upcoming activities related to a specific record. It doesn't show a user's login history, which is found in user management settings. Nor is it used to display a history of field value changes, which are tracked separately in Field History

Tracking. Lastly, the Activity Timeline does not track the performance of marketing campaigns.

3. D: Tasks, events, and emails are all primary types of activities in Salesforce activity management. An Opportunity is not a type of activity. It is a separate object used within sales processes.

4. C: Chatter is not designed to completely replace email communication. While it may reduce email volume by enabling collaboration inside Salesforce, email remains necessary for many types of communication. Chatter does, however, help team members share updates and information, and it allows users to follow records, other users, and groups to receive updates in their feed.

5. B: The Salesforce mobile app allows users to access and update Salesforce data on their mobile devices. It does not provide the exact same functionality as the desktop version. You can both view and update data using the app, not just view it. The mobile app doesn't require a separate license.

6. C: The main benefit of AppExchange applications is that they can extend Salesforce functionality without extensive custom coding. While some are free, many are paid solutions, so the primary benefit is not cost related. These apps can reduce the need for custom development, but they don't completely eliminate it. AppExchange apps are not installed automatically.

7. B: Enabling Chatter Feed Tracking for an object allows users to see updates and changes to those records in their Chatter feed. It does not automatically create new records. While it provides updates, it doesn't replace the need for detailed reports on the object. Lastly, enabling Chatter Feed Tracking does not affect or restrict record access.

Chapter 10 Answer Key

1. C: The Salesforce Data Export service allows organizations to schedule or run on-demand data exports, ensuring data is backed up regularly. It is not for exporting metadata. Additionally, this service doesn't facilitate real-time data synchronization, which requires APIs or other integration tools.

2. A: When using the Data Export service, the exported data is delivered as a downloadable link sent via email. The link leads to a ZIP file that contains individual CSV files for each object selected for export. The service does not send files as direct email attachments. It also doesn't use JSON format for exports, as Salesforce provides the data in CSV format. The service is for periodic backups and doesn't provide a real-time feed to an external data warehouse.

3. B: A key difference between exporting reports and using the Data Export service is that the Data Export service provides data backup, while report exports are based on specific filters. Both reports and data exports can be scheduled, but the

Data Export service doesn't allow for conditional delivery. Both methods also generate CSV files, and neither uses JSON format for standard exports. The Data Export service supports both standard and custom objects, depending on what is selected for export, and is not limited to just custom objects.

4. B: An administrator would use a converted leads report to analyze which marketing campaigns led to the most successful conversions. Deleted leads are not included in this type of report. The report is not used for tracking leads that have been reassigned to a new owner, which is done through lead owner change tracking. Similarly, the report isn't used to measure the average response time for new leads; that's usually tracked with case reports or automation.

5. C: While Case history, login history, and Setup Audit Trail reports are all available in Salesforce, a dedicated Chatter Feed Tracking report is not. Case history reports track changes on Case records, such as status and ownership. Login history reports provide insight into user login attempts, including successes and failures. The Setup Audit Trail logs administrative changes. Although Chatter activity can be reported on, there is no specific history report for Chatter Feed Tracking.

6. B: A report subscription lets users receive scheduled emails only when specific conditions are met, which is useful for proactive monitoring, whereas data exports are sent on a fixed schedule without conditions. Therefore, conditional delivery is only available for report subscriptions, not for data exports. Data exports can provide full org-wide data backups, while report subscriptions only distribute predefined reports. Standard users can subscribe to reports if they have access, but administrators control data exports.

7. C: The running user determines whose data permissions apply when the dashboard is viewed. While a user's security settings do control overall data access, dashboards specifically display data based on the running user's permissions. Filters can refine the data that is displayed but do not determine overall visibility. The underlying reports provide the source data, but the dashboard's visibility is ultimately based on the running user's settings.

8. D: For a widget to display data, it must be linked to a report. While users must have access to the report, the linking of the report to a widget is the required step for display. Dashboards update at scheduled intervals or manually, but this doesn't affect the display of individual widgets. Non-admin users can also edit dashboards as long as they have the proper permissions.

9. B: The purpose of a dashboard filter is to adjust the way data is displayed on the dashboard without modifying the source reports. Dashboard filters do not impact security settings, which are what control access to reports. Additionally, dashboard filters are not related to the scheduling of dashboard refreshes or email delivery.

10. C: When a report that a dashboard widget relies on is deleted, the widget will display an error message indicating that the report is missing. Salesforce does not automatically generate new reports to replace deleted ones. Deleting a report does not delete the entire dashboard, but it does affect related widgets, and the widget will not simply remain unchanged.

11. C: Matrix reports support two row groupings or a row grouping and a column grouping, making them ideal for visual comparisons like quarterly revenue. In contrast, Tabular reports are basic lists that lack the row and column groupings needed for comparisons. Summary reports allow row grouping but not the column-grouping required for a visual comparison. Joined reports can compare separate reports side-by-side, but they don't offer the integrated visual comparison of a Matrix format.

Chapter 11 Answer Key

1. B: Record-triggered Flows activate when a record is created, updated, or deleted, while schedule-triggered Flows run automatically at specific, predefined times. Both types of Flows have the ability to create, update, or delete records. Neither type supports Screen elements, as they operate in the background without requiring user interaction. The context in which a Flow runs is a configurable setting for both types and is not their primary distinguishing factor.

2. B: When a record is submitted for approval, it is automatically locked to prevent edits during the process. This locking mechanism is the default behavior to maintain data integrity, though administrators can configure limited exceptions. The submission does not automatically alter sharing settings, clone the record, or route it to a queue for processing.

3. C: The Loop element processes records from a collection one at a time . Collection process is not a valid element in Flow Builder; For Each is a general programming concept, not a label in Salesforce; and Iterator is not used in Flow Builder.

4. C: A fault path in Flow Builder is designed to handle errors that occur during a Flow's execution. It provides an alternative route for the Flow to take when an element fails. Fault paths are not used to bypass validation rules or skip elements due to insufficient user permissions. They also do not create shortcuts for experienced users.

5. A, C: Salesforce provides two wizards for creating approval processes: the Jump Start Wizard and the Standard Setup Wizard. The Jump Start Wizard is intended for creating simple approval processes, whereas the Standard Setup Wizard offers full customization. The Advanced Configuration Wizard and Quick Setup Wizard are not valid Salesforce tools.

6. C: When a new version of a Flow is activated, the previously active version is automatically deactivated. This ensures that only one version of a Flow is running at any given time. Manual deactivation is not required, and the version change takes effect immediately without needing to be scheduled.

7. B: To create a guided process for sales representatives to qualify leads, you would use a screen Flow. Screen Flows are specifically designed to support user interaction. Record-triggered Flows, schedule-triggered Flows, and autolaunched Flows all run in the background and do not involve user screens.

8. A: Approval steps are executed in the order they are listed in the Setup page. At each step, Salesforce evaluates the entry criteria to determine if the step should run. The entry criteria themselves do not define the order of steps, but only whether a step applies when reached. The hierarchy level of approvers has no effect on the sequence of steps. There is also no "priority" field that influences the execution order in an approval process.

9. C: A key advantage of using Einstein with Flow Builder is its ability to analyze existing Flows and generate human-readable descriptions of their functionality. This feature helps explain Flow logic in plain terms. Einstein does not perform Flow testing, make decisions using machine learning, or eliminate the need for administrators to understand Flow concepts.

Chapter 12 Answer Key

1. B: Salesforce Trailhead is beneficial for exam preparation primarily because it offers hands-on experience with the platform, which is crucial for understanding concepts. While networking with other professionals is valuable, it isn't the main purpose of Trailhead. Trailhead Academy, not Trailhead, is used to schedule exams. Relying on memorizing practice answers is less effective than active, hands-on learning.

2. B: To manage your time effectively during the exam, you should make a quick first-pass answer and mark questions for review. This strategy helps you quickly tackle the easier questions, saving the more challenging ones for later. Answering the easiest questions first also helps build confidence and secure points early on. Reserve reviewing all questions only at the end, as you might run out of time. Additionally, don't spend an equal amount of time on every question; you should allocate your time based on how difficult each question is.

3. B: Being well-rested before the exam is important because it ensures sharp reasoning and recall. A well-rested mind performs better cognitively. Cramming the night before is less effective than being rested. The primary benefit of being rested is not to reduce the time needed to complete the exam or to avoid the need for breaks, but to maintain mental acuity.

4. A: If you fail the Salesforce Platform Administrator certification exam, you should review and study the areas where you were weak. This approach is the most effective way to improve your understanding and perform better on a future attempt. Failing once is a common part of the process and should not prompt you to change your career path or take a different certification exam, as it is more beneficial to focus on the same exam with better preparation.

5. D: After passing the exam, you can verify your Salesforce certification using the certification verification feature on Trailhead. This feature provides a formal way for others to confirm your credentials as well. While sharing your results on social media can be useful for networking, it's not a form of official verification. Similarly, printing the results or emailing Salesforce support are not the correct methods for official verification when a dedicated feature exists.

6. B, C: To improve your performance on the Salesforce Certified Platform Administrator exam, you should focus on two key strategies: understanding the underlying concepts and taking hands-on practice exams. Understanding concepts allows you to apply your knowledge to different scenarios. Hands-on practice exams give you practical experience and reinforce what you've learned. Memorizing questions and answers from practice tests is less effective than truly understanding the concepts. Also, skipping difficult questions entirely will reduce your chances of passing.

Chapter 13 Answer Key

1. B: To fulfill the request, you must create a private Chatter group and add the project team members. A private Chatter group ensures that only invited members can view and participate in project activity, keeping the information restricted to the team. Creating a public Chatter group would not meet this request, as it would be visible to everyone in the organization. While project management apps are available on AppExchange, they aren't necessary to meet the specific request for a Chatter-based collaboration space. The request can be fulfilled in Salesforce, so the answer is not "Nothing; this cannot be done in Salesforce".

   Knowledge Area: Productivity and Collaboration.

2. C: The administrator should use Lightning App Builder to configure the custom Lightning record page. This tool provides a drag-and-drop interface that allows for the customization of Lightning record pages, including the placement of key details, related lists, report charts, and Quick Actions. While page layouts determine the arrangement of fields and related lists, they don't control the placement of Lightning Components like report charts. Compact layouts are used for key fields on the mobile app and hover details, not for customizing Lightning record pages. Record types control picklist values and page layout assignments but aren't used for configuring the page's components or layout.

Knowledge Area: Object Manager and Lightning App Builder.

3. B: To compare this quarter's revenue to the previous quarter's revenue with a stacked bar chart, the source report must be in the Matrix format. Matrix reports are the only format that supports multiple groupings, which is necessary for a stacked bar chart dashboard component. Tabular reports are simple lists of records without any groupings, so they don't support this type of chart. Summary reports allow for a singular row grouping, making them unsuitable for stacked bar charts. Joined reports combine multiple report blocks but lack the grouping structure required for this specific chart type.

Knowledge Area: Data and Analytics Management.

4. B: To create a guided, step-by-step troubleshooting process that dynamically adjusts without coding, the administrator should use a screen Flow. Screen Flows are ideal for interactive, user-driven processes because they can include screens, fields, and decision points that respond to user input. In contrast, record-triggered Flows and autolaunched Flows both run in the background without any user interaction. Schedule-triggered flows are used for batch updates at specific times or intervals and are not suited for real-time, interactive processes.

Knowledge Area: Workflow/Process Automation.

5. C: The best field type to create for this request is a roll-up summary field. A roll-up summary field automatically calculates and aggregates values from related child records, such as summing the amount of all won Opportunities for an account. A text field is used for nonnumeric data and cannot perform calculations. Currency and number fields store monetary or numeric values but do not calculate or roll up data from related records. A formula field can perform calculations on the same record or parent records, but it cannot aggregate values from related child records, which is required in this scenario.

Knowledge Area: Object Manager and Lightning App Builder.

6. B: To immediately prevent the departing administrator from logging in without deactivating their account, you should freeze the user account. Freezing the account immediately blocks login access while keeping data, scheduled reports, and dashboard ownership intact, giving you time to reassign these assets. Assigning a read-only profile will restrict their ability to make changes but won't prevent them from logging in, which is the immediate concern. Changing their role only affects record access based on the role hierarchy and does not prevent login. Monitoring their login activity is a reactive measure that won't stop them from logging in and accessing data.

Knowledge Area: Configuration and Setup.

7. B, D, E: During the Lead Conversion process, a new Contact, Opportunity, and Account record can be created. The purpose of lead conversion is to transform a

lead into these standard Salesforce objects to represent the individual (Contact), the company (Account), and a potential sales deal (Opportunity). Leads cannot be created during this process since they are the source record. Cases are used for customer service and support, not for the sales-focused Lead Conversion process.

Knowledge Area: Sales and Marketing Applications.

8. B: As a Salesforce administrator, you can fulfill the user's request by changing the language setting of the user. This setting, found on the user's detail page, controls the language in which the Salesforce user interface is displayed. Changing the locale only affects date, time, number, and address formats, not the display language. Salesforce supports multiple languages, so it's not true that it is English-only. Changing the default language setting in the company profile affects new users, but not existing ones, who must change their preference individually.

Knowledge Area: Configuration and Setup.

9. B: To display key metrics and related lists at the top of a Contact record page for quick reference, the administrator should use the Highlights Panel. The Highlights Panel is specifically designed to prominently display important fields, actions, and related lists at the top of a record page. Page layouts determine the arrangement and visibility of fields, but they don't provide this dedicated summary section. A compact layout controls which key fields appear in the mobile app and hover details, not the layout of the main record page. Related list quick links only provide navigation to related lists and don't display metrics at the top of the page.

Knowledge Area: Object Manager and Lightning App Builder.

10. A: The administrator should use case assignment rules to automatically assign incoming Cases to support agents based on the product category. These rules route Cases to specific users or queues based on defined criteria. Escalation rules are used to trigger actions when a Case remains unresolved for a certain period of time, not for initial assignment. Auto-response rules send automated email confirmations to customers and do not handle Case assignment.

Knowledge Area: Service and Support Applications.

11. A: To create a private collaboration space for the sales team, the administrator should use a private Chatter group. This is the correct solution because it is an invitation-only environment where only members can view and participate in discussions, ensuring the space remains private and confidential. A public Chatter group would not meet this need, as it is visible to anyone in the organization. Opportunity teams allow for collaboration on specific records but don't provide the dedicated, centralized discussion and file-sharing space that a Chatter group does.

Knowledge Area: Productivity and Collaboration.

12. A: The administrator should use a permission set with an expiration date to grant temporary access to modify specific fields. This feature allows for the temporary extension of permissions without changing a user's baseline profile, and the expiration date ensures the access is automatically revoked. The role hierarchy controls record-level access and does not grant temporary field-level security. A user's profile determines their baseline permissions and is not practical for short-term, temporary access, as any changes would affect all users assigned to it. Sharing rules extend record access but do not modify field-level security or allow temporary assignments.

Knowledge Area: Configuration and Setup.

13. A, C: The administrator should use organization-wide defaults and role hierarchy to meet this requirement. First, set the organization-wide defaults for Opportunities to Private, which ensures sales representatives can only edit the Opportunities they own. Then, configure the role hierarchy so that sales managers are above the sales representatives, allowing them to automatically inherit access to their team's opportunities. Grant access using hierarchies is enabled on all standard objects in Salesforce and cannot be disabled. Sharing rules are not needed because they are used to extend access, not restrict it. Permission sets grant additional permissions but do not restrict access, and public groups are used for group-based sharing and not for object-level access control.

Knowledge Area: Configuration and Setup.

14. A, C: To update related records in a Flow, the administrator should use the Loop and Assignment elements. A Loop element is essential for iterating through a collection of related records, such as all the contacts tied to an account. The Assignment element is then used inside the loop to modify the field values of each individual record before the changes are saved. While a Decision element can be useful, it is not required for the basic process of looping and updating records. A Screen element is only used for interactive Flows, and a Subflow is used to call another Flow, neither of which are necessary for this automated process.

Knowledge Area: Workflow/Process Automation.

15. A: To update a Case's priority at specific time intervals, the administrator should use scheduled paths within a record-triggered Flow. Scheduled paths allow the Flow to delay execution until a specified time condition is met, such as a certain number of days after the record was last modified. A Loop is used to iterate over a collection of records and does not allow time-based delays. A Subflow is used to call another Flow and does not control the timing of execution. A Screen element is only used in interactive screen Flows and is not applicable for this automated, background process.

Knowledge Area: Workflow/Process Automation.

16. C: The correct setting is Session timeout, as it's specifically designed to automatically log users out after a period of inactivity, which directly addresses the security requirement. IP restrictions control where users can log in from but don't affect session duration. Similarly, single sign-on (SSO) simplifies the login process via an external provider but does not enforce automatic logouts. Lastly, Login Hours restrict the times users can access the system but do not end active sessions due to inactivity.

Knowledge Area: Configuration and Setup.

17. A: To ensure an Opportunity is created during lead conversion, the administrator should instruct users to leave the "Create Opportunity" checkbox selected. This checkbox is selected by default in Salesforce, but users can deselect it if they do not want an Opportunity created. An autolaunched Flow could technically automate Opportunity creation, but that approach adds unnecessary complexity to a standard function. There is no "Opportunity Auto-Creation" option in Lead settings, and validation rules can only enforce conditions and prevent record saves, not create records.

Knowledge Area: Sales and Marketing Applications.

18. B: A Quick Action is the most effective tool for creating a custom button that generates a related quote from an Account record. This feature is designed to allow users to perform specific, predefined actions with a single click. While a Lightning component could be used for more complex customizations, it is not the simplest solution for this straightforward task. Page layouts control the visibility and arrangement of fields but can't create custom buttons for actions. A validation rule is used to enforce data entry requirements and cannot provide interactive functionality like generating a new record.

Knowledge Area: Object Manager and Lightning App Builder.

19. B: To report on Accounts with their related Opportunities and the Contacts involved in those Opportunities, you must build a custom report type with Accounts as the primary object. You then add Opportunities as a related object, and from there, you can include Contact Roles as a related object to Opportunities. Summary reports allow grouping and subtotals, but they don't define the relationships between objects, which is a prerequisite for this report. Joined reports can combine data from unrelated blocks, which is not necessary for this scenario since the records are related. Tabular reports are simple lists and cannot display related records in the required format.

Knowledge Area: Data and Analytics Management.

20. C, E: To create a Flow that dynamically updates a Customer Score field based on related records, the administrator needs to use both the Get Records and Assignment elements. The Get Records element is essential for retrieving the related Cases and Opportunities, providing the data needed for the calculation. The

Assignment element is then used to store and update the calculated value of the Customer Score field. A Pause element is not required as it's typically used in scheduled or waiting Flows, not for this type of calculation. A Decision element evaluates conditions but doesn't retrieve or modify records itself. A Screen element is only needed for user input or output in a screen Flow and isn't necessary for a background automation.

Knowledge Area: Workflow/Process Automation.

21. A: To ensure each user sees dates, times, and currency formats specific to their country, the administrator should configure locale settings. This setting specifically determines how these values are displayed based on the user's country. Language settings only change the user interface language and have no effect on formats for dates, times, or currencies. Currency management handles multiple currencies but doesn't control the display format of dates and times. Finally, the Company information setting sets the default locale for the entire organization but can be overridden by individual user preferences.

Knowledge Area: Configuration and Setup.

22. A: A lookup relationship is the correct choice because it creates a loose association between the custom Contract object and the standard Account object. This ensures that when an Account record is deleted, the related Contract records are not automatically deleted, which is the desired outcome. A master-detail relationship is not appropriate because it would enforce a tight relationship, causing the child Contract records to be deleted along with the parent Account record. A Junction object is used for many-to-many relationships, which is not the case here since each contract is linked to only one account. An external lookup relationship is only used to link Salesforce records to external data sources and is not relevant to this scenario.

Knowledge Area: Object Manager and Lightning App Builder.

23. C: Flow is the best way to enforce the business logic that an Opportunity's Close Date must be within 90 days of its Created Date when it enters the Proposal Stage. This tool can automatically update a field based on specific criteria. A validation rule can prevent a record from being saved if it doesn't meet the criteria, but it doesn't actively update the field for the user. An auto-response rule is used to send automated email responses and is not suitable for updating field values. A case assignment rule is specifically for routing support cases and is not applicable to this scenario

Knowledge Area: Sales and Marketing Applications.

24. B: To ensure a dashboard displays data according to each user's access level, the administrator should use a dynamic dashboard. This type of dashboard ensures that users see data based on their own security settings, such as seeing only their own records or their team's records. Standard report filters can refine data but do

not automatically adjust what is visible based on the user's permissions. Dashboard components are the visualizations themselves, such as charts and gauges, and do not control record visibility.

Knowledge Area: Data and Analytics Management.

25. C: The best feature to ensure different sales teams only see fields relevant to their jobs is page layouts. By assigning different page layouts based on a user's profile and record type, administrators can control which fields are visible to specific groups. Record types are used to control available picklist values and which page layouts are applied, but they don't directly determine field visibility on their own. Field History Tracking logs changes to fields and does not control their visibility. Validation rules enforce data entry requirements and cannot hide or show fields for different users.

Knowledge Area: Object Manager and Lightning App Builder.

26. A: The correct answer is Login Hours, which allows administrators to restrict when users can log in to Salesforce, and automatically logs them out when the permitted time window expires. Session timeout only defines how long a user can be inactive before being logged out. IP restrictions limit where users can log in from based on their IP address, not the time of day. Lastly, multi-factor authentication adds an extra layer of security but doesn't restrict when users can log in.

Knowledge Area: Configuration and Setup.

27. B: Lead assignment rules are the correct feature to use because they automatically route leads to the appropriate user or queue based on specific criteria, like company size, ensuring enterprise leads go to the Enterprise Sales Team. Web-to-Lead is used to capture lead information from a website, but it doesn't assign the lead. Field mapping links fields between objects (like Lead, Account, and Contact) but doesn't control assignment. Auto-response rules send automated email replies to new leads but don't handle their assignment.

Knowledge Area: Sales and Marketing Applications.

28. A: The administrator should use Web-to-Case to create a public-facing web form that automatically generates a Case in Salesforce when submitted by a customer. Email-to-Case is an alternative that allows customers to submit Cases via email, but not through a web form. Case assignment rules are used after a Case is created to determine who receives it, not to create the Case itself.

Knowledge Area: Service and Support Applications.

29. B: To ensure that deleting an Account record also deletes all associated Project records, a master-detail relationship is the correct choice because it enforces a cascading deletion. A lookup relationship links records without enforcing ownership or cascading deletion, so the Project records would remain even if the

Account record were deleted. An external lookup relationship connects Salesforce records to outside data sources and doesn't enforce cascading deletion. A many-to-many relationship uses a Junction object and is not applicable for this scenario.

Knowledge Area: Object Manager and Lightning App Builder.

30. A, B: To design a Flow that updates a Contact's status only if it meets certain conditions, you need the Decision element to evaluate whether the criteria are met and the Assignment element to set the new field value. In a record-triggered Flow, the Contact record is already available, so a Get Records element is not required unless you need to query additional related data. Screen elements are only used in screen Flows for user input, which is not part of this scenario.

Knowledge Area: Workflow/Process Automation.

31. B: A formula field is the correct choice for calculating the number of days between two dates on a single record. A roll-up summary aggregates values from related records, not values within the same record. A text field stores alphanumeric data and a number field stores static numeric values, neither of which can dynamically perform calculations like a formula field.

Knowledge Area: Object Manager and Lightning App Builder.

32. B: The correct report type to measure the lead conversion rate is Leads with Converted Lead Information because it includes data on converted leads and the resulting Opportunities. The Opportunities with Contacts report focuses on Opportunities and contacts, not the conversion of a lead. A Sales Pipeline report tracks the progress of Opportunities but doesn't relate to lead conversion. Opportunity History reports on changes to an Opportunity's stage, not how leads are converted.

Knowledge Area: Sales and Marketing Applications.

33. C: To send immediate email confirmations when a customer submits a new Case, an administrator should use auto-response rules. Escalation rules are for Cases that remain unresolved for too long. Case assignment rules determine which user receives a Case but do not send automated responses to the customer. Web-to-Case enables the creation of Cases via a web form but requires auto-response rules to send the email confirmation.

Knowledge Area: Service and Support Applications.

34. B: A roll-up summary field is the correct choice because it can calculate values from related Opportunity Products and display the results directly on the Opportunity record. A formula field cannot aggregate values across child records, while Number and Text fields only store values entered by users and do not calculate totals automatically.

Knowledge Area: Data and Analytics Management.

35. A, C: To automatically update a related Opportunity's close date when an account's contract end date changes, the administrator should use a Record-triggered Flow and the Update records element. The record-triggered Flow ensures the automation runs in real time when the account's date changes. The Update Records element then modifies the existing Opportunity record. The Assignment element is for updating Flow variables, not records in Salesforce. A Screen element is for collecting user input in screen flows and is not applicable for this automated process.

Knowledge Area: Workflow/Process Automation.

36. B: Component visibility rules should be used to display dynamic components on a Lightning record page when an Account has high revenue because they allow administrators to conditionally show or hide components based on field values. In contrast, App Builder filters organize components but don't dynamically display them, while record types control page layout variations rather than showing or hiding components based on data, and page layouts determine field arrangement but don't support dynamic component visibility.

Knowledge Area: Object Manager and Lightning App Builder.

37. A: A record-triggered Flow is the best solution for automatically creating a Contract record when an Opportunity is marked closed-won, as it can automate record creation based on field updates. Lead assignment rules are not applicable since they route leads, not create new records. An approval process requires manual steps and does not automatically create new records. Workflow Rules have been retired by Salesforce, in favor of Flows, and could only create new Task records and not Contracts.

Knowledge Area: Sales and Marketing Applications.

38. B: Web-to-Case is the correct feature for automating the creation of Cases from website inquiries. Campaign Influence tracks campaign effectiveness but does not create Cases, and Collaborative Forecasting is for sales forecasting, not Case creation.

Knowledge Area: Service and Support Applications.

39. A: Historical trend reporting is the appropriate feature for sales managers to view and compare sales data from different time periods within the same report, as it's designed to track and compare report data over time. A summary formula calculates values within a report but doesn't compare different time periods. Report filters limit data but don't provide a way to compare across multiple time periods, and a custom report type defines object relationships but not time-based comparisons.

Knowledge Area: Data and Analytics Management.

40. A, D: A schedule-triggered Flow and the Update Records element are the correct choices for a Flow that runs nightly to update overdue Opportunities. The schedule-triggered Flow allows the automation to run at a specific time without being triggered by a record update, and the Update Records element is necessary to change the status of the identified Opportunities. The Assignment element is only for setting Flow variables, not for modifying records directly. The Screen element is not applicable as it is used for user input in screen Flows, and this process runs automatically.

Knowledge Area: Workflow/Process Automation.

41. A: The Add Multiple Users option in Setup allows administrators to create several users at once and automatically generate system emails with login credentials. This is more efficient than creating users individually. Manually creating each user one at a time will also send system emails but is inefficient at scale. Permission sets are applied after a user is created, not before, and Chatter groups cannot create users.

Knowledge Area: Configuration and Setup.

42. A: Field-level security should be used to restrict user access to specific fields on an object. This feature allows administrators to control who can view or edit sensitive fields based on a user's profile or permission set. A profile determines object-level permissions, not field visibility. Sharing rules extend record-level access but do not control field visibility, and role hierarchy only affects record ownership visibility, not field visibility.

Knowledge Area: Configuration and Setup.

43. A, B: Case assignment rules can automatically route cases that meet certain criteria to a designated high-priority queue for handling. Escalation rules are then used to monitor cases in that queue and, if they remain unresolved beyond a specified time, send a notification to the support manager or reassign the case. Case teams allow groups of users to collaborate on cases but do not provide automated assignment or notifications. Web-to-Case is for capturing customer issues from a website, not for routing or escalation.

Knowledge Area: Service and Support Applications.

44. C: A Joined report allows you to view data from the same or different objects in multiple blocks within a single report. This makes it the best option when comparing Opportunities from different record types in separate sections. A summary report can group by record type but displays the results in a single block. A matrix report adds grouping in rows and columns but still does not provide separate blocks for comparison. A tabular report is a simple list of records and offers no grouping or block-level comparison.

Knowledge Area: Data and Analytics Management.

45. B, C: The Get Records and Decision elements are required to build a Flow that checks for existing related Contacts before creating a new one. The Get Records element retrieves existing related Contacts to check if any exist. The Decision element then evaluates whether any related Contacts were found, ensuring a new Contact is only created if necessary. The Assignment element is used to set Flow variables and does not check for related records, while the Screen element is only used in screen Flows for user input, which is not applicable here.

Knowledge Area: Workflow/Process Automation.

46. B: Company Information is where multicurrency is enabled at the organizational level, allowing various currencies to be used. User Personal Customizations only allows individual users to customize their personal preferences, and it does not enable multicurrency for the entire organization. Opportunity settings do not activate multicurrency, as they are used to control forecasting and Opportunity Stage settings. Currency management allows for adding exchange rates and managing active currencies, but it requires multicurrency to be enabled first in Company Information before it can be used.

Knowledge Area: Configuration and Setup.

47. D: The administrator should use case teams. Case teams allow multiple agents to work together on a single Case, ensuring each member has access to it and can work efficiently. Case assignment rules automatically route cases to a specific agent or queue, but they don't allow multiple agents to collaborate. Entitlements define support agreements and track customer service eligibility, while escalation rules reassign Cases based on time-based conditions.

Knowledge Area: Service and Support Applications.

48. B: To allow sales users to collaborate on accounts, share files, and communicate in real-time within Salesforce, the administrator should use Chatter. Chatter is a built-in Salesforce collaboration tool that allows users to post updates, share files, and discuss records in real time. The Activity Timeline provides a history of interactions on a record, but it doesn't allow for real-time collaboration. Email-to-Case is a feature for creating Cases from emails for customer service and isn't intended for internal collaboration.

Knowledge Area: Productivity and Collaboration.

49. A: To automatically update a related Account's custom field when a new Opportunity is created, a record-triggered Flow should be used. This type of Flow runs automatically when a record is created or updated, making it the best solution for this automation. Screen Flow requires user interaction for guided experiences, which isn't suitable for this automated process. An autolaunched Flow only runs when called from another process, so it wouldn't trigger automatically upon Opportunity creation. An approval process automates approval routing and doesn't update fields when records are created.

Knowledge Area: Workflow/Process Automation.

50. A: To configure a many-to-many relationship where a vendor contract can be associated with multiple accounts and vice-versa, the administrator should create a Junction object with master-detail relationships to both accounts and contracts. This allows a many-to-many relationship where multiple accounts can be linked to multiple contracts through the Junction object. Using a lookup relationship or a master-detail relationship creates a one-to-many association and wouldn't be able to establish a true many-to-many relationship. Lastly, external sharing is used to control record visibility and doesn't establish object relationships.

Knowledge Area: Object Manager and Lightning App Builder.

51. A: To create a report that only includes Opportunities where the Amount is greater than $50,000, the administrator should use a filter. A filter is used to include or exclude records from a report based on specific field values, making it the correct option for this requirement. A summary formula allows for calculations within a report but doesn't filter which records appear. A cross filter is used to filter based on related objects, such as Opportunities with or without related Activities, and isn't needed here.

Knowledge Area: Data and Analytics Management.

52. A: The Salesforce administrator should update the company name, default locale, and fiscal year settings in Company Information. This section allows administrators to make global, organization-wide updates. Business Hours determine when users can access support features, but they do not affect company-wide settings like name, locale, or fiscal year. While Fiscal Year setup allows for configuring fiscal years in more detail, the default fiscal year is controlled in Company Information. Finally, Locale settings control regional formatting for individual users, not company-wide defaults.

Knowledge Area: Configuration and Setup.

53. A: To ensure that only users from the company's office network can access Salesforce while allowing executives to log in from any location, the administrator should use IP restrictions. This security setting allows administrators to define a range of allowed IP addresses, preventing users outside that range from accessing Salesforce unless an exception is granted, which is ideal for executives. Login Hours restrict when a user can log in, but not from where. Multi-factor authentication enhances security but doesn't restrict logins based on location. Trusted devices reduces the need for authentication but doesn't prevent users from logging in from outside locations.

Knowledge Area: Configuration and Setup.

54. B, C: To design a Flow that evaluates an incoming Case's priority and routes it to the correct queue without user input, an administrator should use both the Deci-

sion and Assignment elements. The Decision element is used to evaluate the Case priority and determine the appropriate queue for routing based on predefined logic. The Assignment element is then used to set the correct queue for the Case based on the outcome of the Decision element. A Pause element is used to delay Flow execution and isn't necessary for immediate routing. A Screen element is only used in screen Flows, which require user interaction, so it's not applicable here.

Knowledge Area: Workflow/Process Automation.

55. B: To ensure different teams see different picklist values for the Lead Source field based on their business process, the administrator should use record types. Record types allow administrators to assign different picklist values to different teams, ensuring each team only sees the relevant values for their process. Field-level security controls who can view or edit a field, but it doesn't change the available picklist values based on a user's role. Validation rules enforce data quality but don't determine which picklist values are available. Page layouts define the arrangement of fields on a record but don't control which picklist values appear.

Knowledge Area: Object Manager and Lightning App Builder.

56. B: Chatter Feed Tracking allows administrators to designate fields on an object, such as Account, so that changes to those fields automatically post updates in the record's Chatter feed. This ensures users following the record can stay informed without manual posts. Chatter Groups provide a space for users to collaborate but do not track record field changes. Chatter Streams let users consolidate updates from multiple feeds into one view but don't generate the updates themselves. Chatter Publisher Actions allow users to quickly create or update records from the Chatter feed but do not monitor field changes.

Knowledge Area: Productivity and Collaboration.

57. B: To track how long it takes to close Cases and to automatically escalate those that remain open for over 48 hours, the correct feature to use is escalation rules. Escalation rules track a Case's age and automatically escalate it if it remains open past a specified time frame. Case assignment rules route incoming Cases to an agent or queue but do not monitor Case duration for escalation. Case teams enable multiple users to collaborate, but they don't provide automated escalation based on time. Support Processes define the stages for managing Case status, but they don't trigger automatic escalation based on how long a Case is open.

Knowledge Area: Service and Support Applications.

58. B: To automatically assign new Opportunities to the correct sales representative based on the Opportunity's region, the administrator should use an assignment rule. Assignment rules automatically assign records, like Opportunities, Leads, or Cases, based on predefined criteria, ensuring they are routed to the right person as soon as they are created. Workflow rules have been retired and are not

recommended for new automation. An approval process is used for review and approval before a record can proceed, not for automatic assignment based on criteria like region. Sharing rules are used for controlling record visibility, not for automatically assigning them to users.

Knowledge Area: Sales and Marketing Applications.

59. B: To ensure that certain fields on the Opportunity object are only visible to specific profiles, the administrator should use field-level security. Field-level security determines which profiles can see or edit specific fields, ensuring sensitive information is only visible to authorized users. Record types control which page layouts and picklist values are available but don't restrict field visibility based on the user's profile. Page layouts control the arrangement and visibility of fields within a record but do not restrict access based on the user profile. Role hierarchy determines record visibility based on a user's position in the organization, but it does not restrict access to individual fields.

Knowledge Area: Object Manager and Lightning App Builder.

60. C: For importing a large volume of records, such as 60,000 leads, the best tool is Data Loader. Data Loader is designed to handle large data volumes efficiently and allows for bulk imports. The Data Import Wizard is more suitable for smaller data sets of 50,000 records or less. Data Export is not a viable option because it only supports the export of records and cannot perform data imports.

Knowledge Area: Data and Analytics Management.

Index

(see also field history)

U

update rights, 105
updates, 335
upserts, 336
URL fields, 167
user accounts
  accessing, 76-77
  All Users screen, 76
  creating, 78-80
  deactivating, 85, 464
  deleting, relationships and, 481
  freezing, 85-86, 476
  listing, 76
  locked, 83-84
  login history, 77-78, 464
  login troubleshooting, 78, 465
  password policies, 81-82
  password reset, 84-85, 465
  personal customization, 88-90
    display, 90-92
    layout, 90-92
  Service Cloud User, 248
User Interface Settings
  App Menu, 54-55
  declarative configuration, 52
    App Menu, 52
    global actions, 52
    Lightning App Builder, 52
    list views, 52
    UI settings, 52
  Enhanced Profile User Interface option, 101-102
  global actions, 67-68
  Lightning App Builder, 68-71
  list views
    accessing, 56
    chart creation, 62
    creating, 58-59
    display formats, 65-67
    fields, 60-61
    filtering, 57
    inline editing, 64
    mass updating, 64-65
    pinning, 56
    printable view, 61-62
    sorting, 56
    visibility, 59-60

User Interface screen, 53-54
User Management, 75
  logging in, 464
  logging in as any user, 86, 87-88
    enabling, 86-87
  login history, 77-78
  login troubleshooting, 78, 465
  MFA (multi-factor authentication), 82-83
  password policies, 81-82, 465
    best practices, 80
  password reset, 84-85
  personal customizations, 88-90
    display, 90-92
    layout, 90-92
  user accounts
    access, 76-77
    creating, 78-80
    deactivating, 85
    freezing, 85-86
    locked, 83-84
usernames, 78
users
  create rights, 105
  delete rights, 106
  read rights, 105
  update rights, 105
Users screen, 99

V

validation rules, 324-325
variable resources, 398
variable stage, 399
variables, Flow, 399-401
verifying certification, 428, 475
version management, 409
Visualforce email templates, 385

W

Web-to-Case, 251, 469, 481, 483
  enabling, 277
  HTML Generator, 278-280
Web-to-Lead forms, 186
Workflow Rules, 379, 480
Workflow/Process Automation, 380, 478
  approval processes, 381-391
  Automation Home, 380
  Flow, 391-419

About the Author

Mike Wheeler holds eight Salesforce certifications and has worked professionally on the Salesforce platform as an administrator, developer, and consultant. Since 2016, Mike has been teaching hundreds of thousands of students online on how to use Salesforce, attain certifications, and launch their careers. He is the founder of Rapid Reskill, focused on Salesforce and AI training, and Velza, a Salesforce and AI consultancy.

Colophon

The animal on the cover of *Salesforce Certified Platform Administrator Study Guide* is a green-billed malkoha (*Phaenicophaeus tristis*). Found throughout the Indian subcontinent and Southeast Asia, this nonparasitic cuckoo can be heard chirping from trees in dense forests and thickets year-round.

Green-billed malkohas are so called because of their prominent pale-green bill, which has a natural curve to help them catch prey. Their plumage, while mostly blue, includes a salty gray patch on their necks and a red mask around their eyes. Their tails, which are remarkably long, are white at the tip. These birds usually measure between 50 and 60 centimeters and weigh a mere 3.5–4.5 ounces. While they tend to creep through foliage like squirrels, green-billed malkohas are actually agile fliers and are quick to disappear into trees when threatened by predators.

Unlike some cuckoos, green-billed malkohas are nonparasitic, meaning they build nests to raise their own young (as opposed to parasitic cuckoos, which lay their eggs in the nests of other bird species, relying on those birds to raise their young instead). These birds feed mostly on small insects, but they sometimes feast on slugs, snails, spiders, and even small lizards.

Currently, green-billed malkohas are classified as Least Concern by the International Union for Conservation of Nature. These birds are very common throughout their range and are an adaptable species, which means their population is not threatened. All animals featured on O'Reilly covers are important to the world.

The cover illustration is by Monica Kamsvaag, based on an antique line engraving from *Lydekker's Royal Natural History*. The series design is by Edie Freedman, Ellie Volckhausen, and Susan Brown. The cover fonts are Gilroy Semibold and Guardian Sans. The text font is Adobe Minion Pro; the heading font is Adobe Myriad Condensed; and the code font is Dalton Maag's Ubuntu Mono.

O'REILLY®

Learn from experts.
Become one yourself.

60,000+ titles | Live events with experts | Role-based courses
Interactive learning | Certification preparation

**Try the O'Reilly learning platform
free for 10 days.**